Self and Society

Sixth Edition

Self and Society

A Symbolic Interactionist Social Psychology

John P. Hewitt
University of Massachusetts—Amherst

Allyn and Bacon
Boston • London • Toronto • Sydney • Tokyo • Singapore

Senior Editor: Karen Hanson
Editor-in-Chief, Social Sciences: Susan Badger
Series Editorial Assistant: Sarah Dunbar
Editorial-Production Administrator: Annette Joseph
Editorial-Production Service: Holly Crawford
Manufacturing Buyer: Louise Richardson
Cover Administrator: Linda K. Dickinson
Cover Designer: Suzanne Harbison

Library of Congress Cataloging-in-Publication Data

Hewitt, John P.
    Self and society : a symbolic interactionist social psychology /
John P. Hewitt. — 6th ed.
        p.   cm.
    Includes bibliographical references and index.
    ISBN 0-205-14679-1
    1. Social psychology.   2. Symbolic interactionism.   I. Title.
HM251.H494   1993   93-19222
302—dc20   CIP

Printed in the United States of America

10 9 8 7 6 5 4 3 2 1   98 97 96 95 94 93

Contents

Preface

When I first conceived of *Self and Society* in the early 1970s my goal was to write a concise, straightforward, and theoretical introduction to the symbolic interactionist approach to social psychology. I wanted to make it accessible and useful to readers with a variety of interests and at several levels of study, and to do so in the best prose I could muster. As this book has evolved through subsequent revisions I have kept these goals in mind, striving to keep its portrayal of symbolic interactionism within the mainstream of this tradition, always trying to improve the clarity of the exposition. This edition is no exception. I have refined discussions, excised outdated illustrations and introduced some new ones, added new references, and continued to polish the writing.

Over the past few years many symbolic interactionists have flirted with — and some have been swept off their intellectual feet by — postmodernism and postmodern social theory. Like many others, I have thought deeply about the issues these theoretical movements raise for symbolic interactionism and deliberated on how I would deal with them in this edition of the book. My first thought was to expand the discussion of other perspectives on social psychology in Chapter 1 to include postmodern approaches. The more I considered this strategy, however, the more obvious it seemed that it would be premature to do so. I have yet to see a coherent account of postmodernism, postmodern social theory, or the postmodern condition that could be communicated with any clarity within a few pages. Outsiders' efforts to characterize postmodernism seem generally to be met with scorn by the faithful. Moreover, I remain unconvinced of the intellectual durability of these movements, which are in significant ways inimical to the interactionist approach to social life. Like the philosopher Richard Rorty, I believe their proponents will find Mead, Dewey, and James at the end of the philosophical road they are traveling. I have, however, completely rewritten Chapter 8, partly in an effort to answer some of the implicit and explicit challenges these movements raise for symbolic interactionism. In this task I eschewed a point-by-point response, thinking it more useful, particularly for undergraduates, to reassert the pragmatist spirit that lies at the heart of symbolic interactionism.

Thank you to the reviewers whose comments assisted me in the preparation of this sixth edition: Peter Adler, University of Denver; Richard Butsch, Rider College; Nancy J. Herman, Central Michigan University; and Ray Schmitt, Illinois State University.

Many people have helped me in my work over the years, but most of all my wife. Expressing gratitude to her has become so much a fixture of my prefaces that it may seem a mere ritual. It is not. Children grow up and leave home; students arrive, sometimes learn, and quickly depart; colleagues come and go. For the last thirty years Myrna Livingston Hewitt has been the friend without whom I would not be who I am.

Self and Society

▶ 1

Social Psychology and Symbolic Interactionism

We human beings live in a world of names for ourselves, for others, and for our activities. These names announce who we are, what we are doing, and why we are doing it. When I call myself "professor," for example, I invite others to identify me as that role, to interpret what I do as relevant to its requirements, and to trust that I have good "professorial" reasons for my words and deeds. The names we call ourselves also shape the identities of others and the conduct we expect from them. If I am the "professor," the others to whom I address myself are "students," whose actions and motives I will scrutinize to see if they are appropriate to their identity.

Two names — *social psychology* and *symbolic interactionism* — identify the author and purposes of this book. To say that one is interested in social psychology tells other social scientists something of one's professional activities and commitments; to assert that one pursues social psychology from the perspective of symbolic interactionism adds another layer of meaning. Yet these names are ambiguous and possibly misleading. "Social psychology" labels diverse scholars and activities, and "symbolic interactionism" names a sociological perspective that can be understood in several different ways. Hence, the first task in developing a symbolic interactionist social psychology is to explore these labels, their origins, and their implications. Later in this chapter I will compare symbolic interactionism with other perspectives in social psychology and develop a systematic statement of its major tenets.

WHAT IS SOCIAL PSYCHOLOGY?

Some of the ambiguity in the term *social psychology* stems from the fact that it is used in differing but partially overlapping ways in two disciplines. Psychology and sociology have shared custody of the term since 1908, when two books were published, each with *social psychology* in its title. One, written by the psychologist William McDougall, argued that in order to understand how human beings are affected by society, it is necessary to study what he called the "native basis of the mind."[1] Like other scholars of that era, McDougall relied on the concept of *instinct*. He believed that it was necessary to discover the "innate tendencies of thought and action" that characterize human beings in order to explain the influences of society on them. The other book, by sociologist Edward A. Ross, placed more emphasis on social forces, arguing that certain processes come into existence because human beings associate with one another. Ross felt that the spread of fads and fashions, for example, cannot be explained simply by the nature and structure of the individual mind. The very fact of human association creates processes that cannot be reduced to the study of individuals.[2]

McDougall and Ross sounded themes that can still be heard in the work of social psychologists, for the members of each discipline are still oriented to their own traditions of theory, ways of doing research, and basic images of human behavior. Psychologists do not deny that social and cultural forces shape the environment within which such basic psychological processes as learning, cognition, or emotion take place. But their main interest is in the processes themselves rather than in their social setting. As a result, psychological social psychologists make the *individual* their central abstraction and main unit of analysis. Sociologists, on the other hand, seek to describe and explain patterns of conduct among larger aggregates of people – groups, communities, social classes, and even whole societies. Without denying the importance of the mind or of processes that operate at the individual level, sociological social psychologists give priority to the fact of human association and make society their chief abstraction and beginning point of analysis.

A look at the typical theoretical and research interests of psychological and sociological social psychologists will clarify the similarities and differences in their approaches. Psychologists emphasize such topics as conformity, interpersonal attraction, the attribution of causality, aggression, altruistic behavior, and attitudes and their impact on behavior. Conformity – how the group shapes the thoughts and actions of individuals – has been a favorite topic. Studies of conformity have asked, for example, under what circumstances individuals can be induced to change their opinions or to adopt a judgment they know to be wrong merely because group pressures are applied to them. In the classic experiments of Solomon Asch, subjects were induced to misjudge the relative length of lines (a task that should be a matter of objective judgment) by pressures to agree with the erroneous judgments of confederates of the experimenter. The confederates, whom the real subjects of the experiment thought were also subjects, intentionally gave wrong answers in an effort to induce the naive subjects to conform to their opinions.[3] More recently, in his studies of obedience, Stanley Milgram found that he could readily induce people to obey directions that required them to inflict apparent harm upon others. Milgram showed that he could create laboratory conditions in which subjects would administer what they believed were electric shocks to other subjects, even over strong protests and expressions of pain. The shocks were not real, of course, but the experiment was carefully staged to create the impression that they were.[4]

Although psychological social psychologists conduct much of their research in a social setting, they typically focus on individual behavior. They have little interest in culture or in the ways in which individual conduct is socially organized and directed. The approach is summed up in Gordon Allport's classic definition of social psychology as the "attempt to understand and explain how the thought, feeling, and behavior of *individuals* are influenced by the actual, imagined, or implied presence of others."[5]

Sociologists approach social psychology differently. Many sociological social psychologists study the same topics as psychologists — topics such as interpersonal attraction, causal attribution, and the relationship between attitudes and behavior. But they are also interested in a broader range of phenomena, including social roles, processes and contexts of socialization, intergroup behavior, collective behavior, deviance and social control, social structure and personality, and public opinion.[6] In their work in such areas, sociological social psychologists focus on the social world itself, treating social structure, culture, social roles, groups, organizations, and collective behavior not simply as environments within which individuals behave, but as crucial levels of reality in their own right. Their ultimate goal is not to explain what individuals do and why they do it, but to understand how organized social life is possible, how it works, and how it changes over time.

The topic of *socialization,* for example, is of very great importance in sociological social psychology. But sociologists are not typically interested in how *individuals* learn what they learn, but in the content of socialization, the social contexts (groups, such as the family or peers, and organizations, such as the school) in which it occurs, and the nature of the process as it occurs at different periods in life. A sociological study of socialization by peers during adolescence, for example, might examine the nature of the friendship bond and explore the kinds of learning that occur in this relationship. In his study of the socializing influences of friends, Gary Alan Fine discovered that the relatively egalitarian and tolerant nature of adolescent friendship provides a context in which the social skills of self-presentation and impression management can be practiced and mastered.[7] Such studies focus on what transpires *between* people rather than within the person, and they pay considerable attention to the wider social and cultural context in which conduct occurs.

There is little to be gained by arguing about which approach to social psychology is the better one. The disciplines of psychology and sociology have both common and different goals. Sociologists can find much of value in psychologists' studies of conformity, person perception, causal attribution, obedience, leadership, and the many other topics they pursue. Indeed, the interests of psychological and sociological social psychologists frequently overlap to the point where each can gain by attending to the research and theory of the other.[8] Yet the sociologist also finds limitations in psychological social psychology. Because much of their work ignores the facts of cultural variation, psychologists are prone to create culture-bound, ethnocentric explanations of human conduct. And because they often focus on the individual in the microscopic social context of the laboratory or small group, ignoring the much larger framework of social institutions, power, and other constraints that affect human conduct, they can seem naive and inattentive with respect to issues of power, coercion, freedom, and other matters with which sociologists are concerned.

My goal in this book is to present and develop a perspective, called *symbolic interactionism,* that provides a distinctively sociological way of understanding human social conduct and group life. Although its concerns are not limited to social psychology — for it regards culture and social structure as critical phenomena — symbolic interactionism is centrally concerned with the issues that have preoccupied social psychologists. Among the several approaches to social psychology that sociologists have used, it is the one most identified with sociology and best suited to the needs of the discipline.

Individual and Society

We can begin to understand the distinctive perspective of symbolic interactionism by examining the sociological view of the relationship between the person and the social world. At the heart of this relationship is a paradox.

Briefly stated, the paradox is this: Only individuals *act*. Everything else — society, culture, social structure, power, groups, organizations — is ultimately dependent on the acts of individuals. Yet individuals can act only because they acquire the capacity to do so as members of a society, which is the source of their knowledge, language, skills, orientations, and motives. Individuals are born into and shaped by a society that already exists and that will persist long after they are dead; yet that same society owes its existence and continuity to the conduct of its members.[9]

The paradox of individual and society has dictated some of the major questions asked by sociologists as well as the problems they have encountered in answering them. How does the individual acquire from society the capacity to be an active, functioning member? Indeed, *what* does the individual acquire — what skills, knowledge, orientations, and motives? How do the individual and cooperative acts of its socialized members create and sustain a society? How can society shape the very individuals on whose actions its existence depends, and how can it live on when its members die?

Questions such as these are particularly important because, in the sociological view, biologically programmed instincts or drives have been supplanted by learning as the most important factor underlying human behavior. The human world is primarily cultural, and human conduct is shaped by the knowledge, skills, values, beliefs, and ways of living held in common by the members of society. Thus, an orderly and persisting society is not guaranteed by our biological programming, but by what we have learned. And, by the same token, individuals are not guided by instinct, but must themselves rely upon society and culture for their own survival.

Simply to assert that behavior is culturally transmitted is not to explain how culture actually influences or shapes individual conduct. Human sexual behavior, for example, is profoundly influenced by culture: What human beings find sexually arousing, the situations in which they find it so, and the choice of others with whom to engage in sexual activity are not matters of human nature, but of cultural patterning. But *how* does culture shape human sexual attitudes and conduct? How does what we learn about sexual activity work its way into our sexual behavior?

Sociologists have adopted varied attitudes toward the problem of linking society and culture to actual conduct. Some have argued that our attention should be focused on *culture* and *social structure* rather than on conduct itself. Those who adopt this position argue that patterns of conduct are so stable and repetitive that the question of how culture and social structure actually shape behavior can safely be ignored. After all, they assert, much of social life is quite routine: People perform the same tasks over and over, the situations and social relationships in which they find themselves are pretty much the same from one day to the next, and their culture essentially provides ready-made ways of behaving. As a result, explaining how culture and society actually shape conduct is less interesting and important than explaining the origins and persistence of cultural patterns and social structures.

Sociologists who adopt this point of view have developed numerous concepts designed to describe and help explain social phenomena. To take but one example, the concept of *social class* refers to the fact that societies are typically divided into segments whose members have a similar position in the division of labor, comparable education and incomes, and similar views of themselves and their place in the world. One social class, for example, might consist of small business owners, another of manual workers, another of factory owners. In each case, there are likely to be greater similarities among the members of the class than between the members of that class and those of another. Class is a structural concept; its focus is on the patterned and repetitive conduct and social relationships that can be observed within and between various groups in a society at any given point in history.

A structural perspective has many attractive features. Human social life is highly repetitive, and it is often necessary to look beyond the details of individual behavior and its formation in order to see patterns and regularities. Moreover, although society ultimately depends upon the conduct of individuals, their actions and interactions typically have consequences they do not foresee and do not recognize. The everyday actions of people as they work, eat and drink, play, make love, socialize, vote, take walks, and attend meetings *do* seem powerfully influenced by social class, and these actions have the cumulative effect of sustaining and reproducing class structures, even though people do not necessarily intend to do so nor recognize that they are doing so.

Looking only at social and cultural patterns and regularities, however, has limitations. Social life is highly repetitive, but it is not totally so because patterns change over time, sometimes slowly and sometimes quite dramatically and quickly. The social division of labor between men and women (along with cultural definitions of men and women) in the contemporary United States or Canada, for example, are not the same as they were a century ago. Today men and women inherit social roles and images of one another that were crafted during the nineteenth century, but have been periodically modified since then. Although some still believe women should be confined to the domestic sphere because they lack the political or intellectual skills for public life, the majority now reject those beliefs. In part because of the women's movement, which challenged such ideas, what once seemed to many to be an eternal fact now seems antiquated; and patterns that once seemed entrenched have changed.

The fact of social change makes it difficult to regard human conduct as simply determined by existing forms of society and culture. We must look at conduct as shaped not only by these external forces, but also by the efforts of people who work within, and sometimes *against,* an inherited culture and existing social arrangements. People are not thoroughly and passively socialized to accept and reproduce culture and society. Under many circumstances they resist and rebel, finding ways to escape from the patterns of conduct that are urged upon them.

A great many sociologists, therefore, have abandoned the position that they can concentrate on social structure and culture and ignore conduct. They recognize that they must have a basic *theory of action*—that is, an account of how people actually form their conduct in everyday life—that can be related to the society and culture their conduct both sustains and modifies.

The main task of social psychology is to create such a theory of action. Its job is to examine the details of action and interaction, to show how people are influenced by society and culture, but also to show how their everyday actions both sustain and change these larger realities. To do so, the social psychologist must concentrate on such topics as socialization, the nature of the person, and the actual formation of conduct in everyday life. At the same time, however, culture and social structure cannot be ignored: The person is created and transformed, and everyday life takes place, within a framework provided by society and culture.

A theory of action can be based on a great variety of theoretical perspectives. The theory to be developed here — symbolic interactionism — has been influential, and often controversial, within sociology. My next task is to show in a general way how symbolic interactionists approach a theory of action that can account for the influence of society and culture on the person, as well as to explain how action and interaction both reproduce and change society and culture.

WHAT IS SYMBOLIC INTERACTIONISM?

Symbolic interactionism is a distinctively American sociological perspective whose roots lie in the philosophy of pragmatism.[10] This philosophical tradition, identified with such scholars as Charles S. Peirce, William James, John Dewey, and George Herbert Mead, contains an important clue to its outlook in its name, *pragmatism,* the commonplace meaning of which is "practical." Proponents of this approach to philosophy view living things as attempting to make practical adjustments to their surroundings. As philosophers, they are interested in the fundamental questions of philosophy: What is truth? What is good? What is knowledge? How do we acquire knowledge? How do we know that we know the truth? In seeking answers to these questions, they argue that the truth of an idea or the meaning of a statement is dependent upon its practical consequences — an idea is true if it works. Pragmatists see all living organisms as oriented to meeting the demands of their environments in practical ways. They view knowledge as continually confronting practical tests of its usefulness. The lens through which they view truth thus emphasizes the consequences of ideas rather than their logical elegance or internal consistency.

Pragmatists see living things as probing and testing their environment. Truth is, therefore, not absolute, but is always relative to the needs and interests of organisms. An idea — for example, the idea that the sun rises in the east — is true if it leads to empirical predictions that help people adjust to the requirements and circumstances of their world. Questions of how members of a species know and interact with their environment are, for pragmatists, matters of great moment, not merely peripheral concerns. Knowing and acting, in the pragmatist view, are intimately linked: We act on the basis of our ideas about the world. The reality of the world is not merely something that is "out there" waiting to be discovered by us, but is actively created as we act in and toward the world.

How does philosophical pragmatism relate to social psychology and symbolic interactionism? A brief overview of the work of George Herbert Mead can help answer this question and convey the general flavor of the symbolic interactionist approach to social psychology.

George Herbert Mead was a pragmatist philosopher whose intellectual stature was equal to that of John Dewey, although he did not become as widely known as the latter. Mead's work covered a great deal of philosophical ground, but he is best known and remembered among social scientists for his theory of mind. This work comes to us primarily through Mead's students at the University of Chicago, who assembled their notes on his courses in social psychology into a book, *Mind, Self, and Society,* after his death in 1931.[11]

Mead's theory of mind attempts to account for the origins and development of human intelligence by linking it to the process of evolution, by viewing mind and conduct as inescapably linked, and by showing that the origins of human mind lie in human society. Mead felt that human intelligence emerged from a process of evolutionary change. Moreover, he was convinced that the mind is not a separate, disembodied entity, but an integral aspect of the *behavior* of the species. He sought to avoid the *dualistic* view of mind and body that had plagued philosophy, a view that led people to separate the physical organism from intelligence and to imagine the latter as existing within some ethereal realm of ideas. For Mead, mind, body, and conduct are inseparable aspects of a process of evolution that has produced a uniquely human life form.

All organisms come into existence and persist (or fail to persist) in interaction with their environments. Their physical structures and their capacities to act do not exist in a vacuum, but are created under specific environmental conditions. Nor are organisms merely the passive receptors of stimuli that emanate from their surroundings. Each organism has a set of capacities to respond to its world; bees, for example, are sensitive to the angle of light coming from the sun and use this knowledge in locating and returning to food sources. Humans are sensitive to the nuances of language and employ this capacity in everything they do. Such capacities have evolved over long periods of time as environmental conditions have changed, mutations have appeared, and new structures have developed. An organism's capacities to respond to the environment help to make the environment what it is. The sun is an important part of the bee's environment, for example, because the bee has the capacity to respond to its position. To be able to respond to the environment is also to be able to act upon it. The human child who learns how to react to the parental "no" is acting upon his or her parents, obeying their demands in order to influence their acts and thus secure personal needs for nurture or praise, every bit as much as he or she is being acted upon by the parents.

Mead found the major explanations of human mind and conduct prevalent in his day to be inadequate. On the one hand, he saw that human conduct was far too complex to be explained by instincts. Although the complex individual conduct and social coordination of the insect society—the beehive, for example—might be explained by genetically programmed (and therefore unlearned) forms of behavior, there is too much cultural diversity, novelty, and complexity for instincts to be a satisfactory explanation of human conduct. So, Mead rejected the instinctivist sociological and psychological theories of the time.

On the other hand, Mead also found much to criticize in *behaviorism,* whose foremost exponent was the psychologist John Watson. The behaviorists insisted that the true path to the explanation of human behavior (or any animal behavior) lay in paying strict attention only to what the scientist could *directly* observe— both behavior and environmental events (stimuli) associated with the behavior. They emphasized that behavior was learned, and they sought to uncover the laws that governed the learning of behavioral responses to environmental stimuli. The behaviorists eschewed any concept of mind, saying that what is essential in conduct is not what people think they are doing but what they observably do and how they are rewarded for doing it. Mental events—thoughts, ideas, images—are for them mostly irrelevant because, they believed, such events cannot be observed.

Although the emphasis on behavior struck a responsive chord in Mead, he felt that behaviorists had gone too far in excluding consideration of internal, mental events. Covert they might be, Mead argued, but they are nevertheless crucial to the explanation of behavior and can, contrary to Watson, be made accessible to observation. We can talk about our inner experiences, and in this way they become observable. Moreover, behaviorism had far too individual a focus for Mead's taste. Although it is true that it is the individual who behaves, individual behavior is rarely disconnected from the acts of others. Human behavior is socially coordinated, often in very complex ways over extended periods of time, and an explanation of behavior that fails to take this fact into account is doomed from the start. Most individual acts are a part of more complex, socially coordinated activities involving several people. Shaking hands, for example, is not merely a bit of behavior in which one person extends a hand in response to the stimulus of the extended hand of another, but is a socially coordinated act in which the past experiences and future hopes of two individuals, as well as established social conventions, are important. Shaking hands to seal a business agreement differs from shaking hands in a situation where one of the individuals was hoping for a kiss. To abstract the individual's part of an act from a more extensive social act is to attempt to explain far less than what we can and must explain.

It was Mead's genius to provide an explanation of the nature and origins of human intelligence—mind—that could deal with inner experience and at the same time take into account the social nature of human life. Although a full account of his theory and its application in contemporary symbolic interactionism will have to await chapters 2 and 3 of this book, the outlines of Mead's contribution are sketched here.

Many nonhuman living things exist in association with others of their own kind and are profoundly affected by this fact. Other mammals vary in their gregariousness, for example, but all have at least some forms of association with one another, whether as members of a herd or of a small band of primates whose social organization and interdependence are more complex. Mead argued that the basis for human interaction differs substantially from that of other animals, including our primate cousins. Among other animals, interaction takes a form that Mead called the "conversation of gestures." Each individual, in beginning an act, engages in overt and visible actions that can be detected by others and serve as stimuli to their responses. A dog, beginning a fight with another dog, bares its teeth and assumes an aggressive stance; its physical gestures are stimuli that key an aggressive response from the other. Interaction thus proceeds between the animals, with the control of each dog's behavior effectively in the hands of the other. In no sense does either decide or make up its mind to act in a certain way.

Human interactions are very different as Mead so incisively saw and explained. First, the most important gestures for people are *linguistic*. Humans are animals who possess language and whose conduct occurs in a world of words. We are attuned not just to the overt bodily movements of others, but to a complex set of vocalizations that precede and accompany their acts and our own. Second, these vocal gestures — acts of speech — have the unique property of arousing in the one using them nearly the same response as they arouse in those to whom they are directed. They are, in Mead's words, "significant symbols." Shouting the word "Fire!" in a public place, for example, does not merely elicit a flight response from those present. The word creates, both in the crowd and in the one who shouts it, a certain attitude — a readiness to act in a particular way, an image of the conduct appropriate to the situation, a plan of action. It is this creation of a common *attitude* in both symbol user and symbol hearer that makes possible the individual's control of his or her own conduct. People who, by anticipating what others will do in response to their acts, are able to plan their own subsequent acts have attained *control* over their own conduct. For example, anticipating the possibility of panic flight if I hastily alert a crowd to the presence of fire, I may decide instead to attempt a more subdued, quieter warning that will improve the chances for safe evacuation. When I do this, I exert control over my behavior.

The significant symbol not only affords humans a degree of control over their own conduct that other animals do not possess but also gives them a form of consciousness not found elsewhere: consciousness of *self*. Our capacity to employ symbols in imagining the responses of others to our own acts also gives us the capacity to be conscious of ourselves. To use a term to be developed in greater detail later, we are able to become *objects* to ourselves; that is, to act toward ourselves as we act toward others, to be one of the many things, ideas, persons, experiences of which we are conscious and toward which our activity is directed. We can name ourselves, think about ourselves, talk to ourselves, imagine ourselves acting in various ways, love or hate ourselves, feel proud or ashamed; in short, we can act toward ourselves in all the ways we can act toward others.

Mead's account of human behavior, mind, and self is a significant milestone in human self-understanding. His theory stresses the explanation of human conduct in scientific terms on the basis of scientific observation. At the same time, it admits inner experiences as capable of observation, for we are able to report and communicate to others about our private experiences and feelings by using significant symbols. His theory recognizes the sociability of human beings as a primary fact of their evolution and existence and uses this fact to explain how human beings mind their environment in distinctive ways. His theory puts the human experience of self on center stage. Human beings are not conceived as puppets controlled by environmental strings, but as creatures whose evolution has yielded a capacity for the self-control of behavior.

Chapters 2 and 3 of this book build upon these basic Meadian ideas, elaborating on the evolutionary development of human behavior and developing a conceptual framework for a symbolic interactionist social psychology. As a preface to these tasks, the remainder of this chapter will develop a general overview of contemporary symbolic interactionism, first by showing its major points of difference with other theoretical perspectives, and then by stating its major tenets.

OTHER THEORIES OF SOCIAL PSYCHOLOGY

Contemporary social psychologists have looked to several different philosophical and theoretical traditions for answers to the questions Mead addressed in his social psychology. Although only a few of these alternative theories can be reviewed here, a brief comparison of them and the Meadian perspective will add to our developing understanding of contemporary symbolic interactionism. Four contrasting perspectives are discussed here: learning theory, exchange theory, phenomenology and ethnomethodology, and psychoanalytic theory. Each of these approaches has points of view in common with symbolic interactionism, but also points of sharp difference. Each addresses basic questions of interest to social psychologists and answers them in different ways.

Learning Theory

The behaviorism of John Watson, which we have already mentioned in discussing the ideas of Mead, provided the foundations for a major contemporary school of psychological thought, which is variously known as *behaviorism, learning theory,* or, in its more explicitly social psychological form, *social learning theory.*[12] This school has, in common with Watson, a general aversion to unobservable, "mental," and "subjective" phenomena and pays attention to directly observable behavior and environmental events. Although its theories and research findings have been enormously elaborated since Watson's day, it still generally finds notions of mind, voluntary conduct, and subjective experiences foreign to its thinking about human behavior.

The basic ideas of behaviorism are familiar to students who have studied psychology and know something of classical (or respondent) conditioning and operant conditioning. *Classical conditioning* is typified in the work of Ivan Pavlov, who demonstrated that a response, such as a dog's salivating in the presence of food, could also be elicited by an unrelated stimulus, such as the sound of a bell, if the bell were rung each time the food was presented to a hungry dog. After a certain number of trials in which food and a bell are presented simultaneously, the bell alone will produce the salivation response. This response is involuntary (the dog has no control over it), but it can be associated by the dog with a stimulus other than the one, food, that usually elicits it. *Operant conditioning* focuses on more voluntary behavior—that behavior over which the organism has some control and that it can produce in order to yield a certain effect. In this form of conditioning, for which the psychologist B. F. Skinner is the chief architect of ideas, the stimulus *follows* the response. That is, some behavior (such as a pigeon pecking on a certain spot on its cage) is followed by a specific event (such as a kernel of corn being released into the cage). If the organism values the event (stimulus) positively, it will be more likely to repeat the behavior in the future. Under these conditions we would say that the behavior has been positively reinforced.

How do the principles of classical and operant conditioning provide a basis for social psychology? The basic idea is that the individual's environment, including the other human beings with whom interaction occurs, is the source of stimuli—both those that trigger classical, involuntary responses and those that serve as positive and negative reinforcement or as punishment for its voluntary activities. Thus, one might say that the child learns a repertoire of behavior from his or her parents, who provide reinforcements or punishments for the child's behaviors. The child learns to brush teeth or say "Thank you," for example, because he or she is positively reinforced for doing so and perhaps punished for not doing so. An important extension of learning theory is the recognition that learning in social contexts is frequently vicarious: By observing the behavior of others and the rewards their actions earn, we are able to learn what they are learning without making any actual trials ourselves. The child can learn that he or she will get praise for being polite to adults by observing other children experience this reinforcement. The child can then enact this behavior, get the reinforcement, and thus experience what has been called *model learning.* This theory of *social learning* expands the basic ideas of learning theory and adapts them to the realities of social life as we observe it: People learn by observation and imitation and not simply by blind trial and error.

The symbolic interactionist finds much that is appealing in behaviorism. The perspective makes learning an important process, and symbolic interactionism finds no fault with that. Nor can the existence of involuntary responses be doubted—not only do we ordinarily not have control over such responses as salivation, but we have more complex responses, such as emotional ones, to various situations and stimuli, and these may also be beyond our capacity to control with any ease. For instance, we may become habitually angry when we deal with persons in authority, and yet not know why we react in this way nor be able effectively to bring such reactions under voluntary control. Moreover, there is much in the behaviorists' ideas about operant conditioning that the symbolic interactionist likes. The idea that a future stimulus (namely, the reward associated with an activity) can control a behavior is an important one because it is a way of conceiving behavior as being goal oriented. Much of what we do seems designed to produce some desired future effect.

In the eyes of symbolic interactionism, behaviorism also has some serious flaws. Although both classical and operant conditioning can be found in human behavior, the symbolic interactionist also finds evidence of processes that are not observed in other animals. The interactionist would say, for example, that we can become *aware* of our conditioned responses, whether they are respondent or operant. We can, for example, become aware of a tendency to respond with anger to persons in authority, and we can and typically do become aware of the relationship of present conduct to future events. Much of what we do is intended to influence what will happen to us in the future—whether in the next moment or the next year. *Self*-awareness is crucial to intentional behavior, for it is the person's capacity to be conscious of his or her own present and future actions that makes it possible for these actions to be controlled. Becoming *aware* of the tendency to respond with anger to persons in authority is the first step in acquiring the capacity to control that response. And a person's ability to govern behavior so as to secure some goal depends on the capacity to imagine himself or herself acting in alternative ways so that one particular act can be chosen.

Moreover, although contemporary behaviorism conceives the social environment as an important source of stimuli, it still tends toward a microscopic view of behavior in which the complexities and real significance of that environment are ignored. Think of our earlier example of a child learning that politeness and obedience produce such rewards as praise and affection. To apply behaviorism in a very strict manner, we have to assume that the child, whether gradually on a trial and error basis or more quickly and vicariously, learns to behave in ways that produce the desired results. Symbolic interactionists argue that there is more to the process of learning than the reinforcement of specific acts. People seem to be guided not merely by rewards but also by more general ideas of how their own conduct is expected to be fitted to the conduct of others. Although in the earliest stages of our experience these ideas may be fairly concrete ("If I eat all my food, my mother will be happy with me"), they become gradually more complex and abstract as the person grows older. Our conduct comes to be guided by more general principles rather than by discrete reactions to concrete situations.

For the symbolic interactionist, the individual's conception of self in relation to the social group of which he or she is a part underlies the capacity to be aware of his or her own responses, to control these responses, and to formulate hypotheses about the expectations and responses of others. People develop an awareness not just of the specific behavior that will produce a particular result in a given situation, but more generally of their place in the life of the group as a whole. People know that they will be called upon to play various roles, that these roles must somehow mesh with the roles of others, and that they must control their own acts so that these fit with the acts of other people. Thus, the interactionist conception of how conduct is learned is more global, more complex, more social, and more dynamic than that posed by a simple learning model.

Exchange Theory

A sociological theory of social psychology that draws upon some of the elementary principles of learning theory as well as upon an explicitly economic model of human conduct is called *exchange theory*.[13] This approach, elaborated in the work of such sociologists as Peter Blau and George Homans, takes learning theory as its starting point. Its basic idea is that what people do is a function of what they get for doing it. To the extent that people are rewarded for their activities, Homans maintains, they will be inclined to repeat those activities in the future.

Sociological exchange theory is more elaborate and social than learning theory, however, because it incorporates an economic model of human beings and their interaction. First, it views people as making rational profit calculations, deciding what they will do on the basis of the likely costs to them of a particular form of behavior as against the rewards the behavior will earn them. Thus, for example, if I am deciding how much time I will devote to my spouse and family, my behavior will depend on the rewards I expect to get for spending time with them (love, respect, attention) as against the costs to me of not doing something else, such as working harder at my job. I may decide to restrict the amount of time I spend with my family because the rewards for being with them are outweighed by the costs—not advancing as rapidly in my job, getting paid less, and receiving less attention and respect from my peers.

Second, exchange theory takes into account the crucial fact that people provide one another with rewards and punishments. Social reinforcements—

acceptance, love, status, respect, approval, and the like—are viewed as crucial by exchange theorists, although they fail to explain just why some things are rewarding and others are not. Moreover, the theory recognizes that people who interact with one another are typically providing mutual rewards and reinforcements. Thus, a relationship between husband and wife might be analyzed by looking at the reinforcements their mutual patterns of conduct provide for one another. Sometimes this leads to a cynical view of human relationships. An exchange theorist might say that a man enacting the "traditional" role of husband provides economic support and social status in return for his wife's provision of sex, affection, and housework.

Exchange theory thus posits that people enter into and maintain social relationships in order to secure rewards. To the extent that their behavior is rewarded, people continue to interact with one another in established ways. If rewards are not forthcoming, people consider terminating their relationships or changing their behavior toward others. People maintain social relationships and established patterns of behavior if it is profitable to do so.

From the perspective of symbolic interactionism, exchange theory has one major virtue: It posits a fairly explicit and complex set of cognitive processes that underlie behavior. In order to calculate their profits and losses and govern their behavior and relationships accordingly, people must be able to imagine alternative lines of conduct, anticipate the responses of others, and thus exert control over what they are going to do. Yet exchange theory does not have an elaborated theory of the self. It assumes that something like the self-control of conduct must operate, but it does not give us an explanation of how it is created or how it operates.

Another serious problem with exchange theory lies in its single-minded emphasis on profit and loss calculations. For exchange theorists, all seems to hinge on the bottom line. This amounts to an assertion that there is but one motive, one meaning underlying all human conduct. We are economic beings, neither more nor less. Symbolic interactionism posits a much more varied, more diverse, and more social schedule of human motives. People calculate their profits and losses, to be sure, but in varying circumstances (and differently in different cultures) they act with altruism, in a cooperative spirit, or with commitment to relationships in spite of the bottom line. Thus, a symbolic interactionist would not be surprised to find someone deciding in favor of a commitment to spouse and family even in the face of sure knowledge that occupational costs might be incurred. I know that if I decide that my family is more important than my job, my success at work might be affected; yet, even so, I may choose in favor of my family.

An exchange theorist would register a strong objection to this criticism, claiming that my choice of family over job in fact confirms exchange theory. I have decided in favor of my wife and family, they would say, because I value those rewards more than I value occupational rewards. This answer, however, converts the propositions of exchange theory into tautologies. Unless we can predict what rewards people will value and thus predict their behavior, we have said virtually nothing of use in explaining their conduct. Exchange theory *assumes* that people do what they do because they are rewarded for doing it — but the proposition becomes true by definition, for the exchange theorist will say that there *must* be something that is rewarding in *any* act, even if those rewards cannot be identified or described.

Symbolic interactionists take a different approach. Rather than explaining what people do on the basis of *assumptions* about their motives, it examines what people say about their motives and looks at the real contexts of interaction in which people actually form their conduct. Instead of assuming in advance that behavior is propelled by a single set of meanings — a devotion to the maximization of rewards — symbolic interactionists *study* the meanings people construct as they go about their affairs. Their focus is on the observation of people as they construct their conduct rather than on a priori assumptions about motivation.

Phenomenology and Ethnomethodology

Two perspectives closely related to one another — phenomenology and ethnomethodology[14] — deal more directly and explicitly with the meaning of human conduct than either learning theory or exchange theory. Phenomenology is a philosophical perspective whose founder was the German philosopher Edmund Husserl. As an approach to sociology and social psychology, its ideas have been adapted in the work of Alfred Schutz as well as in that of Peter Berger and Thomas Luckmann. Phenomenological sociology makes the subjective standpoint of individual actors its central focus of attention. Unlike a more objectivist approach, which views the social world as a reality that exists independently of any individual's perception of it, phenomenology sees that reality as constituted by our view of it. There is, therefore, not a single, objective social reality that can be analyzed in the same manner that a scientist might analyze physical reality. Rather, there are multiple realities; indeed, pushed to an extreme, one might say that there are as many social realities as there are perspectives from which to view them. A phenomenological approach asserts that it is impossible to say that there is some objective reality called "American society" or "John Smith's family" whose existence is so clear and straightforward that it can be literally described and explained. "John Smith's family" is a different reality to each of its members, as it is to a variety of outsiders who come into contact with it and perceive it. To John Smith, it may be a source of pride and satisfaction; to his wife, it may be a chafing set of restrictions; to his child, it may be a haven from a cruel world of teachers and peers. It is a different reality to each. The phenomenologist accounts for human conduct by attempting to "get within" and to describe the subjective perspectives of people, on the premise that one can only understand and account for what people do by understanding the reality they perceive and act toward.

Ethnomethodology is a variant of phenomenology. Like phenomenologists, ethnomethodologists are interested in the perspectives of actors, in how they view and act in their world as they see it. The main concern of ethnomethodologists is with the methods people use to produce meaning. Ethnomethodologists assert that meaning lies in the accounts people give of their experiences and interactions with others. These accounts are verbalizations, and they attempt to introduce order, sense, rationality, and predictability into the social world. For example, an ethnomethodologist might study the way in which people are diagnosed as schizophrenic. The ethnomethodologist does not assume that there is some real disease called schizophrenia, nor that its diagnosis is merely a matter of applying medical knowledge so as to ferret out the category of illness into which a given patient belongs. Instead, the ethnomethodologist suspends judgment on such questions and focuses on how the psychiatrist *explains* the diagnosis—the behavior he or she says is important, the rules he or she invokes to justify calling that behavior schizophrenic, and the like.

Underlying this approach is the belief that people are constantly engaged in a process of creating appearances—making it appear that their behavior is correct or appropriate, that they are being sensible and normal human beings doing things in the usual way. The perspective argues that culture does not provide a specific set of rules that guide people in their everyday behavior, but that it provides the resources that people make use of in creating the illusion of normality and meaning in their everyday lives. Pushed to an extreme, ethnomethodology appears to take no interest at all in what people do, nor in explaining why people do what they do, but concerns itself only with how people make sense of what they do.

Symbolic interactionists find some features of phenomenology and ethnomethodology to be interesting and useful additions to its approach (we will discuss some of these later in this book), but reject these perspectives as the basis for a comprehensive social psychology. Although symbolic interactionism, like phenomenology, views the person's perspective and perceptions as very important, the former avoids the extreme subjectivity into which the latter is prone to fall. Symbolic interactionists argue that people act on the basis of meanings, so that one's actions in a particular situation depend on the way that situation is perceived. For example, if I believe the world is out to get me, I will interpret the actions of others in accordance with my belief and act accordingly. Yet the world external to the individual does not simply become what the individual thinks it is—there are limits to the person's capacity to imagine that the world is what it is not. My view may be that of a paranoid, and my actions may even cause other people to dislike me and to act in ways that confirm my paranoia, but their perceptions do not necessarily accord with mine—the world, as they see it, is different, and their actions have different meaning for them than I attribute to them. An external world confronts and constrains the individual regardless of how he or she perceives it.

The major contribution of ethnomethodology is the insight that people construct the illusion of meaning and sensibility through their conversations. Although symbolic interactionists emphasize the meanings that people share as they interact with one another, it is easy to overemphasize the extent to which meanings are fully and genuinely shared. Ethnomethodology emphasizes that shared meaning is often an illusion and not actuality, that people have ways to convince themselves that they agree with one another or that they share the same motives when in fact they do not. Beyond this insight, which will be incorporated in this book, ethnomethodology is too limited in its scope to constitute an adequate foundation for social psychology as a whole. By reducing everything to the question of how people create appearances, ethnomethodology ignores such important matters as how people actually decide to act in particular ways, how interaction influences conduct, and how selves are formed. By paying attention only to what people say about their actions, ethnomethodology ignores the actions themselves — and it is what people *do* that is the central concern of social psychology.

Psychoanalytic Theory

Few social psychologists work explicitly from a psychoanalytic perspective, but the influence of Sigmund Freud and his intellectual followers upon the social sciences as a whole and upon our everyday, commonsense ideas about psychology has been considerable.[15] We must, therefore make some effort to convey the essence of this perspective. There is much more to Freud's theory than the ideas presented here, of course, but these are the ideas of most immediate interest to sociologists.

Freudian theory has a view of both the nature of society and of the development and vicissitudes of the individual personality. Freud poses the individual and society explicitly against one another, and one can grasp the dynamics of society and culture, as well as the place of the individual in society, only by understanding the dynamics of personality.

Freud's conception of personality divides it into three components. The *id* is the source of the individual's drives, instincts, and behavioral energy. The forces that move behavior — such as sexuality or aggression — are biological and universal; they are exceedingly powerful; and they are the central fact with which the individual as well as the society must contend. The id is the source of motivation and supplies the person with images of those objects that will meet its needs. It is, for example, the source of both the sexual drive and images of sexual activities or partners that will satisfy that drive. The second component of personality is the *ego,* which is a kind of operating mechanism that searches in the external world for opportunities to meet the organism's needs. The ego lives in the real world; that is, it confronts the external world and attempts to secure objects that will actually satisfy the person's drives. In a sense, the ego is driven by the id, for it attempts to accomplish what the id wants. In doing so, it must also cope with the third component of personality, the *superego,* which is the internalization of society and culture in the individual. The superego represents what society stands for, as opposed to what the id wants, and it is as powerful and demanding a force as the latter. It represents morality, perfection, and the socially necessary as against the unremitting biological imperatives of the id. The ego can thus be thought of as the negotiator or manager that is caught between these two powerful forces. The ego has the difficult tasks of trying to satisfy both the id and the superego simultaneously, and in doing so it must rely on many defensive techniques (defense mechanisms), the objectives of which are to deceive the id and superego into thinking that their imperatives are being met. One of the more common mechanisms is repression, whereby potentially dangerous ideas or wishes are pushed out of the conscious part of the mind and into the unconscious. For example, if the values of the society view sexuality negatively, the ego may deal with the insistent sexuality of the person by repressing it, pushing sexuality out of consciousness.

Symbolic interactionists, like other sociological social psychologists, have generally either ignored psychoanalysis or rejected it because of its weakest features instead of attempting to grapple with the problems it poses for social theory. In particular, most social psychologists reject Freud's biological and instinctual theory of motivation—his image of human beings as seething pots of impulses barely contained by a thin veneer of civilization. Symbolic interactionists have felt that the relationship between society and the person is more cooperative, that culture does not battle biology. In their view, humans are animals without instincts; culture replaces the biological guidance that the human species has lost in the course of its evolution. As a result, culture guides human beings rather than restraining their antisocial impulses. If this is so, much of the force of Freud's theory seems to be lost.

It is possible, however, to reject a theory of instincts and of culture and biology as hopelessly pitted against one another without also rejecting some more important and valid insights of psychoanalysis. Donald Carveth argues that the instinctual basis of motivation can be rejected without discarding other aspects of Freud's theory. Indeed, according to Carveth, the theory of instincts *must* be rejected in order to get to the really important insights of psychoanalysis.[16] In a general sense, Freud's theories strongly caution against an "over-socialized" conception of human beings. Although culture does take the place of instinct, it does not automatically or mechanically dictate conduct. There is no lack of conflict between people or between the person and society, and what people do often seems unpredictable and inexplicable.

Moreover, it is not necessary to posit antisocial biological drives in order to explain how society and the individual come into conflict. In both psychoanalysis and symbolic interactionism, there is a basis for viewing the individual and society as in a natural state of tension with one another, although not in a constant state of war. Like Freud, symbolic interactionists say that acts have their beginnings beneath the level of consciousness. Psychoanalysis posits an unconscious with a life of which the individual is unaware and does not control. Symbolic interactionists have been reluctant to adopt this conception, but do acknowledge that people only become aware of the nature and directions of their acts after they have begun, thus acknowledging that some part of mental life is unconscious. Symbolic interactionists also imbue the person with the capacity to inhibit and redirect incipient acts — to say "no" to the impulses that arise within them, impulses that are derived from culture as well as from individual plans and purposes. The result is that the individual is no puppet of society, but an active creature struggling for self-control and sometimes developing plans and purposes that run counter to what culture demands or encourages.

MAJOR TENETS OF SYMBOLIC INTERACTIONISM

What then is the essence of symbolic interactionism? Although there is more than one version of symbolic interactionism, most symbolic interactionists would subscribe to the following general principles.[17]

- The task of social psychology is to account for the formation and varieties of human social conduct.

Like all sociologists, interactionists are interested in the patterned regularities of human social life. Human conduct is social and cannot be explained merely as the result of idiosyncratic individual efforts. The fact is that our conduct does have a great deal of regularity; it is, as sociologists say, socially structured. But symbolic interactionists also believe that patterns and regularities cannot be fully grasped without understanding the social processes in which they are created. The regularities of social class or gender, for example, do not persist of their own accord or through sheer inertia, but because human beings actively construct their conduct in particular ways.

Like the phenomenologists and ethnomethodologists, symbolic interactionists believe that individual and joint methods of interpreting and perceiving reality are important. Human beings spend a great deal of time interpreting their own conduct and that of others, striving to make sense of the circumstances in which they find themselves. But human beings do not only define situations, they also *act* in them. They do not only interpret the actions of others, but also use their interpretations as the basis for their own actions. They do not merely strive to explain the circumstances in which they find themselves, but also to base actions on those explanations. In short, human beings are practical creatures who strive to make sense of their world so that they can take actions that have some chance of furthering their goals or fostering their adaptation to the world.

Like exchange theorists, symbolic interactionists believe that calculations of cost and gain must be taken into account in explaining conduct. Human beings are goal oriented, and they do what they are rewarded for doing. Explaining what human beings find rewarding and why they find it so, however, is a complex and difficult task. We are not driven merely by economic considerations or by status, sex, or a desire to form and maintain positive self-images, although all of these goals are important, and securing them is likely to reinforce patterns of conduct. At bottom, it appears to symbolic interactionists that human beings are motivated not by any specific drives or motives, but more generally by meanings.

- Human conduct depends upon the creation and maintenance of meaning.

Unlike the behavioral psychologists, who see meaning as either nonexistent or irrelevant, symbolic interactionists say that conduct is predicated on meaning. Unlike many sociologists who believe that culture and society dictate meanings to people, interactionists see meaning as variable and emergent. Meaning arises and is transformed as people define and act in situations; it is not merely handed down unchanged by culture. This emphasis on meaning "means" several things.

First, it means that people act with plans and purposes—that when they get in the car or speak words of love to someone, they do so with purposes in mind. Human conduct is directed toward objects, which is to say that it always looks toward some goal or purpose. People do not always pursue their purposes single-mindedly once they set their conduct in motion, for they are often deflected from their intended paths by obstacles or by more appealing objects. Nor are people conscious of their purposes or of how they will attain them at every moment; much of what they do depends upon habit. When I get in the car to go to the store, I do not have to constantly think of the store or of the techniques of automobile driving I have learned. Habit takes over many tasks. I may sometimes speak words of love out of habit, not really intending what I am saying.

Second, the interactionist approach emphasizes that meaning and intention are two sides of the same coin. For symbolic interactionists, meaning lies in intentions and actions, and not in some ethereal realm of pure meanings or interpretations. Meaning is found in conduct, both in conduct that is overt and therefore visible to others and in plans and purposes that are formulated and verbalized only silently and are thus not observed by others. Our conduct is meaningful because it is fundamentally purposeful; it can be purposeful because it rests on meaning.

Third, symbolic interactionists stress the possibility of meaning being transformed, and they recognize individual as well as shared meanings. Clearly human beings are restricted to certain kinds of meaning by the words they learn, because words represent the objects they can imagine. People cannot act toward that which they cannot name. Symbolic interactionists say not only that humans live in a named world, but also that naming is an activity that is central to the way they approach the world. People have the capacity to think of new ways to act by inventing new objects — new names. Although they may not do so frequently, they have the capacity to do so, and this guarantees that sometimes they will do so. Faced with novel situations or obstacles to conduct under way, human beings think of alternative goals and alternative methods. Thus, the meanings on the basis of which we act are never fixed or final, but emerge and change as we go about our affairs. Furthermore, these meanings — the objects of our actions — are personal as well as social, for human beings rather easily learn to pursue goals that are inimical to the goals pursued by others.

- Human conduct is self-referential.

The individual human being is both an acting subject and an object in his or her own experience. Unlike other animals, who regard the world from the center of their own being, but can never themselves be a part of the picture, human beings have self-consciousness. They act toward themselves with purpose much as they act toward the external world with purpose. They take themselves — their feelings, their interests, their images of self — into account as they act.

The self is a valued, indeed crucial human object, a major source of the purposes that people bring to their environment. Human beings do not merely wish to act in concert with others to secure the things they are taught by culture to value, but to find a sense of security and place — a sense of social identity — by participation in group life. They do not merely take themselves into account as they act, but seem to want to develop and sustain coherent images of themselves. And they want to attach a positive value to the self, to regard themselves favorably, to maintain and enhance their self-esteem.

Consciousness of self thus confers not only the capacity to exert control over conduct, but also to make the self an important focus of conduct. Human beings are capable of very precise social coordination; they are able to consider their own acts from the vantage point of the group as a whole and thus to imagine the consequences of their acts for others. They are also capable of considerable self-absorption and of putting their own interests before those of others. A person can attain a coherent self and maintain self-esteem by cheerful cooperation with the organized life of a community, but can also obtain these ends through more individualistic means.

- People form conduct as they interact with one another.

Psychologists, particularly the learning theorists, have typically emphasized the individual's history of rewards and reinforcements as a way of explaining individual conduct. Many sociologists have emphasized the determining effects of roles, norms, social class, and other aspects of our membership in society. The former often seem to depict a human being imprisoned within his or her own previous patterns of action and reward; the latter, an individual fully shaped and determined by society and culture. Without denying the importance of either individual histories of reward or of social and cultural variables, symbolic interactionists emphasize that conduct is formed in real time as people form plans and purposes, take themselves into account, and interact with one another.

Most human acts, interactionists think, are not individual acts but social acts, requiring the coordinated efforts of several individuals. Although individual capabilities affect the capacity of individuals to perform their parts in social life, the actual performance of such actions as shaking hands or delivering a lecture is sustained not just by individual skills, but also by their maintenance in a social setting. The audience is as important to the lecturer as his or her own speaking skills—a disinterested audience can flatten even the liveliest speaker. Although the social acts we perform are handed down to us by our society, they do not persist by themselves, but through the interaction of people who use their understandings of these acts as templates to reproduce them. A handshake exists not only in a name or an idea, but also in the actual pressing of one sweaty palm to another.

Symbolic interactionists thus regard the actual outcomes of any given episode of social interaction as potentially novel. Most of the time, we human beings shake one another's hands or deliver or hear lectures in a routine fashion. It is unusual for a social encounter to follow a truly novel course. It is unusual, but not impossible. Human beings do encounter situations they have not faced before; they find their paths are blocked by one obstacle or another; they misunderstand one another, failing to define situations as others do. In these and a variety of other ways, routine situations can become novel. People must find new meanings—new purposes and new methods—and they must reach into their stock of individual skills and socially acquired knowledge for general principles that can help them deal with novel situations. Thus, skills learned in other contexts are generalized as people encounter problematic situations; roles that cannot be performed in the routine way are performed in new ways.

- Society and culture shape and constrain conduct, but they are also the products of conduct.

In common with other sociologists, symbolic interactionists emphasize the prior existence and impact of society and culture. We humans are born into an already existing society and culture, and we are quickly swept into its flow. We are surrounded by others who define reality for us, showing us the objects in their world and in some ways requiring us to make them our own. The child, for example, learns that there is a god, or that there are many gods, and that one must tread carefully in his, or her, or their presence.

Yet we human beings do not have to reproduce the society and culture we inherit, and sometimes we do not. Regardless of what is at issue — belief in the powers of the gods or in the importance of drinking beer cold or being faithful to a spouse — the persistence of a belief or social practice rests on individual and collective action. Society is not a self-perpetuating, autonomous system of roles or social relationships. Rather, as Herbert Blumer has said, society consists of people interacting with one another. Culture is not an invariant set of lessons from the past, but the environment in which we all live, an environment composed of objects whose persistence depends upon our continuing to take them into account, even as our survival depends on coming to terms with them.

SUMMARY

• Social psychology is a specialty within both sociology and psychology, and the theoretical and research interests of the parent disciplines influence the topics studied and shape the questions that are asked. Psychologists make the individual their main abstraction and thus want to predict what individuals do under varying conditions of group life. Sociologists begin by assuming the paramount importance of society and culture and are less interested in explaining individual conduct than in depicting the operation of social and cultural processes. These disciplinary concerns are reflected in the typical activities of sociological and psychological social psychologists.

• Sociological social psychology stresses the complex and even paradoxical relationship between the individual and society and culture. Because human beings are cultural animals, individuals acquire the knowledge and skills they need for survival through membership in a society that exists before they are born and that will outlive them. This very society on which they depend is also dependent on them, however, for society is nothing more than the coordinated actions of its members, and its culture is transmitted from one generation to the next only through their actions.

Sociologists have often been tempted to emphasize only one side of this complex relationship, viewing the individual as a product of society and culture and taking it for granted that what people actually do produces and reproduces the latter. Because of the powerful constraining influence of society and culture, and because group life seems so highly patterned and repetitive, it has often been thought possible to ignore individual conduct and everyday social interaction on the grounds that the larger patterns of culture and social structure *essentially* determine what people do.

Social psychologists reject such one-sided determinism. Because culture and social structure change over time, we have to explain not only how they are sustained, but also how they change. Even more important is the nature of life, especially human life. Following Mead and the other pragmatists, symbolic interactionists view living organisms as actively engaged with their surroundings, trying to take advantage of opportunities and to overcome challenges by using the tools with which evolution has endowed them. To explain how any form of life exists and survives in its environment, we have to grasp the fact that organism and environment constantly shape one another. For human beings, society and culture *are* the environment, and the main tools we use are significant symbols. Human beings are creatures who act on the basis of symbols, which give them the capacity for self-consciousness and for the deliberate control of conduct. Society and culture — the human environment — are themselves constantly the products of human symbolic activity as well as factors that constrain what people can do.

• Sociologists have used a variety of theoretical perspectives, including learning theory, exchange theory, phenomenology, ethnomethodology, and psychoanalysis, as a basis for their approach to social psychology. The symbolic interactionist perspective has some points of similarity with each of these approaches, but also differs from them in important ways. Like learning theorists, symbolic interactionists emphasize the study of actual conduct. However, interactionists feel that individual acts should be studied as whole entities that are almost invariably a part of social acts rather than broken down into minute stimulus-response units. Like exchange theorists, symbolic interactionists recognize that human beings respond to rewards and typically calculate the benefits of alternative courses of action. Interactionists, however, further argue that social psychology must have some way to explain *how* people estimate potential costs and benefits and *why* they find certain actions more rewarding than others. Like phenomenology, symbolic interactionism stresses the importance of what people intend to do; and, like ethnomethodology, it emphasizes the fact that human beings strive to make sense of the social world in which they live. Symbolic interactionism has a more complete account of how people formulate their plans, and it does not try to reduce everything humans do to an effort to make sense. Finally, symbolic interactionism has some points of similarity with psychoanalysis, although just how compatible the two perspectives are remains to be seen. At the very least, psychoanalysis offers an in-depth account of *unconscious* processes as well as insight into the tension that exists between the person and society.

• Symbolic interactionists believe their task is to explain the actual formation of conduct in social interaction and not to assume that social and cultural patterns by themselves explain conduct. In this task, they emphasize meaning, arguing that people act on the basis of meanings they construct in social interaction. Among the most important meanings are those related to the self, for interactionists conceive human beings as self-referential creatures for whom the self is among the most important objects. And symbolic interactionists view human beings not only as shaped by culture and society, but also as capable of shaping them. In the last analysis, culture and society depend upon human actions constructed on the basis of meanings formed in everyday social interaction.

ENDNOTES

1. William McDougall, *Introduction to Social Psychology* (London: Methuen, 1908).

2. Edward A. Ross, *Social Psychology* (New York: Macmillan, 1908).

3. Solomon Asch, "Effects of Group Pressure upon the Modification and Distortion of Judgments," in *Groups, Leadership, and Men,* ed. H. Guetzkow (Pittsburgh: Carnegie Press, 1951), pp. 177–190.

4. Stanley Milgram, *Obedience to Authority* (New York: Harper and Row, 1974).

5. See Gordon W. Allport, "The Historical Background of Modern Social Psychology," in *The Handbook of Social Psychology,* vol. I, eds. Gardner Lindzey and Elliot Aronson (Reading, Mass.: Addison-Wesley, 1968), pp. 1–80.

6. For a survey of sociological social psychology, see *Social Psychology: Sociological Perspectives,* eds. Morris Rosenberg and Ralph H. Turner (New York: Basic Books, 1981).

7. Gary A. Fine, "Impression Management and Preadolescent Behavior: Friends as Socializers," in *The Development of Friendship,* eds. S. Asher and J. Gottman (Cambridge: Cambridge University Press, 1980).

8. This seems to be true, for example, with respect to *attribution theory,* which is a product of psychological social psychology, and the study of *motive talk* and *presentation of self* in sociological social psychology. See Kathleen S. Crittenden, "Causal Attribution in Socio-cultural Context: Toward a Self-Presentational Theory of Attribution Processes," *The Sociological Quarterly* 30 (1, 1989): 1–14.

9. Peter Berger and Thomas Luckmann discuss this issue as the dialectic of individual and society. *"Society is a human product. Society is an objective reality. Man is a social product."* For their discussion, which is related to, but not identical with, an interactionist analysis, see their *Social Construction of Reality* (New York: Doubleday Anchor, 1967).

10. The literature on pragmatism and symbolic interactionism is vast. For a recent review and analysis, see Dmitri N. Shalin, "Pragmatism and Social Interactionism," *American Sociological Review* 51 (February 1986): 9–29. For a discussion of Mead as a social reformer in the political context of his time, see Shalin, "G. H. Mead, Socialism, and the Progressive Agenda," *The American Journal of Sociology* 93 (January 1988):

913-951. For a variety of other views of Mead and his ideas, see the commemorative issue on Mead of *Symbolic Interaction* 4 (Fall 1981) and another issue of *Symbolic Interaction* 12 (Spring 1989); the latter contains an article by Randall Collins, "Toward a Neo-Meadian Sociology of Mind," and a variety of critical responses. Those interested in the relationship between pragmatism and critical theory should see the "Special Feature: Habermas, Pragmatism, and Critical Theory" in *Symbolic Interaction* 15 (Fall 1992). For a historical review of Chicago sociology, see Berenice M. Fisher and Anselm L. Strauss, "Interactionism," Chapter 12 in *A History of Sociological Analysis,* eds. Tom Bottomore and Robert A. Nisbet (New York: Basic Books, 1978).

11. See George Herbert Mead, *Mind, Self, and Society* (Chicago: University of Chicago Press, 1934); *The Philosophy of the Act* (Chicago: University of Chicago Press, 1938). Also see *George Herbert Mead: On Social Psychology,* ed. Anselm L. Strauss (Chicago: University of Chicago Press, 1964); David L. Miller, *George Herbert Mead* (Austin: University of Texas Press, 1973); John D. Baldwin, *George Herbert Mead: A Unifying Theory for Sociology* (Beverly Hills, Calif.: Sage, 1986); Mary Jo Deegan, ed. *Women and Symbolic Interaction* (Boston: Allen and Unwin, 1987); Hans Joas, *G. H. Mead: A Contemporary Re-examination of His Thought* (Cambridge: M.I.T. Press, 1985).

12. The major statement of social learning is that of Albert Bandura. See his *Social Learning Theory* (Englewood Cliffs, N.J.: Prentice Hall, 1977).

13. For presentations of exchange theory, see George C. Homans, *Social Behavior: Its Elementary Forms,* rev. ed. (New York: Harcourt Brace Jovanovich, 1974); Peter M. Blau, *Exchange and Power in Social Life* (New York: Wiley, 1964); and Richard M. Emerson, "Social Exchange Theory," in Rosenberg and Turner, *Social Psychology,* pp. 30-65 (Note 6).

14. Berger and Luckmann (*Social Construction of Reality,* Note 9) present an essentially phenomenological perspective. For the work of Schutz, see *Alfred Schutz: On Phenomenology and Social Relations,* ed. Helmut Wagner (Chicago: University of Chicago Press, 1970). For a recent symbolic interactionist view of ethnomethodology, see Mary J. Gallant and Sheryll Kleinman, "Symbolic Interactionism versus Ethnomethodology," *Symbolic Interaction* 6 (1, 1983): 1-18.

15. General discussions of Freudian theory and social psychology can be found in C. S. Hall and G. Lindzey, "The Relevance of Freudian Psychology and Related Viewpoints for the Social Sciences," *The Handbook of Social Psychology,* 2nd ed., eds. G. Lindzey and E. Aronson (Reading, Mass.: Addison-Wesley, 1968), pp. 245-319.

16. Donald L. Carveth, "Psychoanalysis and Social Theory: The Hobbesian Problem Revisited," *Psychoanalysis and Contemporary Thought* 7 (1984): 43-98. Carveth's article is a difficult but exciting appraisal of the importance of psychoanalysis for social theory, written in a way that is sympathetic to symbolic interactionism and incorporates many of its insights.

17. For an important statement of an avowedly more social structural version of symbolic interactionism, see Sheldon Stryker, *Symbolic Interactionism: A Social Structural Version* (Menlo Park, Calif.: Benjamin-Cummings, 1980). For another statement of this view and its relation both to role theory and symbolic interactionism more broadly, see Sheldon Stryker and Anne Statham, "Symbolic Interactionism and Role Theory," Chapter 6 in *The Handbook of Social Psychology,* 3rd ed., eds. Gardner Lindzey and

Elliot Aronson (New York: Random House, 1985). See also Stryker, "The Vitalization of Symbolic Interactionism," *Social Psychology Quarterly* 50 (1, 1987): 83–94. Although there are some differences between Stryker's version of symbolic interactionism and mine, in my view there are even more similarities and points of fundamental agreement.

▶ 2

The Evolution
of Human Capacities

Every living thing exists in an environment, a set of surrounding conditions, events, and other organisms that provide the materials for its sustenance and influence its activities. The protozoa cultured in a laboratory, the bear in its habitat, the human being in society and culture — each responds to and acts on a specific environment. The microorganism occupies a small space, has a brief life span as a single individual, and is affected by a comparatively restricted set of physical and chemical forces. Complex organisms such as mammals occupy a correspondingly complex environment, which consists of other organisms and their behavior as well as physical conditions and events. The human environment includes symbols as well as material things, and its features are as crucial to an analysis of human conduct as are the features of the amoeba world or the bear world crucial to an explanation of the behavior of amoebas or bears.

ORGANISMS AND ENVIRONMENTS

The distinction between organism and environment leads to a number of interesting questions: How has a particular species come to exist in its habitat? How are its physical structure and behavioral capabilities related to the setting it inhabits? How well can it survive under different or changing environmental conditions? What impact does the species itself have on its environment?

Zoologists focusing on the American alligator, for example, might look at it in a specific habitat such as the Florida Everglades. They would attempt to locate the predacious alligator in the food chain, discovering its typical prey and its food sources. They would examine its physical adaptations to a water environment — its ability to swim, its ability to submerge for long periods of time, and its cold-bloodedness. The zoologists would link the behavior of the alligator to environmental conditions, stressing, for example, the relationship between the yearly cycle of wet and dry seasons that prevails in southern Florida and the alligator's patterns of migration. And they would emphasize the alligator's role in keeping its own pond free of mud and weeds, a behavioral pattern that contributes to the survival of many forms of life other than the alligator itself, including some of its prey.

A description of the relationships between alligators and their environment reveals a complex, dynamic, and constantly evolving web of interdependency. The alligator is affected by its surroundings — by water supply and levels, by the number of fish and turtles available as food, by ponds and their locations, and even by the number of mosquito larvae. The alligator, in turn, affects its environment. For example, it keeps its own pond clear and is a major predator of fish and turtles, thus influencing the location and numbers of other species.

At first glance, the ecology of the Everglades alligator seems to have little connection with the social psychology of human beings. The ecosystem in which the alligator is implicated is intricate, but nonetheless concrete, and relationships between the alligator, its behavior, and its habitat seem easily discernible. In contrast, the physical structure of humans is more complex, the range of their behavioral capabilities is far wider, and their habitat cannot be portrayed as concretely as for most other animals. Nevertheless, there are important similarities. Human societies are tied to an ecology every bit as much as a population of alligators, and the behavioral capabilities and dispositions of people are just as inseparable from species' habitat.

Alligators and people both illustrate a fundamental principle of life: *Organisms and environments determine one another.* It is tempting to look at the alligator simply as the product of a particular environment. After all, this animal occupies a relatively fixed position in the natural world. It seems to have evolved to fill a specific environmental niche, and its every act takes place in response to events within this narrow world. If there is a dry spell, the alligator must seek deeper pools of water with fish to provide itself with a supply of food. Because it is a cold-blooded animal, it must warm itself in the sun and seek the warmth of the water on cold winter days. Everything the alligator does seems determined by an environment that lies beyond its control.

But matters are not so simple. In both contemporary and evolutionary terms, the alligator has a hand (or a tail!) in shaping its environment. It *actively* keeps its pond free of weeds, for example, so as to have a place to live and nest. But in doing so, it also provides a suitable habitat for the very fish that are a key part of its food supply, particularly during the dry season when other wet places have dried up and the fish move to ponds maintained by alligators. The evolutionary processes that have adapted the alligator in its particular environment took place with the active cooperation of many generations of alligators — not, of course, because alligators intended to evolve in a specific direction or to become key to the survival of fish, but because at every point along the way the structure and behavior of the organism itself influenced the way the environment could affect it.

Living things are naturally active, and they possess a set of capabilities that they use to their advantage in dealing with their environments. Given this fact, we cannot sensibly speak of environment as determining either the structure or the behavior of organisms. Rather, a complex set of dependencies exists between the two, and the naturally active and sensitive organism is every bit as important as the constraining and limiting environment in which it lives.

To put this in a slightly different way, the structure and sensitivities of an organism determine its effective environment. Is water a part of the alligator's environment? Yes, of course it is, but it is so because of the alligator's particular sensitivity to and need for water. And what is true of alligators is also true of humans: Whatever is environmental to people is so because of and in relation to the particular needs, sensitivities, and dispositions of members of the species. This fact marks a point of difference as well as of similarity between human beings and other living things. There is considerable variation in the way various species attend to, respond to, and act on the environments in which they are typically located. To grasp the nature of human behavior in the human world, we must understand how humans differ from other organisms as well as how we resemble them.

LEVELS OF RESPONSE TO THE ENVIRONMENT

Species differ from one another in many ways — in size, method of locomotion, visual acuity, physical structure, capacity to manipulate objects, nervous system organization, and strength, to name only a few. It is beyond the scope of this book and of social psychology itself to develop a comprehensive description of the human species, particularly with respect to physical characteristics and capabilities. Nevertheless, we can point to some broad differences between human beings and other animals that enable us to understand what is distinctive about the human environment. These differences have to do with the general response capacities of humans as compared to other animals — how we attend to and react to significant objects and events in our environment.

All organisms are not alike in the way they respond to stimulation from the environment. Some seem to be able to perceive and react only to things and events that are nearby; others have more elaborate and sensitive mechanisms of sight, hearing, or smell that enable them to respond to things that are farther away. Some seem to be bound to and rather tightly controlled by an immediate environment, while others appear to have more mastery over a spatially larger environment. Some seem able to process only a limited amount of information, while others can respond to complex and subtle combinations of stimuli.

The differences in response capacities among organisms, as well as the distinctive features of human beings, can best be understood in terms of a number of advances that seem to have occurred in the course of evolution.[1] Four levels of response to environmental stimulation can be portrayed in the order in which they appeared during evolution. Each advance from one level to the next is characterized by a growth of mastery on the part of the organism and less determination by its surroundings. In each stage, organisms attend to and act upon their environments in a way that makes for more flexibility in the organism-environmental linkage than was possible in the preceding stage.

The simplest form of response, and the first to appear in the evolution of life, occurs when an organism's response to environmental stimulation is immediate and *direct*. A microorganism, for example, may simply ingest a bit of food it encounters or move around an object that is not food. There is no sense in which an organism such as an amoeba "chooses" whether it will respond to the food by ingesting it. If the object is of a size and composition that it can be engulfed and digested, it will be; if the object is too large or if it is chemically offensive, the organism will move away from it. In either case, the organism acts immediately and directly. The object is food because of the makeup of the microorganism, and it is present at the whim of the environment. As Ernest Becker wrote, in the case of such direct linkages as this, the "organism is a slave . . . to the properties of the object itself."[2]

Although direct responses are characteristic of the simplest forms of life, they play a role in more advanced creatures as well. The human knee-jerk reflex is a direct form of response "wired into" the nervous system; as long as the nervous system functions properly, the reflex occurs in response to the appropriate stimulus. But in more complex forms of life, direct responses become less important relative to more complex modes of response.

Among these other modes is the *conditioned* response. Here, the organism first responds directly to a stimulus; next, an unrelated stimulus is associated with the first; and finally, the organism is able to respond in the same way to the second stimulus as to the first, even when the latter is not present. In the familiar example of Pavlovian (classical) conditioning, a dog responds to the sight and smell of food by salivating. The food is a stimulus because of the dog's need or liking for it, and the response of salivation occurs directly and immediately when food is presented. Now, however, a new element is introduced: When food is presented to the hungry dog, a bell is rung. The dog continues to salivate on presentation of food, but as the bell is rung each time food is presented, the dog soon responds to the sound of the bell and salivates even when there is no food. One stimulus, a bell, has come to be associated with another, food, even though the former is in itself of no particular interest to the animal. That is, nothing in the physical condition of the animal makes the sound of the bell an intrinsically important stimulus, whereas food is related to its organic needs.

An organism that has the capacity for conditioned responses is no longer merely a slave to the properties of stimuli that are relevant to its needs. Liberated from the need to respond directly and immediately to stimuli, the organism can respond to the *signs* of objects. A sign is anything that stands for or signifies something else. In the case of Pavlov's dog, the *bell* is a sign — an indication — that food is coming, and the dog has learned to respond to the sign in the same way as to the actual presence of food.

The ability to respond to the *signs* of organismically important stimuli marks a fundamental advance in the evolution of life. The organism that is capable of conditioned responses is far more powerful and autonomous in its world, even though the environment itself is the source of signs and to a great extent the controller of the conditioning. In the natural world, important events and objects — important as stimuli essentially because they are related to food, comfort, danger, and other biologically crucial circumstances — tend to occur in association with events and objects that are themselves not important. The smoke that occurs with fire may sometimes be of no importance itself, except that its association with fire makes it a *sign* of fire.

The capacity for respondent conditioning marks a heightened and more complex sensitivity to the environment. Even though it represents a major forward development of what we would call intelligence, however, the animal is still limited to the whim of natural occurrence. The animal that has learned to respond to the sign of a biologically crucial event — Pavlov's dog, for example — has not itself *created* the empirical association between the sign and what it signifies. *Pavlov* made the bell ring when food was presented to the dog. What the dog did — and it is significant — was to *learn* that such a connection existed, but it did so without in any sense choosing to do so. The environment presented itself and the dog responded.

Not surprisingly, then, the next evolutionary advance entails the development of the organism's capacity to make connections *on its own* between events and conditions in its environment. The third level of response is marked by a greater alertness to a problematic situation — a heightened awareness of the environment in such a way that the organism itself actively searches for connections between things and events that are relevant to its needs and activities. There is a striking contrast, for example, between the behavior of a hungry dog and a hungry chicken confronted with a similar situation. A chicken will pace back and forth in frustration alongside a fence that separates it from food; a dog in the same situation will see a break in the fence a few feet away, run along the fence, through the break, and back to the food. The dog sought and formed a connection between things in its environment, but the chicken did not. Both are motivated — that is, both are sensitized to the food because of hunger — but the dog is better able to master the situation by seeing how various features of its environment are connected.

For the dog who sees a break in the fence, or the chimp who uses a stick to knock down a bunch of bananas, there is a *delay* between stimulus and response during which complex internal processing occurs. Indeed, the progression through the first three levels appears generally to involve an alteration of the temporal relationship between stimulus and response. In the first level, the response immediately follows the stimulus. The chief transformation involved in the second level is that the organism gains the capacity to respond *before* the relevant stimulus is actually present, since it can react to the sign of an event or object, a stimulus that may well occur in advance of (or at a distance from) the object itself. In the third level, we have a further alteration of the spatial and temporal structure of behavior, namely a time delay during which the organism associates events and objects in its environment.

Behaviorists have a useful way of thinking about how the temporal ordering of events is altered in this third level, although their conceptions of *respondent* and *operant conditioning* do not neatly correspond to our second and third levels of minding. In operant conditioning, the stimulus is said to *follow* the response. For example, the pigeon emits a response (pecking at a spot in its cage) *in advance* of the stimulus (a bit of food). This form of behavior might be said to be stimulus-seeking, in the sense that behavior occurs in advance of and with the expectation of the occurrence of a desired stimulus. Still, we would not (nor would behaviorists) speak of this as purposive behavior. It is inappropriate to use such terms from human vocabulary to characterize the behavior of such animals.

Although operant conditioning is an idea that helps us understand the various levels of response, it does not correspond clearly to our third level, nor does it go far enough in distinguishing it from the preceding level. Operant conditioning does portray an organism that is more active with respect to its environment — it acts upon the environment more clearly and more directly. It should be emphasized, however, that there is considerable variation in the capacity for operant conditioning. Pigeons are capable of this form of conditioning, but they do not compare well with dogs or many other mammals in the ease with which they can "see" connections in the environment and act upon them. Among mammals, the primates, a group in which humans are classified, have the most highly developed capacities for sensitivity to habitat and for establishing complex and subtle connections between objects and events.

The advances achieved in the evolution of the first three levels of response are important, but they pale by comparison with what happens at the fourth level. The animal capable of second- and third-level responses — able, that is, to respond to the signs of important stimuli in advance of those stimuli and to delay an immediate response so that several stimuli can be processed — has gained some mastery of the environment because of its capacity for anticipation and delay. It still inhabits a fairly concrete world: The "here" and "now" are stretched somewhat in duration and extent, but still the organism reacts to and acts upon given, particular, and concrete things and events in nature.

At the fourth level, a new element comes into play that dramatically transforms the response capacities of the organism. This element is the *symbol,* which is a sign created and given significance by organisms themselves. In the first three levels of response, organisms react to real, concrete things and events—sometimes directly, sometimes indirectly through the mediation of naturally occurring signs, sometimes by processing complex combinations of signs. At these levels of response, however, the organism always responds to a concrete and very particular world. At the fourth level, organisms respond to symbols, which are arbitrary signs of objects that can stand in place of the objects themselves. Thus, as we shall see, at a symbolic level of response, organisms act toward a world they take an active part in shaping, a world that is inherently abstract rather than concrete, a world that is in some sense imaginary.

A symbol is an *arbitrary* sign because it is associated with what it signifies solely by virtue of the agreement of those who use it. The word "house" is a symbol that stands for a physical object in which people reside only because a community of speakers (of English) agree that the two are associated. Symbols, therefore, are not merely a form of sign behavior engaged in by the individual, for their very existence and meaning depend on their use in a social context.

Symbols take many different physical forms—linguistic, body postures or movements, objects such as flags or paintings. The verbal symbol, produced by organs of speech, is of the greatest consequence for human behavior. This is the case for at least two reasons. First, verbal symbols are unique because those who produce them hear virtually what anybody else hears. Utter a sound and you hear nearly what others hear—the sound can be a stimulus to you just as it is a stimulus to others. In contrast, hand gestures and facial expressions (although they too can function in a symbolic mode) do not present a nearly identical stimulus to the one using them as they do to those witnessing them. The view from behind the face differs from the view in front of it. Second, the audio/oral channel of communication has the advantage of being relatively clear. That is, sounds have no other function than communication, whereas we use our hands for many purposes. We can speak at the same time as we perform tasks with the hands; if we had to rely on gestures for our symbols, we would often have to interrupt activity for communication, and vice versa.

Whatever their form, symbols are *conventional,* or social, in their meaning. The natural sign has a meaning that exists because the individual organism has learned to associate the sign and what it signifies. Symbols have meaning because a community of symbol users adopts the convention of using given symbols consistently, and because individual members of the community learn the conventions. "House" always stands for a particular kind of structure in a community of English speakers.

The capacity to use and respond to symbols has revolutionary consequences for the species that develops it. The framework of space and time within which action occurs is further expanded and complicated. At the same time, the actions of individual members of the species become more intricately linked together, since the use of symbols to represent things and events makes it possible not only to experience the environment in more complex ways, but also to share that experience with others. And, finally, the very character of the environment itself—of what is or may be environmental to the organism—is expanded. Human beings do not just respond to things and events, but to the symbols that stand for these things and events. And, as we will see, symbols do not merely represent a fixed reality, but in significant ways they create the reality—the environment—that confronts us.

SYMBOLS AND THEIR CONSEQUENCES

The evolution of response capacities has generally thickened and extended the spatial and temporal framework within which behavior takes place. The capacity for conditioning enables organisms to anticipate the future by responding to the signs of events yet to occur, and it enlarges the area within which the organism acts. The capacity to process many stimuli necessarily requires the organism to suspend time by inhibiting its action while the processing occurs. The capacity to make and use symbols carries these developments even further.

Characteristics of Symbols

First, symbols make it possible to *name* things in the environment and to manipulate these names rather than the things themselves or visual images of them. Symbols provide a rather powerful and efficient code—or shorthand— for internally representing and dealing with a world of things and events. Although we sometimes say that "a picture is worth a thousand words," it is in many respects far more efficient to manipulate words rather than visual images. Words—symbols—provide a method whereby humans can bring external reality within the sphere of their imaginations, where they can manipulate "house," "dog," and "table" rather than either the physical things for which these names stand or visual images of them.

Symbols thus alter the nature of our spatial world by bringing the environment "inside" us. Signs and stimuli are a part of the external world and are under its control; the organism responds to them as best it can. Symbols designate things in the external world, to be sure, but they are our property; we own and control them. Symbols change the external world from something that merely *is* what it is to something that can be *imagined*. They are the means whereby we import the external world into our minds and bring it under our imaginary control.

A second and closely related characteristic of symbols is that they make it possible to experience objects and events without their physical presence. The word "food" (the symbol) can be invoked and used by an individual apart from the actual presence of food (the real thing). Because we control symbols and do not require the actual presence of the things or events they stand for, we can imagine anything well in advance of and at considerable distances from its actual occurrence. Symbols, therefore, enable us to manipulate the environment imaginatively or hypothetically at times and places of our own choosing. This constitutes a major advance because we can anticipate things and events and decide what to do about them well before they occur.

Finally, symbols are inherently general and abstract. The direct experience of the world is an experience of the particular. Food, danger, prey — whatever the organism perceives — is a particular thing at a particular time and place. The development of symbols gives rise to categories of things, to classes of objects, to food in general rather than *this* food here and now. To name an object or event once is merely to attach a symbolic designation to it; to attach the same name to a similar object or event is immediately to create a *category* of similar objects or events. Symbols thus encourage an *attitude* of generalization and categorization; we humans do not approach the world as a set of discrete and unique things, but as a set of things that fit into various categories.

The Social Nature of Symbols

These developments in themselves, signal as they are, would not count for much if the use of symbols was merely a process internal to the *individual* organism. Symbols are crucially important because they are *social*. Symbols have meaning because they are used by the members of a group in a consistent way; and their use by the members of a group profoundly influences their behavioral capabilities. How is this influence exerted?

Symbols make possible the transference of mental states from one organism to another. A person who shouts "Fire!" in a public building, for example, is attaching a symbolic designation to the situation. As he or she shouts, others become aware of the situation in a way they previously were not aware of it. The mental states of these other people have become similar to that of the person who shouts "Fire!" Moreover, the individual who warns the others reacts to this warning in much the same way they do; that is, hearing his or her own voice, the person doing the warning takes an attitude toward the situation —

such as forming a desire and a plan to get out of the burning building — that resembles the attitude of the others.

In this example, one individual has noticed a feature of the environment, such as smoke issuing from part of the building. But instead of responding individually to this sign of fire — instead of simply leaving — the person responds socially. The individual symbolically designates the event taking place as a fire and utters the word so that others can hear it. In doing so, the individual calls forth the response of flight in himself or herself as well as in others. He or she designates a stimulus and anticipates action not only for himself or herself but also for others.

This is an example of social interaction; to be more specific, it is an example of *symbolic interaction.* It is what George Herbert Mead had in mind when he distinguished between the "significant symbol" and the "conversation of gestures."[3] (See the earlier discussion in Chapter 1.)

What Mead had in mind by the conversation of gestures is well illustrated by two dogs encountering one another. One may growl and bare its teeth; the other responds in like manner and begins to advance; the first dog then lunges at the other, and the fight is on. Each animal seems to respond to features of the other's behavior — in particular, to the initial parts of its act. The very beginning of a growl seems to set off a response in the other dog, and the beginnings of its response key the response of the first dog.

This is called a conversation of gestures because the beginning part of the act of one individual is a gesture — a sign — that indicates or signifies the impending act and keys an appropriate response in the other. Interaction at this level depends upon responses to signs, where each sign is actually a small, initial fragment of an entire act that is to follow. Given a growl, the dog is conditioned to respond by attacking, because the growl is a sign of an attack on it. There is no reflection, however, no "choice" on the part of the dog as to which response it will undertake. Given the gesture, the response is fixed, whether by conditioning or genetics.

The possession of symbols gives rise to a new form of social interaction — to what Herbert Blumer coined *symbolic interaction.* Suppose we have two (human) boxers in the midst of a bout. One begins to move his arm in the initial phase of a body blow and the other responds automatically with a defensive reaction, perhaps lowering an elbow to fend off the blow. If only this happens, we still have a conversation of gestures. But something else may occur: The boxer may see his opponent's fist move in a certain way, decide that it is not indicative of a body blow but is instead a ruse designed to throw him off balance so another punch can be landed, and react in a way calculated to counter the ruse.

If the latter occurs, we have an instance of symbolic interaction in which one boxer has *interpreted* the actions of the other. To say he has interpreted is only to say that he has designated the other's movements symbolically — he has thought to himself "ruse" and acted accordingly, rather than responding blindly. The *movement* is objectively there, but its *intent* is designated by the boxer, who responds *to his own designation* of the stimulus rather than to the raw stimulus itself.

The impact of symbols on interaction among symbol users is quite substantial. Events that occur in the environment can be designated by symbols by one individual, and his or her mental state thus transferred to others by the utterance of words. Moreover, individuals can respond symbolically to one another's acts, designating them (internally in the imagination) with one symbol or another and acting accordingly. Indeed, the roots of human conceptions of truth and falsity lie here: If individuals can designate environmental things or events with symbols, and if they can designate the intentions of one another's acts, they also can designate designations. That is, one person may shout "Fire!" and another may interpret the shout as a joke, a mistake, or even a lie.

Symbolic interaction and the transference of mental states from individual to individual depend on the complex set of symbols we call *language*. For it is in the vocabulary it provides as well as in the rules for combining elements of vocabulary that the facility for the designation of events, things, and persons is grounded. Language provides a medium for designating important stimuli that are present at any given time. The designation is done internally (the individual inwardly *names* stimuli) as well as externally, since names may be vocalized and made accessible to others who understand the language.

One consequence of the use of symbols remains to be explored. The distinction between the organism and its environment is fairly straightforward for animals that do not use symbols. Mutual determination of organism and environment aside, the two are clearly separate from one another; the environment is what lies outside the individual animal, and the line of demarcation between the two is clear.

The symbolic capacity introduces a strikingly new element into the relationship between organism and environment. If organisms can create and use symbols to designate their external environment, they can also use them to designate — to name — one another as entities in their environment. Their propensity to do so leads to another tendency, namely for individual symbol users to use their own names as designations for themselves. In this way, the symbolic capacity makes the organism itself a part of its own environment. Because it can name itself, it can act toward itself.

It is not surprising that animals who have learned to use symbols to deal with their environment would use them on one another. Since they are social animals (recall that symbols are inherently social since they require consensus for their meaning), the coordination of their activities would be improved if they could *name* one another. However, implicit in the practice of naming is the possibility that a given member might himself or herself use the designation others have applied to him or her. If a given member is called XYZ, that is a name he or she can pronounce as well as hear. To use a name for oneself is to acquire a *self,* to become one of the objects in the environment toward which the individual can act and, indeed, must act.

Such a development, the full implications of which we will explore later, is as revolutionary as the symbol itself. By participating in a community of symbol users in which a person is designated symbolically, and in which he or she can use the symbol for self, the individual takes on a completely new relationship to his or her own existence. He or she no longer is just an organism acting in relation to an external environment, but a person who acts toward an environment he or she is part of. Indeed, it is when the capacity to respond to oneself as a part of the world develops that we can speak of a dawning of consciousness, for it is only then that we can think of organisms as being aware of their own actions. The organism that minds itself is aware of itself as a part of the world and has gained an important capacity for control over its own acts. Just as it can anticipate the behavior of others of its species, it anticipates (imagines) its own acts as well.

THE DEVELOPMENT OF LANGUAGE

How did the capacity to employ linguistic symbols emerge in the course of human evolution? A definitive answer to this question is impossible, for the problems that generally attend the reconstruction of evolution are even greater when it comes to language. Anthropologists can point to bones in their effort to reconstruct the physical development of our species, but the organs of speech involve the soft tissues of the mouth, larynx, and brain, and there are no physical remains. Consequently, we can speculate and infer, but we can never really know with much certainty how language evolved.

Nevertheless, some understanding of how speech might have developed is important. Just as the structure of organisms and their characteristic modes of behavior can best be understood by placing them in an evolutionary context, so also with language. Our species evolved over a long period of time, and it is clear that an intelligence based on language has been intimately linked to our development. Therefore, to grasp how we behave in our present state of evolutionary development, it may be helpful to have at least a plausible understanding of how we got to be what we are.

Symbols and Communication

Before examining what this evolutionary process might have been, we must explore the relationship between the use of symbols and communication.

Communication is so frequently confused with the capacity to use symbols that the two must be more clearly delineated.

Communication in itself does not necessarily rely on symbols. Our earlier discussion of the conversation of gestures referred to one form of communication, in which organisms respond to the early phases of one another's acts as signs of the whole act. A cursory look at animal behavior will confirm that a variety of forms of communication exist that do not employ symbols. Bees communicate the direction and distance of sources of nectar with great precision by means of physical movements — "dances" — oriented to the location of the food in relation to the sun.[4] Killer whales sound warning calls over long underwater distances, a feat made possible by their "sonar" devices and the way sound is transmitted under water.[5]

In the case of both bees and killer whales, however, we see communication that occurs by means of what can be termed *calls* rather than by means of symbols. For each biologically important situation, there is a distinct call that is used only when that situation actually exists. (Calls usually are sounds, but as the case of bees and their flight patterns illustrates, they need not be.) Each situation has its own call, and only one call can be used in a given situation.[6]

It is communication that takes place, to be sure: Killer whales will come to the aid of another from miles around, and bees will flock accurately to the source of food following the "message" of the communicating bee. The message is transmitted, but communication is limited, since the number of calls is finite and their linkage to situations is genetically fixed. Nonetheless, information is transmitted from one organism to another in such a way that behavior is affected; the essence of communication lies in the capacity of one organism's messages to change the behavior of another.

• Symbolic communication, in contrast, entails a flexible, modifiable capacity to use sounds or some other physical means of expression. The nature of this capacity can best be seen by contrasting human speech with animal calls. First, language constitutes an *open* system in comparison with the closed system of calls characteristic of animal communication. Many animals — gibbons and prairie dogs, to name two very different species — have a system of calls, but the system is closed because each of the situations for which a call exists can bring forth only that particular call. Thus, if there is a call for danger and one for food, the animal who encounters a situation in which both are present can respond only with one call or the other. Language, in contrast, is an open system because it permits a mixed situation to be met with a precise response. The situation in which both food and danger are present can be symbolically designated. Language permits any situation to be met with a great variety of utterances tailored to the specific nature of the situation. Among other things, this means that the organism can also meet new situations by inventing new utterances.

Second, modifiability means *displacement*. In a call system, the specific call — for food, danger, or anything else — is tied to the immediate situation to which it is a pertinent response. Language, however, displaces the use of a symbol from the immediate situation; it makes it possible for language users to talk about a situation even when it is not immediately there. This is a significant difference: The call system ties its user to the present since it can "talk" only about what is present. The language system admits of past and future, of "here" and "somewhere else," because its designations, or symbols, can be used with displacement.

Third, the call system is unmodifiable because its units of sound are *global* in character; that is, the organism responds to calls as total entities and not to several individual units of sound that are assembled into a call. This is a difficult concept to illustrate. Since we are so accustomed to hearing the discrete units of sound that make up words in our language, it is hard to imagine hearing sounds globally. In a word like "father" we can discriminate two syllables, and we can separate the various sounds making up the word from one another. Linguists call this quality of language *duality,* which refers to the fact that language contains elementary units of sound, each meaningless in itself but capable of being combined with others to make units of meaning. Calls are heard globally, which limits the number of calls that can be differentiated within any given system. The duality that characterizes language makes it possible to produce a relatively large number of words and enables language users to distinguish clearly and certainly among them.

The Evolution of Language

How could such a flexible system of language have come to be? Although no definitive answer is possible, Charles Hockett and Robert Ascher speculated on a sequence of evolutionary developments that seems plausible in the light of the archaeological, fossil, and geological record, as well as in terms of the similarities of physical structure and behavior between people and their nearest nonhuman relatives.

Their reconstruction of evolution depends on the existence among the ancestors of the human species of a call system such as we described earlier. It would have been a closed system, without displacement or duality of patterning, comprising a half dozen or so distinct calls, "each the appropriate vocal response—or the vocal segment of a more inclusive response—to a recurrent and biologically important type of situation."[7] Such a call system might include calls for food, danger, friendly social contact, mother-child contact, and the like.

At the time of their evolution in the Miocene period in Africa, the prehominids from whom both apes and humans later were to evolve encountered changing climatic conditions that caused the amount of forest area to shrink. Some were thus forced to abandon the trees, and as they did, they developed an upright posture and bipedal locomotion. The latter developments were related to the survival value of carrying food and weapons in a new environment, the earth's surface, in which food was hard to come by and predators were plentiful. As the animals learned to make excursions for food from a sheltering grove of trees, the habit of carrying back bits of food in the hands may have developed, and as it did, bipedal locomotion would have been encouraged. Whatever it was in the genetic structure of those animals that enabled them to make excursions and carry back food, its survival advantage meant that their descendants would have the same capacity.

With upright posture and the use of hands for carrying and feet for locomotion—developments that took place over a very long period of time— the mouth and teeth became unoccupied. Previously used for grasping and carrying (as well as for chewing, of course), they were now relatively idle. The result was startling:

> It can quite safely be asserted that if primate and hominid evolution had not transferred from mouth to hand first the grasping and manipulating function and then the carrying function, human language as we know it would never have evolved. What were the hominids to do with their mouths, rendered thus relatively idle except when they were eating? The answer is: they chattered.[8]

Thus it was that the movement from trees to ground and the adoption of upright posture favored the development of a call system. Chattering, which became possible with these changes, would tend over time to become an important means of signaling. Since these hominids were already social—we were social animals *before* we acquired language and became human—the coordinated search for food and defense against predators would tend to confer an evolutionary advantage. Coordination required some means of communication, however, and vocal signals have the advantage that the animals using them can easily divide their attention, paying heed to the calls of their fellows, for example, while watching the activities of their enemies.

How could a system of calls, which probably developed on the basis of genetic changes, be transformed into language? The reconstruction by Hockett and Ascher postulates that even though the call system was essentially closed, the situations of real life were not so simple. Food and danger, for example, were two conditions often present simultaneously and very closely balanced in their intensity. We can easily imagine that our ancestors frequently were very hungry and encountered food and enemies at the same time. Even though the tendency to respond to such situations with a single call would be strong, it is conceivable that at some point a *composite* call (that is, one that combined aspects of each of two separate calls) would be used. If this happened frequently enough, and others were able correctly to interpret the composite calls (that is, could behave in ways appropriate to a mixed situation), the tendency to use and to respond to the new call would be reinforced.

When a new call is produced by combining parts of two existing calls, a radical change occurs. We can illustrate the significance of the change by using nonsense syllables to stand for the calls (keeping in mind that the calls are heard globally and not as syllables). Suppose we have the following two "calls":

FIDO = the call meaning "food here"
TALA = the call meaning "danger coming"

We might represent a combined call, which an individual might emit in a situation in which food and danger were equally salient, in the following way:

FILA = the composite call meaning "food and danger"

Such a composite call would tend to be used habitually (that is, the members of the species would become conditioned to use it) if it proved advantageous to do so. But, in becoming a habit in the group, this composite call would forever alter the character of the innate calls on which it was based. The old, globally heard calls out of which the new call was built are no longer quite so global, but have become composites themselves. Now there are four elements, each with a more or less distinctive meaning:

FI = "food"   TA = "no food"
DO = "no danger"   LA = "danger"

Creating a composite call has the effect of altering the meaning of the original calls, splitting each of them into two meaningful parts.

Over thousands of years, an expanded system of calls would tend to become established if it conferred an evolutionary advantage—that is, if it gave its possessors a survival advantage over competitor species. It can be presumed that a call system did provide such an advantage—that it enabled group activities to be coordinated more effectively, with more precise responses to the environment.

If such an expanded call system were to become established, it would have to be on the basis of learning rather than simply genetics. This is so, first, because an expanded system of calls would be too complex for genetic control. If a species has only ten calls that it produces instinctively, it has the ability to produce a system of one hundred composite calls whose significance its members must learn. And second, because the system would be too complex for genetic control, the young of each generation would have to learn the system anew. Encountering adults who used a variety of calls—a few of which the young could themselves produce and perhaps understand instinctively, but most of which they could not—the young would be obliged to infer the meaning of calls from the behavioral contexts in which they were used. Such an inferential process, which is precisely how young human beings learn language, would tend to encourage selection over the long run for whatever capabilities for teaching and learning were already present in the species. If the expanded call system were itself adaptive, the members who could use and learn it best would be at a reproductive advantage. As selection for learning ability took place, presumably, the call system would become more complex, and additional selection for learning ability would occur.

As the expanded system came to depend more and more on learning, it would become increasingly difficult for the whole system to be learned in the real situations in which it would be used. Rather, it might be expected that some learning of the call system would begin to occur at a distance from real situations of use. Many animals engage in "play" activity, and the young learn adult forms of behavior first by engaging in play. We might expect, therefore, that the call system would become implicated in this play. With this development of the habit of learning the system in playful activity and not in real situations, we have the beginnings of displacement — that is, the use of calls in the absence of the real things or events they represent. Moreover, the development of displacement entails a new distinction, between the "real" and the "imaginary" — between "food and danger" that are real and present and "food and danger" that are only present in the animal's imagination.

At this point, the various calls in the system began to be more like what we know as symbols. Even though the call that is produced instinctively as the initial phase of an animal's response to a situation is not a symbol, the call that combines elements of several calls and can be used apart from real situations really is a symbol. Its meaning depends on learning and on the common recognition of it (and its meaning) by a group of individuals. It is genuinely a way of representing or *naming* objects and events in the species' environment.

One further development is required for the emergence of language — *duality of patterning*. As a call system expands, the "acoustic space" becomes more densely packed — that is, there are more and more calls; and even though each is a composite, they still tend to be heard globally in distinction from others. With increasing numbers of calls, it becomes more difficult to distinguish one from another in this way. Thus, so long as calls are listened to and heard as total units, there is a limit to the number of calls that can be effectively used.

At some point, according to Hockett and Ascher, users of an expanded, opening, and displaced call system began to listen to the component units of sound making up the call system, rather than to the calls as global sounds. They began to hear smaller units of sound and to assemble them into units of meaning. That is, they began to hear "FI-LA" rather than "FILA." The result was that the call system could become fully open, for now there was essentially no physical limit on the number of calls that could be produced. Language — or at least prelanguage — had arrived.

This account of the evolution of language is, of course, speculative and not literal. We cannot know with certainty the exact time span or sequence of evolutionary developments that led to language, and this reconstruction will undoubtedly be modified or replaced by others as we learn more about human origins. It has been argued, for example, that the language of early hominids was not based on speech, but on gestures.[9] Hand and arm gestures can be used to designate objects in the environment and relate one to another — that is, indeed, what takes place in the use of sign language by the deaf. The development of language based on such gestures could possibly have taken place more quickly than one based on speech, for the former would seem to require less anatomical change than the latter. The capacity to speak rests on extensive modifications in the mouth and throat, whereas gestural language could have been implemented by our ancestors without anatomical changes. This is an important form of argument in evolutionary terms, for evolution proceeds in an essentially conservative way — that is, genetic selection tends to favor those characteristics that enable the species to survive in its habitat, not necessarily the development of very new characteristics that enable it to expand or to do better. As gestural language became established — if this line of thinking is correct — it would have favored selection for brain development in the same way as speech. Ultimately, however, speech took over as the major form of language because it provided a clearer channel than the physical gesture. Regardless of which came first, it is worth noting that even at present our speech is supplemented by an extensive "vocabulary" of physical gestures — shrugs, frowns, and signs made with the hands.

Regardless of whether language was first vocal or gestural, the biological and cultural destinies of human beings have been intertwined for a very long time, and the development of language was a key part of their relationship. Through language, humankind acquired new capacities for response to the environment — as well as a biology that came to be dependent upon these capacities. The paramount fact of our evolution is language and the capacity for flexible and novel response to the environment that it has bestowed upon us. We have become freed in large part from the tyranny of immediate response, we have acquired a capacity for social coordination that goes well beyond that of our primate cousins, and we have brought our environment within ourselves where it can be manipulated in the imagination.

The close association between the evolution of the human brain and anatomy and the development of our language-based behavioral capabilities gives rise to two important questions, both of which are being debated in the social and behavioral sciences at present:

- If language developed in the course of evolution, should we not find some similarities between ourselves and our contemporary primate relatives? If we share our origins, should we not also find that we share some capabilities, including the use of language?

• If biology and culture are so closely intertwined, can biology ever be excluded from the analysis of human conduct? Are the claims of sociobiologists worth the consideration of symbolic interactionists?

These issues are worth discussing, for they help to put the symbolic interactionist perspective into the broader framework of contemporary social thought and research.

LANGUAGE, BIOLOGY, AND CULTURE

Few ideas appeal to human beings as much as the possibility that we are more like other animals than we have thought — or that they are more like us. There appears to be a profound wish to impute human characteristics to animals — to suppose that cats and dogs think like we do, to believe that animals have feelings, or to imagine that chimpanzees or porpoises have language. In recent years, a considerable amount of serious scientific research has focused on such questions, particularly on the cognitive and linguistic capacities of chimpanzees and gorillas. At the same time, considerable interest has been directed to the animal origins of human conduct. Scholarly and popular studies have explored the view that humans are innately aggressive or territorial, and sociobiology has emerged as a discipline that seeks to explain much of human behavior and social organization in terms of genetic control.

Social scientists and many biologists are highly skeptical of efforts to see animals and people as alike in the major determinants of their behavior. In great part, their skepticism reflects the long battle against biological determinism fought by social scientists. Biological explanations of human conduct have long been appealing, and it was a major accomplishment of anthropology and sociology in the nineteenth and early twentieth centuries to establish the idea that social and cultural factors had largely supplanted biology as an explanation of the forms and varieties of human conduct. The reemergence of explanations grounded in biology has been viewed with justifiable alarm, for biological explanations lend themselves very easily to political justifications of the status quo. If men and women, or blacks and whites, are thought to be biologically unequal in their mental or physical capacities, then efforts to improve and equalize their position and treatment can be resisted on the grounds that "it's only human nature" that they be treated unequally.

There is another reason why social scientists look askance at efforts to reintroduce biological thinking into sociological explanations, or to reduce the latter to the former. Because of their long battle against biological determinism, the social sciences have kept a distance from biology, and the chasm between the two has widened. Sociologists generally feel that they can ignore developments in biology, since the primacy of society and culture in human affairs is established. Similarly, biologists remain largely ignorant of sociology, sometimes seeing it as hopelessly unscientific, but more often simply paying it no attention. Thus, sociologists generally remain in the dark about developments in the biological sciences. Symbolic interactionists, in particular, are not very interested in primate studies, regarding their conclusions as having little bearing on the concerns of social psychologists. At the same time, when biologists speak of human conduct and social organization, they do so in terms that are hopelessly simplistic and naively ill-informed from the vantage point of sociologists.[10]

In the concluding pages of this chapter, we try to assess the implications of work on primates and some aspects of sociobiological theory for symbolic interactionism. Although studies of primates, we will argue, show them to be more similar to us than we had imagined, the work of sociobiologists remains largely unimpressive.

Symbol Use among the Great Apes

Considerable research in recent years casts new light on the question of whether our primate relatives possess the capacity to use symbols and even, to some extent, on the nature of this ability.[11] Although some of this research has been misconstrued as "proving" that chimpanzees and gorillas "have language," a careful look suggests a more conservative, but still important, conclusion. Under certain conditions, it seems possible to induce other primates to behave in ways that seem to require at least some degree of symbolic capacity. Although the research does not permit the conclusion that chimpanzees use symbols, it does point to some impressive similarities between them and us, and it helps to clarify the ways in which we are very different from them.

Many readers of this book have heard of primates that have been taught to use one or another system of symbols or quasi symbols. Washoe, for example, was a female chimpanzee trained by Allen and Beatrice Gardner to employ the American Sign Language. Washoe learned to produce and recognize some fifty signs and to combine them into "sentences" that were, in many cases, novel combinations, not merely repetitions of those she had been taught. Similar success was reported by David Premack, whose chimpanzee, Sarah, learned to manipulate colored plastic shapes (and later a computerized keyboard) in order to identify objects, respond to questions, and ask for what she wanted. Along similar lines, the gorilla Koko and the chimpanzee Lana spontaneously asked questions of their trainers, after having been put through a similar procedure, which equipped them with a graphic means for designating and responding to things, events, and relationships in their environments.

These studies appear to present sound evidence that chimpanzees and gorillas are capable of behavior that rests on at least a rudimentary symbolic capacity. These apes do not possess a natural language of their own, to be sure, and the capacities they have are elicited only with careful training by their keepers. Yet, they do seem to possess cognitive abilities that social scientists have always thought were exclusively human. What is the evidence for this assertion?

First, these apes seem cognitively more like humans than suspected in a very crucial respect. Language is thought to depend on the capacity for what is called *cross-modal perception,* which refers to the coordination of information acquired through one sense with information acquired through another. Cross-modal perception is evidenced by the ability to recognize an object that is only touched as the same one that previously had only been seen. Speech depends on sight-sound cross-modal perception, since one must be able to coordinate objects that are seen with their representations in sound, their names. It may also be that language requires the capacity to associate a sound heard with an internal visual image of the object it represents. It appears that chimpanzees have a capacity for cross-modal perception. They can associate the picture of an object with the real object that they can touch, but not see; that is, they can choose the correct picture for an object they are touching, but not looking at. Chimpanzees who have been taught the use of plastic symbols also seem capable of learning to associate the sounds of English words with the appropriate plastic shape. This does not imply that they "understand" English, but only that they can associate a global sound with an object.

Second, the preponderance of evidence suggests that apes' use of various symbolic media does not amount merely to successful conditioning. One of the most important criticisms directed against the studies of primate symboling is the charge that what is accomplished amounts to nothing more than very subtle and complex conditioning. In this view, chimpanzees choose the correct plastic disk to associate with an object only because they have been reinforced for certain combinations and only because experimenters communicate subtle cues to their animals that lead them to make the correct choices. Thus, it has been alleged, experimental animals merely learn expected responses to stimuli, and this is certainly no indication that they have the capacity to understand or use symbols.

It appears that the research findings cannot be so easily dismissed, however. For one thing, we find evidence of displacement — that is, of the use of symbols in the absence of the objects that they designate. On some occasions, an animal employs a symbol that it has learned even though the object itself is not present. This indicates that the animal has partially loosened the bonds that tie it to concrete, here-and-now things and events. The spontaneous use of a symbol is a far different matter from its use to label an object on the demand of an experimenter. Moreover, there is evidence that the apes' use of symbols tends toward abstraction; that is, they use them to refer to categories of things and even to intangible relationships, not just to material things. When the propensity for abstraction and displacement is put together with observations of apes us-ing the symbols they have been taught as a means to communicate with one another, it is impossible to dismiss their conduct as simply the result of conditioning.

One additional bit of evidence on the cognitive capacities of the apes in-volves their responses to mirror images of themselves. Unlike monkeys, which respond socially to mirror images of themselves (that is, they respond in a way that leads one to believe they think there is another monkey present), apes seem to recognize that they are seeing themselves in mirrors. They use mirrors, when they are available, for grooming, and they have learned what the image in the mirror really is. Moreover, the symbols apes appear capable of using include symbols designating their fellows and themselves.

Do such studies indicate that apes possess language and selves and that we must abandon our idea that humans are unique in their possession of these at-tributes? Powerful as the evidence is, the answer to this question can only be "no." The significance of such studies does not lie in their demonstration of language in the apes nor in the discovery that apes have selves, but in their capac-ity to refine our ideas about the significance of language in human life and the nature of the capacities on which it rests.

The first point to be stressed is that apes have not been taught nor have they themselves evolved anything like a language as we apply this term to human language. Apes do not spontaneously use graphic symbols to represent their worlds. They do not have mirrors in their world. They do not have the capacity to create computer keyboards or sign language or plastic disks. They seem to have the basic cognitive abilities that are required to enable them to learn to use symbols of a certain kind when they are created and painstakingly taught to them by humans. They can associate cross-modally, they can form and hold visual images, they are social animals, and they have adequate hand-eye coor-dination. The apes did not evolve a language, however, nor can they be taught (at least on the basis of present evidence) a symbolic code that comes anywhere close to that mastered even by fairly young human beings.

These studies of primate symbol use point up the importance of several cognitive capacities for the use of symbols, but they also underscore the vast gulf that exists between the capacity to employ rudimentary symbols and the power of a full-blown language. Humans and apes share a common ancestry, and so it should come as no surprise to learn that we and they possess some of the same cognitive capacities. That is what the symbolic capacity is — *cognitive,* a certain ability to process information and relate environmental things and events. We humans can do this by using sounds as our graphic means of rep-resenting the environment. The apes seem to share some of this representational capacity, although it appears to be largely confined to visual rather than auditory senses. (Sign language and plastic symbols alike are perceived visually and related to other visually perceived objects.)

A symbolic capacity, however simple or complex, is one thing; language is quite another. The apes embarked on an evolutionary course different from ours. Our biological nature, unlike theirs, evolved in tandem with our elaboration of a symbolic capacity into a full-blown language. Our speech came to be controlled by the cerebral cortex, while the vocal call systems of other primates remained under the control of the more ancient limbic system. We developed a refined, biologically based capacity to produce, hear, and reproduce sounds, whereas they did not. Our brains grew larger than theirs. And while we became progressively more dependent upon learning and language use in a complex social environment, their development left them still dependent on a call system and with simpler modes of social organization.

The Limits of Biological Explanation

Our account of the origins and development of human language emphasized the process of evolution. Symbols and language, in this view, emerged over a long period of time and made humans more adaptable — that is, capable of surviving and flourishing in a wider variety of environments and in the face of considerable environmental change. In view of this emphasis on the evolution of our species, it is reasonable to ask how symbolic interactionists view the present role of biology in human conduct. Recent years have seen a revival of efforts to explain human conduct in biological terms, and it is important to understand where symbolic interactionists stand on such matters.

Symbolic interactionists share the dominant view of the social sciences that the human environment is cultural and that cultural factors have largely supplanted innate controls over human conduct. We do not live in a world of physical stimuli that are given in nature and for which we come equipped with a complex set of genetically determined responses. Instead, our environment is a cultural one, composed of ideas, values, knowledge, norms, and symbols. Our responses to this cultural environment are learned rather than inherited. Culture, which is grounded in our symbolic capacity and our use of language, is the source of what we know about the world, what we value, and how we think we should act. It is the repository of our practical knowledge about farming and hunting and building and other means of providing food and security for ourselves. It is the source of our ideas about what is worth striving for, whether it be material well-being or individual happiness; and it provides us with definitions of what is normal and right and what is deviant and wrong in our everyday conduct and in our relations with one another. Culture, to put it simply, is both our environment and the source of our responses to it.

We humans are cultural creatures *because* of our biology — that is, because of a sequence of evolutionary developments that left us standing upright, speaking, carrying things with our hands, and using our comparatively large brains to store and retrieve a large number of learned responses to complex environmental situations. Our symbolic and cultural nature is itself a biological characteristic, for as biological creatures we are dependent on culture. We have reached the point in our evolution where culture is essential to our survival, where we do not have a clear-cut genetic patterning of behavior.

From an interactionist perspective, many recent attempts to reintroduce biological ideas into the analysis of human conduct are thus seriously flawed. This is the case, not because culture has made biology completely disappear, but because many such efforts seem to ignore the cultural nature of humankind.

One crude form of biologism in recent thought, for example, takes the view that human beings possess various innate dispositions, such as aggressiveness, territoriality, or male bonding, that are the basis for observable human behavior and social arrangements.[12] Reasoning that all humans have a tendency toward aggressiveness, for example, the proponents of this form of biological determinism take the view that common human forms of behavior, such as war, simply mirror our biological dispositions.

Such formulations do not stand up to close scrutiny, for they are easily refuted by the facts of human behavior. Although war is held to be the result of human aggressiveness, it appears that those who fight in wars are frequently anything but aggressive in their attitudes. Soldiers may be bored, preoccupied with their families at home, or simply terrified by the horrors of battle, but they are not simply acting on the basis of aggressive motives. This is not a surprising fact, since it is clear on examination that wars are the outcome of relationships between national states, not between individuals, and that the psychic states of individuals are typically irrelevant to the causation of war. It would be more accurate to say that war *causes* aggressiveness. Men and women can be induced to have feelings of hatred toward their enemies when a nation becomes embroiled in a war, but it is the war that mobilizes the emotion rather than the emotion that produces the war.

Moreover, as anthropologists have demonstrated, variations among human societies are too great to permit gross characterizations of human beings as aggressive. There are very peaceful societies. There are societies so warlike that aggression against outsiders is a constant preoccupation. There are societies which, after enduring violent civil wars, return to a peaceful state of existence. In the face of such variation, it makes no empirical sense to characterize human beings as aggressive.

The fundamental error in this kind of biological thinking is to equate a form of human activity with a presumed underlying motivation. Marshall Sahlins puts it quite eloquently:

> Observing warfare, the sociobiologist concludes he is in the presence of an underlying aggression. Seeing an act of food sharing, he knows it as a disposition toward altruism. For him, the appearance of a social fact is the same thing as its motivation; he immediately places the first within a category of the second.[13]

Sahlins goes on to express a position that is similar to that taken by symbolic interactionists: Human acts are meaningful acts, and we do not simply act out of particular biological motivations. Each action is mediated by the symbols we have learned, so that even those acts, such as eating, that respond to concrete biological needs tend to be wrapped in layers of social meaning. Thus, we respond to the act of another human being not on the basis of its innate biological meaning—such as aggressiveness or altruism—but because we symbolically designate that act as aggressive or altruistic. As Sahlins argues, and as we shall make clear in later chapters, any given act of which human beings are capable can have multiple meanings and can be instigated by a variety of purposes. Is the sharing of food innately altruistic? Do we do favors out of a simple propensity to be helpful to others? Such acts may be motivated by an altruistic concern for others without regard for the self, but they may have other bases as well. Doing things for others can be motivated by a need for approval; it can be a means for buying loyalty and cooperation; in some cultures, it can be a subtle form of aggression.

Another problem associated with such biological explanations is the lack of direct evidence for genetic control of conduct. If one argues that human behavior (and thus also human social arrangements) are under some kind of genetic control, then it behooves one to show that there are genes for altruism or aggressiveness or whatever quality is being explained. But there is no direct evidence for such genes. Although it is sometimes difficult to determine just how committed the sociobiologists are to a strong genetic determination of behavior, it appears that many of them are so committed. As Stephen Jay Gould wrote of the work of Edward O. Wilson, one of the chief architects of sociobiology, one has to see his work as an expression of the view that genes control ". . . specific and variable traits in human behavior—including spite, aggression, xenophobia, conformity, homosexuality, and the characteristic behavioral differences between men and women in Western society." And what is the evidence for such direct genetic control? Gould is blunt: "At the moment, the answer is none whatever."[14]

One of the favorite arguments of the sociobiologists, for example, is to explain the existence of altruism in terms of what has come to be called *kin selection theory*. This theory, when applied to the animal world, supplies an elegant and simple explanation to what is otherwise a puzzling fact about behavior. Individual animals under threat, at least in some species, will sound a warning call and thus alert others of their kind to the danger. In doing so, however, the individual animal is apt to expose itself to greater danger. The animal at the watering hole whose call alerts others in the group to the presence of a predator may save others, but is itself thereby more likely to be the predator's victim. This is puzzling, for if natural selection operates at an individual level, the animal is acting in a way that makes its own survival less probable, and so also in a way that makes the survival and reproduction of its genes less probable. But if this is so, how does a genetically controlled pattern of response, such as a warning call, persist? Natural selection would seem to favor silence, which would be of maximum value to the individual. Kin selection theory argues that the animal that transmits the call actually helps to insure the survival of its genes, since its close kin are apt to hear the call. Since they share a good part of its genetic makeup, its genes are apt to be reproduced even though the individual may not survive.

Sociobiologists tend to transfer reasoning such as that contained in kin selection theory to human beings. They would argue, in effect, that there is a gene for altruism that is transmitted in human populations in the same way as in animal populations. That is, altruistic behavior may harm the individual, but contribute to the survival of the family and thus of the individual's genes. There is, however, no direct evidence for a gene for altruism — its existence is inferred, not demonstrated. Even among animals, what seems to be genetically controlled is a very *specific* behavior, namely a vocalization that occurs as a part of the animal's response to a situation of danger, rather than a more diffuse disposition or motive, such as "altruism." Among humans there is no evidence of comparably specific behavioral responses.

Moreover, there is a far simpler cultural explanation of altruistic behavior that pays closer attention to the varieties of human motivations and that does not require us to postulate the existence of specific genes for specific forms of behavior in a species whose whole evolutionary development has been toward generalized adaptive capacities. Sahlins gives the example of Eskimo families who abandon their elderly on ice floes when times get rough, leaving them to fend for themselves and to die relatively quickly. Since the elderly accept this fate gracefully, it might be said that here is evidence of an altruistic gene at work. A simpler explanation is that Eskimo families have learned that such a pattern of behavior is necessary if they are to survive difficult times when the elderly would be a drain on scarce resources. The cultural pattern persists because those families that either do not learn it or refuse to follow it have a tendency over time not to survive, and so do not live to pass on their traditions to subsequent generations. Here is an instance of cultural rather than natural selection. It does not require us to postulate the existence of genes that exert their influence on behavior in some unconscious way; instead, it recognizes that humans learn patterns of behavior, that they may resist some patterns because they call for painful decisions, and that when they do resist these patterns, their capacity to survive and teach their children is reduced.

Symbolic interactionists take the view that human beings are biological organisms, and that their conduct and capabilities have to be looked at in the context of their evolution as creatures. But this evolution has proceeded in the direction of progressive liberation from biological restraints and guidance. Our species' evolution has yielded an expansion of our capacities to act on the environment, a change in the nature of that environment from purely material to symbolic, and the replacement of genetic controls with cultural controls over behavior.

As a result, symbolic interactionists see little merit in studies that try to explain very general sorts of behavior, such as aggressiveness or altruism, by reference to genetic controls. Because there is no direct evidence for such control, because such approaches see more uniformity in human conduct than can be demonstrated, and because simpler explanations are available, such studies seem to hold little promise. At the very least, symbolic interactionists would argue, the burden of proof is on sociobiologists to demonstrate the merits of their approach.

The rejection of sociobiology does not mean that symbolic interactionists dismiss all possibility of biological influences on conduct. It is one thing to argue against the more naive formulations of the sociobiologists; it is quite another to rule out in advance any possibility that patterns of behavior that we now explain in sociological and social psychological terms might one day be explained in biological terms. Like other social scientists, for example, symbolic interactionists have attempted to examine the origins and consequences of mental illness. Increasingly it appears that genetic and organic factors play a major role in the etiology of mental illness, particularly its more severe forms. The proper interactionist response is not to refuse to believe the evidence, but to use it to amend and enrich their theories. The confirmation of an essentially physiological explanation of severe forms of mental illness would free symbolic interactionists from the need to explain some very complex and difficult forms of behavior. Moreover, it would allow them to concentrate on the task of explaining how the ill are dealt with by the social worlds of which they are members. Schizophrenics, for example, do not cease to be social beings — their emotional troubles are apt to interact with their relationships with other people and the meaning of their troubles is apt to be shaped by the culture of which they are a part.

The symbolic interactionist model of the person in society is open to biology in a way that many other theories are not. In George H. Mead's analysis of the self, there is a spontaneous, partly biological component to the self, a component he designated as the "I." Although there has been considerable disagreement about what Mead meant by this term, it seems clear that one of his intentions was to leave open the possibility that social and cultural factors could not account for everything in behavior. There seems to be a spontaneous, unsocialized, and impulsive element in our initial responses to many situations. Although we eat or make love in accordance with culturally acquired meanings, we experience hunger or sexual tension fundamentally because we are biological creatures. How we respond to such urges is, of course, a matter shaped by our culture. Whether we eat cows or ants, or have sex every day or once a week, is not dictated by biology but is shaped by our cultural framework. This, in the final analysis, provides the best way of understanding the relationship between culture and biology: They are interactive, not only in the evolution of our species but in day-to-day conduct. Although the attention of the social psychologist is naturally drawn to the social and cultural aspects of everyday behavior, we should not forget that, at bottom, it is a biological life form whose behavior we are attempting to explain.

SUMMARY

- In order to explain human behavior, we must look at the environment in which humans live and see how it is similar to and different from the environments of other organisms. All organisms both shape and are shaped by their environments, and the capacity of organisms to be aware of and respond to their environments provides the key to understanding the relationship between the two. Evolution seems to have gradually produced forms of life that can respond more flexibly to and exert more control over their surroundings. More advanced forms of life can delay immediate responses, react to stimuli that are not themselves significant but that signal events that are important, and process complex combinations of stimuli. In addition to possessing these capabilities, humans are able to create and use symbols, which are arbitrary signs that take their meaning from the agreement of those who use them.

- A symbol is a sign—typically a word or combination of words—that means approximately the same thing to all members of the community for whom it is a symbol. In other words, when a symbol is used by one member of a group, that member can respond to his or her own use of the symbol in a way that resembles the responses of others. If I say "house," for example, I hear myself use the word and I can respond to myself—say, by forming a mental image of a house—in a way that is very similar to the way others around me respond. Symbols thus make possible a fairly precise form of communication. Because all members of a community have essentially the same response to a symbol, it is possible for members to transfer mental states from one to another. The situation perceived by one member can be described and thus, also be perceived by others; the behavior in which one person is about to engage can also be described and that person's intentions can be communicated to others. Symbols, therefore, enhance the capacity to communicate and make humankind, the symbol-using species, a thoroughly social species.

- The importance of symbols also lies in the way they transform the environment. Not only do symbols make human beings an even more social species than our primate cousins and ancestors, but they radically change the nature of the environment in which people live. Symbols bring the external world *within* the person, for they enable the individual to perform imaginative manipulations of things in that world. Instead of being limited to visual images, humans can also use the more compact code provided by symbols as a means of imagining and thinking about their world. Moreover, the use of symbols widens the world in which we behave because it makes it possible to imagine and respond to things and events that are not physically present. Human beings can think about distant things and events; even when faced with the need to solve an immediate problem, they can respond to objects that are not present. Faced with a car that refuses to start on a cold winter day, for example, I can imagine alternative courses of action, many of which involve objects — such as jumper cables, spare batteries, telephones, and tow trucks — that I either do not possess or that are miles away from me. As a result, human beings, because they use symbols, live in a world that is spatially and temporally larger than the world inhabited by other animals.

• There is another important consequence of the use of symbols: the development of self-consciousness. The members of a social species such as humankind are environmental to one another — each individual is a part of the surrounding conditions to which others respond. Thus, the members of a group are as likely to be designated by symbols as any other important part of the world. Each member of the group is likely to acquire a name, a unique label that others in the group can use to designate that individual.

The possession of a name makes it possible for the person to become a part of his or her own environment, the same environment that is named by the symbols used by the community. A name creates a new object, the self, that can be experienced, imagined, and manipulated in the same way as other objects. Animals that lack a symbolic capacity have physical sensations, to be sure, but they do not have the capacity to experience themselves as a part of the very world in which they live. They have a direct experience of their sensations and of the stimuli that impinge upon them, but they lack the capacity for that indirect experience of the self as a part of the world in which it lives that is the distinctive characteristic of human beings.

• The direction of human evolution, then, is away from biology and toward culture. This does not mean that human beings cease to be biological creatures, of course, or that biology plays no part in shaping human conduct. Human beings continue to be creatures who need food and protection from the elements and who also have sexual appetites. But, by and large, although we are creatures whose cultural nature is built on a biological foundation, biology does not explain our behavior. The human ability to invent and use symbols, rely upon learning, and achieve a considerable degree of mastery over — and freedom from the sheer whim of — the environment gives our behavior a complexity and malleability that far exceed that of other creatures.

Thus, humans need food as much as any other biological creature, but it is through the symbols we use to designate the world that we know what food is; the manner in which we eat food and the kind of food we eat is as much or more a matter of culture than of biology. The precepts of various religions that make some foods taboo, as well as the common association of food consumption with sociability in our own culture, are evidence that there is more to eating than biological survival. The same may be said of sex: Human sexual urges and practices are not simply and perhaps not even mainly biological, for we experience sex not only directly as physical urge or sensation, but as a part of the self of which we are conscious. In this, as in other spheres of their existence, human beings act not simply as biological creatures tied to an immediate world of stimuli, but as creatures who imagine, dream, anticipate, and delay as they act in and toward a world of symbols.

ENDNOTES

1. This discussion of levels of response follows that of Ernest Becker, which is adapted from Leslie A. White. See Ernest Becker, *The Birth and Death of Meaning* (New York: Free Press, 1952), especially chapters 2 and 3; and Leslie A. White, "Four Stages in the Evolution of Minding," in *The Evolution of Man,* ed. Sol Tax, vol. 2 of *Evolution After Darwin* (Chicago: University of Chicago Press, 1959).

2. Becker, *Birth and Death of Meaning,* p. 16 (Note 1).

3. See George H. Mead, *Mind, Self, and Society* (Chicago: University of Chicago Press, 1934, 1962), especially pp. 61–75.

4. See Martin Lindauer, *Communication among Social Bees* (Cambridge, Mass.: Harvard University Press, 1963). Such modes of bee communication have some of the qualities of open call systems, since the bee can adjust its communicative behavior fairly precisely to the location of food. This is somewhat less limiting than the association of very specific calls and situations.

5. For an informative discussion of killer whales and other cetaceans, see *Audubon* 77 (January 1975).

6. Our discussion of animal call systems and their evolution into language is adapted from Charles F. Hockett and Robert Ascher, "The Human Revolution," *Current Anthropology* 5 (1964): 135–168. This lucid and carefully written article is an excellent introduction to evolution for students of social psychology.

7. Ibid., p. 143.

8. Ibid., p. 148.

9. See Gordon Hewes, "Primate Communication and the Gestural Origin of Language," *Current Anthropology* 14 (1973): 5–24.

10. See, for example, Edward O. Wilson, *Sociobiology: The New Synthesis* (Cambridge, Mass.: Harvard University Press, 1975).

11. The following discussion of the topic leans heavily on David Premack, *Intelligence in Ape and Man* (New York: Wiley, 1976); Horst D. Steklis and Michael J. Raleigh, "Requisites for Language: Interspecific and Evolutionary Aspects," in *Neurobiology of Social Communication in Primates,* ed. Horst D. Steklis and Michael J. Raleigh (New York: Academic Press, 1979), pp. 283–314; and Davydd J. Greenwood

and William A. Stini, *Nature, Culture, and Human History* (New York: Harper and Row, 1977). The last book is an especially well written and informative introduction to the topic of human evolution and language written by two anthropologists.

12. See, for example, Konrad Lorenz, *On Aggression* (New York: Harcourt Brace Jovanovich, 1966); Lionel Tiger, *Men in Groups* (New York: Random House, 1969); or Robert Ardrey, *The Territorial Imperative* (New York: Atheneum, 1966). My discussion owes a great deal to the work of anthropologist Marshall Sahlins, *The Use and Abuse of Biology: An Anthropological Critique of Sociobiology* (Ann Arbor: University of Michigan Press, 1977).

13. Sahlins, *Use and Abuse of Biology,* p. 14 (Note 12).

14. Stephen Jay Gould, "Biological Potential versus Biological Determinism," in *The Sociobiology Debate,* ed. Arthur I. Caplan (New York: Harper and Row, 1978), p. 45.

▶ 3

Basic Concepts of Symbolic Interactionism

The preceding chapters discussed the general orientations of symbolic interactionists to human conduct and the human social world. Now it is time to move from the general perspective to a more precise set of concepts for depicting and understanding the phenomena in which social psychologists are interested.

Every scientific discipline develops a set of basic concepts that delineate its way of looking at the world. In classical physics, for example, such terms as mass, acceleration, and gravity provide a basic vocabulary for talking about the world and describing what is interesting about it from the perspective of the physicist. Such concepts are abstractions. Out of the great complexity and uniqueness of immediate objects and events, they distill a limited number of characteristics, attributes, or processes that seem especially noteworthy. No one can see force, but we can conceive of force as an abstraction and relate it to the mass of a body and the speed at which it travels.

Concepts enable us to depict a particular slice of reality, whether the physical reality of the physicist or the social reality of the symbolic interactionist. No set of concepts is concerned with every aspect of reality, nor can it be. A concept is a way of selecting for special scrutiny those aspects of the empirical world that a discipline feels are important—and it is also a way of ignoring aspects it thinks are less significant. Thus, the physicist's conception of mass or energy has nothing to say about several of the sensations that are important in our everyday perceptions of physical things—their shape, color, or aesthetic appeal. The concept of mass does not deny that we have these experiences or that they are important in their own way. In ignoring them, it implies only that they are of no importance in discussing the relationships among physical bodies.

Concepts are the elementary building blocks of theories. Although the term *theory* has several meanings, our usage is simple and straightforward. A theory is an organized set of statements expressing the relationships among concepts. The function of concepts is to depict what is important about some aspect of the world; theories link concepts together in order to make statements about the world. Thus, $F = MA$, the equation of classical mechanics that states that force is equal to mass multiplied by acceleration, can be seen as a theory. An attribute called "force" is related to two other attributes called "mass" and "acceleration" by this equation, which portrays the relationship among these attributes in the real world. That is what a theory is—a set of statements that portray the world by showing how its various processes or characteristics are related to one another.

There is no easy place to begin to present the basic concepts of symbolic interactionism. Like any other scientific perspective, symbolic interactionism utilizes an interlocking set of concepts. Each basic concept is tied to and its meaning is dependent on one or more other concepts. Thus, no single concept can be grasped fully without understanding the others. Nevertheless, symbolic interactionists have been preoccupied with a few basic issues in developing their basic concepts:

- What does the environment look like from the perspective of the behaving person?
- How is behavior organized and controlled by the person?
- And how does the person coordinate his or her conduct with that of others?

The basic concepts of symbolic interactionism result from the effort to answer these fundamental questions about human behavior.

OBJECTS

Symbolic interactionists rely on George Herbert Mead's concept of the *object* to portray the way in which people perceive and act upon their environment. Human beings live in a world of objects—of symbolically designated things, ideas, people, activities, and purposes. The environment they experience and toward which they act is neither an undifferentiated blob of sensory experience nor a microscopically perceived stream of stimuli. It does not consist solely of the material world that we can see and touch. Instead, people live in, pay attention to, and act toward a world of objects.

What Is an Object?

The term is not easy to grasp, perhaps because symbolic interactionists use it in a way that differs from its everyday meaning. Ordinarily, when we talk about an object, we mean something that has material existence—a table, a rock, a screwdriver—and that we can see or touch. Indeed, the first definition of *object* found in the *Random House Dictionary* says that it is "anything that is visible or tangible and is stable in form." Symbolic interactionists use the word more broadly and in a way that reflects a more subtle conception of how things and events in the environment become visible or tangible as well as stable in form.

After defining *object* in the way mentioned above, the same dictionary goes on to list four additional meanings:

2. anything that may be apprehended intellectually: *objects of thought.*
3. a person or thing with reference to the impression made on the mind or the feeling or emotion elicited in an observer: *an object of curiosity and pity.* 4. a thing, person, or matter to which thought or action is directed: *an object of medical investigation.* 5. the end toward which effort is directed; goal; purpose.

These definitions convey two basic meanings that are superficially different, but actually very closely linked to one another. These meanings help convey an essential symbolic interactionist (and pragmatist) idea, which is that the very nature of the human environment is shaped by the activities and intentions of acting human beings.

The first of these two meanings emphasizes the process of indicating, referring to, or acting toward whatever is in some sense "out there" in the environment that can be symbolically designated. The cup of coffee I as an author pick up and drink from as I write is an example of an object in this sense. It is something external toward which attention can be directed, that can be designated by a symbol, "coffee," and in this case something I can also act toward by making it an example in a book on social psychology. The cup is, to be sure, a material thing, but it becomes an object when it is symbolically designated and acted toward. Moreover, the "cup of coffee" is really more than one object. As the thing I act toward by drinking, it is one object—something to quench my thirst or keep me awake; as something I act toward by writing about it, it is quite a different object, something I use to illustrate a point. An "example" can assume a variety of tangible shapes and forms: I could just as easily have used a "pencil" or a "microcomputer" as an "example" in order to make my point. Nonetheless, the "example" is something we designate and act toward when we try to explain something, just as "a cup of coffee" is something we act toward when we try to stay awake.

The second meaning conveyed in the dictionary definitions conveys a sense of an object as a goal or purpose of activity. In this sense of the term *object* a cup of coffee or an example is not merely something toward which a person can act by picking it up and drinking it or by writing about it. It is also something a person picks up or writes about in order to "have a cup of coffee" or "give an example." This meaning of the word *object* is closely related to the preceding one. An object is not only something given shape and significance because the person designates and acts toward it, but also and simultaneously a *goal* of the person's action. Human beings live in a world of objects that they constantly create and recreate through their symbolic designation of and action toward. Their orientation to the objects that constitute the environment at any given time is purposive and goal oriented. Human beings fashion a world of things and stimuli into a world of objects because they act with purpose toward it. In this sense, cups of coffee and examples exist as objects in the human world because people act with intent, with the purpose of having a cup of coffee or giving an example.

This view of objects as both created by human activity and as the goals of that activity has two important implications:

- Human beings live in a world of objects, not of things or stimuli.
- Human conduct is oriented to goals and purposes.

Because their conduct depends on symbols and language, people act toward objects they designate and do not merely respond to stimuli that impinge upon them. In Herbert Blumer's words, from the standpoint of people acting at any given moment, "the environment consists *only* of the objects that the given human beings recognize and know."[1] As this book is being read, the reader's environment consists of what he or she is immediately designating and acting toward, primarily these words—unless, say, it is a spring day and the reader is distracted or bored. Things are abundant, but at any given moment only a few of them are transformed into objects by the attention given them by people who act purposefully toward them.

The concept of an object becomes clearer (and more powerful) when we realize that physical things are only one category of object that people designate and toward which they act. Symbols, we said, make it possible to designate things that are not present and even things that do not physically exist. A child, for example, can designate the shadows that play on the bedroom wall as ghosts and act toward them as if they were real—jumping under the covers or into the parents' bed for protection. This is an example of the creation of an object by symbolic designation. No "thing" exists (apart from shadows on the wall) that is made into the object "ghost." Yet the child acts toward the ghost as if it were as real as any physical thing.

The concept of an object becomes even more significant when we move from an individual to a social level of analysis. The child who treats shadows as ghosts has designated an imaginary object that is nonetheless treated much as any physical object. When the child acts toward the ghost by seeking parents' company and reassurance, the child and they jointly create a new object.

This new object—let us call it "reassurance"—is a *social object* created by a *social act*. The object comes into existence because parent and child act toward one another for the purpose of giving and receiving reassurance. The act is social because its object is social; that is, the parent and child are able to coordinate their separate individual acts because each can keep the social object of "reassurance" in mind to represent the purpose of their conduct.

It may seem strange to think of something so abstract as "reassurance" as an object. Reassuring and being reassured that ghosts will do no harm seems to be of a different order than action toward other objects, particularly physical objects. Reassurance cannot be tasted, touched, or painted. Yet we indicate and act toward many such social objects in our daily lives, and we do so as if they were as real as any material thing. Jobs, marriages, political philosophies, love affairs, deadlines, responsibilities, projects—the list could be extended indefinitely—are not material or tangible. Yet each exists and is made real in the coordinated actions of individuals toward it. A "deadline" is no thing, but it exists because a newspaper editor and reporters coordinate their activities by attending to it and acting as if it must be met. "Responsibility" shapes our behavior, as when we work hard to fulfill an occupational obligation, even though no one can touch or taste responsibility.

This view of objects also shapes the way symbolic interactionists view human *motives* and *purposes*. Both individually and socially, human action is typically oriented toward goals. More precisely, whether we speak of the individual as acting alone or in concert with others, actions typically "look toward" an end state or object. The child seeking parents' company on a windy night when the moon is full anticipates the completion of a joint action with them, namely, being reassured that the ghosts will not get him or her. Action generally moves toward an end state—toward the completion of an object. Bernard Meltzer, summarizing Mead's view of the object, writes,

> An object represents a plan of action. That is, an object doesn't exist for the individual in some pre-established form. Perception of any object has telescoped in it a series of experiences which one would have if he carried out the plan of action toward the object.[2]

Thus, the world of objects that surrounds the human being at every moment is not an inert set of things, but is intimately linked to and, in fact, represents and reminds us of the variety of experiences we have had with that world and of the motives and goals we have in relation to it. The objects that make up the human world embody the purposes and experiences human beings have in that world, and they invite us to act toward them in familiar ways.

Objects and Language

The world of objects in and toward which we act is not created anew each time people encounter and interact with one another. Instead, each of us is born into a world of objects that already exists in the conversations of others. Snow, automobiles, happiness, toothaches, beer, liberation, and thousands of other words that are known by, or at least capable of being known by, a speaker of English are not made out of fresh interpretations each time individuals act. Rather, each of us is born into a community of individuals who speak English and who — by using this language to designate and act toward the world — also enclose us within it. When we learn the names of the things around us, we take it on faith that things exist, that they are what they are called, and that they are important. This may not seem obvious in the case of concrete things — many of our words seem simply to name the material things we can see and touch around us. But, of course, the world of objects contains more than concrete things such as rivers, snow, and tomatoes. It also contains more abstract objects, such as love and liberty, whose existence we must infer and believe in because they are words used by other people.

Moreover, even the array of material objects that are present can be labeled in different ways. Vocabulary is related to culture in the simple sense that there are likely to be more names for things that are important in the life of a people than for those that are less significant. If camels are used for transportation, food, and other purposes, there are likely to be several words for naming and talking about camels. If a group lives in the Arctic, there will probably be fine distinctions among various kinds of snow, as there will be also among cross-country skiers, who must wax their skis differently depending on the temperature and moisture content of snow. It is reasonable to say that camels are different objects for the Bedouin than for the Israelis of Tel Aviv, and that the snow that rarely falls in the American South is a different object from that which falls on the Eskimos. Language, we might say, is a repository of the objects that have proved important in the life of particular peoples.

Despite the fact that individuals are born into a world of preexisting objects, embodied in language and conversations, it is not accurate to see them as imprisoned within this world. Objects are provided for us by language, but they also can be created by us as we use language. Speech and written language give us the capacity to relate objects in the world to one another in ways that are familiar, but also in new and different ways. Thus, it is possible to say the familiar — "The professor is carrying the book" — but we can also say the unfamiliar or the absurd. "The book is carrying the professor" is a strange expression, one that appears to arrange objects in relation to one another in a way that makes no literal sense. Yet, of course, if we think metaphorically and not literally, a book carrying a scholar may make sense after all: Some people write books that are so well received that the reputations they earn their authors "carry" them for the rest of their careers, providing royalties, invitations to speak for large fees, and so forth. The metaphorical use of language—using familiar words in strange, but meaningful new ways—is a major way in which new meanings are created and new relationships among old objects imagined.

Language is creative of reality and not merely reproductive also because new words can be coined and defined. The words that make up a language constitute a system—each word can be talked about, if not fully defined, by using other words. Hence, it is possible for us to agree to use old words in new ways or to coin new words and agree on how we will use them. In either case, language helps create new objects just as much as it embalms a world of objects created by others before us.

Finally, although we are born into a community of speakers of a particular language, the continuity of that language and the world of objects depends on us as much as on them. Speech exists in acts of speech; the objects designated by speech continue to exist only so long as they are talked about. Thus, if language is a prison that confines us and shapes our view of the world and its objects, we, its inmates, must constantly construct and reconstruct its walls and bars.

ACTS AND SOCIAL ACTS

Our discussion of objects and social objects referred to acts and social acts without defining these terms precisely. Now we must turn our attention to these concepts, for they represent the symbolic interactionists' view of how individuals organize their conduct in relation to objects in the environment. The *act* is an elementary unit of conduct that represents the smallest meaningful unit we can abstract from the stream of human behavior. For behaviorists, as we pointed out in Chapter 1, the stimulus-response linkage is the basis for defining the basic unit of conduct. We suggested that this unit is too small, and our task now is to specify a larger and more useful unit—the act.

If we were to attempt to describe an individual's behavior during the course of a day, we would need to make some decision about how to organize the description. The person's behavior might well seem to involve constant activity, a stream of conduct without visible seams or joints, but we would be hard put to describe it that way. Instead, we would make some effort to describe the various "things" a person did. The same is true if we attempt to describe our own individual behavior: When I got up this morning, for example, I first "went to the bathroom," then "washed and shaved," then "ate breakfast," then "read the morning newspaper," then had a "second cup of coffee" with my wife, and then "went to my office" to write these words. In providing this description, I break my stream of activity into a number of discrete parts and label each on the basis of some major purpose or object in relation to which I was acting.

An act is such a discrete unit of behavior. It has a more or less definite beginning point and usually an identifiable end point. It is related to one or more objects. "Eating breakfast" is an act, so conceived. It begins at a particular point when I sit down at the table, and it ends when the eggs are finished, the toast is gone, the coffee cup is empty, and I get up from the table in order to begin some other act. Its object is "breakfast." It is a functional unit of conduct in that it seems to have some relation to my purposes. It has a coherent, identifiable relationship to what I must do to stay alive and healthy, to accomplish other goals, or to satisfy the expectations of other people.

We may define an act as a functional unit of conduct with an identifiable beginning and end that is related to the organism's purposes and that is oriented toward one or more objects. As we shall see, it is not always easy to determine when a given act begins or ends, and sometimes it appears that acts are contained within acts in the manner of boxes within boxes. But, in general, it is a useful definition that enables us to identify a slice of conduct upon which we can focus and whose structure we can describe.

Phases of the Act

Acts have beginnings and endings, and so the task is to examine what makes them begin, what moves them along, and what brings them to a conclusion. To do so we turn once again to the work of George Herbert Mead, whose analysis of the act provides a major foundation of symbolic interactionism. Mead found the beginnings of the act in what he termed *impulse,* and he examined the act as it proceeds through the stages of *perception* and *manipulation* toward the final stage of *consummation.*[3] An act starts with an impulse, which occurs when our existing adjustment or line of activity is disturbed. It proceeds quickly to a stage of perception in which we begin to name or designate objects and thus give our acts direction. It proceeds through a stage of manipulation, when we take concrete steps to reach our goal. And it ends with consummation, when our original adjustment or line of activity is restored.

The nature of an impulse can be seen most clearly with an example. Imagine three persons engaged in a conversation at a cocktail party, one of them a new assistant professor, the others more established professors. As one of the older professors makes a remark, the colleague covertly winks at the assistant professor, who notices the wink; something is strikingly altered in the young professor's perception of the situation. The young professor previously had been intent on the topic of the conversation, but now focuses attention on the wink and its significance.

As the young professor notices the wink, he experiences an impulse to act. The wink disturbed the situation — it made problematic or uncertain a conversation that was previously running smoothly in its course. The young professor thus feels an impulse to act — a desire to respond in some way to the wink, whether by ignoring it, returning it, laughing at it, commenting on it, or merely making a mental note to try later to figure out what it meant.

This view of conduct does not imply that the person is merely a responder to outside stimuli, remaining motionless and inactive unless and until something impinges and sets an act in motion. It is more accurate to think of people, and indeed all animals, as constantly and naturally active in some way. At any given moment, we are engaged in a particular line of conduct, but we have within us the capacity to respond to a great variety of stimuli, for there are many impulses "striving" to be released. The balance among our internal sensitivities changes from time to time; we may be very receptive to winks at one point but more interested in food at another. Sometimes we are interested in sex, whereas at other times erotic stimuli are less important than our wish to create a favorable impression in another person or merely to get a few hours of sleep. Some of the internal changes that affect our sensitivity to stimuli are more or less periodic — such as those associated with food and hunger — and are not under our conscious control, whereas others reflect conscious developments as well as our ongoing interactions with our surroundings. In any case, we should not think of living things as simply aroused by external stimuli, but also as seeking such stimuli as a result of events going on within them.

Given that the person develops a readiness to act in response to a stimulus, what happens next? What will the young professor say or do? To ask this question is to jump the gun, for we cannot talk about the results of an impulse until we specify how the person perceives the stimulus. What object will the young professor designate? What will be the goal toward which he directs his act? The wink alerts and sensitizes the person to the need to act, but it does not itself define the object of action.

In order to act, the individual must interpret or designate the wink in a meaningful way. He must attach a name to it and in doing so create a goal for himself. But doing so is at least potentially problematic. Was the wink meant as a reminder of a secret shared between the older and younger professor? Was it intended to convey a covert opinion of what the speaker is saying? If so, was the opinion positive or negative? Or was the wink just an involuntary muscle spasm?

How the young professor perceives the wink depends on his relationship to the others as well as his internal condition. If he is anxious to make a good impression in order to improve his chances of earning tenure, he is likely to treat the wink as relevant to how the others are viewing him — he may think it a signal to respond in some way to what the speaker is saying. More generally, we can say that *impulse* and *perception,* as successive phases of an individual's act, are inextricably linked: The perception and designation of objects and stimuli are strongly influenced by the condition of the organism, so that the actions it initiates stem both from its own internal states and from the presence of external events or stimuli.

Let us assume that the young professor is anxious to make a good impression and treats the wink as an indication that the speaker has made an error that he should point out. The next phase of the act, which Mead labeled *manipulation,* requires an overt action. Suppose the young professor interrupts the speaker and says, "I disagree with you." This is the overt portion of the act — it is the external manifestation of a process that, until now, has gone on internally.

What happens next depends on the social response to the overt act. If, for example, the older professor jumps in and confirms the significance of the wink by saying, "Yes, I think he is right — you're wrong," then the act has reached *consummation.* That is, the younger professor's adjustment to the situation, which was disturbed by the wink, has now been restored. He can, at least for the moment, turn his attention back to the conversation and away from the wink.

But suppose the young professor's assertion meets another response. Suppose he has an affair going with the other professor, and that her wink was intended somehow to remind him of their romance rather than to refer to the conversation in which they are both engaged. In this case, perhaps, interjection of disagreement does not receive her approval, and he is put on the spot to explain why he disagrees. If so, his act has not restored an adjustment to the situation, but instead has put him on the track of another act designed to get him out of an awkward spot. Indeed, what may be disrupted is his affair with the other professor, in which case he begins to construct an act in order to restore that adjustment. It may be difficult in such an instance for an observer to determine just what act the young professor is trying to consummate!

Mead's approach to the act neatly solves the problem of the "meaning of meaning." For the young professor, the older professor's wink is an object — it is something he indicates to himself and attempts to act toward. The meaning of the object at first lies in the individual's initial readiness to act toward it in a certain way. The wink's meaning is not inherent, however, for it can be interpreted and acted toward in a variety of ways. Nor is the young professor's understanding of the wink merely a matter of remembering past occasions on which people have winked, for he knows that winks may signify many different things. The professor, of course, *intends* the wink in a certain way, anticipating a certain response to her act; but her intent does not control the young professor's interpretation.

For symbolic interactionists, then, meaning is anchored in behavior. The meaning of an act is neither fixed nor unchanging, but is determined in conduct as individuals act toward objects. As acts proceed, meaning may be transformed. Initial readiness to act toward an object in a given way does not mean that action will necessarily follow that course. A person may change his or her mind, redesignate the object, and act in a different way, or may find that the act gets him or her nowhere, that he or she must adjust by getting ready to act in a different way. As the individual's actual conduct toward an object changes, the meaning of the object likewise changes.

In analyzing the individual's act in this way, Mead meant to call our attention to the necessity of seeing human behavior in terms of both its external manifestations and its internal processes. The individual's act does not consist merely of what may be observed by others, but also entails an internal process of control in which the individual directs conduct toward some goal or object.

In the preceding example, there are both individual and social objects, as well as individual acts and social acts. By attending to and acting toward another's wink, the young professor constitutes it as an object—it becomes something his behavior must take into account. At the same time, he participates with the others in the creation of a *social object*, which is an object created and sustained by coordinated or social acts. A conversation is such a social object—it is something toward which the attention of participants is jointly directed in a social act. They begin it, try to keep it going, and perhaps feel badly if it is interrupted.

People are themselves social objects to one another as they interact. When the young professor in our example has to decide whether to treat the professor as a participant in a conversation or as someone with whom he has a secret affair, he really is deciding what object the person will be. The "reality" of the other person, at that moment, depends on how he constitutes her as an object. What or who people are is a function of the way we jointly designate them as we interact.

Social objects are created as people engage in *social acts*. In Mead's words, a social act is one that involves "the cooperation of more than one individual, and whose object as defined by the act . . . is a social object."[4] Social acts depend on social interaction and interpretation; that is, in order for individuals to cooperate with one another in the creation of social objects, they must orient their conduct to one another. Each must take into account the possible response of the other to his or her own impending act and assume that the other will do the same. Such a process of mutual orientation in completing social acts is what we mean by social interaction—whether the social act in question has as its object a conversation, as in the preceding example, or something very different, such as a baseball game or a debate.

In order for people to engage in social interaction, and thus complete the social object of a social act, they must be able to interpret one another's acts. The individual engaged in interaction with another must be able to assign meaning to the acts of the other in such a way that he or she can act appropriately. An individual engaged in a conversation must be able to interpret—assign meaning to—what the other says so that he or she can make an appropriate reply. In a baseball game, the pitcher must be able to assign meaning to the catcher's signals, so that he or she can throw the appropriate pitch.

The interpretation of others' acts generally focuses on their intent. We ask ourselves what someone intended by what she said, and the pitcher asks himself what pitch the catcher intended to call for. There is nothing mysterious about the close association of meaning with intention, because, so far as the orientation of people to one another is concerned, "meaning" really has to do with the question of what we are going to do, what others will do in return, and what we will do in response. In this sense, meaning is *triadic,* to use Mead's term: When an individual acts (by making a statement or command, shaking a fist or turning away, or even by means of a facial expression), she indicates to the other what she plans to do, what the other is expected to do in return, and what social object is being created by them. The catcher who signals for a given pitch is indicating what the pitcher is to do, what the catcher is prepared for, and what he expects will happen as a result — a curve, fastball, a change-of-pace, or an intentional walk.

One additional fact about the symbolic interactionist approach to conduct needs to be stressed: It is the *problematic* event or situation that makes it necessary for people to orient themselves self-consciously to objects and to try to interpret the meaning of each other's acts. Much of what we do in our everyday lives is routine — we awake and dress, make coffee, drive to school or work, and conduct a variety of activities in much the same way from one day to the next. Accordingly, a great deal of what we do can be explained in terms of *habit,* and we need not invoke more complex conceptions such as those we have just been considering. Some of these habitual forms of conduct involve basic skills, such as standing erect and walking, that are so ingrained and repetitively exercised that we never have to think about them unless disease or disability interfere with our capacity. Other habitual forms of activity, such as driving an automobile, are more complex and involve response to the acts of others as well as the exercise of basic skills.

However simple or complex the habit, when something interferes with the progress of an act toward its usual object, we become more keenly aware of the object itself and of the most appropriate ways of designating and responding to the acts of others. For the young professor responding to a wink, it was the ambiguity of a wink that made it necessary self-consciously to designate its meaning. For the driver of an automobile, it is when the vehicle refuses to start or when other drivers do not act in accordance with expectations that habit becomes an insufficient basis for conduct, and the environment and the individual's plan of action toward it must be more self-consciously designated. "What is going on?" we are apt to ask. "Why did the other person do that? What should I do?"

It is thus true, in a limited sense, to say that we human beings sometimes act as if we were merely responding to stimulation from the external world. When we encounter red lights at intersections, we do not have to engage in a conscious process in which we designate the meaning of a red light. We more or less automatically and habitually respond by putting on the brakes. Yet at some point in the past when we were learning to drive we did have to designate the meaning of a red light and learn explicitly and consciously how to respond to it. Moreover, there are many occasions, even in such simple activities as driving an automobile, when our habitual responses are not adequate and we must actively designate the objects toward which we are acting. Other cars fail to stop as they should for red lights, traffic signals break down, and we sometimes fail to see a red light in time and have to decide what to do. In the face of such problematic occurrences, our capacity to designate and interpret is crucial to the success of our actions.

SELF AND THE CONTROL OF BEHAVIOR

The human capacity to exert control over conduct — to coordinate behavior with that of others and create complex social acts and social objects — is linked to a uniquely human phenomenon, the possession of *self*. Symbolic interactionists use this familiar word in a distinctive way to designate both an object that is created as we interact with others and the process through which this object is created. Both as a process and as an object, the self is a crucial part of the way humans regulate what they do.

Self as Object

The essence of the symbolic interactionist concept of self lies in the idea that human beings can be objects to themselves. Each person can be an object in his or her own experience — that is, an object that he or she can name, imagine, visualize, talk about, and act toward. Humans can like or dislike themselves, feel pride or shame in real or imagined activity, and, in general, act toward the self within the same range of motives and emotions that shape actions toward others. This, for symbolic interactionists, is a fundamental fact of human existence.

How is it possible for people to constitute themselves as objects? How can individuals become conscious of themselves and so become a part of their own experience, of the very environment in which they live and act? And what does this capability imply about the nature of human conduct?

Answers to these questions turn on the special nature of the act when it is symbolically organized. The characteristic human response to situations is the inhibition of an immediate response until an act can be constructed that seems to fit the situation. Noticing his professor wink, the young professor in our earlier example felt impelled to act, but did not do so immediately. Instead, he checked his own response until he could decide what to do. He considered several alternative objects, selected one of them, and then acted.

In the evolution of the human species, such inhibition of the individual's act naturally occurred in social situations, since human beings were social animals before they were symbolic. In the course of becoming human, our ancestors were doubtless faced with many circumstances in which individuals had to check their own acts in order to consider the possible results of those acts — not only in terms of what the natural environment might do next, but also in terms of what their fellows might next do. Indeed, to function effectively in a group setting, say in the pursuit of food, individuals would have to imagine not merely the possible actions of the prey and of their fellows, but also their own actions in response to alternative possible events.

But how could individuals anticipate their own acts? From the perspective of an individual organism, the world is outside itself, and the organism is not a part of that world at all — it merely responds to and acts upon it. Thus, in saying that individuals would have to anticipate their own actions and see them in relation to the actions of others, we seem to be imposing an impossible requirement. But not really, because individuals do have a way of anticipating their own conduct, for visualizing themselves as a part of their environment, and for seeing their own acts in relation to those of their fellows, namely *the symbolic designation of others and self.* Members of a species that can name objects can name each other. Since one hears one's own name, and not only the names of others, one can *use* one's own name. To hear and speak one's own name — to designate oneself as an object just as others designate one — is to alter not only one's relationship to the social world, but also the very nature of that social world.

However it first happened, the individual who first used the group's name for himself or herself managed to internalize the whole group of which he or she was a part. By naming self as well as the others, the individual could internally represent not only others and their behavior but also his or her own responses and their responses in turn. Without a symbol for self, the individual can represent others and their acts; with a symbol, a name, the individual can represent self as implicated in their acts and thus imagine and depict the activities of the group as a whole.

By naming group members and themselves, human beings import the social process within the individual mind. As individuals participate in group life, each can represent the activities of the group within his or her own mind and act according to how he or she thinks others will act. Indeed, not only does one represent the activities of the group as a whole and imagine various scenarios taking place, but one also interacts with oneself. This can be accomplished because the act of giving oneself the name that others give one makes one an object in one's own world. One does not merely symbolically represent a world of social objects — people — of which one is a part, but one acts toward (and interacts with) those objects, including oneself.

The evolutionary significance of naming the self was that the coordination of group activities could become more precise and flexible if each individual could imagine alternative scenarios of action. By taking self into account as a factor in the situation, the individual is better able to control his or her own acts and better able to anticipate the outcomes of alternative acts. Furthermore, as precision of control over self and of coordination with others increased, the competitive position of a group using such procedures must have been significantly improved.

However self-designation and self-interaction arose in evolution, we see the operation of these processes in our everyday lives. "Talking to oneself" is an everyday experience. It is also a necessary activity, for "thought" — which is the name we give to such internalized conversation — cannot take place unless individuals treat themselves as social objects with whom they can conduct a conversation. In conceiving of thinking as an internalized conversation, we are in effect saying that what we call the human "mind" or "consciousness" is really the incorporation of social process within the organism. People have "minds" because they are able to act toward themselves, talk to themselves, and take themselves into account as they act. "Mind," therefore, is not some mysterious entity that is distinct and separate from the "body." What we call "mind" is a form of behavior like any other kind of human behavior, for it is inherently a social behavior that depends upon the human symbolic capacity.

When humans mind themselves, they constitute the self as an object. Each time we imagine ourselves doing something — whether saying "no" to a party invitation, achieving a promotion on the job, or getting an "A" in a social psychology course — we are acting toward ourselves as objects. When I say to myself, "I'm going to work hard to earn an 'A' in this course," I am creating and acting toward an object — myself. This object, me, is a crucial object in my life, for it is implicated in my every act. Although it may be transformed, modified, or revised as I interact with different people and find myself in different situations, it is always an object that figures in my conduct.

It is important to stress that the self as object does not refer to the body. It is not only the corporeal existence of the person that we have in mind when we talk about the self, but also, and more importantly, a great many intangible attributes and characteristics. People are mothers or farmers or criminals. They are moody or kind or capable or strong. They are self-confident or insecure, anxious or relaxed. They are, in short, whatever kind of objects their own acts (and, we will see, the acts of others) indicate them to be. When we constitute others or ourselves as objects with such attributes and characteristics, we are dealing in abstractions. We are talking about objects and not simply about the material thing that is the body.

This is an important point to grasp, particularly since some of the terms we use to discuss the self — the very word "self" as well as two other terms, "I" and "Me," to be discussed shortly — incline us to think of the self as something tangible. To some degree our language forces us into such a misconception. Since objects are designated in English by nouns, we are led by our linguistic habits to think of them as things. As generations of English teachers have pounded into our heads, nouns are the names of persons, places, and things. Very well, we are inclined to think, the self is a thing, a structure in the mind. It is not; it is an object we create and recreate as we act toward it.

Self as Process

The preceding discussion has hinted at the nature of the process in which the self is objectified. These ideas can be made more precise, however, by turning once again to Mead's ideas about the self, and particularly to his distinction between the "I" and the "Me."

Mead (as well as William James) used the personal pronouns "I" and "Me" to describe what we can think of as two phases of the process whereby the self is created and recreated. "I" designates the "subject" phase of the process, in which people respond as acting subjects to objects or to the particular or generalized others in their situations. "Me" labels the "object" phase of the process, in which people imagine themselves as objects in their situation.

The significance of the "I" and the "Me" can be grasped by putting these terms within the general framework of the act as Mead described it. An act begins when the individual's adjustment to a situation is disturbed. The initial, impulsive tendency is to react to a disturbance in some way; if the telephone rings, if the significance of a wink is unclear, or if what someone says is not understood, the individual is spontaneously moved to respond. Typically, conduct already underway is interrupted and attention is turned toward the new stimulus. If one is reading a book and the telephone rings, the impulse to react to the sound occurs because one is distracted from the activity of reading.

Mead intended the concept of the "I" to capture this immediate, spontaneous, and impulsive aspect of conduct.[5] The initial part of any act, whatever the source of impulse, involves an acting "subject" who is becoming aware of the environment and the objects within it toward which action must be directed. Action always is initially unorganized and undirected, so far as the conscious awareness of the person is concerned, for it represents a response to something, and the person cannot become aware of that response until it gets underway. The person cannot designate an object and begin an act toward it until he or she has become aware of the initial, impulsive response to a stimulus.

The individual's awareness of his or her own initial response to a stimulus signals the beginning of the "Me" phase of the self. Consider a mother disciplining her child: Deemed guilty of misconduct, the child is told she is banished to her room until dinner. She begins to protest her exile, but checks herself and goes off quietly. The child has begun to protest, has imagined her mother's likely response, and has realized that biting her tongue and keeping quiet is the best way to avoid further difficulty. In such occurrences, we see the emergence of the "Me." The child in this example has responded to the imagined attitudes of the other (her mother) toward her own possible response to a situation. We call this the "object" phase of the self because the individual takes herself into account as an object. In taking the point of view of her mother, the little girl becomes a "Me." Indeed, it is at such a moment that she may use the objective case of the personal pronoun, saying to herself "She'll only be more angry with me if I object!"

The "I" and the "Me" continually alternate in ongoing conduct. At one moment, the individual acts as an "I," responding to a particular situation and to the objects it contains; at the next moment that response becomes a part of the past and so is part of the "Me." Because the response has passed into recent memory, it is now available as an object of reflection. The person further responds as an "I" to this image of self—this "Me"—which was itself a moment ago an "I." A parent sometimes shows anger toward children, beginning to speak harshly to them; in so doing the parent is acting as an "I." A moment later, becoming aware of this harshness by imagining how he or she looks from the perspective of the children, the parent becomes a "Me," and then may respond to this "Me" by apologizing or by speaking less harshly. In doing so the parent again becomes an "I," this time responding to an image of self rather than to something outside of the self. And so the alternation between "I" and "Me" continues. (Again, it is important to stress that the "I" and "Me" are states of consciousness, not entities, in spite of the fact that our language leads us to speak of them as if they were things or parts of the self.)

This constant alternation of "I" and "Me," of action and reflection, is the way human beings achieve control over their conduct. The "I"—or impulse—phase of conduct is not under the person's control, for human beings do not really know what they are going to do until they begin to act. Our impulses to respond harshly or angrily to another's act, for example, can be brought under control only after they have started; a person cannot really control his or her temper until he or she has started to lose it. Impulses are governed by the state of the organism itself, that is by its sensitivities to its surroundings, and these are not themselves directly accessible to consciousness. Physiological states such as hunger, conditioned responses to a variety of stimuli ranging from reactions to red light to facial expressions, and perhaps many other matters affect how the individual selects and impulsively responds to a given stimulus. As the person responds, of course, his or her conduct usually can be brought under control, and we can think of the alternations between "I" and "Me" as successive approximations to an act desired by the individual and the others present. As the father checks his temper and responds evenly to his son, the son relaxes, and the father, in turn, responds to this relaxation with fatherly advice rather than punishment.

We see this process of self-formation also at work in the internal conversation that takes place when, for example, we feel caught between what we want to do and what others want us to do. Suppose a person has been invited to a party, but would really prefer to spend a quiet evening at home. "If I go," she might say to herself, "I won't have a good time, because I'm tired and I don't feel like partying. But if I don't go, I'll hurt his feelings. Well, maybe he'll understand if I explain that I'm tired. No, he'll remember I also refused an invitation last week. Perhaps I can go but not stay long. But that might also hurt his feelings or make him angry." In this internal dialogue we also see the alternation of "I" and "Me." The person imagines how she will feel if she goes to a party, then imagines herself refusing to go, and then imagines various alternative responses and the way in which her inviter might respond to them.

This is the essence of the self as process. There is an impulse to act, imagined responses to such an act, imagined alternative actions, and some eventual resolution of the inner dialogue into some overt course of action. The dialogue may not always be as verbal and explicit as we have portrayed it here, for we do not always formulate precise verbal descriptions of our conduct and others' responses. Instead, we can also carry on this dialogue in swiftly formed and dissolved images, in fleeting glimpses of ourselves and others. Nor is our attitude necessarily a coldly disinterested, rational one. Frequently we do not merely imagine how another will react to us, but actually feel the sensations and emotions we attribute to them.

The successive "Me's" that enable the individual to gain a measure of control over conduct are possible because the individual is able to imagine the perspective of another. In the moment-to-moment alternation between "I" and "Me," the person successively imagines his or her appearance in the eyes of the other and is able to control the direction of the act by responding to that imagined appearance. This may seem to be simply a way of showing how the individual is able to conform to social expectations, because with each successive "Me" the person appears to come closer to an act that the other expects and wants. However, matters are more complicated than this. Although it is true that the "Me" in a sense guides the person toward acts that are more or less in conformity with the expectations of others, human beings are not simply conforming creatures. They are also capable of considerable novelty, creativity, and sheer self-interest. There is tension as well as cooperation between "I" and "Me."

This is so, first, because the capacity of the person to exert control over conduct depends on the inhibition of the initial, impulsive response to a situation. The father who begins to respond in anger must be able to prevent the angry impulse from turning into an overt angry word or deed. Clearly this is not always possible; impulses are sometimes so powerful that they carry forward into overt conduct before we can get hold of them and check them. To lose one's temper is, in effect, momentarily to fail to exercise control, to permit an impulse to issue unchecked into conduct. Thus, people are forever doing things they do not wish to do and that others do not like simply because the capacity to control conduct is not perfect.

Moreover, people make mistakes in their efforts to control their acts. They do so, for example, by misperceiving the expectations of others or of society as a whole. Each "Me" is the result of an effort to imagine how we appear from the perspective of the other, and is thus susceptible to failures or errors of imagination. The father may fail to control his anger simply because he does not see himself as harsh; that is, he imagines himself as just in the eyes of his misbehaving child, and so feels no need to check his impulse to respond angrily. And, some mistakes in control are simply the result of simple errors of perception or of muscular control. The outfielder in a baseball game may realize quite well that he is supposed to catch a fly ball but fail to do so because he misjudges its location or path. Similarly, a person may fail to see the flicker of doubt or hurt in another's face and thus miss a cue that would assist in the imagination of that person's response and the formation of an appropriate "Me."

Finally, the capacity to control conduct confers an ability to choose an act other than that which is socially expected and approved. Because human beings can inhibit their responses, form images of themselves, and then choose an act, they can refuse to act as they are expected, choosing inappropriate acts instead. To put this another way, because they have the capacity for the self-conscious control of conduct, human beings also have the capacity to act in self-interested ways and to choose alternative and even socially disapproved ways of doing so.

SOCIAL ROLES AND THE DEFINITION OF SITUATIONS

Our discussion of basic concepts up to this point has equipped the person with the capacity to act, to coordinate acts with those of others, and to anticipate acts and thereby bring them under control. The analysis has glossed over some of the most important details of social coordination and self-control, however. We have not shown how it is possible for acts to be socially coordinated, for several individuals to act in such a way that each fits his or her own line of conduct to that of others. This is the next and final task of this chapter.

Since social coordination rests on the capacity for self-control, which depends on our ability to become objects to ourselves, we can begin to fill in the details of social coordination by looking more closely at self-objectification. Earlier we suggested that the person, by having a name for self as well as others, can "get outside" of the self and include the self in calculations about the group and its activities. But this is a vague formulation. What does it mean to "get outside oneself"? Where does one go and where does one stand in order to have a vantage point from which to look at oneself?

These questions are not meant literally, to be sure, for the experience of self does not rest on "out of body" experiences! It does, however, rest on the capacity to have some perspective other than one's own from which to view self as well as the situation one is in. We do not experience ourselves directly and intuitively, nor is our grasp of the circumstances that confront us limited to our own point of view. Instead, we see ourselves from the vantage point of others. We know ourselves indirectly and socially by imagining the responses of others to us. Likewise, we are able to grasp the situation of which we are a part by temporarily adopting the perspectives of others.

How are we able to do this? We say, for example, that a child anticipates the response of her parents to her actions and takes this into account in her relations with them. A daughter wants to stay out until two in the morning for a big dance, but a father is reluctant to give her permission to do so. Although her impulse may be to argue with him or to stalk angrily from the room when she is denied permission, she imagines her father will not respond positively to that behavior and that it might even make him intransigent. Thus, imagining herself acting in a way that might destroy all hope of getting what she wants, she elects to try some other approach, perhaps engaging her father in a calm and reasoned conversation about his reluctance to allow her to stay out so late. But the questions remain: How can she anticipate her father's responses to her possible acts? How can she predict that he will respond more favorably to reason than to anger?

Part of the answer—but really only a small part—lies in the fact that the daughter has had other such experiences with her father. She has learned how to ask permission to do things he will only reluctantly allow her to do, and she knows which of her actions will make him angry and which will appeal to his sense of reason and fairness. Although experience helps explain the daughter's behavior, it is not a good general explanation of how people are able to anticipate one another's acts. Much human interaction occurs among people who do not know one another, who have not established a fund of experience on the basis of which they can predict one another's behavior. We interact successfully with store clerks, lawyers, students, and many others whom we have never met. Moreover, we interact with familiar others in novel situations, where we must rely on something more than past experience to enable us to anticipate their actions.

People are able more or less successfully to anticipate one another's actions for two main reasons:

- First, at nearly every moment of our activity we know the *situation* of which we are a part. We know what we are doing, what is expected and forbidden,

what is typical and what is atypical, what others are doing, and what we are doing with them because we have a *definition of the situation.*
- Second, we know *who* the others are with whom we are interacting. We know not only what is happening but also who is making it happen, because we have knowledge of the *roles* contained in the situation in which we find ourselves and we know which role is ours and which roles belong to others.

Situations

Conduct does not occur in a vacuum, but in specific, concrete, and usually well known situations that present us with a familiar configuration of acts and objects. This configuration is termed the *definition of the situation,* which may be thought of as an overall grasp of the nature of a particular setting, the activities that have taken place there and are seen as likely to occur again, the objects to be sought or taken into account, and the others who are present. More formally, a definition of the situation is an organization of perception in which people assemble objects, meanings, and others, and act toward them in a coherent, organized way.

People act on the basis of their definitions of situations. Where a situation is familiar and its configuration of meaning is known, people organize their own conduct and their expectations of others in relation to its definition. Students and professors in a classroom, for example, usually act on the basis of a familiar definition of a situation. They know that the situation contains professors and students who will act toward such objects as questions, explanations, lectures, exams, and grades. Where there is no definition of a situation to start with — where people find themselves without confident knowledge of who is present or what is going on — they must first focus on establishing a definition. If, while driving along a highway a person encounters stopped vehicles and people standing around, the person attempts to define the situation — to decide, for example, whether there has been an accident and, if so, how recently it has occurred — so that he or she can know what to do.

The concept of the definition of the situation stresses the fact that acts do not occur in an abstract, rootless, or mechanical way. Human conduct is always situated. Our acts, along with the expectations and interpretations on which they are based, are rooted in our cognition of the situations of which we are a part. To return to an earlier example, people do not interpret even such bodily gestures as winks in an abstract way, but rather within particular situations such as cocktail parties where they know who is present and some things that are likely to occur and some that are not. People know, for example, that there are limits on what constitutes a proper topic of conversation at a party — although their sense of what is proper will vary along such lines as social class or religion. It is permissible in many circles to tell off-color jokes, but not to reveal intimate facts about one's own sex life. Knowledge of what others will find tolerable or desirable is an important part of the definition of the situation. Similarly, the definition of the situation encompasses a sense of who is present and what they will do together. We know, to continue the example, that a cocktail party will contain others who are more or less our social equals, that it will involve drinking alcoholic beverages, and that we will be expected to carry on polite conversations. Knowing in advance what a cocktail party is and who will be there, we are able to make more-or-less correct interpretations of others' acts and to construct acts they will find acceptable.

The definition of the situation does not only allow us to anticipate or understand the actions of others, but also is an important basis for our capacity to see ourselves. Because we have a definition of the situation, we can see ourselves as a part of it. That is, because we know what is going on and who is making it happen, we have a basis for seeing not only who others are and what they are doing, but also who we are and what we are supposed to be doing. The "Me" that arises as we grasp the meaning and direction of our own acts is always a situated "Me." That is, we do not generally have a global image of ourselves, but a specific image that arises in a specific situation. We see ourselves in classrooms, at cocktail parties, driving our cars, and in countless other concrete, defined situations in everyday life.

When we see ourselves in these situations, we are in essence using the definition of the situation as the platform on which we stand to have a view of ourselves. Or, to shift to a different metaphor, the definition of the situation can be thought of as a map with "You are here" prominently marked at the place where we are supposed to be standing. When we hold a map in hand and visualize our place on it, we do so in order to determine how to get where we want to go. When we contemplate a definition of the situation and visualize our place in it, we do so in order to decide what we can or should do. In both cases, we rely on an abstract representation of the world as a device to locate our position in it.

Situations contain a great many elements and their definitions convey a great deal of knowledge about them and about ourselves. Most important for the analysis at present is what the definition of the situation conveys about who is present — about the roles that the situation conveys.

No matter what the situation in which we find ourselves, we have a grasp of the way in which its activities will be socially organized. We know, more or less, who will be responsible for doing what, who is allowed to do what, who must do what, and who cannot do what. For example, if we are playing baseball, we know that the catcher crouches behind the plate and is responsible for catching pitched balls (as well as having a few other responsibilities). If we are going to a cocktail party, we know that there are different categories of persons there, called hosts and guests, and we know that each has certain responsibilities for the success of the party as a whole. Guests must circulate, talk, consume food, and drink, and yet not drink too much or allow their conversations to become too serious.

Another way of putting this is to say that we approach each situation with a sense of how it will be organized, and that this sense of its organization is expressed in terms of *roles*. For symbolic interactionists, the concept of role provides a key link between the perspective and behavior of individuals and the social situations in which they find themselves. Moreover, just as the definition of the situation provides one platform from which we can achieve glimpses of ourselves, the roles contained within the situation provide another, crucially important platform.

Role

Role is among the most widely used concepts in social science. Unfortunately it is also among the more difficult to grasp, for its use by many sociologists differs sharply from the way symbolic interactionists use it. Because of this fact, it seems reasonable to explain the conventional usage first, and then show how the interactionist approach to role is different.[6]

In the conventional sociological view, a role is defined as a cluster of duties, rights, and obligations associated with a particular social position (or, as it may be called, status). This approach emphasizes the normative requirements of a particular role. That is, a position such as *professor* involves certain obligations—to show up in class to teach students, to assign them work and grade it promptly, to keep up to date in the specialty. These normative requirements constitute the professor role. Just as there is a professor role, there is a reciprocal student role, with its own set of normative requirements—to come to class, take notes, participate in discussions, and show up for examinations.

The conventional sociological approach to role sees these normative requirements as providing guidance for individuals as they try to construct their conduct. That is, they know what to do—how to "play" their role—because the norms that define the role provide a script for any given situation in which they are called upon to play the role. A role requires them to read the lines it provides, doing and saying what they must in order to live up to the normative requirements of the role.

This is a very misleading portrayal of the way people actually form their conduct and of the significance of roles in this process. It is so, first, because it exaggerates the importance of conformity to social norms in the construction of conduct. Human beings follow and make use of norms, to be sure, but, for the most part, their moment-to-moment conduct as they "play" roles does not depend on efforts to conform to norms, and their attention is not focused on obligations or rights. Their attention is ordinarily focused on objects and social objects and on individual and collective efforts to reach them. Only occasionally—when they are uncertain of what to do or when someone challenges their conduct—do people focus explicitly on norms. And often when they do think of what they ought to do in the performance of a role, it is after the fact rather than before; people act and then consider whether they have done what they should, rather than starting with a norm and proceeding to construct their act. Moreover, a normative approach to social role is unrealistic because even the simplest roles human beings enact would be difficult to describe or summarize with any list of duties, rights, and responsibilities.

The symbolic interactionist approach to role does not emphasize a position to which a fixed list of duties is attached. Instead, interactionists emphasize two related ideas. Both ideas stress the pragmatic and creative capacities of human beings rather than their tendencies to adhere to rigid schedules of conduct.

First, they emphasize that the participants in any social situation have a sense of its *role structure*. That is, when a situation is defined, so that the participants know who is present and what will occur, they can cognitively structure the situation in terms of roles. If an individual knows he or she is in a social psychology course, for example, he or she knows there will be students and a professor. When a situation is defined (and thus also named), its participants are also known and named, and the names used are the names of roles — student, professor, host, guest, physician, patient, and the like.

The second idea is that a role is a configuration or gestalt — not a list of duties, but rather an organized set of ideas or principles that people employ in order to know how to behave. The role of a professor doesn't consist of a list of things a professor must do, but rather a set of more general ideas about how professors and students are related to one another in various situations in which they interact. This sense of role as a whole thing rather than a set of parts is closely linked to the sense of role structure people have in defined situations. That is, to have a grasp of the situation as a whole and of the way its joint activities are parceled out to various participants (identified by their role names) is to have a grasp of several configurations or gestalts, those of others as well as of oneself. The catcher in a baseball game has a sense of the overall role structure of the game (as played by batters, pitchers, infielders, outfielders, catchers, etc.), of his own location in that structure and its implications for what he will be expected to do, and of the locations and operating principles of others in the game.

We can sum up the interactionist conception of role by suggesting that a role be defined as a *perspective* from which conduct is constructed. A role is not a concrete list of behavior, but a more abstract perspective from which the individual participates in a social situation and contributes to its social acts and social objects. A role is thus a place to stand as one participates in social acts. It provides the perspective from which one acts — just as the roles of others, through our acts of imagination, provide perspectives from which we view both their conduct and our own. The catcher acts by grasping the baseball game as a whole through the eyes of a catcher, but also by occasionally transporting himself into the perspectives (roles) of the pitcher or batter in order to anticipate or make sense of their acts.

This approach to role recognizes that roles constrain conduct, but also that the more fundamental human tendency is not merely to accept the guidance of a role, but cognitively to structure situations into roles. Our attitude toward social situations of all kinds is to organize or structure them in our minds. In other words, we look for order or meaning in the situations in which we find ourselves, and where we cannot easily find it by assigning the name of a familiar situation, we work hard to create order. Thus, if we encounter a situation in which it is not clear who occupies what positions and who enacts what roles, we turn our attention to figuring out these matters. We are role-structuring and situation-defining creatures. We decide who around us has authority over us, to whom we are supposed to address a question, and who we are or seem to be in the eyes of the others who are present. And if we find ourselves in a situation that is so ambiguous that there is no structure, we create one. A newly formed group, for example, may be quite undifferentiated, but before it has been in existence very long, some people will be leaders and others followers, some will be active and some will not, some take on this task and others that one. In short, we look for structure, and where we do not find it, we create it.

For symbolic interactionists, it is the fact that our knowledge of roles provides us with a grasp of structure and organization that is important, not the particular structure provided by a given set of roles. People, we will see, act within their roles, but in a manner that permits them far more latitude and flexibility than that provided by an actor's assigned role in a play. Although roles provide them with a sense of the structure of social situations, people are capable of altering the structure when it seems necessary or desirable to do so. We are not locked within particular role structures, but have the capacity to create new ones.

Definitions of situations, together with the role structures associated with them, provide human beings with two important capacities:

- We gain the capacity to anticipate or predict the actions of others with whom we are interacting.
- We gain the capacity to make sense of the actions of others, even those actions we did not anticipate.

Our knowledge of who is doing what permits us to make reasonably accurate predictions about the actual behavior of others. We enter a physician's examining room, for example, knowing who is the patient, who is the physician, and who is the nurse. We know that medical talk and activity will occur, and that we may be asked to disrobe or to sit on a table or to take deep breaths as the physician listens to our chest with a stethoscope. We can anticipate what the physician may ask us to do, what questions will be asked, and what her manner will be. This is not to say, of course, that we routinely catalog all possible happenings in our minds before entering such situations, so that we are prepared for anything and everything. We do not, in fact, imagine everything that will take place, nor do we attempt to do so, nor could we do so. But we do entertain at least some ideas about what may occur—we imagine what is going to happen—and we get our ideas about what may happen from our knowledge of the perspectives provided by roles and situations.

But our capacity for sense making is as important as our capacity to predict. Although much that actually transpires during a situation could have been anticipated had we taken the time to do so, we do not anticipate everything. Yet there is little that occurs that does not make sense in terms of the definition of the situation and its associated roles. Knowledge of situations and roles gives us a sense-making as well as a predictive capacity. To put this another way, we can make retrospective "predictions" so that, whatever does happen in a defined situation, we can make sense of it in terms of the definition of that situation and its roles. When we enter a physician's office, we assume that she is acting within her role as physician and that we will act within our role as patient. This is a very powerful set of assumptions, for it disposes us to interpret whatever the physician does as an instance of her role. The physician's behavior—the things she asks us to do, the questions she asks, the comments she makes—makes sense to us (even though we may not have anticipated it) because we treat that behavior as an instance of appropriate physician-role behavior. We can interpret it as behavior that makes sense from the perspective of a physician. Obviously we cannot treat everything the physician does in these terms, for it is always possible for people to fail in their roles—that is, to act in ways regarded as inappropriate and as not interpretable as an expression of a role. As a rule, however, our expectation that people will do what is appropriate for their roles is powerful and it stretches to cover a very considerable amount of variation in what they actually do. To put this another way, behavior sometimes has to get quite far out of alignment with its role before we challenge its propriety.

The predictive and sense-making capacities roles give us are crucially important when it comes to our grasp of *our own behavior* in the situation. The same sense of organization and structure that enables us to predict and make sense of the behavior of others also enables us to do the same thing with respect to our own. We can get outside of ourselves and anticipate and make sense of our own conduct by putting ourselves imaginatively in the shoes of others in the situation. The roles contained within a situation as well as the definition of the situation as a whole give us a place to stand and provide us with a perspective from which to view *ourselves*.

Consider again the example of going to see a physician. The same knowledge of roles that lets us imagine what the physician might do and that gives us reason to interpret her behavior as plausible also allows us to imagine our own possible responses. A male, for example, who goes to a female physician for a routine physical examination will likely anticipate various parts of the examination, including the need to disrobe and submit to some intimate probing. He will perhaps wonder if he will be embarrassed or uncomfortable during the experience. He will also probably imagine the physician's disapproval were he to show much discomfort or embarrassment. After all, he might imagine her saying that women routinely submit to internal examinations by male gynecologists.

It is our hypothetical male's organization of the situation into the roles of patient and physician, as well as the roles of males and females, that leads to such imagined events and his own imagined response to them. By anticipating the possible actions of the physician, and by looking at his own reaction to the situation from her vantage point, he is able to get control of his conduct. It is by standing in the role of the physician that this man is able to see both his own possible behavior and her possible reactions to it. Only when these possibilities are known is the person able to choose which line of conduct to pursue—whether to disregard the physician's gender or to be embarrassed because he is a male and she is a female.

As the foregoing example suggests, individuals sometimes must act within or in relation to more than one role in a situation. This is often the case with respect to gender roles, for no matter what other specific roles individuals have, they are almost always visibly male or female. As a result, gender roles are available as perspectives on which to base one's own conduct or to interpret the conduct of others. Where occupants of a particular role—such as an occupational role—are predominantly or overwhelmingly of one sex, a special problem arises when we interact with someone whose gender is not typical of that role. In American society, physicians are still predominantly men, and so the female physician presents the male patient with an atypical situation where he must, so to speak, stand naked before a female adult in a nonsexual situation. For women, accustomed to male physicians, it is more likely to be defined as "normal" to expose the body to a man in this situation. The female physician faces a different and more serious problem because she is apt to be treated differently than are male physicians—perhaps with less respect—and sometimes may have difficulty even convincing others to regard her as a physician. Hospital patients, for example, may assume that she is a nurse, not a physician, since nurses are predominantly female.

Role Making and Role Taking

Two concepts capture the essence of social interaction and conduct formation as they are shaped by social roles.[7]

- *Role making* is the process wherein the person constructs activity in a situation so that it fits the definition of the situation, is consonant with the person's own role, and meshes with the activity of others.
- *Role taking* is the process wherein the person imaginatively occupies the

role of another and looks at self and situation from that vantage point in order to engage in role making.

These two processes are intimately linked. There can be no role making without role taking, for an individual cannot construct a role without at some point occupying the perspective of the other and viewing self and situation from that vantage point. And there can be no role taking without role making. As interaction proceeds, the acts of self and of others document the roles that are being made. That is, each act observed in self and in others serves as evidence that the roles we think are being made are actually being made. Only to the extent that we feel confident that we know the role of the other can we momentarily adopt their perspective in order to see ourselves as they are seeing us.

Symbolic interactionists speak of role *making,* rather than role playing or role enactment, in order to stress two important aspects of the process. First, behavior "in role" is not a matter of the routine enactment of lines in a script, where each action is well known in advance and where there is little latitude in what is said and done. Roles are not packages or lists of mandatory behavior, but perspectives from which people construct lines of conduct that fit the situation and the lines of conduct of others.

In other words, roles provide an organizing framework that people can use to *make* a performance that will meet the needs of a particular situation. Each performance of a role has to be oriented to the particular demands of the situation and to the social acts that are being constructed there. It has to be tailored to meet particular conditions. Thus, for example, a physician encountering an automobile accident along the highway has to face a different situation than she does when examining a recalcitrant male patient in her office. On both occasions, she is engaged in making her role as a physician, but the way she does so must fit the situation and its demands. There is no single script that provides all the required directions for action. Role making thus becomes a self-conscious activity in which the person is creatively engaged in making an appropriate role performance, not a blind activity in which a script is routinely enacted.

Second, role making is a self-conscious activity. In order to make an adequate role performance—one that others will interpret as appropriate and that will also be acceptable to the one making it—there must be consciousness of self. The person must be aware of his or her own role performance in the making so that it can be adjusted to suit personal goals, the demands of the situation, and the expectations of others. This is where role taking enters the picture. To be conscious of their own role performance, individuals must have a way of conceiving it, and this is attained by assuming the perspective of others. To know where to throw the ball so that he can get the runner out, the catcher must know where the second baseman expects him to throw it. If he fails to grasp the infielder's expectations, he may throw the ball past him into the outfield, allowing a runner to advance and perhaps to score a run. He knows what the second baseman expects by taking his perspective and by looking at the play from his perspective. Thus, seeing a runner on first making his move to steal, the catcher signals the second baseman, then gauges the latter's movement so that he can aim the ball appropriately. The catcher has used his grasp of the other's impending role behavior to control his own action.

Role taking always involves cognitively grasping the perspective of the other whose role is taken, and sometimes it also involves identification. The catcher in the foregoing example uses the perspective of the second baseman to control his own conduct, but this is essentially a matter of cognition. The second baseman's role is the source of a factual prediction about what he is likely to do. In contrast, the child who responds to parental discipline—as in the case where the child apologizes and resolves to try to do better in the future after having been called to account for some transgression—engages in role taking in which affect and evaluation are significant and identification is clearly evident. The child not only makes a factual prediction that the parent will be pleased with an apology and a resolution to do better in the future, but also may identify with the parent's perspective. That is, the child both grasps and accepts the parent's point of view, viewing what he or she did as inappropriate and viewing the parent's imposition of punishment as just. His or her subsequent conduct is thus an effort to rebuild and maintain a favorable conception of himself or herself as someone the parent will like. This constitutes role taking just as much as the more neutral, factual conduct of the catcher in relation to the second baseman.

Role Taking as a Generalized Skill

The central idea of role-taking is that the individual can imagine a situation from a perspective other than that afforded by his or her role in the situation. A role provides the person with a vantage point from which to view the situation and from which to construct his or her own action. As we have seen, to make his or her own role performance, a person must be able to grasp the situation and himself or herself from the vantage points provided by the roles of others. This ability to see the world through a perspective other than his or her own is a generalized skill: Human beings not only see things from the vantage points of others' roles, but also from perspectives provided by the situation itself, by specific acts in the situation, and by what Mead called the *generalized other*.

We suggested earlier that the situation itself offers us a place to stand and view the situation as a whole. When we assert that a definition of a situation gives us a sense of how roles structure its activities, we are in essence saying that the definition is a "platform" on which we stand to view the whole scene. If we encounter a situation and do not know at first what is happening and then assign a label to the situation—for example, by saying "this is an automobile accident in which there are injured people"—this is what we do. We "take the role of the situation," as it were, surveying the events taking place before our eyes from the "perspective" of the situation as a whole.

Moreover, specific social acts or sequences of social acts also provide us with a platform from which to view and assess what is taking place. Consider two children constructing a scenario by means of which they hope to persuade their parents not to get rid of a kitten that has been destroying the household's plants and furniture with its claws. "When Mom says they're going to give the kitten away," one child might say, "I'll start to cry, and then you come into the room with the scratching post and explain how you made it so the cat will leave the furniture alone, and then Mom will say that we can try it for a few days." The child constructing the scenario is taking the role of the mother, to be sure, anticipating how she is likely to respond to a tearful child and to the other child's act of building a scratching post. But the child is also adopting the "perspective" of a social act, looking at what should or must occur in the behavior of each participant in order for that act to be carried out successfully. Here, it is the child's conception of the social act itself that provides the perspective from which the situation can be viewed.

Finally, we are afforded a place to stand and a perspective on our own and others' conduct by the generalized perspectives of the groups to which we belong or to which we aspire to belong. Our behavior is always situated, shaped by the perspective of our role in a particular social situation, whether we are playing baseball, eating dinner with our family, or attending a lecture. But situations and roles are anchored in a larger context of organized group life. Baseball games occur within such larger organizational contexts as Little League Baseball or Major League Baseball. Eating a family dinner presupposes the existence of a durable group called the family. Lectures are given and attended in such larger organizational settings as colleges and universities. And these groups and organizations themselves exist within the still larger context of community and society.

Not only do situations, roles, and social acts provide us with perspectives, therefore, but so do groups, organizations, communities, and societies. The physician examining a patient, for example, adopts the perspective not only of the patient and of the specific situation in which the examination occurs, but also of the profession of medicine itself. That is, she takes into account not only the patient's definition of the situation but also the views of other physicians, who have expectations as to how an examination should be conducted – of how the patient should be treated, what tests ought to be conducted, and what forms of behavior are inappropriate.

Similarly, the child who has done something of which he knows his parents will disapprove may feel impelled to try to escape punishment by denying that he did it, and yet ultimately decide to tell the truth about his actions. To some extent the child tells the truth because he has taken the role of his parents, identified with their expectation that he will tell the truth, and thus modified his conduct to meet this expectation and earn their approval. But there is a more generalized process of role taking at work here, for "telling the truth" is not an expectation specific to this child in relation to his parents, but is a more generalized expectation of the community or society in which the child lives. Thus, in addition to taking the role of his parents, the child also takes the role of what Mead called the *generalized other,* by which he meant the generalized perspective of the group, community, or society as a whole.

The generalized other is, like a role, a perspective that the person must imaginatively adopt in order to take it into account in forming his or her own conduct. It is made up of standards, expectations, principles, norms, and ideas that are held in common by the members of a particular social group. In a complex society, there is not one generalized other, of course, but many. Although some very general ideas about conduct seem to be held in common by all members of the society and thus represent the perspective of the society as a whole, others are confined to specific religions, ethnic groups, social classes, or even regions of a country. Thus, in their everyday lives people may at various times take different generalized others into account in constructing their behavior. Each generalized other represents the unique perspective of some community, organization, group, occupation, religion, social class, or ethnic group.

The generalized others whose perspectives the individual assumes need not be confined to groups of which he or she is a member. *Reference groups,* defined as those social groups that provide generalized others to whom the individual refers his or her conduct and against whose standards that conduct is evaluated, may include groups of which the individual is not an actual member as well as groups to which he or she belongs.[8] Thus, for example, a higher social class than the one of which an individual is a member may serve as a reference group for that individual and provide him or her with a generalized other whose views must be taken into account. Persons with aspirations for upward social mobility typically take higher occupational or status groups as their reference groups, using them to establish patterns of behavior appropriate to the kind of persons they hope to become.

SUMMARY

• This chapter outlines the basic concepts of the symbolic interactionist approach — ways of looking at the world that shape what the social scientist sees and how he or she sees it. These concepts are interconnected, each one building on and dependent on another. Taken together, they define the social world from the interactionist perspective and serve as the basis for more elaborate discussions in subsequent chapters of this book.

• The human world is a world of objects, which are things we designate by means of symbols and toward which we act. Objects are not only material things, such as articles of clothing, toward which we can direct attention and make the focus of action; objects can be anything that we can designate symbolically. Therefore, abstract conceptions, such as love or justice, are objects just as much as more tangible things.

• The world of objects in which human beings live is given to them in their language, which names the world and thus directs our attention to the objects for which it has names. At the same time, language is creative — it allows people to invent new names for new objects in their world and to devise new ways of acting toward old objects. Science can invent new concepts — for the concepts we use to depict reality in this book are, in fact, a kind of object — just as people more generally can imagine a future that is different from the present. And familiar objects can take on a variety of different meanings as we act toward them in different ways. The cup I drink from as I write these words is thus an object in two senses: I direct my attention toward it as I drink a liquid from it (a "cup of coffee") and I direct my attention to it as I try to explain the concept of an object (an "example").

• An object both invites and resists action. An object invites action in the sense that it "contains" a variety of acts that may be undertaken toward it. When I walk into my office, for example, my chair invites my sitting down in it and my desk invites my using it as a place to put my books and papers. Of course, I can also use my chair as a ladder to reach a book on a high shelf and my desk as a place to rest my feet. These latter potential acts are contained in the object just as much as the former. Objects may thus issue a variety of invitations to my conduct, and it is the act I choose that determines just what object the thing will be at this particular moment. And although objects invite conduct they also resist it, because objects sometimes get in our way and we must move around them in order to reach other objects. I must open my office door, walk around my desk, and steady my chair as I sit down in it. Each of these things has an obdurate reality of its own that I must take into account as I act. I cannot walk through material things, and my chair has casters and will slide out from under me if I am not careful.

Just as tangible objects both invite and constrain, so do the more abstract and social objects that are the product of social interaction. Another person's smile invites me to consider its meaning and, in deciding what that meaning is, to act toward that person as a certain kind of object — as a potential friend, an ally, a future spouse or lover, or as a treacherous individual whose facial expressions are put on in order to deceive me. Similarly, the conversation that is the object of the attention and actions of others when I enter a room is something that constrains my conduct; it has a reality in their eyes that I must take into account and respect, unless I do not care how they feel about my interrupting it. Abstract and social objects, just as much as material things, are the objects of individual and collective attention, and they both invite and constrain conduct.

• For social psychology, the most important and interesting objects are social objects, which are indicated and become the focus of attention and action as people interact with one another. Most of the time, people act in one another's presence and the objects that are the focus of their attention are the products of their joint efforts. "Parental reassurance," "a conversation," and "a physical examination" are examples of social objects toward which people act as they participate in a social act. The child gets reassurance and the adult gives it in a context in which both have "reassurance" in mind as the common focus of their action. Similarly, a conversation is something toward which two or more people jointly act, as is a medical examination.

• The special quality of human behavior that makes it different from the conduct of other living organisms is its dependence on the self-conscious control of conduct. As people act, both individually and jointly, they designate objects and then attempt to act in ways that bring them closer to attaining their objects. This process of control depends on the capacity of the individual to inhibit an impulsive response—to keep the impulses that arise as we respond to the external world from turning immediately into overt acts. In order to exert control over conduct, the father acting toward the object "discipline" must prevent impulsive actions, such as anger, from erupting into overt action long enough to form an image of the direction the act is taking him so that this direction can be checked or altered if necessary.

• Human beings derive their capacity to inhibit an impulsive response from their ability to act toward themselves as objects—to take the perspective of the other toward themselves and to become a self-conscious "Me" rather than an impulsive "I." We are able to become "Me's" through the process of role taking, in which we imaginatively insert ourselves into the perspective of the other (or even of the situation itself or of the social group) in order to ascertain how we appear and how our conduct will be greeted if we respond in the direction our impulse is taking us. Role taking requires that we know something of the expectations and orientations of others. In other words, to take the role of the other we must know something about this role so that we can understand the perspective from which the other acts.

• The capacity for role taking depends on the person's grasp of the situation in which he or she is interacting with others and of the roles that are characteristically found there. In order to devise a performance that fits my own role in a situation, I must know the situation in which I find myself. If I am to make the role of professor, for example, I must know that I am in a classroom, that there are students present, and that this situation ordinarily contains such objects as lectures, questions, answers, examinations, and grades.

On the basis of a definition of the situation, I grasp what other people are present and what social objects are to occupy our attention. The specific perspectives of the others whose roles I grasp, the definition of the situation itself, and the more general perspective of the society as a whole or of some important group provide a variety of perspectives from which I can become aware of the directions and implications of my own impulses and attempt to bring them under control. As I begin to respond to each event that occurs, I can form an image of myself — a "Me" — from the perspective of another and decide whether it fits with the situation in which I find myself and with my role in that situation or whether I must revise the direction of my conduct.

Because human beings act within defined situations and on the basis of their roles in them, what we do is subject to a great deal of control. Situations and their social roles and social objects are constraining realities that shape and limit what people can do. Yet, it is important to understand that, from the perspective of symbolic interactionism, there is nothing inevitable or automatic about this social control of individual conduct. A considerable part of the control others exercise over us is possible because we voluntarily govern our conduct to fit with the demands of situations and roles. The individual always has the capacity to resist, to say "no" to such demands and to act on the basis of self-interest or on the basis of a different interpretation of what the collective interest demands. There is always the chance that the individual will misunderstand the expectations of others or simply be unable to hold contrary impulses in check.

As a result, creativity, novelty, and conflict between the person and others are as important in human affairs as conformity. Thus, the basic concepts of symbolic interactionism are not a recipe for explaining conformity, but an effort to depict a human world in which social controls work most of the time, but by no means perfectly. Human beings are resisting as much as conforming creatures, and the relationship between society and the individual is one of tension just as much as of cooperation.

ENDNOTES

1. Herbert Blumer, *Symbolic Interactionism: Perspective and Method* (Englewood Cliffs, N.J.: Prentice Hall, 1969), p. 11.

2. Bernard N. Meltzer, "Mead's Social Psychology," in *Symbolic Interaction: A Reader in Social Psychology,* ed. Jerome Manis and Bernard Meltzer (Boston: Allyn and Bacon, 1972), p. 15.

3. See George Herbert Mead, *The Philosophy of the Act,* edited and with an introduction by Charles W. Morris (Chicago: University of Chicago Press, 1938), pp. 3–25.

4. George H. Mead, *Mind, Self, and Society* (Chicago: University of Chicago Press, 1934), p. 7.

5. Ibid., pp. 173–226 and 273–281.

6. There has been considerable debate, even among symbolic interactionists, about the status of the concept of role. The conventional sociological view has its clearest and most sophisticated expression in the work of Robert K. Merton and William J. Goode. See Merton, "Sociological Ambivalence," pp. 3–31 in his *Sociological Ambivalence and Other Essays* (New York: Free Press, 1976); and Goode, "A Theory of Role Strain," pp. 97–120 in his *Explorations in Social Theory* (New York: Oxford, 1973). Warren Handel and Jerold Heiss have argued—mistakenly, I think—that there is more similarity between interactionist and normative approaches to role than my analysis portrays, and that the two perspectives have converged. See Handel, "Normative Expectations and the Emergence of Meaning as Solutions to Problems: Convergence of Interactionist and Structural Views," *American Journal of Sociology* 84 (1979): 855–881; and Jerold Heiss, "Social Roles," pp. 94–129 in *Social Psychology: Sociological Perspectives,* ed. Morris Rosenberg and Ralph H. Turner (New York: Basic Books, 1981). For an effective rebuttal of their arguments, see Ralph H. Turner, "Unanswered Questions in the Convergence Between Structuralist and Interactionist Role Theory," pp. 23–36 in *Micro-Sociological Theory,* vol. 2, ed. H. J. Helle and S. N. Eisenstadt (London: Sage, 1985).

7. The classic symbolic interactionist statement on role is by Ralph H. Turner, "Role-taking: Process versus Conformity," pp. 20–40 in *Human Behavior and Social Process,* ed. Arnold M. Rose (Boston: Houghton-Mifflin, 1962). For an excellent recent statement, see Peter L. Callero, "Toward a Meadian Conceptualization of Role," *Sociological Quarterly* 27 (Fall 1986): 343–358.

8. See Tamotsu Shibutani, "Reference Groups as Perspectives," *American Journal of Sociology* 60 (1955): 562–569; Shibutani, "Reference Groups and Social Control," pp. 128–147 in Rose, *Human Behavior* (Note 7); and Ralph H. Turner, "Role-taking, Role-standpoint, and Reference Group Behavior," *American Journal of Sociology* 61 (1956): 316–328.

▶ 4

Socialization
and the Self

Self is a pivotal concept in the symbolic interactionist analysis of human behavior and social relationships. The preceding chapter outlined the essential elements of self-theory, explaining the process whereby the self becomes an object to itself. This chapter looks in more detail at this process, its outcomes, and its impact on the person's behavior, beginning with an examination of acquisition of self in the process of socialization.

THE ACQUISITION OF SELF

There is no self at birth, only an organism capable of acquiring selfhood. The neonate does not yet have language, and so lacks the developed symbolic capacity necessary for self-designation. Hence, the infant neither acts toward itself as an object, nor is its behavior regulated by a dialogue between "I" and "Me." These capacities lie in the future.

Obviously, babies are not inert, for they respond to events in various ways, nursing at their mothers' breasts, crying when they are uncomfortable, and responding to the sound, smell, and touch of other humans. They are capable of and engage in immense amounts of learning in their early months. But neither their learning nor their behavior is characterized by self-consciousness. Whether their needs are satisfied depends largely on the inclinations of their parents or other caretakers. Others act toward the infant in a symbolic way, for they interpret its cries and coos as expressions of its needs or of its pleasurable or angry feelings when these needs are met or thwarted. But the actions of the infant are not symbolically organized. The face it presents to the world is not under self-conscious control. The infant cries when it is hungry, of course, but does not self-consciously cry *in order to* persuade adults to meet its needs. Rather, adults interpret the infant's cries (sometimes correctly and sometimes not) as expressions of the infant's needs and then act in accordance with their interpretations. The symbolic interaction taking place is very much one-sided.

Children of five or six are remarkably different creatures. First-graders are capable of speech. They can do much of the work necessary to care for themselves and meet their everyday needs—dressing themselves, feeding themselves, using the toilet. They have a far more sophisticated repertoire of conduct and a reasonable degree of control over it, so that for brief periods of time they can be left unattended by adults. How do such changes come about? What happens in the first few years of life to endow the child with a vastly expanded range of behavioral capabilities?

Clearly, physiological and psychological growth and development—what we might call maturation—are an important part of what takes place. Newborns can do very little, but during their first year infants develop the ability to hold their heads up, to roll over from stomach to back, to sit up, to crawl, and, eventually, to stand erect and take their first steps. They learn to coordinate information gained through the senses and begin to distinguish between themselves and the external world. Through toddlerhood and early childhood, additional developmental processes are at work and considerable learning takes place.

Without denying the importance of growth and development, however, symbolic interactionists believe that it is the development of self that forms the most crucial aspect of this part of the child's life. Although physical maturation brings the capacities needed to serve as a member of the human group, it is the acquisition of self that ties the individual to the group and makes the group a part of the person being created.

Language and the Self

Developing the ability to act toward the self as an object depends on the acquisition of language, for it is in language that our symbolic capacity is imbedded and upon which self-reference depends.[1] Language is crucial to the acquisition of self in two major ways. First, language provides the system of names for self and others that makes possible the individual's participation in group life as well as the incorporation of group life within the individual. Language confronts the child with an organized society of his or her fellow human beings. Second, language provides a vast array of labels for other important objects, so that the child is brought into contact not just with the group but also with the environment in which the group lives. That is, language confronts the child with culture.[2]

Learning the Social World

The child is born into a social world, an ongoing network of interpersonal relationships among parents, siblings, other kin, and wider circles of others outside the family. This world is already in existence and confronts the new arrival as a massive, natural fact. The individuals in this world are linked to one another in a variety of role relationships, and each relationship is named. There are parents and children, brothers and sisters, husbands and wives, grandmothers and grandsons, cousins, friends, and many others. Just as the relationships among people in this network are named, so the individuals in the network are named as well. Thus, "father" is also "Daddy" and "John," and "cousin" is also "Debbie" or "Andy."

This social world confronts the child with a considerable array of objects about which the child at first knows nothing because he or she has no names for them. Gradually, the child learns to make sounds, to imitate the sounds that adults make, and to associate these sounds with particular sensations. Of paramount importance, the child learns the sounds associated with significant others—for example, "Mama" and "Daddy"—and eventually the name by which they refer to him or her.

Two momentous discoveries are involved here. The first is that *things have names.* The child learns that sounds are regularly associated with the things he or she encounters, including people, and that rewards are to be earned by learning and using these names. The child's first efforts to name people and things are met with positive responses by caretakers, who reward this behavior with praise or in whatever ways are culturally appropriate. This is a development we take for granted; that is, by the age of about one we expect that a normal child will begin to use words and within the next year begin to develop simple sentences. Yet it is also something we greet with excitement—a child's first words and sentences are often recorded and remembered—as well as a measure of relief, since it indicates normal development.

The second discovery, perhaps even more momentous, is the child's discovery that *he or she has a name.*[3] Only after this crucial development occurs does the child begin to possess a self. This name is the child's way of getting outside his or her own perspective and viewing self from the perspectives of others. When the child learns that he or she is the object to which others make reference when they use a certain name, and that he or she also can use this name, the child has made a significant leap toward the acquisition of self.

Yet the mere knowledge of a name and the capacity to use it to refer to self yields a relatively undifferentiated self. True, the individual now has the capacity to visualize himself or herself as a separate and distinct object among many objects in the environment. And, as a result, the child's capacity to control his or her own conduct, including bodily movements, is thereby enhanced. Acquiring knowledge of one's name helps to carry forward a general process of differentiating body and self from the external world. But the self that develops initially is relatively simple, for it can be no more complex than the child's conception of the social world of which he or she is a part. Initially, this conception is rather simple.

Developing a more complex capacity for self-reference involves learning one's native language and then mastering its procedures for referring to self and others. The reality presented to the child by important others and their various names and titles is complex and must gradually be deciphered. Important social objects such as the child's mother and father have more than one name. They are "Mama" and "Daddy" to the child, but they are also addressed by other terms of reference. Thus, "Daddy" is also "Robert," "Bob," and "Mr. Jones." The child is confronted with alternative personal names as well as titles. Overlaid on these names and titles is a complicated set of personal pronouns. Thus "Daddy" talks about himself using words like "I" and "me" and is referred to by others using words like "you," "he," "his," and "him." The child also uses these terms and has them applied to him or her by others.

It is not surprising, therefore, that children at first make mistakes in their use of pronouns. Sometimes they refer to themselves using their first name, at other times shifting to a pronoun, but often the wrong one. A child may refer to herself as "you" because she has heard herself referred to in this way. Gradually, children's usage becomes more accurate—not only in the sense that they learn to use the grammatically correct form of a pronoun ("he" or "she" as the subject of a sentence, for example, and "him" or "her" as the object), but also, and more significantly, because their usage comes to reflect the complexities of social relationships. That is, their pronoun usage comes to reflect a more sophisticated grasp of relationships between people and of the variety of perspectives from which these relationships can be viewed. Children learn a multitude of things: that "I" and "me" refer to oneself, and that anyone can use these terms to refer to self; that "he" and "him" refer to males, while "she" and "her" refer to females; that older adults, if they are male, may be fathers, but that only one adult is "Father"; that just as "Sam" is a brother, so also they may be brothers or sisters to Sam.

Among the earliest facts about the social world that children learn about and incorporate as a basic part of their conceptions of themselves is that the social world is *gendered.* That is, they learn that there are several pairs of terms—boy and girl, male and female, man and woman—and that these terms refer to a fundamental and apparently important principle of social classification. They do not learn about the meanings of these terms immediately, but gradually as others act toward them as male or female children. Nor do children immediately grasp the basis on which others treat them as male or female; although the child is classified at birth as either male or female on the basis of external genitalia, at various points he or she may think clothing, hair length or style, or the presence or absence of a beard is the crucial determinant of this classification. The child does learn, however, that this classification is important and that it is in many ways crucial to his or her membership in society. As Spencer Cahill has pointed out, adults seem to speak and act as if babies "do not mature into 'big kids' but into 'big girls' and 'big boys.'"[4] No matter how children learn about gender and at whatever rate, the conception of self they develop is from the start a gendered conception.

Along with increasing accuracy in the use of pronouns and relationship terms, as well as a grasp of sex and age as basic social categories, comes an increasingly more complex conception of self. The more the child masters these terms, the better able he or she is to represent these relationships internally, thus incorporating the social world into himself or herself. Because he or she can represent others and their perspectives symbolically ("Mommy wants me to be a good boy"), the child gains in capacity for self-control, but also becomes more susceptible to social controls. No longer simply an organism that receives care from others and is controlled directly by them, the child becomes an increasingly self-governed entity, representing to himself or herself the perspectives of others and taking them into account as he or she constructs conduct.

Learning the Culture

Acquiring language opens up not only membership in the group, but contact with the group's world—with the tangible and abstract objects that, taken together, constitute its culture. As the infant moves into and through childhood, he or she learns not only his or her own name, gender, and relationship to others, but also the names of the objects recognized by the group or society to which the child belongs. The child learns the names of tools, ideas, places, buildings, activities, plants, vehicles, and myriad other objects that constitute the surrounding culture. Children learn a common set of objects—and thus a common culture—regardless of social class or the region of the country in which they live, but they also learn about additional objects and define some objects in different ways depending upon whether their parents are wealthy or poor, farmers or urban factory workers.

The child learns about the objects of culture partly by attaching names to things, so that the tangible objects within sight or reach can be talked about. Parents make an effort to teach their children the names of such objects, and children themselves are curious. Having grasped the idea that things have names, they seek to learn the names of the things they can see; indeed, they often seem driven to do so.

Learning the names of things is only one side of this aspect of socialization, however, for it is equally and perhaps even more significant that children learn the "things of names."[5] Material things within reach or view are only a small part of the vast world of objects designated by our language. Many objects have names, but are not tangible or cannot be immediately apprehended. Thus, for example, children learn the meaning of words like "hot" or "no," which are not labels for material things. They learn something of their parents' conception of the supernatural, even though for most people in our culture there are not thought to be any tangible, directly visible manifestations of a deity, by whatever name he or she is known.

The child's capacity to name and learn the meaning of intangible objects stems partially from the systematic nature of language. One of the characteristics of language is that terms can be defined in relation to other terms. In other words, we can designate and thus interpret words that are unknown to us. Parents and clergy can discuss the attributes of God, conveying the significance and nature of this unseen object through indirect means. Thus, statements like "God will punish you if you misbehave" or "God is the good that lies in all of us" are indirect ways of conveying the meaning of an important object.

There is more to learning the meanings of objects—the things of names— than simply being able to talk about them. The meaning of a tangible thing goes beyond its name, and the meaning of a more abstract object entails far more than using other words to define it. Fundamentally, meaning lies in the actions people have taken, are prepared to take, or can imagine taking toward objects. Thus, to learn the meaning of an object is to learn not only its name but also the ways in which people are prepared to act toward it. So, for example, the child learns the meaning of "hot" not just as a label for a certain sensation but also as a term that implies certain kinds of actions. People avoid "hot" stoves, drink "hot" coffee, wear clothes of "hot" colors, say they are "hot" when they are warm but also when they are sexually aroused, and report "hot" cars to the police. The meaning of a word expands as the behavioral possibilities covered by that word are discovered. Similarly, children learn not only that "God" is the name of an unseen being, but also that this being is treated very differently from most objects—with a special sacred attitude, not the casual, matter-of-fact attitude with which most other objects are approached.

As the child learns the names of things and the things of names, he or she comes to grasp each object as presenting several behavioral possibilities. Each object can be implicated in a variety of social acts, and a major part of the socialization process entails the child's learning what these acts are and how to decide in any given instance which act is most salient. Linguistic socialization thus goes far beyond the learning of words, their definitions, and their possible grammatical relationships. It involves learning the relationships between words and deeds, between the system of labels for objects (as well as the rules for combining these labels into sentences) and the range of social acts that are possible in the world in which the child lives. In short, the child learns how to represent his or her own conduct and that of others linguistically, to represent the world linguistically, and also how to link the two together.

Learning the meaning of objects applies to the self as much as to any object in the environment. The self is an object, but not one that is grasped intuitively or directly. Rather, as we suggested, it is an object grasped from and through the perspectives of others. Thus, children learn the meaning of this very crucial object, the self, on the same basis as they grasp the meaning of any other object: The meaning of the self is found in the way others act toward it. They learn the thing of this very important name by observing the way others act toward it and, gradually, by learning to act toward it themselves in the same ways as do others.

The child is, after all, an object to other people. He or she has, in their eyes, certain characteristics, abilities, limitations, and natural tendencies. The child is something toward which they act — by providing care, teaching, disciplining, loving, or even wishing the child would grow up and go away. The child thus has a meaning to parents and to other adults. This meaning consists of a set of beliefs and attitudes they hold toward the child and their readiness to act toward the child in certain ways. Thus, whether a child is felt to be strong or weak, intelligent or stupid, or wanted or unwanted, will influence how parents act toward it. Such beliefs will shape what they demand of the child, the pattern of rewards and punishments they administer, and what they permit (or require) the child to do.

Beliefs about a child's attributes and characteristics stem from two major sources. First, they emerge in a particular family on the basis of a history of interaction with the child. Although widely held beliefs about children in general are a major force shaping the way adults act toward children, it is nonetheless true that each child and each family is unique in some ways. Each child has an individual history of activities, as well as a given temperament that affects the way he or she is received within the family. Moreover, the belief systems of families often include the notion that certain children take after particular kinfolk — for example, that a son is strong-willed like his father or that a daughter is destined to be crazy like her Aunt Carol. These beliefs can be both positive and negative, but in either case they influence the way parents and others act toward the child and so will shape the kind of object the child becomes to itself.

The second and more important source of beliefs and attitudes toward children is culture itself. Each culture makes the child into a different kind of object at various points in the life cycle, just as each culture objectifies men and women in distinctive ways. Thus, in one culture children may be defined as special objects, having qualities and characteristics that differentiate them sharply from infants and adults. Children are viewed this way in American or Canadian society, which treats children as a special and identifiable category. Other societies see children differently, viewing children very much as miniature adults and seeking not to prolong childhood as a carefree and pleasant time of life, but to move individuals toward adult responsibilities as quickly as possible.

Thus, both the pace of socialization and the kinds of human beings it produces are dependent on cultural definitions of such objects as child, childhood, adolescence, male, female, and human nature. Whether a particular individual experiences childhood as a pleasant time of play, or adolescence as a time of upheaval and stress, depends not just on the unique characteristics of individual temperament or the idiosyncrasies of his or her family, but also on the more general beliefs on the basis of which his or her parents act.

Whether they originate in the general culture or in unique family experiences, definitions of the child held by important others such as parents and siblings affect the social treatment accorded the child and so also affect the child's grasp of himself or herself as an object. Self-definitions are powerfully shaped by social definitions. Although individuals do develop defenses against definitions they do not like, and although they acquire some degree of autonomy from others, people nevertheless generally mean to themselves what they mean to others, because they see themselves as others see them.

Not only the individual's capacity for self-control, but also the very meaning of the self as object, depends on interaction with others. In particular, it depends on the process of role taking. For the child to learn its own meaning as a social object, it must adopt the perspective of others toward itself. It must be able to imagine them acting toward itself in various ways and to infer its own meaning to them from these imagined actions, as well as from their real acts toward it. In order to do this, the child must have a grasp of the group of which the child is a part—initially the family, later other groups—and of the various perspectives that exist within it. The child must, in short, grasp the role structure of the group and use it as a way of imagining the possible actions of others toward it. How does the child acquire this capacity?

Stages of Socialization

Fully developing the capacity for self-reference depends on the acquisition of a sense both of the content and the organization of the family, other groups, and the community as a whole into which the child is born. That is, the child must learn who and what may be found in the world and must discover how these objects are related to one another. According to Mead, this process takes place in two stages—"play" and "the game."[6]

In the *play stage,* which occurs once the child has begun to acquire a vocabulary by means of which people and objects can be designated, the child plays at various roles made evident by others, their activities, and their use of language. The child plays at being a mother, a police officer, or a mail carrier. Having observed the activities of such persons, the child duplicates their words and deeds in play. Imaginary floors are swept, punishments meted out, mail delivered.

By playing at the roles important others perform, the child is not merely learning a repertoire of acts associated with these roles. The little girl who observes mother and father go off to work each day, and who observes and sometimes participates in their talk about work at dinner, is not merely learning words and acts that later can be replicated. Rather, by engaging in play words and deeds, she is coming to have a sense of herself as an object in the world – indeed, as several possible objects – with specific qualities, capacities, motives, and values.

Playing at roles, as Mead wrote, "is the simplest form of being another to one's self. It involves a temporal situation. The child says something in one character and responds in another character, and then his responding in another character is a stimulus to himself in the first character, and so the conversation goes on."[7] Being another to oneself is not merely imitative behavior – not simply learning how to act – but a process that shapes the child's view of self. Just as the meaning of all objects both lies in and shapes acts undertaken toward them, so it is with the self. The play acts of the child toward self shape the meaning of that very crucial object.

The ability to play at roles rests on the fact that the child recognizes particular others who are named and whose activities can be watched and later imitated. Knowledge of their roles is acquired gradually, of course, and in many respects incompletely or inaccurately. Gregory P. Stone relates the report of a colleague who watched two young children playing house.[8] The little girl engaged in a variety of domestic activities in an area in the front yard of her home. The little boy, in contrast, would ride his tricycle to the back of the home, stay there a while, and then return to the playhouse area and pretend to sleep. Clearly, in families in which the father works away from the home and the mother stays at home, little girls learn more of their mothers' work than boys learn of their fathers'. The fathers are observed to be absent periodically, but what they do is unknown to the child in any realistic way.

In the play stage, the child is always responding to and imagining himself or herself to be a particular other – just as the child's early experiences with others tend to be with particular people, and often sequentially rather than in an organized group fashion. The child's needs are tended to by others, but the child is viewed as incapable of many organized activities by parents or siblings and so is not included. For the self to be developed fully, a further stage of development must take place, in which the child comes to participate in more organized activities and to respond to self from the standpoint of the generalized other.

This second stage in the acquisition of self is called the *game stage,* for the organized game epitomizes what must be done in taking the role of the generalized other. Playing catcher in a game of baseball – in contrast with playing at being a mother or a mail carrier – requires the child to take the perspective of the team as a whole toward himself or herself as a particular player. To conceive of oneself as a catcher, one must have a composite, simultaneous idea of a baseball team, the various positions involved, the object of the game, and the relationship of the catcher's position to the activity as a whole.

The constitution of self as object from the vantage point of the generalized other gives the self its unity. The child playing at roles is a different self in each instant at which a role is assumed. The child in a baseball game, and later the child who is able to develop a conception of self as a member of a family and community, is able to view himself or herself as one individual who makes a variety of roles on different occasions in relation to specific others and to the community as a whole.

The acquisition of self is thus a sequential process in which each phase makes possible the one that follows. The development of language, including a name for self, makes possible the process of playing at and taking the roles of specific others. This in turn paves the way for the integration of the self in the game stage, in which the person acquires the capacity to respond to self from the standpoint of the generalized other. In this manner, as the child acquires a richer sense of the content and structure of group activities, he or she also develops a fuller sense of self.

Although many scholars have attempted to do so, it is difficult to attach any specific age levels to the development of the self through these stages.[9] As the historian Phillipe Aries reminds us, conceptions of the *child* as distinct from the infant or the adult are a historical creation.[10] It seems reasonable, given the fact that people have expected different things of children in different historical periods, to argue that the rate at which the acquisition of self will occur is dependent on such expectations rather than on developmental factors that have to do with physical maturation. Beyond the earliest stages of physical and neurological development, and except for the period of puberty, the acts of others exert more influence on the acquisition of self than internal biological changes.

Not everybody who comes into contact with the child has an equal influence on the child's acquisition of self. Because a child is exposed to its parents (or to those who take their place) from virtually the moment of birth and becomes thoroughly dependent on them for physical care and emotional nurture, they are far more significant in the child's development than are other adults. Thus, the structure of the family and of the other groups that the child comes to know later is not grasped simply in cognitive terms. Rather, some people in the social structures confronted by the child are emotionally more important to the child than are others, and role taking in relation to these *significant others* naturally has a greater impact on the self. Significant others include parents, siblings, other members of the extended kin group (such as grandparents, aunts, and uncles in North American culture), and, during later stages of socialization, teachers and peers.

The way in which the sometimes competing influences of various agents of socialization are balanced is a topic to which we shall return later in this chapter when we discuss influences on self-conception. For the moment, it is important to stress that the socializing influences to which the child is exposed, particularly in a complex society, do not necessarily work harmoniously with one another, nor is the child merely a passive recipient of these influences. It is erroneous to conceive of the child as a sponge that merely soaks up what is presented by adults. Instead, opposition between various agencies (between parents and peers, for example) may be a patterned aspect of socialization. In American society, children are strongly under the influence of a peer culture by the time they reach junior high school age. Its influences — the activities and attitudes it rewards — may be sharply at odds with parental values. Under these circumstances, we must conceive of the child as having somehow to select among various socializing influences, choosing to emphasize the perspectives of some and to reject or downplay those of others.

This latter point is particularly important. When social scientists speak of socialization, the image conveyed is frequently of a one-way process in which adults act and children respond. Although adults have power and authority over children, it is not accurate to conceive of children merely as reacting to what adults do. Instead, children — like people of all ages — play an active role in their own socialization. They do not only react to parental initiatives and directives, but themselves initiate socialization experiences. Moreover, socialization involves considerable cognitive activity. The child does not merely understand as he or she is told to understand, but actively engages in interpreting the meaning of what adults say and do.

To be a child is to be inquisitive. Naturally, societies differ in the extent to which they permit children to explore their worlds freely or in the extent to which they encourage children to ask questions. Even so, wanting to fill in gaps in knowledge, to attach names to things, and to understand what one is supposed to do are all part of the existential condition of childhood everywhere. Children, by definition, have incomplete knowledge, and much of the initiative for completing it comes from them. Thus, they ask questions in order both to learn their culture and to learn about themselves. In American society, adolescents also commonly test the limits of parental rules, seeking to learn how far they can depart from expectations before sanctions are imposed on them; but this propensity to resist is fostered more by the culture than any inherent human proclivity to resist socialization.

If one looks at the experience of growing up from the perspective of a child, it is clear that there is a great deal to be figured out. Parents and other adults issue directives and rules, but they are not so clearly defined or precisely formulated as to leave no room for interpretation. Parents may bring rewards and punishments to bear on their children, but the rationale for doing so is not always — perhaps not ever — fully spelled out. Much is left to interpretation. As a result, the child is more or less constantly in the position of making inferences about the meanings of parental actions. "Mom and Dad get angry when I spend a lot of time at Jim's house, but not when I play with other kids," a child might say to himself. "Is it because Jim's family is poor and lives in a run down neighborhood?" The child might be correct or incorrect in making such an inference, but some inference must be made, for parental rationales are often not self-evident and the child needs some basis on which to act in the future.

To say this is to say that *socialization is symbolic interaction.* Once selfhood has been acquired, with the capacity for role taking developed, socialization proceeds on each and every occasion in which the child interacts with others. Each episode of interaction is potentially an episode of socialization, whether it is explicitly labeled as such or not. Each instance of interaction proves an occasion on which the child can make some interpretation of what adults want, expect, or think.

In this sense, socialization never ends, and it is a mistake to think of the process as somehow confined to infancy, childhood, and adolescence. Although the acquisition of self is the most crucial phase of socialization, since all that follows in the individual's life depends on it, it is not the end of socialization. Fundamentally, all of life is socialization, and the process ends only with the individual's death.

With the acquisition of the capacity for self-reference, we can justifiably speak of "the person." Conceptions of what the person may be at any given age are, of course, variable within and between societies, so that the particular forms that self-reference takes, as well as its relation to conduct, will vary with sex, age, and group membership. The basic fact of personhood, however, is the capacity to number one's self as among the objects in the world.

THE NATURE OF THE PERSON

We must extend the basic Meadian analysis of the self and develop it more systematically in order to show the complex and subtle relationships between the person and society. Three fundamental ideas will guide our analysis.

• *People are both situated and biographical objects.* The self is a *situated* object, for as people engage in role making and role taking in everyday life they become objects to themselves in the particular situation. One is a child, student, or friend, each within a particular situation and the role it calls upon us to perform. But the self is also a *biographical* object, for one's activities span many situations in the course of a lifetime, and one becomes an object shaped by one's experiences as a whole rather than by any particular situation.

• *The self is an object to itself through role taking, but it is simultaneously an object to others.* One is the object of one's own acts as one tries to construct an appropriate performance as a student, but one is also an object of the acts of professors and of other students. One has a reality in their eyes as well as in one's own. The fact that we are the objects of others' acts as well as of our own is crucial because we and others do not always agree on who and what we are. A student may expect an "A" in a course, only to learn that a professor regards the work as deserving only a "B." When this happens, self-objectification and objectification by the other do not agree, often with significant implications for one's conduct and self-regard.

• *Although the experience of self as object ordinarily has a seamless quality in everyday life, we can analytically divide the self into three aspects.* People have location in relation to one another—they are linked and placed by roles, group memberships, and communal and societal ties, and thus acquire *identity.* They develop a sense of their qualities and characteristics and how these fit together into some coherent whole—they acquire *self-images.* And, they respond affectively to themselves—they have positive or negative emotional responses to self and thus acquire some level of *self-esteem.*

Situated and Biographical Self

Every social situation makes a self available to each of its participants. In a defined situation where participants know who they are and what they are to do, each has a situated self that is linked to the person's role in the situation. Each has a *situated identity*—a sense of location relative to others in the situation—because he or she has a role that is systematically related to the roles of others. The professor knows where he or she is because the presence of students in a classroom locates people with respect to one another. Each also has a *situated self-image* and *situated self-esteem,* for the role the person is called upon to play emphasizes or brings out certain skills or characteristics and subdues others, and he or she feels either positively or negatively about the role performance.

Is the person anything more than a situated self? One could argue that the answer is no—that the experience of personhood is really only the experience of a series of masks that we don in each successive situation we encounter. Indeed, it is interesting to note that the English word *person* in fact derives from the Latin *persona,* meaning a mask or character, as in a play. It might be argued that there is nothing more to the reality of the self than a series of characters—or masks—and that there is no essential core of being that differentiates us from others or makes us in any sense unique. Instead, there is only a set of roles to be performed.

This is a distorted portrayal of the self. In the first place, many of the attributes and characteristics we claim for ourselves seem to transcend particular situations. We do not think of ourselves as articulate only when we write or as strong only when we perform manual labor. Instead, human beings seem to claim such characteristics for themselves and to think that they define them as they are generally rather than only in particular roles. Much the same is true of self-esteem. It is true that human beings have good or bad feelings about themselves as a result of how they perform in particular situations. But we also tend to like or dislike ourselves in general and not only in relation to particular performances. Self-esteem is a more general and global feeling, not only a situated feeling.

Second, our sense of location relative to others is not provided only on the basis of social role. Human beings belong to groups, organizations, communities, social movements, and societies, and it is in these organized social contexts that particular roles and situations are anchored. *Identity* thus derives not only from the role one has in a particular situation but also from one's sense of membership in social units of various kinds. One is "located" or "identified" by one's religion, ethnic group, social class, college or university, state, town, neighborhood, and a variety of other social characteristics as well as by one's situated role.

In short, identity, self-image, and self-esteem are not only derived from the particular situations in which people act, but are also brought to these situations. These aspects of the self do not only derive from our performance of roles in situations, but, as we will see, they are crucial to our capacity to assume and perform roles.

We speak of a biographical self because people have memories and because they use them to take stock of and keep track of the self. The person remembers the past, other roles that have been made, special successes and failures, hopes and disappointments. However much we become absorbed in the situation and role of the moment, we also tend to link the situated performance to past and future. The professor compares today's lecture with last week's or last year's. The student tries hard to do well on an assignment in order to get a better grade—and thus think better of himself or herself—in the future. The self is never merely an object in the particular situation, but is also an object linked to past and future.

Acts of memory are themselves situated, of course. At particular times and places, such as in meeting old friends after many years, attending family reunions, or in daydreaming or meditation, we explicitly link what we are now to what we were then or to what we hope to be. In the same way, to recount one's life history to a biographer or to a therapist is also to constitute oneself as a biographical self. Memory is far from perfect, for much of what occurred in the past is remembered not in any detail but is retained in images that codify and simplify the actual experience. Much is forgotten, much is remembered selectively, and much is repressed because the memory of it is too painful. Nonetheless, situations in which we remember—as well as those in which we anticipate—are critical to our construction of self.

It is not merely memory of the distant past that is important. People remember who and what they are in the present—in the midst of one situation they do not entirely drop from consideration the question of what they might be next or were last. Instead, people are aware of a continuity of themselves from role to role and from situation to situation; that is a basic part of their personhood. Continuity is a central part of the person's experience of self because it is an important part of our experiences in general. Because human beings are meaning-driven creatures, we look for connections between things and events over time. We tend to interpret what we are doing now as related to what we were doing earlier and to what we will be doing in the future. As I look at my notes in preparation for teaching a class, for example, I remember what I talked about last and anticipate where I will be at the end of today's class. Indeed, I think about whether I accomplished what I wanted to last time and try to devise ways to be more effective today. If a class I think will go very well instead turns out very badly — or if I forget where I am during a lecture and begin to repeat myself — I experience some discontinuity in myself and I must work to restore it.

Human beings experience themselves within both shorter and longer spans of time. In each situation, the role the person is called upon to make is a major basis for the experience of continuity. Each "Me" that arises in the flow of role taking can be linked to preceding and subsequent "Me's" because it is seen as a manifestation of a self that is largely defined by a particular role. As people move from situation to situation, or as they reflect more broadly on the course of their lives or think about the future, their feelings of personal continuity depend in part upon their sense of membership in groups, organizations, and other collectivities, as well as on their identification with the members of these social units. These are matters we take up in more detail later in this chapter.

The Multiple Realities of the Self

When social interaction occurs, individuals take the roles of others toward themselves and so become persons — objects — to themselves. As a professor lectures to a class, he or she takes the role of the students and so governs conduct — deciding what to say, checking inappropriate or irrelevant conduct, responding to imaginary questions or comments. In doing this, the professor becomes an object in his or her own experience; but the students also are acting toward the professor and thus constituting him or her as an object. Some are listening intently and asking questions; others are gazing out of the window or sleeping. Some are shaking their heads in agreement or confusion; others are motionless and barely give evidence that they are alive. In fact, the professor is simultaneously several persons, one for each of the students who is present. In each of their eyes, the professor is a different object to be taken into account — for some, an obstacle to sleep; for others, a source of wisdom; and, for still others, scarcely relevant.

The person thus has a multiple rather than a single reality. One is a person in one's own experience, both in the immediate situation and in relation to one's life as a whole. And one is a person in the experience of others, not only those immediately present, who may hold differing views, but of many who are elsewhere. One is at a particular moment a professor writing a book, but one is also a spouse expected home at a particular hour, a parent upon whom children depend in particular ways, and a child of elderly parents who have memories of a child or adolescent.

There is no reason to expect that all of these views of the person will fully correspond or agree. It is, of course, on the basis of one's self-objectifications that one acts, and it is through role taking that one attempts to grasp the views of others so that one can take them into account. However, others may well view one in ways of which one is not aware, so that their actual perspectives are not what one imagines them to be. Parents, for example, may continue to see their children as they were years ago, even though the adult child has changed in significant ways. Children see their parents through eyes formed in childhood and may not easily grasp how their parents have themselves changed.

The significance of the multiple reality of the person lies in the potential conflict or tension between how the person sees himself or herself and how others see him or her. The person's social identity, for example — his or her sense of membership in and attachment to others — is not merely a function of how the person sees himself or herself. For the person to have identity, he or she must not only feel and claim attachment to others, but also have such claims validated by those others. In order for our identity to be complete, others must identify us as we identify ourselves. They must in some way confirm our attachment to them for the identity to be fully meaningful to us.

The reality of the person is thus both individual and social, and it is anchored in the numerous situations of everyday life and created anew in each situation as well as in biographies people construct for themselves or have constructed for them by others. To ask what a person is like — what his or her interests and values may be, how that individual will probably act in a given situation — is to request a complex description of a person and surrounding others, rather than a simple description of "personality," "traits" fixed in the organism, or roles made on various occasions. An individual is born into a family, becomes subject to the influence of a variety of others — teachers, friends, enemies, judges, clergy, lovers, employers — and proceeds through life, becoming a person to self as well as to others, with a biography that is partly self-made and partly the production of other people.

One major task of social psychology is to introduce some theoretical order into such complexities as these. If the person is both a product of the moment and of a biography, how are these two components related to one another? How does everyday experience add to or subtract from the person as a biographical entity? How does biography influence present conduct? If persons are objects both to themselves and to others, how are the two related? How does the person's perception of self reflect the appraisals of others? How are these appraisals determined? Who are the others whose judgments and acts count most heavily in the formation of the person?

ANALYZING THE SELF

If we are to answer such questions we must begin to look more closely at the variety of ways in which people experience themselves. Social psychologists have invented a great many concepts to assist in this task, but three are of special significance:

- *Identity* refers to the person's location in social life; we can distinguish *situated identity, personal identity,* and *social identity* as the major forms of identity.
- *Self-image* refers to the qualities and attributes that the person perceives in or claims for himself or herself.
- *Self-esteem* refers to the positive or negative sentiments that people attach to themselves as a result of their experiences in social life.

Identity

We can begin the task of portraying how people experience themselves by focusing on the way they locate themselves in social life, as well as on the way social life locates them. Human beings are role-making and role-taking creatures who typically see themselves as members of one or another social group or collectivity. They derive a sense of what they should do as well as the energy for doing it from their sense of likeness with others and their participation in joint purposes. They can also define themselves in opposition to the group and derive a sense of location and energy from their perceived differences from others. The concept of identity speaks to both of these experiences.

Gregory P. Stone defines identity as a "coincidence of placements and announcements." When a person has identity, "he is situated, that is, cast in the shape of a social object by the acknowledgment of his participation or membership in social relations."[11] If, for example, a man goes into a department store to make a purchase, he has the identity of a customer in his own eyes and in the eyes of the clerk he approaches. By asking a clerk for assistance, he in essence claims or announces an identity, and by giving the assistance, the clerk places him in the identity he has claimed. As this example suggests, a *situated identity* such as that of a customer is ordinarily based on and requires a role; both clerk and customer in this example have identities conferred on them by their roles.

Identities are important because they organize and energize our conduct in the situation. A role in itself is lifeless, an unplayed part that has no substance until the individual claims it for his or her own and breathes life into it through identification with it.[12] To identify with a role is not only to see oneself in that role but also, for the duration of the situation in which the role is found, to appropriate the role as one's property and virtually to equate it with oneself.

Thus, in a sense, to make a particular role is to be that role for a period of time and to exclude from one's sense of self all those other roles that one claims at other times. To have an identity is thus not only to have a sense of how one is located relative to others in a situation, but also to gain energy and direction in one's conduct by adopting the perspective and purposes of the situation and of one's role in it as one's own.

Identity is not a simple product of situated role, however, for the sense of social location that underlies our everyday activities is anchored in a variety of situations and roles and links us to (as well as differentiates us from) various groups and collectivities. Thus, in addition to the concept of *situated identity,* we must have a concept of identity that refers to the person's larger and more durable sense of social location that is linked to a variety of roles, situations, and groups over a longer period of time. The concepts of *social identity* and *personal identity* address this need.

Social identity refers to a sense of self that is built up over time as the person participates in social life and identifies with others. Its frame of reference is not the immediate situation and its role, but rather a *community,* the set of real or imaginary others with whom the person feels a sense of similarity and common purpose. To have a social identity is to identify with some set of people with whom one feels an affinity, in whose company one feels comfortable, and whose ideas and beliefs are similar to one's own. One feels real and whole as a person in relation to this community, and one also has a place in the larger society as a result of one's membership and identification with it.

A community may be defined by place, as is true of the small town and sometimes the urban neighborhood. Such places are often made up of people who resemble one another and who share a sense of attachment and mutual responsibility. An ethnically homogeneous neighborhood in a city, for example, is a place where people resemble one another because of common ethnic origins, and often social class and religion. Their relative homogeneity, along with the fact that members may spend a considerable proportion of their time within the neighborhood, fosters a sense of self as a member of the community, one whose essence as a person is defined by those ideas and beliefs members have in common and whose biography makes sense in relation to one's membership in the community.

In contemporary society, a great many groups, organizations, and collectivities may have the same function as the small town or urban ethnic community in providing social identities for their members. A nuclear family, a social movement such as the women's movement, a religious experience such as being "born again," or even a generation, such as the "baby boomers," may provide the basis for the feelings of similarity and common purpose on which social identity rests. Whatever the basis for identification with others, however, the real or imaginary community locates the person in society. One has location within the larger society because of one's membership in that community — and one also has a place within the community itself.

Along with social identity, people form a sense of *personal identity.* Where the former is anchored in a sense of belonging and of likeness to others, the latter involves a sense of separateness and difference. Personal identity is a sense of self built up over time as the person embarks on and pursues projects or goals that are not thought of as those of a community, but as the property of the person. Personal identity thus emphasizes a sense of individual autonomy rather than of communal involvement. It gives one a sense of location within a community or the larger society because of one's distinctive or unique characteristics, rather than because one shares the goals or characteristics of others.

Both social identity and personal identity can be found in contemporary life. Some people seem to emphasize the pursuit of social identity, others personal identity, and still others some degree of balance between the two. Both, however, are forms of biographical identity that underlie and, in a sense, make possible the variety of situated identities the person assumes. It is an underlying sense of the continuity and essence of the self, expressed either in social identity, personal identity, or both, that permits the person to become temporarily absorbed in a situated identity. Each situated identity — student, daughter, customer, client, group leader, friend — can be treated as a manifestation or facet of the person that underlies these situated performances. It is social and personal identity that arrange and order various situated roles, causing us to give priority to some and to relegate others to a lesser position. Sheldon Stryker has theorized that identities are organized into hierarchies of salience, and that the more prominent an identity is the greater the person's propensity to seek out opportunities to act in terms of that identity.[13] Thus, if I emphasize a social identity based in an ethnic community, I am apt to give the most time and energy to roles that express this identity and to give lesser priority to others. Therefore, I may invest most of my time in family or church and be less interested in my work or in political participation in the wider society. If I emphasize a personal identity based on a desire to achieve great success, my choice of the situated identities to which I give priority will be different.

Self-Image

A second dimension of self is captured in the term *self-image,* which refers to the qualities, attributes, and characteristics the person attributes to himself or herself. Whether we focus on the particular situation in which the person identifies with a role or on the underlying social and personal identities, the perception of self involves more than social location. Husbands and wives do not regard one another merely in terms of their respective locations in the family, but as loving, competent, nagging, abusive, exploitative, sensitive, or in terms of myriad other adjectives and characteristics. Such adjectives are often applied with reference to specific roles (one is a "loving husband" or a "competent professor"), but they are also applied with reference to the person himself or herself (one is simply "loving" or "competent").

Why are the images people form of themselves important in a sociological account of the person? The reason lies in the fact that people develop images of themselves and of one another in relation to those qualities and attributes that are important to their social roles and their sense both of identification with and difference from one another. Images of self are positive or negative, to be cultivated or avoided, desired or undesired. Although the question of how self-image motivates conduct is complex, it seems reasonable to postulate that human beings would rather have positive or socially valued than negative or despised images of themselves. They wish to be thought of and to think of themselves as intelligent rather than stupid, brave rather than cowardly, handsome rather than ugly.

Culture presents us with the qualities that are deemed important and that people feel they ought to possess or seek. Thus, there is a powerful link between the person and the society, for it is social life that provides not only the standards people are expected to emulate but the means of doing so. It is through the situated roles provided by the society that intelligence, for example, may be cultivated and demonstrated. The social world gains a considerable portion of its influence over the person simply because it controls both the definition of what a person should be and the means of becoming it. This is true with respect to both social and personal identity. That is, to have others reciprocate one's identification with them and feelings of membership in their community, one must to some degree become the kind of person the community desires. But even if one's deepest sense of self is anchored in personal rather than social identity, one wishes to have others accept one's claims to be special or unique, and often this means one must achieve socially valued and "standardized" forms of uniqueness.

Self-Esteem

Finally, the concept of self-esteem is very closely linked to that of self-image. Because people are led to see themselves in negative as well as positive ways through their experiences with others, they respond in affective ways to themselves. They like or dislike themselves, feel proud or ashamed, experience sadness or joy as a result of the ways they come to see themselves. The concept of self-esteem refers to the positive or negative sentiments people attach to themselves.

Self-esteem is thus the affective dimension of self-objectification. Our perceptions of self are not merely cognitive efforts to decide who we are and what we are like, for we have emotional responses to what we see. One is apt to feel a sense of pride or joy when one basks in the praise of others or takes pride in a job well done, and to feel ashamed when one acts in ways that important others condemn. These are affective responses, very much like those feelings of joy, sadness, anger, dismay, and other emotions that we experience in our everyday lives. Self-esteem consists of that class of sentiments whose object is the self: They are aroused in us as we attend to ourselves and see ourselves as we imagine others see us.

Each of these aspects of the self — identity, self-image, and self-esteem — has important implications for the way human conduct is energized and directed. If we are to carry the analysis of self forward, therefore, we must look more carefully at the concept of motivation, which symbolic interactionists have treated in a distinctive way.

THE SELF AND MOTIVATION

Two concerns have been fundamental to social psychologists' efforts to link conduct and the self. The first is to explain how persons come to be what they are. How do individuals acquire their social and personal identities, their self-images, and their customary levels of self-esteem? How do they come to identify more or less consistently with a specific set of others (parents, friends, colleagues, children) or with a more general set (organizations, political parties, or even the society as a whole)? How does the person's treatment by others — the images or sentiments they express toward the person — affect the person's sense of self?

The second major concern is the influence of the person's own conceptions of self on conduct. Does personal or social identity influence the person's decisions about what to do in situations where there is choice? Do the appraisals made by others and perceived by the person have any effect on conduct? Do people orient their conduct to the expectations of others in order to have their identities confirmed or to be positively evaluated?

Motive and Motivation

Questions about the self and conduct cannot be pursued very far without encountering the terms "motive" and "motivation." As we seek to link self-conceptions to others' conceptions of the person, and both to conduct, we quickly discover a need for some organizing principles of conduct that can enable us to explain why persons act one way and not another, why some are successful and others not, why some have high and others low self-esteem. Some people become criminals and others become Supreme Court justices; some manifest an air of good feeling toward self, and others seem constantly plagued by anxiety; some achieve social positions of great eminence, and others are content to perform lesser tasks. Although such different outcomes are strongly influenced by social circumstances and constraints well beyond the control of individuals, they are not fully determined by them. Thus, we need a way of discussing motive and motivation if we are to account for the directions taken by both self-concept and behavior.

Motivation refers to the forces, drives, urges, and other states of the organism that impel, move, push, or otherwise direct its behavior. As most psychologists and many sociologists use the concept, the concept of motivation is typically invoked in an effort to explain the direction of a person's behavior as well as the amount of energy that seems to underlie it. To speak of behavior as "motivated" is to designate behavior that is related to some specific organic drive (such as food or sex), to a conditioned response, to a stimulus, or to some generalized need or disposition of the organism, and to say that the behavior occurs "because" the motivation exists.

Although the concept of motivation is necessary, its use is fraught with peril. It is tempting, for example, to assume that each act can be explained by linking it to a single motive: People eat, we might say, because they are hungry, or they work hard in school because they are motivated to achieve. This assumption is flawed, since the motivational underpinnings of most human acts are more complex than they appear on the surface. We eat "because" we are hungry, but also for other reasons: "because" we are restless and wander to the refrigerator; "because" it is noon and we ordinarily eat at noon; "because" eating makes us gain weight and thus live up to a self-image as a "fat" person. Few acts can be explained by a single motivation. Because the motivational underpinnings of conduct are complex, it is all too easy for the observer to engage in what C. Wright Mills called *motive mongering,* which involves substituting the observer's own account of what motivates conduct for the real circumstances that shape what a person does. Moreover, for the symbolic interactionist to attempt to explain conduct mainly in terms of drives or other such forces would be to violate a major precept of the perspective, namely that people act on the basis of meanings.

For such reasons symbolic interactionists have been wary of the concept of motivation. There is a way to discuss motivation, however, and that is to link it to the impulsive "I" phase of conduct. Motivation, in this approach, refers to the state of the organism at a particular time in terms of which it is sensitive to its environment. To be "hungry," for example, is to be especially receptive to food stimuli. The organism contains a great many impulses, but at any given time some of these are more salient than others. At a particular time, impulses that relate to eating and drinking may be highly salient; if they are, food stimuli are especially important and noticeable, and we can say that the organism is motivated by "hunger."

Such a conception of motivation is a useful way of elaborating Mead's concept of the "I" and showing its relationship to the "Me." Any of a great number of factors can influence the particular sensitivities of the individual at a given time: organic states such as hunger; previous conditioning to various aspects of the environment, ranging from picking up the telephone when it rings to responding to stimuli of which one is scarcely aware, such as others' tones of voice; and, crucially, the imagined responses of others to a completed or contemplated act. Motivations such as these operate at a preconscious level and they determine the impulse, but not the whole act. As the person experiences his or her own impulsive response, it becomes a part of his or her "Me"—the person takes the attitudes of others toward the act. At this point the determining influence of motivation temporarily ends, and the person can bring the act under voluntary control.

Motive, in contrast, refers to what people say about their conduct rather than to the forces that shape their impulses. In everyday speech (and, indeed, in some kinds of social research) we often speak of persons' motives for their actions, ask people "why" they behaved in a particular way, and explain to ourselves and others the reasons for our acts and what we hoped to gain by them. Such motives are verbal phenomena; they exist because people talk about what they do. Motive thus is a concept closely linked to the "Me," for it points specifically to that aspect of self-reference in which the person seeks to explain and to control his or her own conduct.

Just as the "Me" is something to which the "I" responds, so we can say that motives, which are verbalized reasons for conduct, may become motivations. That is, verbalized motives may come to organize the sensitivities of the individual to the environment, and particularly to the social objects in it. If hunger (a motivation) leads a man to snack between meals, he may explain to his wife that he is "hungry because he didn't eat much dinner" (a motive). As he says this, he may respond to his own statement of motive by recalling that he also had a snack before dinner, and by thinking that if perhaps he had fewer snacks, he would have less need for them. Here, a motive has become a motivation. That is, what the man has said about his contemplated act has shaped his sensitivities to his surroundings and influenced subsequent impulses. In Mead's terms, the "I" has responded to a "Me."

Motives are a very important aspect of behavior. Everyday social interaction regularly gives rise to talk about motives as people interrupt one another and ask for reasons and explanations. We devote considerable space to the forms and varieties of motive talk in Chapter 5. The focus in this chapter, however, is on motivation, on the way in which identity, self-image, and self-esteem affect conduct at the level of impulse.

The guiding principle of the analysis is that the person's conceptions of self influence motivation. They affect the state of the person as an organism and thus influence impulsive responses to various objects and events. They shape the person's dispositions, level of anxiety, moods of depression or elation, feelings of joy or sadness, sense of competence or incompetence. These motivations in turn affect conduct by shaping the person's sensitivities to the acts of others, to the world of objects, to the person's own acts. How people respond to various circumstances at the level of impulse—the "I"—is affected by motivational states that are shaped by the self.

Identity and Motivation

How is identity implicated in the motivation of conduct? In general terms, situated identity is the master organizer of the person's sensitivities to events that transpire within the situation. Social and personal identity are more deeply rooted motivational states that shape the way we respond to situated roles and form situated identities.

Consider a patient and a physician interacting within the situation of a medical examination. Each is motivated by his or her respective identity — one person by the identity "patient," the other by the identity "physician." To say that each is motivated by an identity is to say that of the large set of responses each could make to the situation, a subset pertaining to the identity is selected and activated. The patient, for example, has a great many wants, needs, desires, and inclinations. Only some — those pertinent to the patient identity — are activated as the patient interacts with the physician. Others — being hungry for food or affection, wanting a new car, longing for a vacation, wishing one could understand the behavior of a rebellious child — are for the moment given a much lower standing in the person's internal hierarchy of impulses. Events within the examining room that are relevant to the patient's concern about what ails him or her will be attended to closely, but those that may be relevant to other stimuli will be noticed less quickly or perhaps not at all. Thus, the patient will be alert to the physician's facial expressions, but much less interested in the advertisement for new cars in the magazine lying on the table.

It is partly the capacity of an identity to organize the person's attention and impulsive responses in a situation that accounts for its impact on conduct. Having assumed a particular role, one has an identity that organizes relevant impulses and excludes those less important to the activity at hand. To make the role of patient, for example, one needs to attend to the physician's words and deeds. The patient identity provides the motivation to do so.

Ordinarily, the process whereby the person assumes a role and its associated identity is a swift and almost unconscious one, and the identity itself becomes taken-for-granted. The patient submitting to a physical examination has considerable consciousness of *self,* for he or she must interpret the physician's directions and govern his or her conduct accordingly. This consciousness of self occurs *within* a given identity — one does not have to think of the identity itself, only of the things one must do from its perspective.

Yet sometimes a situated identity is a matter of considerable self-consciousness, and when it is, a situated identity may be verbalized and thus become a motive as well as motivation. A young couple may see one another socially a few times, for example, and at first each thinks of the other only as someone with whom to have a good time. But at some point, one may begin to see the other as a potential romantic partner, and thus also redefine self from friend to lover or future spouse. Although often this may occur gradually, at some point one or both become self-consciously aware of the shift in identity. When this happens, self and other are identified in different terms — as lovers, boyfriend and girlfriend, a couple, or in similar terms.

The new verbalized identity, in turn, reorganizes the person's orientation to the situation and to the other. Impulses that were formerly of less importance — sexual impulses, for instance — may now assume greater importance. Characteristics of the other to which one previously paid no attention — such as his or her religion or plans for the future — now become of great significance.

Social identity and personal identity also have significance as motivation and motive.[14] A person does not ordinarily make each role with equal energy or define each situated identity as equally important to the self as a whole. One may throw one's energies into parenting and do the minimum one can get away with at work. One may be an active participant in local political affairs but be content to be a bystander in the affairs of church or synagogue. Some identities, it seems, energize us much more than others, and the force with which we act seems to depend upon the identity we have in a particular situation.

Situated identities are always linked to social and personal identities. If a social identity as an active member of a local community is highly salient, for example, particular situated identities will tend to engross the person to the extent to which they contribute to this social identity. One may respond to an opportunity to run for public office with much greater enthusiasm than a chance to organize a Sunday school picnic. If a personal identity based on professional success is the dominant element of one's self-conception, however, one may greet either of these opportunities for public activity with much less interest than a chance to organize a professional conference. We tend to choose situated identities depending on the ways they contribute to our social and personal identities.

The effects of social and personal identities occur through both motivation and motives. On one hand, we carry social and personal identities with us at every moment, although well beneath the surface of consciousness. These identities organize our receptivity to various kinds of events. The ears of a community leader prick up at hearing that a political office will be vacant, not because the individual thinks of himself or herself as a "community leader" at each and every moment, but because previous designations of self in those terms have organized his or her sensitivities to the world in a certain way. The eyes of a would-be best-selling author light up when he or she hears of a particularly gruesome crime, not because of an interest in the crime but because it represents an opportunity to write a book. One does not need to think "best-selling author" at every moment in order to have this response, but at some point in the past that self-objectification was made and now shapes one's conduct at the level of impulse.

Under some circumstances, of course, people do make it a point to announce their social or personal identities to themselves and to others or to focus inwardly on social and personal identity. A person is apt to do so, for example, when the situated identity he or she has is a socially devalued one. In a study of the homeless, David Snow and Leon Anderson discovered a number of practices whose object seemed to be to maintain a positive sense of social or personal identity in the face of the socially denigrated condition of being homeless.[15] A homeless person is not only placed in a devalued situated identity, but is in a sense stripped of any legitimate social place.

How do the homeless try to sustain a sense of dignity in the face of their predicament? Snow and Anderson found that some homeless people seek to do so by distancing themselves from other homeless people or institutions, in effect claiming that the situated identity does not reveal their true social or personal identity. A person might maintain that he or she isn't really like other homeless people; or that homelessness is only a very temporary condition and he or she is about to return to a normal life; or that unlike other homeless people, he or she fends for himself or herself and doesn't depend on shelters or other institutions for the homeless. Others among the homeless adopt an opposite tactic, making their homelessness into a virtue as best they can by embracing the situated homeless identity and claiming it as the basis of a valued social or personal identity. One might, for example, point to the way homeless people stick together and help one another, thus claiming a valued place in society by virtue of their commitment to the important cultural value of aiding others. Finally, some of the homeless essentially retreat into fantasy or tell stories designed to create the appearance that they really once had and soon will again have better lives.

It is not only social dislocation and derogation that bring social and personal identity to the fore. The performance of every situated identity carries some implications for the person's social and personal identity. Organized sport, for example, provides opportunities for people not only to assume situated identities as athletes but also to achieve particular success or distinction and thus solidify personal and social identities and have them validated by others. The small-town high school football hero, for example, who in the last game of the season in his senior year scores the winning touchdown that upsets the favored rival, achieves not only praise at the moment but also a durable place in his community. He becomes known to others for that accomplishment, and he may make it a central feature of his social identity.

As Raymond Schmitt and Wilbert M. Leonard suggest, sport provides a particularly effective social context for "immortalizing" the self.[16] Those who are interested in sports—whether in a small town or the larger society—talk about sports, rate athletes and their accomplishments, and legitimize sports as an activity worthy of attention. In the small town, the accomplishments of a high school athlete may be the talk of the whole community. In the larger society, those who take a special interest in sports constitute a "social world," which is a community whose members are focused on the activity of sports and that provides a stage on which athletic feats can be accomplished and used as a basis for self-definition. In either context, individual athletic accomplishment can provide the basis for talk that locates the person within the local or wider community and thus validates the accomplishment as the basis of personal or social identity.

In these examples, personal and social identity motivate efforts to talk about one's situated identity and put it in the best possible light. In the face of degrading social conditions, the wish both to have a valued place and to convince others that one has such evidently remains quite strong. Exceptional performances or accomplishments, such as in the world of athletics, become a way of "immortalizing the self," which is to say, of making a permanent place for oneself in some community.

We can also see personal and social identity erupting into conduct in the phenomenon that Erving Goffman called *role distance*.[17] Goffman pointed out that even in the midst of serious situated role performances, such as that of a surgeon in the operating room, people sometimes make light of their roles, act playfully, and engage in self-deprecation. Surgeons and nurses, for example, might joke about the sterility of surgical instruments, in spite of the fact that this is no laughing matter. As Goffman pointed out, such forms of conduct have the important function of easing tensions, making it possible for people to maintain high standards of performance without making the atmosphere oppressively heavy with sanctions. Humor is an effective means of social control, a way to remind people of their responsibilities without directly accusing them of falling short.

But role distance also arises because social and personal identity lie in the background of every act. If they sometimes seem to intrude just at the point where the person is deeply engrossed with the situated role, it may be because the situated identity is threatening to "take over" the self. Taking oneself with less than full seriousness in a role is a way of reminding self and others that there is more to one than just the current situated identity. Especially where that identity is drawing a great deal of involvement from the person, role distancing may be a way of reasserting the significance of other components of the person's identity.

Social identities can also come very definitely to the surface when an event occurs that is not relevant to the situated identity, but that is very significant to a social identity. A professor delivering a lecture may be engrossed in the situated identity and role and be scarcely conscious of his or her ethnic, racial, or religious identity. But should a student make a prejudiced comment, one or more of these social identities may come very quickly to the fore. If this happens, the professor will suddenly become aware of being, say, a Jew, and will begin to approach the situation on the basis of that social identity rather than or in addition to his or her identity as a professor. The professor will become alert to further such expressions and begin to make the professor role with that underlying social identity in mind.

Each time one announces a social or personal identity, one reorganizes the self at a motivational level. That is, one reorganizes one's impulses and thus alters the environment to which one will subsequently be sensitive. The parent who announces that his or her career will require the rest of the family to make sacrifices not only attempts to redefine the situation in which others act, but also to transform the self. By announcing the importance of a career identity, the person is seeking to rationalize subsequent conduct as much in his or her own eyes as in the eyes of others. If one tells oneself that career comes first, one makes career impulses most important and career stimuli most significant, while at the same time one makes it easier to ignore other stimuli.

Self-Esteem, Self-Image, and Motivation

Social psychologists have also given considerable attention to self-esteem and self-image and their role in motivation. Early in this century, the sociologist Charles Horton Cooley used the well-known metaphor of a looking glass to depict the nature and sources of the images of themselves people see reflected in others.

> A self idea . . . seems to have three principal elements: the imagination of our appearance to the other person; the imagination of his judgment of that appearance; and some sort of self-feeling, such as pride or mortification.[18]

How do feelings about ourselves arise out of this process of imagining our appearance in the eyes of the other?

> The thing that moves us to pride or shame is . . . an imputed sentiment. . . . This is evident from the fact that the character and weight of that other, in whose mind we see ourselves, makes all the difference with our feeling. We are ashamed to seem evasive in the presence of a straightforward man, cowardly in the presence of a brave one, gross in the eyes of a refined one, and so on. We imagine, and in imagining share, the judgments of the other mind.[19]

As people interact, guided by their respective identities, they develop images of one another. Indeed, if they have a history of interaction, it is likely that they will bring images of one another to the situation. As these images—of bravery, refinement, tact, competence, intelligence, kindness, cruelty, stupidity, deviousness, and the like—are established, people imagine their own appearance to others in terms of them. That is, the person forms an image of the other, then imagines his or her appearance to the other from the standpoint of that image, and feels good or bad accordingly.[20]

This approach to self-esteem emphasizes the appraisals of others as they are perceived by the individual in the situation.[21] In some instances, of course, others mince no words in telling us what they think of us, so that we have direct access to their opinions of us. Words of praise or condemnation from others encourage us to have specific images of ourselves. Much of the time, however, we must rely on role taking, imagining our appearance to the other. In either case, the result is an affective response to ourselves. Whether we are directly told how the other feels about us or we impute a sentiment to the other, the result is that we develop an attitude toward ourselves.

There is more to self-esteem and self-image, however, than our responses to the appraisals of those others with whom we happen to be interacting at a given moment. Some of the people with whom we interact are important to us and so we are apt to take their appraisals more seriously than those of people whose opinions we do not respect. A child, for example, is likely to give more credence to the views of parents than those of teachers. An adult is likely to put more stock in the views of friends of long acquaintance than those of strangers. Thus, although each situation in which we interact with others has some impact on our overall level of self-esteem, some situations have greater impact than others. The self-sentiments that arise in each situation seem to be filtered through our existing conceptions of self before they add to or subtract from our overall self-esteem.

Moreover, we add to or subtract from our level of self-esteem not just by responding to the real or imagined appraisals of others, but also by comparing ourselves to them. Part of the process of self-objectification, perhaps especially in a culture that emphasizes individual achievement, entails our comparing our own activities and accomplishments with those of others. We see others of our age, for example, who have better grades, greater incomes, or more powerful positions, and these comparative facts affect our self-esteem, most likely for the worse unless we can find some way to explain the difference. Or, in contrast, we observe others doing less well than we are and derive some feelings of self-satisfaction from our better position.

Self-esteem is also influenced by our own appraisals of our performances. In the classic formulation of the psychologist William James, self-esteem is influenced by the "ratio" of success to pretension. The more one aspires to a particular accomplishment or other standard of self-worth, the greater one's successes must be in order to feel worthy. How we feel about ourselves is not simply a result of what other people tell us, but of what we want to be. If you think of yourself as someone who could be a champion athlete, mere athletic prowess or modest success is not enough; you must win in order to live up to your aspirations. As James's formulation suggests, feelings we have about ourselves in particular situations are thus weighed against our aspirations. You may triumph over an opponent in a contest, but if your goal is to be world champion and you have defeated a third-rate contender, the thrill of victory may be tempered by your sense that this particular victory doesn't count for very much.

Self-image and self-esteem are thus not simply the products of particular situations, but also of a continual process of reflection in which the person decides what standards and what others are significant. At any given point in the person's life, we are likely to find that the person has some organized sense of what is important and what is not, of whose appraisals should be taken seriously and whose should be disregarded. Some identities, for example, are likely to be more psychologically central than others. A lawyer who has fallen short of previous aspirations to make a great deal of money may adopt a revised version of occupational identity in which the new goal is to do well enough to be respected in a community and to provide for the needs of a family. A person who succeeds at academic tasks but is uncoordinated on the athletic field emphasizes the academic identity and downplays the athletic one, thus maximizing the chances of feeling positive about self by emphasizing those activities where the most favorable appraisals and comparisons are secured.

Self-esteem provides a major motivational link between the person and the social order. Social roles and group memberships provide the contexts within which our situated identities occur and our social and personal identities develop. Hence, one of the major ways in which we secure self-esteem is through our attachment to and identification with the social world. Human beings seek positively valued identities. They look for ways of behaving that will enable them not only to secure their goals, but also to earn the approval of others. Sometimes they seek the approval of others by emulating them and their behavior. In their formation and pursuit of personal aspirations and in self-appraisals, they rely to a significant extent on the standards and values of the community or society to which they belong. Even when we appraise ourselves, we do so for the most part as we think others would do.

Yet it is important not to lay too much stress on the determining nature of group standards and group judgments. Symbolic interactionists stress that human beings are naturally active and self-conscious creatures who acquire some degree of autonomy along with the self. We act so as to earn the approval of others; we act in ways that let us approve of ourselves because we act as others would have us act. But we also develop individual goals and aspirations. We do not seek only social identities, which locate us comfortably in the bosom of community, but also personal identities, which may entail projects and goals of our own that put us in tension or opposition to others. Thus, to some extent human beings derive self-esteem to the extent that their pursuit of personal identity is successful. Viktor Gecas and Michael L. Schwalbe have expressed a similar idea by arguing for the importance of what they call "efficacy-based" self-esteem, which is the positive sense of self the person derives from effective action.[22] Self-esteem is achieved in part through exercise of our capacities to take effective actions—to solve problems, to create new things or ideas, or to demonstrate our autonomy from the social world.

Moreover, in their quest for the positive appraisals of others, human beings may consciously seek to deceive others rather than emulate them or live up to their expectations. If people sometimes genuinely and spontaneously adapt their behavior to social standards, at other times they may simply try to create the appearance of doing so. Through a variety of techniques of *impression management* they may seek to present a self that seems to be what others wish it to be. People carefully craft their physical appearances to create the impression that they are younger than they really are. Office workers seek to appear busy with work when they are engaged in personal activities. Men and women feign sincere interest in and respect for one another when they are really looking for a one-night stand. In a variety of ways people seek to present a self that seems appropriate to the situation or that meets cultural requirements even though they are inwardly alienated from this presented self. And sometimes, it seems, they may convince themselves as well as others of the validity of their performance. As Erving Goffman pointed out, people may be "taken in" by their own performances, so that what was initially a "false" presentation of self becomes a genuine one.[23]

Self-esteem is a product of our activities and of our experiences with other people, but it is also something we *bring* to each new situation of social interaction. As such, it is a motivational state: Self-esteem affects the way we are sensitive to others in the situations in which we encounter them. One of the key ways it does so is through its relationship to anxiety.

Low self-esteem implies a high level of anxiety—a state of apprehension or psychic tension. Morris Rosenberg found, for example, that low levels of self-esteem are associated with more frequent reports of psychosomatic symptoms, such as insomnia, nervousness, fingernail biting, and sweaty hands. Symptoms of this kind, clear indicators of anxiety, were more frequently mentioned by those who had low self-esteem, as measured by a series of questions designed to tap attitudes toward the self.[24] The condition of being anxious is familiar to everyone and is neither an entirely negative experience nor one caused solely by low self-esteem. Uncertainty, threat, danger, fatigue, pressure, and other circumstances may give rise to anxiety from time to time, and in moderate degree the state of being anxious may be helpful to the person's adjustment to a situation. Being "up" for an examination is probably useful to a student, provided the anxiety is not too severe.

Anxiety is an important motivational state. As a derivative of low self-esteem, it sensitizes the individual to others in a particularly painful way, making the person more vulnerable to the negative judgments of others as they verbalize them and more likely to see others in positive ways and to judge self negatively. Indeed, a vicious cycle can be found: The person approaches contact with others with a high level of anxiety; he or she is likely to be more vulnerable to their criticism and to make condemnations of self; and thus each social encounter produces an incremental reduction in overall self-esteem.

For people with low self-esteem, it would appear, the motivational results work in opposing directions. On the one hand, the person is motivated to conduct that resembles that of others; on the other hand, because low self-esteem promotes anxiety, the person may be unable to present self in a way that leads to positive images. Acute anxiety is a paralyzing condition, one that makes it difficult for the person to act in ways that would present a favorable self to others. As Harry Stack Sullivan wrote, the person with low self-esteem finds it difficult to "manifest good feeling toward another person."[25] Anxiety interferes with conduct. It makes it difficult to show appreciation of others' qualities even when the person wants to emulate them, and it probably interferes with accurate role taking as well. People with low self-esteem thus seem caught between a desire to be like others whose qualities they value and the inability to be like them.

Most people, of course, do not have genuinely low self-esteem; nor do most have extremely high self-esteem. Most people have self-esteem that is high enough to keep anxiety from paralyzing them, but low enough to make them receptive to others' evaluations. As this formulation suggests, both exceptionally low and exceptionally high self-esteem may have important implications for the individual. If very low self-esteem is frustrating because it leads to aspirations for the self that are hard to fulfill, very high self-esteem may be equally consequential because it works to insulate the person from the appraisals of others. The person who approaches every situation with customarily high self-esteem may impulsively select images of others in such a way that only favorable conclusions about self can be reached. The person may always see himself or herself as an object of admiration, regardless of how others actually feel. People with very high self-esteem may, thus, fall beyond the control of others' judgments.

The discussion of self and motivation has largely ignored the larger social context within which social interaction occurs. We have spoken of identity, self-image, and self-esteem as if the person were relatively free to go wherever he or she chooses in the social world and to present the self as he or she sees fit. Realistically, however, the others with whom the person interacts, the images they value, and the conduct that is possible are strongly influenced by culture and society. Our attention must now turn to this topic in order to complete our account of the person.

THE SELF AND THE SOCIAL ORDER

A variety of cultural and social factors constrain the nature and development of the self. The identities people can assume in specific situations are only partly open to their choosing, for often one has no choice about one's situated role. Likewise, one is not entirely free to choose the others with whom one will interact. In many situations of life, people must interact with specific others, regardless of their wishes or the appraisals they expect to receive from them. In addition to these fundamental constraints, people are pulled in different directions by conflicting expectations, they are subject to the influences of the communities to which they belong, and they are shaped by the special nature of modern life. In the following pages, we consider the variety of ways in which culture and society constrain the self.

Ascription and Achievement

Sociologists have long distinguished between two opposite ways in which people come to enact various roles. On the one hand, many roles are *ascribed,* which means that the person is assigned a role by others on the basis of biological considerations (such as age or sex) or birth into a particular family (identified, for example, by ethnicity or religion). Sex is a clear example of an ascribed role (leaving aside physical abnormality or surgical change of sex): The person is born with the genitals of one sex or the other, and that fact alone assigns the person to a role. In any situation in which people define gender as a relevant part of its role structure (and that probably includes most situations to some extent), role making and role taking are influenced by the specific ideas people have about proper, normal, and expectable conduct for boys or girls, men or women. Similarly, religion, age, and sometimes even political affiliation may be matters of ascription. The person is viewed as having a set of characteristics or dispositions by virtue of having been born into a family that sees itself and is seen by others as having those characteristics.

On the other hand, some roles are *achieved,* which means that the right to assume a particular role does not depend on birth, but is voluntary and dependent upon the attainment of a specific set of qualifications. In modern societies, occupational roles are largely achieved: Few individuals are regarded by their families as required to assume a particular occupation merely because they were born into that family, and no legal sanctions are available to force an individual to become what parents wish.

The contrast between ascription and achievement is important because it emphasizes the fact that a person's identity, whether in a specific situation or in a larger biographical sense, is not entirely a matter of choice. Indeed, in many instances the person may have no choice at all. In the United States, historically and presently, the role of a black person is often fixed by race rather than by characteristics germane to the interaction that is to take place. In many circumstances, people react differently to men and women, even though sex is unrelated to the particular activity at hand. In these situations, an ascribed characteristic that is not germane to an activity is used as the basis for establishing identity. A hospital patient may, for example, assume that all black people are orderlies. In thus establishing the situated social identity of a particular person as someone who must be an orderly because he or she is black, the patient approaches interaction with him or her with a preconception of the role structure of the situation. Even when the patient learns that this particular individual is a physician or a nurse, the interaction that takes place is still likely to be influenced by ideas about race.

Identity may be constrained as much by achieved roles as by ascribed roles. Even a role the individual has achieved the right to enact by acquiring the appropriate qualifications — such as an occupational role — subsequently constrains and shapes the self. Acquiring the training necessary to be a professor, for example, means that one foregoes the opportunity to acquire the skills of other occupations, since one has invested so much time and money in preparing for one occupation that changing occupational roles is almost precluded. Moreover, to pursue an occupation is not only to develop a conception of oneself as, say, a physician or a farmer but also to be regarded as such by others and to be entangled in a web of social relationships with others. One is constrained by the self-image one develops in the course of learning and enacting an occupational role, and by the fact that a significant part of one's self-esteem depends upon the successful performance of the role. As Peter Adler and Patricia Adler showed in their study of college basketball players, a role performed with great success and cheered by others can overwhelm the self. Adler and Adler studied the roles and what they termed the "gloried selves" of college basketball players. Engulfed by the athletic role — facing pressures from coaches, fellow students, and boosters to define themselves almost solely as athletes — the players they studied found themselves under strong pressures to define themselves in the same terms. The players concentrated mainly on their athletic role to the detriment of other present and future roles. They became almost totally defined by a role they had achieved. They were in a sense diminished as persons by their very achievements as athletes.[26]

Limitations on the Choice of Others

Just as social life constrains the development of self by providing the roles on the basis of which the self is defined, so too it limits the person's choice of others with whom to interact and his or her ability to regard their appraisals as important or unimportant. These limitations stem in part from the facts of birth and ascription. One's parents are ordinarily not chosen — parents and their children are typically stuck with one another, as are siblings. Furthermore, to be born black or white, male or female, rich or poor, is to be confined to some extent to an existing network of social relationships. Depending on social class, the worlds of men and women may be far removed from one another, so that the others with whom women interact may be limited (often very rigidly) by custom, knowledge, or rules and sanctions laid down by husbands. To be born white in American society is often to be denied contact with African Americans, their values, outlooks, and beliefs. De facto segregation of housing and schools, patterns of hostility between groups, community sentiments, and sheer racism are among the factors that constrain or limit contact between blacks and whites.

Moreover, as individuals in a modern society move through a succession of age roles, from infancy through childhood and adolescence into adulthood, they encounter a series of others whom they do not choose, but who interact with one another because of their social position. Teachers, other children, members of the extended family, gang leaders, social workers, Boy Scout leaders, police officers, college professors, and employers are others with whom individuals interact, sometimes by choice, but often on the basis of chance or the decisions and actions of others over whom they have little or no influence.

The ongoing social order that confronts the individual at birth is thus in many ways an unyielding reality to which the person must adjust. Beliefs about behavior that is normal for boys and girls, the practice of starting school at age six, or a propensity to see black people as capable of filling only menial jobs may be given features of the social world from an individual's standpoint. They exist when the person is born and they shape the formation of the self. They exist only because people form their conduct on the basis of particular beliefs, ideas, and knowledge—because, for example, they have learned to act toward African Americans, girls, or six-year-olds as particular kinds of social objects. From the standpoint of the individual confronting it for the first time, this world of objects is real. It is there as an objective, factual set of conditions that must be taken into account in his or her conduct. That little girls are to be avoided is simply a fact for some little boys, a matter of what is "obviously" real and important.

In order to account for the development of the self, therefore, we must know the person's location in the social order. That is, we must know the world of objects and the social arrangements of the family and community into which the person is born. We must know the beliefs and values found in the family, the attitude taken toward the child in school, the kinds of peers with whom the individual associates, the sort of job attained or college attended. All of these are strongly influenced by the person's social position, whether the person is black or white, male or female, rich or poor, Catholic, Protestant, or Jew, urban or rural, of Polish, Italian, or Norwegian descent.

How does this obdurate social world influence self-conceptions? Both consciously and unconsciously, people arrange their presentations of self in various situations so as to manifest the qualities and characteristics valued in their social world. In a basic sense, the avoidance of low situated self-esteem—or the development of positive self-esteem—sets the terms by which self presentations are managed, since it is by manifesting valued qualities that the person is able favorably to imagine his or her own appearance in the eyes of the other. The impact of the social order on this process is considerable. Desirable qualities and characteristics are personified by others with whom the person is constrained to interact, and the valued attributes of others are themselves a factual, objective part of the world so far as the child is concerned. The adjustment of conduct — which is what the presentation of self is all about — always is an adjustment to a specific set of others and to particular standards of evaluation, and these are a preexisting part of the world, at least so far as much childhood experience is concerned. As one grows older, of course, one may discover that the standards by which people evaluate one another are matters of human creation, not absolutes, and that a variety of other people in the society hold different views of what is natural and proper.

Conflicting Self-Conceptions

Some of the most important constraints on the adjustment of conduct to valued images of others come into play at the point where the child moves out of the exclusive confines of the nuclear family and encounters a more diverse set of others. In a complex society, which divides the labor of socialization among various agents and agencies, what parents expect may well not coincide with the views of teachers. If the child imagines parents to emphasize street savvy and toughness, and teachers as wanting refinement, sensitivity, and attention to school work, the child may be able to manifest both sets of qualities only with great difficulty, if at all. If the child perceives teachers as protective or restrictive, and has already developed a self-image that emphasizes self-reliance and independence, the child may rebel against their efforts to impose controls.

Such conflicts between selves fostered within the family and those encouraged in public contexts such as schools are not uncommon in a society as ethnically, racially, and religiously heterogeneous as American society.[27] Ideal conceptions of the person are not the same for Christians and Jews, for example, nor even for all Christians, and thus contradictions between family and public expectations are inevitable. From the standpoint of the person, this may impose not only limitations on the development of the self, but also a major task for impression management. It can be difficult to live up to parental images or to those of an enclosed ethnic community and at the same time manifest qualities valued by outsiders whom the person may have to please if his or her goals are to be achieved. The African American or the Jew in American society may resonate best to a particular ethnic "soul" and yet be forced to strip away peculiarly ethnic qualities of manner, dialect, or belief on the job and in interaction with nonethnics.

Sometimes the perceived necessity of being a different person within the family or the ethnic community as opposed to the world outside leads to a bifurcation of social worlds and of the self. Inside the protective world of the ethnic family, people can interact with one another by using ethnic slang that would be misunderstood by persons who are not members of the particular group. Indeed, interaction within the group often depends on distinctions between "we" and "they" that would be offensive to outsiders. Within the ethnic context, the person can present a self that lives up to particular conceptions of what the person ought to be. Outside that context, a different self must be presented to others, one that is adjusted to conceptions of the person that are either common to all members of the society or are held and enforced by a dominant group.

The self is thus shaped by ideal conceptions of what the person ought to be, and these vary by ethnic origin, religion, region, social class, and other kinds of social differentiations. It is noteworthy that many of these definitions of the ideal person are not only linked to group memberships, but also depend to some extent on we-they contrasts between groups. The selves fostered among African Americans, Jews, white Southerners, or Polish Americans are defined, not just by the beliefs and values of the group itself, but also by the particular contrasts between themselves and outsiders emphasized by members of the group. To be Jewish is thus not merely to live up to a set of images of what Jews ought to be like, as defined by Jews, but also to avoid certain patterns of behavior or belief presumed to characterize gentiles.

Not all such influences on the construction of the self come from the contrast between familial and other standards. Within the family itself, the child may or may not be able to meet parental expectations. Successful parents may convey an image of competence to the child that exceeds the child's capacity to match. Sometimes parents expect more of a child at any given age than the child can deliver. Not infrequently, parental expectations are not clear — the parents present no clear image in terms of which the child can adjust his or her conduct — and so leave the child to flounder in uncertainty and anxiety.

Whether the influences come from within or outside the family, there are occasions on which the child — or the adult — is confronted with images that cannot be emulated in conduct. Sometimes the child can make no presentation of self that will elicit approval from others. If teachers evaluate the child negatively on the basis of race or class, for example, he or she faces a particularly vexing problem. No presentation of self can avoid the fact of race, and class can also be very difficult to overcome, since the child may be marked by patterns of speech or dress that clearly mark him or her as different. The child who is born unwanted into a family that is already defined by its members as too large can do little or nothing to alter his or her definition by others as an interloper. In such contexts as these, behavior is irrelevant to the judgments others make. The child may form an image of what is desired and present self accordingly, but to no avail, for negative appraisals occur anyway.

What strategies are available to people when self-presentation makes little or no difference? To some extent, when others base their appraisals on grounds that have nothing to do with conduct, the person is free (within limits) to define them as insignificant and their evaluations as irrelevant. The child whose teachers persist in appraising him or her as stupid can cease to take their judgments seriously. He or she may even invert their images and regard as positive whatever they see as negative. The child who has come to see himself or herself as artistically creative may withdraw from emotional attachment to parents if they see this creativity as unimportant or even undesirable.

There are limits on the person's ability to define others as significant or insignificant, however. Parents and teachers must be endured even if their appraisals are painful. Emotional attachment will not develop with teachers who act negatively toward the child, but such attachment to parents occurs to some extent regardless of what the parents do, since the child's earliest experience of the social world has been with them. A man may see his boss's standards as wrong and so not regard the boss as a significant other person, but it is still the boss who calls the shots at work and writes the paycheck.

Moreover, even though withdrawing recognition of others as not significant to the self is a way of protecting the self, such a strategy is not without cost to the person. Even when the negative appraisals of others are labeled insignificant, they may continue to have an impact on the person, because they have raised doubts where there were none before. The child may define teachers as insignificant, but their appraisals have raised doubts about competence that may endure long after the child has forgotten the teachers themselves. An individual with a positive conception of self may, from time to time, encounter others who do not share that image. Even though their appraisals may be defined by the person as insignificant, continued interaction with them, which frequently is unavoidable, is a constant reminder of the low esteem in which he or she is held. One may encounter fellow workers who are very supportive and others who hold one's work in very low esteem. The former will be seen as more significant to self-image and self-esteem, but the latter cannot be totally ignored, because they are present from day to day, and they may be in a position to affect one's advancement on the job.

Withdrawing recognition of others also is costly because it may, in time, lead to a shrinking of the circle of others with whom the person customarily associates and with respect to whose judgments the self is continually reaffirmed. As Hans Gerth and C. Wright Mills indicated, the avoidance of interaction with negative others leads to a retreat to a circle of "confirming intimate others."[28] As the person moves through successive stages in the life cycle, he or she may encounter so many negative images of self that more and more people are seen as insignificant. Eventually, the person may find only a small circle of confirming others in whose company a positive self-conception can be sustained. In the extreme, the person may retreat to a private fantasy world where no real others are encountered, only imaginary others who always give positive appraisals.

Community and the Generalized Other

Finally, the self is constrained because people are members of groups, organizations, and communities, all of which confront them with a generalized other whose demands must be taken into account. Although problems arise when we attempt to apply the concept of the generalized other to complex societies, the concept clearly fits less complex societies. It may be helpful, therefore, to look at such societies in order to understand the self and the forces that constrain it in the complex societies of the present. *Community* is the key concept in this task.

The classic sociological conception of a community is of a territorially based social unit — such as the small town or village — that thoroughly embraces the lives of its members, who feel bound to one another as whole persons and whose sense of identification with one another and with the community is strong. The members of a community resemble one another in most respects; they are committed to the same values, share views of the world, and respond similarly to the variety of situations they encounter in their everyday lives. Accordingly, the impact of the community on the individual member is powerful, for it commands the loyalty of the individual and its claims are difficult to resist. It is the source of a powerful generalized other that is constantly present as a standard by which the person can gauge his or her conduct and that the person recognizes that others also use.

This classic kind of community may be called an *organic community,* for the individual's life is rooted in and dependent upon this social unit. It is the social "soil" in which the person flourishes and to which the person is bound. As a social unit with a shared set of values, it clearly provides the person with a sense of place, with standards for emulation, and with a set of real other persons who will reward or punish in proportion to the person's capacity to live up to community standards. At the same time, however, it is a confining world, for it does not easily permit persons to change their place and it exacts a great deal of conformity as its price for the sense of personal security it provides.

In such an organic community, the generalized other *is* the community. An organic community has clearly visible boundaries, not only because it has a limited territorial expanse, but also because it provides clear psychological horizons for its members. The person is surrounded from birth by familiar and similar others who stand in a known and unchanging relationship. Everyday life consists of a familiar round of activities with these people, and the life cycle is clearly defined, so that one knows the succession of roles one will be expected to assume. Under these conditions, it is not difficult for people to grasp the perspective of the community as a whole. Not only is there a perspective, but that perspective is within the psychological reach of the person.

The generalized other in such communities makes it possible for people to have well-developed social identities, but rather attenuated personal identities. A shared set of expectations, sentiments, norms, and values that people use to examine themselves and their conduct enables them to achieve a sense of continuity and integration by identifying with the community. In such communities, people are able to link the successive "Me's" they experience as they interact with one another, treating each experience of the self as related to past and future experiences. The commonly shared expectations of the group provide an underlying sense of purpose, providing the person with a way to make sense of the successes and failures encountered in everyday life. Similarly, the community and its values provide a perspective from which the self can be integrated: Each of the roles in which the person regularly engages can be seen as related in some way to the values of the community as a whole.

A community that provides so well for social identity makes the construction of a personal identity a difficult task. Because there is a widely shared perspective from which to objectify the self, it is more difficult for the person to find either reasons or ways to define it in different terms. Because the community has a place for the individual and has the power to keep the person there, it is difficult for the individual to resist or escape. Even in the organic community, however, the fundamental nature of human beings is to be active and creative creatures, and not merely passive agents of society. They form personal identities, but with more difficulty and with lesser scope for variation.[29]

The generalized other seems to be a conception well suited to the organic community with its widely shared set of values, beliefs, and expectations. But what of more complex societies, where there are often fundamental disagreements about such matters? In societies like the United States and Canada, for example, inequalities associated with class, ethnicity, or religion seem to produce not a single culture, but many, so that it is impossible to think of the society as a whole as a social unit from whose perspective the individual could develop a coherent view of self. The small farming village of the eighteenth century may well have been an organic community with a clear generalized other. But is it legitimate to speak at all of a generalized other in modern societies, where such organic communities have almost disappeared and people live in the more anonymous world of the city?

Complex societies have a highly specialized division of labor, contain many competing and contending social groups, and create inequalities of income, wealth, and power. As a result, the person has a knowledge of only a few of the many roles the society offers and has little basis for identifying or role taking with those with whose roles he or she is unfamiliar. Even simple societies contain social divisions, such as between men and women, that make role taking and identification difficult. In complex societies there are apt to be many divisions and thus many barriers to the creation of a widely shared culture.

In complex societies people are in many ways unlike one another. The social perspectives of middle-class people are likely to differ from those of working-class people. Protestants, Catholics, and Jews share membership in the society as a whole, but differ in many respects from one another. The social worlds and outlooks of men and women, children and adults, and professors and plumbers are likely to be distinct and different, making it difficult for the members of one category or group to see things from the perspective of the other. People are alike in some respects, to be sure, for even the most complex and stratified society has a core of culture that all of its members share. On the whole, however, the effect of a complex division of labor, social class, and religious and ethnic diversity is to create many ways in which people are different from one another.

In complex societies, then, there seem to be many generalized others whose perspectives the person must take into account in everyday life. Each social group, organization, or other collectivity has its own generalized other and the person to some extent changes generalized others as he or she moves from one social context to another. When with one's family, for example, their perspectives count in making assessments of the self. At work, it is the generalized other of that context that shapes the way we feel about ourselves.

At the same time, it would be a mistake to think that there is no more inclusive generalized other in modern societies — that is, that there is nothing that ties the members of such societies together and thus counteracts the many social forces that separate one community from another. Contemporary people think of themselves as members of societies and citizens of nations; sometimes they even conceive of themselves as human beings without regard to the particularities of community or nationality that set them apart from one another. To the extent that people conceive of themselves as members of such larger social units, they can be said to participate in a common culture that transcends particular community lines and that provides for a more general "generalized other."

The Person in Modern Society

The diversity and complexity of modern life have thus shaped new kinds of persons and a new kind of relationship between the person and society. In order to understand what has occurred, we must look at the nature of community in modern society and examine the way in which persons define themselves in relation to communities.

A modern society is not only a more structurally complex entity than the societies of the past, but it is a larger entity as well, one that contains multiple communities. The organic communities of the past were in many respects self-sufficient entities. The European peasant community of the Middle Ages, for example, was in important ways a world unto itself. It produced the food and fiber on which the lives of its members depended, and a person could live a life without ever leaving the community or encountering the members of other communities. Thus, in effect, the organic community was also a society—a more or less self-sufficient and self-reproducing entity with little dependence on the outside world.

In contrast, a modern society contains a great many communities, few (if any) of which are economically self-sufficient, and most of which are dependent on other communities and on the society as a whole. The rural small town and the urban ethnic neighborhood, for example, have some of the characteristics of organic communities: They are apt to be important in the lives of their members and to be made up of individuals who spend their lives together. But such communities are not self-sufficient and generally not self-reproductive. The residents of a neighborhood live their lives together and identify with one another, but they must work outside the neighborhood and interact frequently with strangers. Small town dwellers may have great loyalty to their town, but the town is economically dependent on other towns and on the structures of government and economy not only of the whole society but increasingly of the whole world.

As a result, the contemporary community provides a psychological world and a place of identification for its members, but it is not the same kind of enclosing and secure world as the organic community of the past. The individual is keenly aware of the existence of a society whose economic and political significance transcends that of the local community. Moreover, the surrounding society is itself a tempting field of opportunities, for it offers other communities with which the person might choose to identify and it is a constant reminder that the community within which one resides is not the only option. A popular song of the World War I era wondered, "How are you going to keep them down on the farm after they've seen Paris?" This is, in fact, the common dilemma of communities in modern society: how to retain the loyalties of members who are tempted by the glamour and opportunities of the outside world.

Another major difference between the organic community of the past and contemporary communities has to do with the basis on which people form communities and thus identify with one another. Modern communities are based on a great many different grounds and not solely on the basis of territory. To be sure, urban ethnic neighborhoods and rural towns retain some of their importance as communities in the lives of their members. Life within such communities still revolves around the regular association of people who know one another well and who are bound by a sense of obligation to one another as well as by their sense of similarity. Modern people, however, because they frequently rub elbows with others who are very different from themselves, must narrow their focus in order to feel a sense of likeness and identification with others. Many people live and work near others who are very different from themselves and, in order to find a sense of community, must either overcome these differences or identify with others who, although they may not be nearby, are similar in some respect.

For each member of a modern, heterogeneous society, there are many possible grounds on which to identify with others. For some people, a shared commitment to a set of religious beliefs provides the basis for identifying with a community. Christians who have had a "born again" experience, for example, have a strong mutual identification based on this experience. For others, membership in a social class may provide the same sense of likeness and common purpose. Modern people may find community in a social movement, identifying strongly with the women's movement, for example, or with the environmental movement; in their professions; and even, in some cases, in their nuclear or extended families. Because there are so many ways in which people are differentiated from one another, there are also many particular ways in which they can feel likeness with certain others.

The kind of community that develops from a sense of identification with similar others is a rather narrowly defined community, and it is often based on quite abstract criteria. For the person whose community consists of those who have been "born again," the sense of similarity is limited to religious conviction and experience. Persons who may be quite dissimilar in social background, ethnicity, formal religious affiliation, occupation, race, and other social characteristics can feel a sense of similarity with one another because they define these differences as irrelevant in the light of their similarity of religious outlook. They identify with one another on the basis of this one characteristic that makes them alike and downplay the significance of other matters. Theirs is, in a sense, a narrow community, one formed not out of the repeated give and take of everyday life with the same people, but out of a more self-conscious selection of others with whom to identify.

Such communities are likely to be dispersed rather than compact. The "born again" Christian may encounter few fellow community members on a day-to-day basis, for even those who are members of one's church are not really members of this community if they have not yet had the "born again" experience. The members of such experiential communities may interact infrequently with one another, relying upon correspondence, revival meetings, or the programs of the "televangelists" that feature preaching or talk about the "born again" experience to confirm the existence of a community and an identity grounded in it.

Modern communities thus rely on the person's imagination as much as on a mundane social life. Contacts with fellow community members may be infrequent, and the sense of community must be sustained by the self-conscious imagining of the nature and scope of the community. This is less the case for communities where there is an existing organizational structure. Individuals who identify with a professional community, for example, usually have concrete social organizations to support their identification. Professional groups, boards, journals, and meetings provide opportunities for those who identify with the community to meet one another and to reinforce a sense of community membership.

Many observers argue that modern society has drastically transformed the nature of the self. Where organic community flourishes, the self is a stable object defined by a strong sense of social identity grounded in and certified by the community. The direction of the person's life seems fixed, the self is given continuity and integration by its place in the community, and people need not devote much energy to securing or maintaining their identities. People know who they are, and thus they know what to do. Their sense of personal identity is subordinate to their social identity as community members.

Where communities have to be constructed by finding some basis on which to identify with others, the nature of the person is transformed as much as the nature of the community. The creation and maintenance of identity requires more self-consciousness; people must decide or discover who they are in order to know what to do. They can, within certain limits, choose who they are; but they are also faced with some degree of doubt as to the choices they make. The person who chooses one community with which to identify is always aware that his or her choice could have been different. There is also a strong temptation to identify with no community — to seek to make community and the social identity it fosters subordinate to a personal identity.

Ralph Turner has argued that modern people are becoming more inclined to look within themselves and to define as the "real self" those impulses and inclinations they feel are genuinely and spontaneously theirs rather than the external dictates of society.[30] Turner's view can be readily interpreted within the framework of social and personal identity. Those who identify strongly with a community tend to feel comfortable with themselves when their impulses and actions live up to the standards of the community. But those who do not have a community-based social identity, who feel confined by community or torn between the demands of several communities, may feel that the only authentic expression of themselves is in a personal identity that permits a considerable degree of autonomy. It is when they feel they are doing what they want to do, and thus pursuing a personal identity, that they feel true to themselves.[31]

Social identity in modern society is much more likely than in the past to be based on a more or less self-conscious selection of a community as its main support. Whatever the basis on which such a community is constructed or imagined, it performs some of the same functions as the organic community of the past. It provides the person with a set of similar others who can support or be perceived as supporting the person's definitions of self. Even when a community is based on rather narrow criteria of similarity, spatially dispersed, and significantly a product of the person's own imagination, it provides for a sense of continuity and integration, linking various situated identities to the social identity it provides.

There are a variety of ways in which people construct social identity through these modern forms of community. Some seek to construct a community that resembles as closely as possible the organic community of the past. The old-order Amish, who maintain very traditional farming communities in Pennsylvania, Ohio, and Indiana, for example, attempt to enclose their members' lives in a way that is very much like the organic community. The whole of life is lived within the boundaries of the community, which rests upon commitment to a traditional set of religious ideas about how people ought to live. Those who live in such communities have some contact with the surrounding modern world, of course, but their identities are almost exclusively grounded in the community itself, which provides a basis for identification with similar others. The outside world is important mainly for the contrast it provides. It confers distinctiveness on the person by virtue of his or her membership in this distinctive community, and it serves as a reminder of what the person should *not* be and how he or she should not live.

The modern person who seeks to ground social identity exclusively in one community need not, however, attempt to construct an organic community. Some participants in social movements, for example, have lives that are exclusively centered in the movement. For them, every act must have meaning in relation to the movement and its goals. The committed member of the women's movement, for example, may lead a life that is as centered in the movement as is that of the Amish person in that community. Yet, whereas the Amish community has many of the attributes of an organic community, the social movement does not; it is not a context within which all of life's needs can be met.

Most people have a more tenuous relationship to a community (or communities) with which they identify. The person may identify with one community — such as a profession or neighborhood — but not so exclusively that everything the person does must somehow be linked to the community. Most people, perhaps, fit this pattern, finding limited forms of community in professions, neighborhoods, religious experiences, or social movement participation, but not devoting themselves exclusively to any of them. The person may thus identify mildly with several communities rather than exclusively with one. The person may also migrate from one community to another, identifying with a number of communities over the course of a lifetime. The person may stand on the margins of two communities, unable either to identify fully with or to ignore either. And, presumably, the person may be unable to find any community with which to identify.

Where identification with a community is less than total, personal identity is a more salient component of the self. Community identification produces social identity, but the coherence and continuity of the person must also be found in the goals, ambitions, dreams, and projects that define personal identity. Thus, people must make plans, assert themselves, keep their eyes fixed on a clear image of what they want to be, and, in general, self-consciously construct themselves as autonomous persons. Some will carry a quest for autonomy to an extreme, eschewing any social identity, but most will seek some kind of balance between social and personal identity.

The modern person is thus in many ways a more self-conscious being than the resident of a traditional community. The self is not simply a spontaneous product of a fixed community that surrounds it from birth and that assigns it a place. It is, instead, something that must be found, constructed, or cultivated. The person must find or make a community, as well as supplement social identity with personal identity.

SUMMARY

• The acquisition of self is closely tied to the acquisition of language and of a conceptual grasp of the social world into which the infant is born. As the child learns the names of things, including itself and important other people as well as material objects, it gradually acquires the capacity to be an object to itself. This acquisition of self occurs in stages. At first the child can only imitate the actions of a variety of others with whom it has contact. Gradually, it develops a more sophisticated grasp of the structure of its family and of the situations in which it is expected to act. As the child does so, the capacity for role taking emerges — that is, the child learns to regard itself and to grasp and control conduct from the perspectives of others.

• The person who emerges from the process of socialization during childhood is a complex being whose nature and prospects are closely tied to society. People are objects to others as well as to themselves; they are creatures of the immediate situation as well as of their own biographies; and they identify with others and their groups, develop and maintain complex images of themselves, and respond affectively as well as cognitively to themselves.

• *Identity,* which refers to the person's place in organized social life, is a crucial aspect of the self. Identity may be *situated, social,* or *personal.* Situated identity is conferred by the person's role in the situation. Social identity is gained as the person identifies with a community and views the self from its perspective. Personal identity is a sense of continuity and integration grounded in an autonomous sense of self rather than in identification with others.

• *Self-image* and *self-esteem* are related aspects of the self. As they make and take roles in situations, people develop a sense of their qualities, which are themselves closely related to the roles they perform. People develop feelings of competence or incompetence, not only with respect to specific roles, but also and more broadly in relation to themselves as persons. As they form images of themselves, both in the immediate situation and in a longer temporal framework, people also respond affectively to themselves — that is, they come to feel well or ill about themselves, to like or dislike the images they form, to have high or low self-esteem.

• Identity, self-image, and self-esteem are important because they link the person to the social order. The individual learns what qualities are desirable by participating in social life — making and taking roles — so that some degree of conformity with social demands becomes an important way in which the person maintains the self as a valued, positively regarded object. Social identity ties the person to others by providing a sense of security — a sense of membership in a social unit of some kind and a sense of purpose and direction in life.

• The self is an important concept because it helps account for what people do, and it helps in this task because it is so closely tied to the motivation of conduct. Symbolic interactionists distinguish carefully between the concepts of motive and motivation. The former refers to what people say about their conduct: A *motive* is a reason or explanation offered by the person as a way of accounting for conduct. *Motivation,* in contrast, refers to the subjective springs of conduct, to the organized sensitivities of the person that determine what the person is attentive or receptive to at any moment.

Self-image, self-esteem, and identity are particularly important at the motivational level. The identity conferred by a role organizes the person's attention to events, and thus shapes impulsive responses. As people interact, they form images of one another, and they compare their performances with ideal conceptions of what they would like to be or to attain. The positive or negative feelings about self that emerge from such encounters affect subsequent actions. Low self-esteem leads to anxiety and may make it difficult for individuals to be accurate role takers or to feel well disposed toward others. High self-esteem may make the person less sensitive to the judgments of others and thus less susceptible to social control.

• Although it is in some ways plausible to argue that human beings seek to develop identities and maximally favorable images of themselves, they are not free to act as they wish. Some social roles are ascribed so that the person has an identity regardless of whether it is wanted. Some standards of achievement are unattainable, at least for some people, who are thus forced to measure themselves by standards that they would rather not accept. Although self-esteem can be enhanced by attending only to positive appraisals, there are limitations on the extent to which the person can select others who will confirm a positive self-image. People are exposed to conflicting demands so that, by earning positive appraisals from one quarter, they earn negative evaluations from another.

• People see themselves not only from the vantage points of specific others in situations but also from the perspective of the group or society as a whole. The *generalized other* is a significant force, for it represents the standards and expectations of society. In relatively simple and homogeneous societies, there is apt to be a single generalized other—that is, one set of general norms, values, and standards held in common by all members of the society. In the more complex and culturally diverse societies of the modern world, there is a generalized other for each group, organization, community, and other elements of the society, but a more inclusive societal generalized other is an elusive creature.

• Because of the complexity of modern society, the nature of the person has been transformed in several important respects. The communities that serve as the basis of social identities are very different from the organic communities of simpler societies. Often people live in the midst of others who are very different from themselves so that physical place is less likely to be the basis for community. Since a community is, in the final analysis, a social entity composed of people who are fundamentally alike, the modern person is forced to settle for a narrower sense of similarity with others. Social identity tends to be based less on identification with those whom one has always known and who share a common way of life, and more on identification with others with whom one has infrequent contact and who resemble one another only in limited ways. Personal identity assumes a more important part in providing meaning and direction for the person's life. The person in modern society is more self-conscious and considerably freer to shift social and personal identities from time to time, but he or she is also much less concretely and securely tied to a fixed social order than were people in the past.

ENDNOTES

1. For a theoretical elaboration of the relationship between language and the self, see Michael L. Schwalbe, "Language and the Self: An Expanded View from a Symbolic Interactionist Perspective," *Symbolic Interaction* 6 (2, 1983): 291-306.

2. Although culture is conventionally defined as the ways of thinking, feeling, and acting shared by the members of a society, it can be defined more usefully as the world of objects shared by the members of society. Culture is thus not behavior itself, but rather the environment within which that behavior takes place. For elaboration of this view, see John P. Hewitt, *Dilemmas of the American Self* (Philadelphia: Temple University Press, 1989).

3. For empirical studies and analysis of childhood socialization, including the use of names and pronouns, see Norman K. Denzin, "The Genesis of Self in Early Childhood," *The Sociological Quarterly* 13 (Summer 1972): 291-314; and Denzin, *Childhood Socialization* (San Francisco: Jossey-Bass, 1977).

4. Spencer E. Cahill, "Language Practices and Self Definition: The Case of Gender Identity Acquisition." *The Sociological Quarterly* 27 (Fall 1986): 302. See also Cahill, "Fashioning Males and Females: Appearance Management and the Social Reproduction of Gender," *Symbolic Interaction* 12 (Fall 1989): 281-299.

5. As Lindesmith, Strauss, and Denzin write in *Social Psychology,* 5th ed. (New York: Holt, Rinehart and Winston, 1977), p. 289: children "discover that names have things—that is to say, that the words they learn correspond to aspects of the real world. In complex types of learning especially, the progression may be from word to things rather than the reverse."

6. See George Herbert Mead, *Mind, Self, and Society* (Chicago: University of Chicago Press, 1934), pp. 135–173.

7. Ibid., p. 151

8. Gregory P. Stone, "The Play of Little Chicken," in *Social Psychology Through Symbolic Interaction,* 2nd ed., ed. Gregory P. Stone and Harvey A. Farberman (New York: Wiley, 1981), p. 254.

9. For a discussion of this problem, see Denzin, "Genesis of Self," (Note 3), pp. 294–295.

10. Phillipe Aries, *Centuries of Childhood: A Social History of Family Life* (New York: Knopf, 1962).

11. Gregory P. Stone, "Appearance and the Self: A Slightly Revised Version," in *Social Psychology Through Symbolic Interaction,* 2nd ed., ed. Gregory P. Stone and Harvey A. Farberman (New York: Wiley, 1981), p. 188.

12. Nelson Foote, "Identification as the Basis for a Theory of Motivation," *The American Sociololgical Review* 26 (February 1951): 14–21.

13. Sheldon Stryker, *Symbolic Interactionism: A Social Structural Version* (Reading, Mass.: Benjamin-Cummings, 1980).

14. Although the approach to identity that I develop here departs in several ways, it also owes much to the work of Sheldon Stryker as well as to the formulations of George J. McCall and J. L. Simmons, who have analyzed the ways in which roles are ordered by the person. See Stryker, *Symbolic Interactionism;* and McCall and Simmons, *Identities and Interactions,* Rev. ed. (New York: Free Press, 1978).

15. David A. Snow and Leon Anderson, "Identity Work among the Homeless: The Verbal Construction and Avowal of Personal Identities," *American Journal of Sociology* 92 (May 1987): 1336–1371.

16. Raymond L. Schmitt and Wilbert M. Leonard, "Immortalizing the Self through Sport," *American Journal of Sociology* 91 (March 1986): 1088–1111.

17. Erving Goffman, "Role Distance," in his *Encounters* (Indianapolis, Ind.: Bobbs-Merrill, 1961).

18. Charles Horton Cooley, *Human Nature and the Social Order* (New York: Scribners, 1902), p. 152.

19. Ibid.

20. For a discussion that shows that Cooley did not see the person as a passive participant in the reflected appraisals process, see David D. Franks and Viktor Gecas, "Autonomy and Conformity in Cooley's Self-Theory: The Looking-Glass Self and Beyond," *Symbolic Interaction* 15 (Spring 1992): 49–68.

21. The literature on self-esteem and its sources is vast. Morris Rosenberg's *Society and the Adolescent Self-Image* (Princeton: Princeton University Press, 1965) is a classic social psychological study. See also his *Conceiving the Self* (New York: Basic Books, 1979) as well as Morris Rosenberg and Roberta G. Simmons, *Black and White Self-Esteem: The Urban School Child* (Washington, D.C.: American Sociological Association, 1972). For recent studies see Gregory C. Elliott, "Self-Esteem and Self-Consistency:

A Theoretical and Empirical Link between Two Primary Motivations," *Social Psychology Quarterly* 49 (3, 1986): 207–218; Richard B. Felson, "Reflected Appraisal and the Development of Self," *Social Psychology Quarterly* 48 (1, 1985): 71–78; and Felson and Mark D. Reed, "Reference Groups and Self-Appraisals of Academic Ability and Performance," *Social Psychology Quarterly* 49 (2, 1986): 103–109.

22. Viktor Gecas and Michael L. Schwalbe, "Beyond the Looking-Glass Self: Social Structure and Efficacy-Based Self-Esteem." *Social Psychology Quarterly* 46 (1983): 77–88.

23. Erving Goffman, *The Presentation of Self in Everyday Life* (New York: Doubleday Anchor, 1959).

24. Morris Rosenberg, *Society and the Adolescent Self-Image* (Princeton, N.J.: Princeton University Press, 1965), Chapter 8.

25. Harry Stack Sullivan, *The Interpersonal Theory of Psychiatry* (New York: Norton, 1953), p. 351.

26. Patricia A. Adler and Peter Adler, *Backboards and Blackboards: College Athletes and Role Engulfment* (New York: Columbia University Press, 1991).

27. For an interesting analysis of the problems of *mixed* ethnic identity, see Cookie White Stephan, "Ethnic Identity Among Mixed-Heritage People in Hawaii," *Symbolic Interaction* 14 (Fall 1991): 261–277.

28. Hans Gerth and C. Wright Mills, *Character and Social Structure* (New York: Harcourt Brace, 1953). This discussion of limits on the selection of others is indebted to their analysis.

29. These issues are explored in depth in Chapters 5 and 6 of John P. Hewitt, *Dilemmas of the American Self* (Philadelphia: Temple University Press, 1989).

30. Ralph H. Turner, "The Real Self: From Institution to Impulse," *American Journal of Sociology* 81 (March 1976): 989–1016.

31. I would dispute Turner's hypothesis that there has been a pronounced shift away from institutional and toward impulsive self-anchorage in the last century. There is little empirical evidence to sustain such a view, and there are many reasons to characterize modern culture as fostering conflict between social and personal identities rather than a shift from one to the other. These issues are explored in Hewitt, *op. cit.*

Social Interaction and the Formation of Conduct

An essential element of the symbolic interactionist perspective is its insistence that human conduct is a product of situated social interaction. We cannot explain what people do merely as the result of social or cultural constraints. Rather, we must study them as they act and interact in specific contexts and circumstances — going to class, having a party, making love, working on a book — where they form their individual and social acts on the basis of their definitions of such situations. This chapter examines the basic processes of situated social interaction.

THE DEFINITION OF THE SITUATION

The idea that people construct their actions based on their definitions of situations, considered briefly in Chapter 3, conceals a great deal of complexity. What is a "definition" of a situation? Where does a definition of a situation exist? How do people define situations? What happens when people cannot find or do not share a definition of the situation? To answer these and similar questions we need to develop a more detailed analysis of situations and their definitions.

The word "situation" is used often in everyday speech in ways that only hint at the more technical meaning of the term we employ here. People speak commonly of this or that "situation," referring to some particular occasion or social context, such as a party, an argument, a predicament, or an event. "It was an embarrassing situation," they might say, or "Here's the situation I found myself in," or "I got out of that situation as soon as I could."

Symbolic interactionists do not think of situations as unusual predicaments from which people try to extricate themselves, but they do employ two commonsense ideas that are conveyed in everyday speech.

- To refer to a situation, whether informally or technically, is to locate activity *temporally* in relation to other activity.

Human activities occur before, during, or after one another, and when we speak of a particular situation we mark off a particular portion of time and give it a name. A "party" may consume several hours, during which people engage in a great many particular acts — dancing, drinking, laughing, flirting, conversing, and the like. When we call a particular situation a "party" we subsume under a single label those activities that have occurred during a particular interval of time.

- The labels we attach to situations also locate the same events spatially.

The event we call the "party" presumably occurred in some well-defined place — at someone's home, for example — and is thus a fairly compact space where people get together and interact. Those assembled for a party conceive of themselves as in the same place. Their sense of where they are is not simply that they are in a particular physical location, but that they are "at a party."

When people conceive or talk about the situations in which their activities occur, they do not use the same clock or yardstick a physicist might use to measure time and space. The significance of time for a "party" does not consist of the passage of a certain number of hours or minutes, nor does space refer to its location on a road map. Time and space are social and not physical dimensions. When people define a situation, they do so from their social perspectives as actual or potential participants. People locate situations temporally from the vantage point of shared ideas about the meaning of events as they occur in time. Thus, a party is something that takes place "after" an especially intense period of hard work, "regularly" on Saturday nights, or "before" someone leaves an organization or moves to another city. Place is likewise defined in social terms. A party is a place where there are "partiers," just as an argument is a place where there are "opponents." It is not geography itself, but rather the roles, acts, and objects found in a place that make it a particular situation.

The temporal aspect of human life, which Mead called *emergence*,[1] thus relates to the way in which people *define* and *experience* their own and others' activities through time. The *present,* the here and now of any particular moment, is experienced in terms of both past and future. What is happening at this moment is understood in relation to what has already occurred and what is expected (or hoped) will occur later. The "present" is specious — it is experienced but does not really exist, for consciousness is always moving through time, always focused either on what has occurred (or on the self as it has acted) or on some imagined future event or act.

Consider, for example, how people construct such events as going to a baseball game. Before taking one's seat or even leaving for the ballpark, one has anticipated the event, perhaps speculating about the lineup or who will be the starting pitcher. At this point, going to the game as a concrete, situated activity is part of the future; yet as it exists in the imagination it shapes present acts. As the teams take the field and the first batter comes to the plate, one may recall past games when the home team beat today's opponent or snatched defeat from the jaws of victory in the ninth inning. Here, the meaning of the present is informed by the past. Today's game becomes an opportunity to maintain a streak or to get revenge for past humiliation. The meaning of the situation has been progressively transformed over time in relation to expectations for the future and experience of the past.

Time is significant in human conduct because meaning is an emergent property of objects and is never absolutely fixed or established. A baseball game that was intended to maintain a streak becomes a disappointment to the fans. At no point is the meaning of "baseball game" fixed, even though the situation has the same name throughout. Rather, meaning is altered with the passage of time. The meaning of the present is shaped by what is expected for the future; as events do or do not occur as expected, a past is created and the meaning of the present is transformed.

Situations are located in social space, and they locate their participants in social space. Each human situation is located within the specific context of a collectivity, group, organization, or some other social unit. "Classes" are held in universities; "weddings" are given by families; "arguments" take place within more diverse social units, but are generally linked to organized social life in some way. Just as the situation has a "place" in a larger social context, it provides a place for the individual participants within it. Their place, of course, is provided by their roles.

Both kinds of location are *relative* and not absolute. People locate themselves — that is, they maintain a cognitive grasp of "where" they are — relative to the situation and to the larger social context in which that situation exists. A cognitive map of the situation itself is given by one's sense of its role structure — of the variety of perspectives from which participants act and of their relationship to one's own perspective. One has a role in the situation relative to the roles of others. One's cognitive map of the situation as a place in the larger scheme of things depends upon the fact that we routinely imagine situations as elements or fixtures of groups, organizations, and other social units. A "class" is situated within a university relative to other situations — other classes, having lunch, writing papers, going to parties, and numerous other situations of college student life.

Under some conditions the relative social and temporal locations of participants in a situation, as well as the larger context within which the situation is itself embedded, can be drastically and swiftly transformed. In a classroom, for example, a student who directs a racist or anti-Semitic remark against another student may set in motion a wholesale transformation of the situation—a change in its definition and role structure. The offending student ceases to be merely a "student" and becomes, instead, a "bigot," just as the target of the remark becomes a "victim." The professor and some of the other students may become "defenders" or "allies" of the "victim," and the situation is itself lifted from its location as a routine instance of a class in the university and becomes, instead, another skirmish in the long struggle against prejudice. It is, in other words, transported from one conceptual domain to another—from one framework of social space and time to another—even while the participants remain in one physical place.

What then is a "definition" of a situation? Who has it? Where is it? How do we know that it exists? The crucial fact about a definition of a situation is that it is cognitive: It is our *idea* of our location in social time and space that constrains the way we act. When we have a definition of a situation, we cognitively configure acts, objects, and others in a way that makes sense to us as a basis for acting. We have a definition of a situation, for example, when we "know" that we are at a "graduation party." There we "know" we will find a graduate, as well as his or her family, friends, and well-wishers who will congratulate and celebrate in familiar ways. Our definition of a situation consists of what we "know" about what will happen and who will make it happen.

Definitions of situations, thus, exist in the minds of the individuals who participate in them. Definitions do not hang from invisible wires in midair, nor do they exist in a mysterious "group mind." Instead, each person acts on the basis of his or her "knowledge" of the situation, role making and role taking in terms of its sensed role structure, acting toward familiar and expected objects, and cooperating in the performance of social acts. Definitions of situations are thus "shared" by participants in the sense that each person acts on the basis of a definition that more or less resembles the definition held by others. Both professor and students in the classroom, for example, share a definition of the situation in which they are together, and each person thus acts on the basis of similar "knowledge" of the situation.

There are limits, however, in the extent to which participants can fully share the definition of a situation. Professor and students, for example, may at one level have a shared definition of the situation: They are in a class together and they share a sense of its role structure and joint activities. The professor, however, may think things are going well, whereas the students are restless and bored. At one level they share a definition of the situation, for each participant acts on the basis of knowledge, and the acts of others confirm that knowledge. Each person, by acting on the basis of a definition of the situation, constructs acts that fit with the expectations of others in the situation. Each person can employ his or her definition of the situation and its role structure to make sense of the acts of others. At another level, however, they do not share a definition. Students, acting on the "knowledge" that this is a boring class, sit through the lectures without saying anything; the professor, acting on the "knowledge" that the students understand everything being said, takes their silence as an indication things are going well. Clearly, definitions of the situation can be somewhat incongruous and still serve as the basis for interaction.

Definitions of situations imply roles and identities. Incongruous definitions of situations imply misidentifications of self and others in relation to the definition of the situation. A man may invite a woman to dinner, for example, and thinking his strong feelings for her are reciprocated, begin to talk of their future together, only to discover sooner or later that she does not hold the same feelings for him. Such incongruous definitions of the situation may persist for some time before they are discovered. As we will see later in this chapter, mutual awareness of roles, identities, and purposes is not always fully open, and when it is not, there are severe constraints on social interaction. For the time being, we will concentrate the analysis on those situations where there are genuinely shared definitions.

Routine and Problematic Situations

The largest part of our everyday conduct occurs within *routine* situations with relatively congruent definitions, such as sitting down to dinner, attending class, driving a car, going to a movie, writing a paper, playing tennis, or doing one's job. These situations are routine because they are familiar. We can easily name them, anticipate the objects they will contain, know what roles people will assume and who will assume them, and expect activities that strongly resemble activities in which we have engaged on previous such occasions.

Everyday life consists largely of a series of routine situations, and many actions in them are quite habitual. If one is accustomed to having dinner at the same hour each day, sitting down and eating seems virtually a matter of reflex. Things are in their accustomed places, the appropriate others are present, food is served on time, and much of what one does requires little self-conscious control. Many situations are so thoroughly routine that we appear to be creatures of habit, or perhaps actors enacting a script, rather than self-conscious human beings making our roles. Definitions of situations seem to provide not only general guidelines of what to expect and what to do but also even our lines and bodily movements. Thus, for example, when two acquaintances exchange greetings, inquiring about one another's health and families, it would seem they are doing little more than behaving in a ritualistic, habitual way. Such routine situations seem completely to determine the actions of their participants.

One could take this perspective further by arguing that it is culture that ultimately provides our definitions of situations. In this view, during the course of socialization we learn a large number of definitions, along with rules for applying them to the concrete situations we encounter. Thus, every circumstance is seemingly anticipated by culture and we can meet it — providing we have been appropriately socialized — by applying the correct definition of the situation.

But matters are not so simple. Although it is true that we learn in advance the definitions of many situations, we do not learn all possible definitions, nor does each episode of interaction merely require us to apply a preestablished definition. The cumulative experiences of human beings as they grow from infancy through adulthood provide them with many scripts, scenarios, and frames in terms of which they can more or less easily construct their conduct. But they are also continually confronted with unexpected and novel events. Every concrete situation is at least a bit different from what we expected it to be. Moreover, openness to new situations and new meanings is an inherent characteristic of human conduct. We do not learn a fixed and closed set of meanings or definitions of situations, but an open system in which interpretation, although it may sometimes be minimal, is always present to some degree and always potentially of great significance.

Language provides a useful analogy. In the process of learning our native language, we do not learn every possible combination of words that we will eventually use, nor do we learn explicitly the rules whereby words are to be combined. We learn a language in such a way that we can say things we have never heard before. We can create sentences that are, to us, completely novel, since we have not previously heard them spoken. It is much the same with culture and its objects and with our definitions of situations. We learn many seemingly fixed and preestablished meanings, which are roughly analogous to words, that are used to form these definitions. We also learn to create new meanings, to consider the possibility that our interpretations of a situation might be wrong, to face the unexpected events that constantly intrude themselves into human affairs.

Thus, no situation is so routine that habit alone suffices to guide conduct. A situation may be well-enough defined that there are few surprises and habit can account for the bulk of what we do there. However, even in routine situations people misunderstand one another, they fail to get jokes, they behave in selfish or unpredictable ways, disagree with one another, seek conflicting goals, compete for scarce resources, and in myriad other ways introduce novelty. When novelty is introduced, no matter how trivial or how readily we deal with it, there is at least some need to substitute the self-conscious control of conduct for habit.[2]

Most of the unexpected events of everyday life are problematic within the boundaries of the defined situation. Indeed, as Mead pointed out, what is problematic is always viewed in contrast with what is not.[3] Is the behavior of a guest at dinner embarrassing? We can think of her conduct as problematic in this sense only by comparing it to our taken-for-granted expectations about the behavior of guests. That a guest is so gauche as to criticize the host's cooking, for example, is problematic in terms of our expectations that guests will politely keep such opinions to themselves. Even though the guest's untoward conduct in this instance will elicit a response from others—the host will be hurt and other guests will express disagreement—it will not as a rule make the definition of the situation itself untenable. That remains the nonproblematic background against which the problematic event is viewed.

In contrast, some situations are themselves problematic or become so. Situations that were defined in one way can be redefined; situations that were defined can become undefined; situations that were defined congruently can become defined less congruously. A party can degenerate into a brawl or an intimate dinner can turn into an argument. People can behave in thoroughly unexpected ways, as for example when they are under the influence of drugs, and by their baffling acts challenge the very definition of a situation. People fall into or out of love with one another at different rates, and so their definitions of social situations can be incongruous. When such disruptions occur, at least some participants will be baffled until they can reconstruct their definition of the situation and thus their place in it.

Problematic situations will be given special attention in Chapter 6. At present, it should be noted that routine and problematic situations represent two end points on a continuum. They are thus ideal types, for no situation is either fully routine or completely problematic; actual situations fall at various points between these extremes.

Role Making and Role Taking in Routine Situations

Role taking, we noted, is the process in which one person momentarily and imaginatively adopts the perspective of another in order to make a role performance that will be coordinated with that of the other. But how does one adopt the perspective of another? How does one know what that perspective is? What must one person know in order to take the role of the other?

A convenient place to begin answering these questions is with the attitudes people bring with them to situations and on the basis of which they begin to construct their conduct in them. People approach routine situations with the attitude that they will be routine—that objects, acts, and others will be much as they usually are and that nothing unusual will take place.[4] Basing his analysis on the work of Alfred Schutz, Peter McHugh suggested that people bring three fundamental assumptions to routine situations:[5]

- People assume that the conceptions they have of a situation are valid. They take for granted that what they "know" as the situation is actually what is taking place. People ordinarily trust their understandings and impressions of what is going on around them.

- People assume that others in the situation share their conceptions of it. That is, although people generally make due allowance for the acknowledged fact that no two people experience a situation in exactly the same way because they occupy different positions in it, there is still a basic assumption of shared perspectives and experiences.
- People rarely bother to check their assumptions about a situation. So long as their definition of a situation works—so long as it allows meaningful conduct to take place—there is no need to question it.

As a student enters a classroom, for example, he or she characteristically assumes that it is the place in which a particular, announced course is meeting and that the group assembled is present for the same purpose. The student acts on the basis of this definition of the situation, assumes others are doing so, and continues to do so unless something occurs to call this assumption into question. If the course is thought to be introductory sociology, but the person identified as the professor begins to teach a lesson in French grammar, the student's assumption is quickly challenged and the definition must be reformulated. But, so long as activities in the classroom can be comprehended through its definition as a routine class in introductory sociology, that definition goes unchecked.

Some care must be exercised in referring to the "assumptions" that participants make in entering and acting in routine situations. An "assumption," after all, sounds rather like a self-consciously formulated thought or announcement. But such assumptions are only occasionally formulated in so many words—the student is unlikely to say before entering a room, "I assume this is the place where Sociology 101 meets, that others are here for the same reason, and that I can act on that basis until there is some reason not to." The assumptions people make about situations exist as attitudes—as ways in which they are prepared to act in and toward those situations—and rarely as verbalizations. People do not often tell themselves (or others) what they think is going on in a situation. In fact, as a general rule of thumb, the more talk there is about the nature of a situation, the more certain we can be that the situation, or something in it, is problematic for the participants.

According to McHugh, people organize meaning in a *thematic* way as they role make and role take in situations. Entering a classroom in which it is assumed a sociology course is being offered, for example, the student assigns meanings to acts, objects, and people by linking them to the central theme "sociology course." This theme provides the basis for interpreting the meanings of acts and events within the situation, each of which serves to "document" the theme. Thus, if the professor hands out a syllabus that is titled "Sociology 101" and begins to explain what sociology is, these acts serve as supporting evidence for the theme. They also reinforce the student's sense of the role structure of the situation—that here is a "sociology professor" talking to "sociology students."

As social interaction proceeds in a routine situation, people attempt to *fit* together the various acts and objects as they attempt to fit together their individual lines of conduct. This process, as we indicated, is a temporal one—what took place a moment ago is presumed to have a bearing on what is now occurring or is about to occur. Students assume, for example, that the outline the professor put on the board a moment ago will serve as the framework for subsequent comments and for discussion. Thus, each of the professor's statements will be interpreted as if it should fall under one of the headings in the outline. So long as this process of interpretation can occur, with each event fitted to the central theme of the situation, the definition of the situation itself remains unproblematic. Over time, the organizing theme of the situation will be *elaborated*—the course becomes not just a sociology course, but a boring one in which the professor sticks to the main point no matter how dull, or one in which the professor frequently drifts off on interesting tangents. So too, the various objects of the situation take on a richer meaning; the professor becomes not just a representative of a role, but a good or bad lecturer, a helpful or indifferent person.

Problematic events do occur within every defined situation. That is, people act in ways that others encounter difficulty interpreting. If, for example, a sociology professor begins to discuss the place of alligators in the ecology of Everglades National Park, students may initially find it difficult to interpret this behavior because it doesn't seem related to sociology. In all likelihood, however, they will attempt to fit this professorial conduct to the central theme of the course. That is, they will find ways to link the ecology of alligators to the social psychology of human beings, thus preserving the definition of the situation.

Within limits, people sustain meaning in defined situations by suspending their judgment on the relationship between theme and particular events. Thus, students may listen for a while to talk about alligators before deciding that the course is not really about social psychology or that the professor is a bit odd. When the professor finally gets to the point—that is, when he or she says something that enables the students to see the connection between alligators and social psychology—the relationship between theme and events is revealed and the definition of the situation is preserved. It may well be, of course, that the meaning of the situation is slightly altered—what was a course in social psychology now becomes, perhaps, an unusual course in social psychology.

The more that objects and events in a situation are problematic because they cannot be readily fitted to its theme, the more strenuously and self-consciously people search for patterns of meaning. This aspect of the definition of the situation—its *authorship* by members —cannot be stressed too much.

Defining situations and maintaining meaning in situations is not merely a matter of responding to objectively present objects and events, to things that are merely there and waiting for people to understand their true meaning. Rather, defining the situation is a process in which we *create* meaning. Human beings are the authors of the meanings on the basis of which they act.

Human beings, we have said, create objects in their environment by acting toward them. Objects do not merely exist, they exist by virtue of people's defining efforts. Thus — within limits — reality is created by intentions. Clearly a proposition such as this should not be carried to absurd lengths, for a flat tire is a flat tire no matter how much one wishes it were not or acts toward it as if it were sound. But in a great many situations of everyday life, the definitions on the basis of which people act create reality.

One of the commonest ways we experience this fact is in the *self-fulfilling prophecy.* If people act on the basis of a given definition of the situation, there is some likelihood that their actions will bring about conditions that confirm the definition on which they have acted, even if circumstances were not originally as they thought them to be. Thus, for example, in the late 1970s, rumors and predictions of gasoline shortages in the United States led many drivers to keep the gas tanks in their cars filled — to "top them off frequently so as not to be caught without gas if there was a shortage. The result was not only to create longer lines at gas stations and thus create the appearance of shortages but also to help produce some actual shortages. Because more gasoline was being carried around in the gas tanks of individual cars, there was less on hand in the wholesale and retail distribution system. Acting on the basis of their definition of the situation, people helped to make it a reality.

Later in this chapter we will examine in greater detail some of the problematic events that can threaten the definitions of situations and show how participants cope with these events. Also, in Chapter 6 we will examine what occurs when situations themselves become problematic. At the moment, however, the task is to examine the process of defining the situation in more detail, paying particular attention to the kinds of "knowledge" people use in making and taking roles.

The Cognitive Bases of Role Making and Role Taking

Symbolic interactionism emphasizes the *cognitive* foundations of human conduct, treating it as dependent on the content of individual minds as they confront and act within a given situation. There are at least two main reasons for stressing that what people *know* and what they *do* are interdependent.

First, people must have grounds for deciding among alternative possible acts in order to control their conduct in interaction with one another. How does an individual determine, for example, if a person encountered on the street is going to be friendly or hostile, and thus whether the proper approach is wariness or trust? How do people anticipate what others are going to say next in a conversation? Clearly people do make predictions about the conduct of others in order to govern their own conduct. The problem is to determine how they do so. What do people know that enables them to grasp the perspectives of others?

Second, an emphasis on the useful knowledge on which people rely carries with it the implication that even in routine situations people must be alert to the fact that there usually are alternative possibilities for others' acts and for their own. Few situations in everyday life have a script so fixed that all an actor must do is to read previously learned and rehearsed lines. To stress the importance of what people know is to stress that they often must use this knowledge to write their lines as the action progresses.

In order to specify how knowledge informs the processes of taking and making roles we must analyze it in some detail. In this task, the phenomenological tradition has made an important contribution. The following analysis is based on that body of work.[6] The basic premise is that the members of a society share a common stock of knowledge, which is not a random assortment of facts and ideas, but a very structured body of knowledge and procedures for using it. This knowledge is not "true" in a scientific sense, which is to say that it has not been produced or tested according to the accepted standards of a community of scientists. It is "true" in a practical sense, however, which is to say that it serves effectively to help people decide what to do and to interpret what others are doing.

Typification

Perhaps the most crucial form of knowledge in the total stock of knowledge is what Alfred Schutz called *typifications*.[7] The idea of typifications is itself quite simple, but its implications for conduct are vast. People know what to expect of one another in particular situations because they "know" that various *types* of people behave in *typical* ways under particular circumstances. Students can understand and predict the conduct of a professor in the classroom, for example, because they share a typification of how professors typically behave under various circumstances. Their typification of the professor consists of a set of expectations and assumptions about what professors usually, ordinarily, generally, or typically do. So long as the professor's conduct falls within this typification, the students can make sense of it, and so the professor's identity and the definition of the situation go unchallenged.

A typification is fundamentally an image or picture that people maintain with respect to a particular role, situation, person, or object and that organizes or catalogues their knowledge of it. On the first day of class, students ordinarily have no difficulty identifying the professor, because that person both looks and acts "like" a professor. If someone thought to be a professor takes a seat with the class, the identity of that person as the professor is undermined, and students will seek a new typification of the person. They may, for example, identify the individual as a "non-traditional student." That is, because the individual does not look "like" a typical young college student and also does not act "like" a professor, they may decide this person is someone who decided to go to college later than usual, perhaps because he or she spent a few years in military service.

As this example suggests, typification proceeds on the basis of visible and auditory *cues*. According to Gregory Stone, all interaction involves two levels.[8] We observe and respond to one another's words and deeds, to what Stone calls *discourse*. These serve as bases for typification and subsequently affect the course of interaction. We also observe and respond to *appearance*—to manners of dress, physical appearance, and demeanor—and these also shape the course of interaction by providing us with typifying cues.

Very little about people is actually visible to observers. Physical appearance (expressed in dress, posture, and facial expression) and a few overt words and deeds constitute all that is directly accessible to others. Thoughts and motives are hidden, and most situations provide an opportunity for people to display few of their talents. There are vast blank spaces in the selves people present to one another. Yet appearances, acts, and words serve effectively as cues on the basis of which others establish the identity of the person and thereby typify his or her acts. For example, it is only on the basis of such minimal physical and behavioral cues as facial recognition, manner of dress, and a few fragmentary acts that one identifies the person who is the physician in a medical office. Yet on the basis of such cues a vast array of knowledge about what physicians do, how they speak and act, and what is usual and unusual in their conduct is made available as a basis of our conduct toward them and the interpretation of theirs toward us.

Appearance is important not only because it provides us with the cues we need to typify someone initially, but also because it assists us in maintaining and refining that typification as interaction proceeds. We assign identity to the physician on the basis of appearance—by dress, demeanor, and conduct in the examining room—but we continue to rely on appearance for other cues that will refine the typification. On the basis of tone of voice, body posture, and facial expression, we may typify the physician as cold or warm, self-confident or uncertain, interested or distracted, about to deliver good news or bad.

Thus, we can say, people act in given situations on the basis of typifications. They are able to predict the conduct of others because they identify them as types of people who are likely to behave in ways similar to others of their type. The very process of role taking depends on this ability to typify. People are able to grasp others' attitudes toward themselves only because they can typify their own acts from the others' point of view. For if people regard the conduct of others as typical of certain roles, groups, or categories of people, they also are aware that they are typified *by* others—that whatever they do themselves shapes their situated social identity.

Seen in this light, role taking is a process in which people are attuned to the typifications others are using to interpret their behavior. Likewise, role making is a process in which the individual seeks to devise conduct that will induce others to make desired typifications. Since some typifications are more desirable than others — better to be an interesting professor than a boring one, for example, or an upstanding citizen rather than a crook — people will seek to present themselves in ways that give others cues on the basis of which to make favorable typifications.

It is, however, only partially correct to assert that people seek favorable typifications through their presentations of self. There are many circumstances in which people contemplate acts that they know or fear will lead to their retypification in undesirable terms. Yet they perform these acts anyway, perhaps because the loss from a possible negative retypification is less than the probable gains from an act others might regard as untoward. A person may steal even though this conduct makes him or her a thief in the eyes of others. Moreover, as discussed earlier, the person's control over conduct is imperfect, so that many acts do not have the benefit of prior reflection about the possible responses of others. Often people don't control the circumstances under which they act — mistakes and accidents affect what we do — and sometimes their impulses produce acts they wish they could recall. As we will see, controlling the typifications others form of us is a common focus of our role-making efforts in everyday life.

Probability
What human beings "know" about the social world (and the natural world as well) is also organized by probability. That is, people carry with them a store of knowledge about the likelihood of various events, and from time to time they refer to this knowledge as they try to make sense of the activities of others or to anticipate how others will interpret their own acts. A police officer confronted with a hostile crowd, for example, must weigh the duty to arrest those who violate the law against the likelihood of increased crowd anger if he or she does so. An officer in this situation might well conclude that arrests would probably incite the crowd to more violence and jeopardize his or her own safety.

Assessments of probability are often secondary to the establishment of typifications. That is, people first employ typifications as they define situations and establish roles and identities in them. Once a situation is defined and typifications of it and its participants have been established, there is still room for uncertainty of action or interpretation. For example, once the police officer has concluded that he or she is faced with a violent crowd and has identified its leaders, the officer still is faced with some uncertainty as to what specifically to do and how crowd members will respond. It is at this point that probability knowledge is brought into play: Given the situation and its participants, what are the alternative possible events and courses of action and what is the likelihood of each?

Causality

Our stock of knowledge also includes propositions about causality. We assume that an event has a cause and that sometimes in order to act appropriately or effectively we must first establish its cause. If an ordinarily cheerful child becomes anxious or depressed, for example, a parent will respond to such atypical or unlikely conduct by attempting to ascertain the cause. Did something happen to upset the child at school? Has the child become involved with drugs? *Why* is the child behaving in this new and unusual way?

The causal propositions brought to bear in such instances vary considerably from one society or community to another. At one time in North America, a great deal of conduct was explained and interpreted in religious terms. A child's anxiety might be interpreted as a sign of a struggle with temptation or as a consequence of sinful behavior. Gradually, people in modern societies have come to view the causes of behavior in scientific or quasi-scientific rather than theological terms. Thus, propositions that the child is anxious because of a learning disability that makes school work difficult or because of involvement with drugs are rooted in social scientific or psychological ideas about the causation of behavior. In another society, the same conduct might well be interpreted and explained as the result of witchcraft or of spirit possession.

Whatever the source of our propositions about causality—and whatever their truth as judged against some scientific standard—they serve as ways of making sense of conduct and of deciding what to do in the face of a problematic event. As with explicit assessments of typicality and probability, it is in the face of the problematic that people assess causality. Where conduct is routine and usual, typifications function largely in the background, our assessments of probability are made rather easily, and there is not much to explain. Where conduct departs from the routine, these forms of knowledge come much more explicitly to the fore.

Means and Ends

Much of the knowledge on which people rely in everyday life takes the form of *recipe knowledge,*[9] which consists of regular procedures people follow in order to secure their ends. Knowledge of relationships between means and ends is crucial to people's capacity to negotiate their everyday affairs and to interact with one another. Knowing how to study effectively, how to take a book out of the library, how to get along with professors, or how to write a good term paper are examples of means-ends knowledge regularly employed by students.

Recipe knowledge has a double function in social life, as do all forms of knowledge. First, it is the basis for individuals' abilities to act toward various objects in their world and to secure their goals. A student who knows how to study, for example, will find it easier to pass a course than the one who doesn't. As we role make in defined situations, following typical lines of conduct as we interact with others, we make use of a great many techniques of conduct. Often we use these techniques habitually; sometimes we must more self-consciously consider what we know in order to select the appropriate technique.

Recipe knowledge is significant also because it provides a frame through which the conduct of others can be interpreted and predicted. Role taking is made possible to a great extent because people are able to treat one another's conduct as means undertaken in pursuit of ends. In a physician's office, for example, many activities are unintelligible to the patient because they depend upon technical knowledge that the average person does not possess. Yet people permit physicians to engage in activities they do not understand because they can attribute purpose to what the physician does. The act makes sense as a means to something the physician wants to accomplish, even if the person doesn't know why it is an efficacious means.

Normative Standards

Another standard against which people measure their own and others' conduct involves their knowledge of normative requirements or preferences. As people interact with one another, taking and making roles on the basis of what they know about typicality, probability, causality, and means and ends, they make judgments from time to time of their own and others' acts in terms of what they feel to be morally appropriate or necessary. Although some of their conceptions of right and wrong are so deeply internalized that their violation leads to intense feelings of guilt or outrage, perhaps the majority are simply matters of knowing what the rules are. Thus, for example, an act of homicide may arouse very powerful feelings of outrage, whereas an act of lying or even theft might receive a far less intense reaction, even though people define both as wrong in their moral code.

The foregoing way of describing the relationship between normative standards and social interaction departs from the usual sociological view.[10] In the standard sociological formulation, norms are held to regulate most conduct, with people socialized into conformity with norms, guided by them in their everyday conduct, and sanctioned by themselves (through feelings of self-satisfaction or guilt) and by others (through punishment and rewards) according to whether they do or do not live up to them. Behavior thus becomes a matter of conformity to norms.

Actually, the relationship between what people do and what they feel they ought to do is not so simple. As our discussion of role making in Chapter 3 indicated, people ordinarily focus their attention on social objects rather than social norms. They are concerned with their goals, with finding and using the right recipe knowledge for pursuing and attaining them, and with making sense of others' activities so that they can participate in social acts with them and carry out their own acts. In other words, usually issues of typicality, probability, causality, and the use of proper means arise before people begin considering the normative status of the acts of others as well as of their own acts.

Norms enter into consciousness — they become objects of discourse — under problematic and unusual circumstances. They do so, for example, when conduct is questioned. When someone acts in a manner that others find strange, unexpected, or untoward, it is likely that a social norm or rule will be invoked at some point. Frequently this is done by implication rather than by explicit formulation: "Why did you lie?" is a question that implies not only a challenge to conduct but also a norm — "People shouldn't lie" — that serves as its premise. Another circumstance in which social norms are apt to be stated (if only in a conversation with the self) is when there is some uncertainty about the course of action to be pursued or about whether a contemplated act will be regarded by others as acceptable.

This approach to social norms makes them a less significant aspect of social life than they are ordinarily thought to be. Rather than the major criterion people employ to regulate their own and others' conduct, social norms are one of several forms of knowledge that people employ in their everyday conduct. The formulation of normative statements is thus a part of role making and role taking, but only a part. People take the roles of others and respond to their own conduct in normative terms, guessing whether others will formulate norms if they act in a contemplated way. It should not be thought, however, that norms are constantly implicated in acts, nor that people behave by finding the appropriate norms that govern each and every social situation.

Substantive Congruency

Finally, the definition of the situation itself is a form of "knowledge" that we routinely employ when we attempt to determine whether the acts of others seem to be based on the same definition as the one we hold. *Substantive congruency* refers to a condition in which various participants in a situation can regard one another's acts as sensible in terms of their own understanding of what is going on in the situation, what objects are present, and who the actors are. Substantive congruency thus denotes a test people apply to one another in the process of making and taking roles. One avenue of role taking is to say to oneself, "What does the situation look like from the other person's point of view?" Here the focus is on the nature of reality itself, and particularly on the question of how a view of reality imputed to another squares with one's own view.

The common situation where one individual regards a "date" as just a friendly social occasion and the other sees it as the first step down the road to romance illustrates how substantive congruency comes into play. Although the two may interact for a time with such incongruent definitions of the situation, eventually one may suspect that the other has a different definition of the situation. The romantically inclined participant may find the other too distant and cold; the friendly socializer may find the other's conversation too intimate. When this occurs, one will consider alternative possible definitions of the situation on the basis of which the other might be acting, and perhaps conclude that their definitions are not congruent. On such occasions, role taking takes the form of a reality test, and role making may well then focus on making definitions of the situation more congruent.

Each of these forms of knowledge — or, perhaps better, ways of knowing — comes into play at various points as roles are taken and made in social situations. Lacking instincts of any consequence and faced with a complex social world, human beings must simply *know* a great deal in order to interact with one another. Considering the vast store of knowledge people must draw on as they act, it is in some ways surprising that human conduct is at all coordinated. The potential complexity of interaction seems enormous in view of the alternatives open to participants in many situations, the possibilities for misunderstanding and misinterpretation, and the sometimes tenuous relationship between outward appearance and inner intentions.

Symbolic interactionists have developed a number of concepts that attempt to cope with this complexity and that speak to people's efforts to give some order and continuity to the apparent fluidity and precarious nature of social interaction. Taken together, these concepts all deal with various forms of *aligning actions* — that is, with the ways human beings attempt to maintain alignment or consistency among their individual and social acts, important cultural objects, and their own conceptions of themselves. These aligning actions constitute the next important topic in our analysis of social interaction and conduct formation.

ALIGNING ACTIONS

The fundamental task people face as they interact is to coordinate their lines of conduct. Whether the social act they are creating is a handshake, a conversation, an argument, or a romantic encounter, each person must fit his or her conduct with the conduct of others through the processes of role taking and role making. Assuming that there is a shared definition of the situation and a shared stock of knowledge, this may seem like a relatively straightforward task. By focusing on the social act to be completed, each person can predict and interpret the conduct of others, know what they expect, and thus make an acceptable performance of his or her role.

The process is more complex than it seems, however, for three essential reasons:

- People perform acts that others do not expect.

For a great variety of reasons, people act in ways that surprise others, and so make the coordination of conduct problematic. People are late to meetings, they tell lies, they perform well beyond our highest expectations, or they fall short of the mark. Whatever the causes of such acts, they interfere with the routine flow of social interaction. When the unexpected occurs, it must be dealt with in some way.

- The self is an object in every social encounter.

People do not focus only on social objects in common with others, but also act with the self in mind. Each individual act has implications not just for the coordination of conduct, but also for the way the person feels about himself or herself — for identity, self-image, and self-esteem, and for the person's pursuit of his or her own goals.

- Culture and its objects constrain every social encounter.

Although human beings neither internalize most social norms nor look for normative guidance at every turn as they interact with one another, they are conscious of culture and its ideal objects of conduct. "Truth," "freedom," "duty," and other key cultural objects are an important part of the environment within which human beings form their conduct. Social interaction is complicated because acts that meet the situated expectations of others, further individual goals, and enhance the self may not accord with culture. When this occurs, people endeavor to link their acts to culture in ways others will accept.

These three sources of complication in social interaction give rise to *aligning actions*,[11] which we may define as largely verbal efforts to create an "alignment" between the substance of social interaction, the self-conceptions of those involved, and the culture they share. Aligning actions are a form of talk that pervades everyday life; they include the accounts, explanations, apologies, disclaimers, and other techniques people employ as they talk about unexpected and problematic behavior, seek to protect or defend themselves from accusations, and attempt to make their conduct appear sensible and desirable in cultural terms.

Social psychologists have identified and studied a number of forms and features of aligning actions. Among those most often employed are *motive talk, accounts, apologies,* and *disclaimers.* Each of these is a discursive technique for sustaining coordinated interaction while also maintaining the self and defining conduct in culturally acceptable, or at least meaningful, terms.

Motive Talk

Talk about motives — requested and offered explanations of why a person acted in a particular way — is a key organizing feature of everyday life and a major way in which potential or actual problematic occurrences are handled in social interaction. Recall the distinction between motivation and motives drawn in Chapter 4. *Motivation* refers to those internal states of the organism that govern its impulsive responses to various stimuli; *motives,* in contrast, consist of statements about conduct. Motivation is generally inaccessible to the observer; the organism's internal states, which govern its sensitivity to environing objects, are impossible to discern directly, because they operate spontaneously and immediately and because they are very quickly transformed by self-consciousness. Motives, in contrast, are very accessible, for they are the stuff of everyday conversation. People are continually avowing and imputing motives, telling themselves and others why they did what they did or intend to do what they intend to do.

In order to examine the significance of motive talk in social interaction, we must examine more closely the circumstances in which it occurs. C. Wright Mills, in his classic discussion of the topic, summarized the essential nature of motive talk in the following way:

> Motives are imputed or avowed as answers to questions interrupting acts or programs. Motives are words . . . They stand for anticipated situational consequences of questioned conduct. Intention or purpose . . . *is* awareness of anticipated consequence; motives are names for consequential situations, and surrogates for actions leading to them. Behind questions are possible alternative actions with their terminal consequences.[12]

In other words, the issue of motive arises when someone interrupts a line of conduct with a question, which may be raised either by the behaving person or a partner in interaction. Behind the question lies someone's view that what is taking place is "questionable"—that is, unexpected, unclear, and perhaps therefore undesired or untoward. An imputation of a motive, a call for another to avow a motive, or an unrequested announcement of a motive are ways in which people respond to such anticipated or actual questions. The goal of motive talk is to lay bare the consequences of a particular line of conduct—to make explicit the object toward which it is proceeding.

We can find an illustration in the common situation where a parent questions a child about his or her conduct: "Why are you going to school dressed in your oldest play clothes?" In the question and the child's reply, "Because we're doing finger painting in art class today," we have a request for and an avowal of a motive. Similarly, we find the same kind of request in the parent's query years later: "Why on earth are you majoring in sociology? What will it get you?" "Because I want to become a professor and do research" or "Because I want to be a social worker" are likewise responses that avow particular motives for the act or acts in question. Questions arise because of something in the child's appearance or the college student's behavior that seems problematic to the parent, who interrupts with a question designed to reveal its consequences and remove the problematic feature.

What is taken as problematic when motive talk arises is a line of conduct that is either unexpected or, from the questioner's viewpoint, has a better or more likely alternative. The parent in the foregoing example had a business career in mind for the child and so raises a question about the decision to major in sociology. Any part of the social stock of knowledge may serve as the non-problematic background against which conduct is viewed as questionable. If a student previously enamored of the fine points of accounting suddenly takes an interest in social psychology, for example, this atypical behavior is the basis for raising questions. Or if the student has displayed a taste for an expensive life style in the fast lane, a career in social work may strike the parent as a strange choice of means to this end.

Questions about motives challenge identity as well as the relationship between the act and culture. To question a child's selection of clothing, for example, is not only to express doubt about the appropriateness or good sense of the conduct, but also about whether the child is acting from an appropriate role perspective. Has the child forgotten that today is a school day and is he or she planning to go out and play? To question the student's choice of academic major is also to question identity: Will this decision enable the child to become the kind of person he or she has wanted to become? Questions about identity raise doubts about the self, doubts that must be resolved.

The motives people offer are designed to explain an unexpected act so that it seems less problematic, to repair the person's identity in his own eyes or the eyes of others, and to find cultural support or justification for the conduct in question. "I'm majoring in sociology so that I can learn more about human conduct and eventually help make the world a better place" is an account that accomplishes all three goals. By attaching a positive cultural value to the decision to major in sociology ("learning" and "helping others"), the motive talker hopes to make the conduct seem sensible to his or her parents and thus also to make a positive impression upon them — to induce them to identify one as someone who wants to do socially worthwhile things.

How do people know what to say when they are asked why they are doing what they are doing? From what source do people acquire a set of reasons for their acts — reasons they can cite on appropriate occasions and that others will accept as answers to their questions? What makes the difference between an acceptable and an unacceptable motive? What determines whether an avowed motive will be accepted by others or rejected?

C. Wright Mills' concept of *vocabularies of motive* provides one way of approaching such questions. People learn to use certain words to explain their acts, but these words are neither shared by all members of the society nor used indiscriminately or at will. Rather, vocabularies of motive are differentiated along at least two dimensions. First, particular sets of motives are regarded as appropriate to specific situations or classes of situations. References to "serving God" or to the attainment of a "state of Grace" are appropriate as avowed motives in religious contexts in contemporary society, but would be regarded as out of place and unseemly in business or government, except in very carefully controlled and circumscribed usages. Thus, a president of the United States might call on "God's help" in an inaugural address, but daily justifications of conduct in terms of divine directives would be seen not only as cause for concern about the separation of church and state, but perhaps also as evidence of an unfit mental state. People learn that in given situations their choices of conduct *and* motives are limited by what others will treat as legitimate.

Second, particular sets of motives hold more or less sway and are treated as more or less legitimate (whatever the specific situation) by various social groups and categories. A conservative U.S. president, for example, might favor reducing or eliminating taxes on capital gains—that is, on income realized from the growing value of stocks or other investments—on the grounds that doing so will give people greater incentive to invest and will thus help the economy grow. Liberal opponents may argue that this claim is a deception, that what the president really wants to do is to give rich people a tax break at the expense of ordinary workers. Among conservatives, the avowal of motives having to do with the stimulation of investment in business is a standard and legitimate way for any given act to be justified when it is questioned. Among those not sharing this vocabulary of motives, "investment" does not evoke such an automatic and unquestioned response. From their point of view, it is an irrelevant and perhaps even an erroneous and deceptive statement designed to distract people from other, less worthy, motives.

The existence of vocabularies of motive that are specific to situations or categories of situations helps explain how people are able to compartmentalize their lives by separating motives important in one sphere from those important in another. It is often noted that gangsters (or, for that matter, corporate executives) seem to lead double lives, acting with ruthless self-interest in their occupational world and with great tenderness and selflessness toward their families. They can do so not only because each of their separate worlds has its own set of objects and acts, but also because each has its own distinct vocabulary of motives, so that conduct that would be unthinkable in one context can be seen as desirable in another.

The differential distribution of vocabularies among various groups in the society—among liberals and conservatives, for example, or physicians and patients—helps explain how various groups attract and hold the loyalties of their members and also how they come into conflict with one another. The capacity of a group to attract and keep members is determined partly by its vocabulary of motives; the more it provides and supports motives that accord with a person's established or desired lines of conduct and self-conceptions, the more it is able to bind the person to it. Families, organizations, social movements, work places, and other social groups provide contexts in which people talk about their reasons for conduct and have their reasons confirmed by others. Thus, for example, a group of alcoholics (such as an Alcoholics Anonymous group) are bound together not just by similar experiences, but also because they share a common way of talking about themselves and their activities. They share a vocabulary of motives that focuses on accepting personal responsibility and maintaining complete abstinence. Similarly, a group of conservative business people may be bound together by a shared vocabulary of motives that emphasizes the ultimate altruism of selfish capitalist acts. The "profit motive" leads to acts that benefit society as a whole, they might say. Although they might be laughed out of a working-class saloon, in their own company such motives are an important way to justify and make sense of their activities.

Motive talk is a common feature of everyday life. It arises whenever people are uncertain of the meaning of others' acts or of how others will interpret their own acts. Other forms of aligning actions — such as disclaimers, accounts, and apologies — also arise in response to problematic conduct.

Disclaimers

A *disclaimer* is a verbal device people employ when they want to ward off the negative implications of an impending act — something they are about to do or say that they know or fear will be regarded as undesirable and discredit them in the eyes of others.[13] Statements such as the following are typical of disclaimers: "I'm not prejudiced, because some of my best friends are Jews, but . . ." "This may seem strange to you, but . . ." "I'm no expert on psychology, but . . ." Each phrase introduces an act or statement that contradicts the premise of the disclaimer. Thus, a person claiming not to be prejudiced may make a racist statement, and a self-proclaimed nonexpert may make a statement only an expert could be trusted to make.

Disclaimers are addressed to a central fact of human conduct. Any act is simultaneously imbedded in a situation, in which it either does or does not fit, and in the identity of the acting person, for which it has either positive or negative implications. A prejudicial statement, for example, typically arises during a conversation and may be quite in place as far as the definition of the situation is concerned. That is, it may fit with the theme of the conversation, be in proper sequence with the statement of a previous speaker, and be an expression of a commonly held sentiment. At the same time, those who hear the racist remark are likely to interpret it as relevant to the identity of the speaker. Because people are generally aware that their acts typify them in the eyes of others, they are frequently careful to disclaim the implications of those acts that, they feel, may get them typified in terms they do not like.

Thus, disclaimers are efforts to carry out an intended act — in this case a racist remark — while avoiding any damage to identity in the eyes of others. By acknowledging that he or she knows that an impending remark could be construed as racist, the disclaiming person hopes to avoid being considered one. The implicit theory on which the disclaimer rests thus seems to be that one who *knows* an act could be discrediting and who disclaims the identity implied by the act should not be discredited. If the disclaimer is accepted, it allows conduct to proceed and situated identities to remain unchallenged. It also aligns conduct with culture, since it establishes that those present are not acting out of prejudice, at least in their own eyes.

Disclaimers are prospective aligning actions. That is, they are employed when, through role taking, the individual anticipates how others will respond to a contemplated act. In effect, then, a disclaimer is an effort to control in advance a definition of a situation and the identities of those present. In contrast, another type of aligning action, accounts, is retrospective, focusing on what has already occurred.

Accounts

What happens when an untoward act occurs without an anticipatory disclaimer? Marvin Scott and Stanford Lyman argue that when the course of social interaction is disturbed by rule violations, unexpected or inconvenient activities, inconsiderate or rude behavior, and other problematic acts, a process of demanding and giving *accounts* takes place.[14] In this process, someone who commits an untoward act is asked to account for it, that is, to explain it to the satisfaction of others present. Although accounts often are demanded explicitly, they are sometimes requested indirectly or by implication, and they may be volunteered when individuals perceive that they may be called to account for what they have done.

Scott and Lyman identify two kinds of accounts, excuses and justifications, each manifesting a particular attitude toward the questioned act and the person's responsibility for it. *Excuses* acknowledge that a particular act is undesirable or wrong, but deny that the individual was responsible for his or her conduct. Asked to explain why he was late for a date, a boy might explain that his car had a flat tire. This excuse admits that being late is undesirable but argues that no blame should be attached, since flat tires are accidents.

Excuses are an important social lubricant. By enabling troublesome situations to be passed over, put aside, and treated as unfortunate past history, they prevent each and every untoward act from becoming a major issue. Since much does go wrong in everyday life, excuses make it possible for definitions of situations and identities to be maintained, as well as for people to see themselves and to be seen by others in positive ways. At the same time, excuses help preserve the rules, standards, and expectations by means of which people ordinarily judge one another's acts. Excuses lay the blame for untoward conduct on someone or something other than the individual held to account, but they unmistakably preserve the definition of the conduct as undesirable. Being late is being late, even if the particular person isn't blamed for this bad act.

Justifications, in contrast, are a form of account in which the person accepts responsibility for an act but denies that it should be seen as untoward or wrong. A good illustration of a justification is a *denial of injury,* which is often used by young delinquents to account for their misdeeds. A person who takes a car on a joyride and later returns it, for example, may claim that since no one was hurt by this act—the car was returned unharmed—he or she did not really steal a car and should not be so charged. A denial of injury reasons that since there was no harm done, no violation of a rule or law has occurred, even though a willful act did take place.

Justifications also lubricate social interaction and attempt to protect identity. Although social norms and laws forbid certain activities, either categorically or under certain circumstances, the status of any particular act as proscribed is never a matter of absolute certainty. As we see in Chapter 7, when untoward conduct occurs it is not necessarily met with an automatic allegation of rule violation or deviance. Rather, there is flexibility, both in everyday life and in the formal procedures of the law, in determining whether a particular act is or is not a violation. The existence of a vocabulary of justifications is one basis for this flexibility. Justifications provide a means by which people can decide whether particular acts constitute infractions. Equally important, the outcome of a particular effort at building a justification for an act—whether it is successful or not—bears on the kind of identity the person is able to claim. If an act is justified, then the person's identity will not be transformed; if it is not successfully justified, then a new identity, perhaps as a deviant or troublemaker, may be in store for the person.

Other Aligning Actions

Motive talk, accounts, and disclaimers do not exhaust the aligning actions people employ in everyday life.[15] Another common form is the *apology,* in which the person who has committed a challenged act admits the untoward nature of the act, accepts responsibility for it, and expresses remorse: "I'm sorry I lost my temper—it was wrong of me to act that way and I sincerely regret it; please forgive me." An apology of this sort pays homage to cultural values and attempts to maintain social interaction by assuaging the anger or irritation of those whom the violation has offended. It also attempts to restore the good identity of the offender by reminding the audience of his or her knowledge of the untoward nature of the act. Implicit in any apology is the claim that one who readily acknowledges an offense, sincerely expresses regret, and begs forgiveness should not be treated the same way—that is retypified and given an undesirable identity—as one who neither recognizes the nature of the offense nor tries to make amends. As Nicholas Tavuchis points out, an apology places the fate of the offender and his or her identity in the hands of the person to whom it is offered. Only the offended person can bestow forgiveness and thus restore the offender's identity and his or her place in the social world.[16]

In his classification of aligning actions, Christopher Hunter also points out that aligning actions can focus on unexpected desirable acts as well as on undesirable acts.[17] Human beings may sometimes fall short of what is expected of them, but occasionally they may do better than they must. They perform heroically, do good deeds and special favors, and in other ways do more than one would expect of them in their assigned roles. Such actions "beyond the call of duty" also lead to aligning actions, for in their own way they can be as problematic as untoward acts. That is, they have consequences that weren't anticipated and have to be assimilated to the situation and its definition; they alter established situated identities; and they stand in contrast to cultural objects by doing more than is ordinarily expected.

Thus, for example, someone who goes out of his or her way to aid a colleague at work, perhaps by pitching in at a time when the work load is especially heavy, creates a situation in which various alignment processes may occur. The helper may, for example, want to have the act defined by others as central to his or her identity as "someone who can be counted on when the going gets tough" or "someone who has the interests of others constantly in mind." If so, the helper may use what Barry Schlenker has called an *entitling acclaimer,* which is an effort to emphasize his or her contribution. "Remember, I was the one who was there for you when others didn't care!" the helper may say. The helper may also use an *enhancing acclaimer,* which is an effort to stress the importance of the contribution: "You'd have been in real trouble with the boss without my help," he or she might say.[18] As with other kinds of aligning actions, acclaimers such as these are efforts to maintain the flow of interaction, to sustain or enhance identities, and to link conduct to important cultural objects.

Moreover, acclaimers illustrate another important property of aligning actions, namely the negotiation of meanings in the situation. Those who use acclaimers typically want to put the best face on their conduct, as do those who use accounts and disclaimers. But the audience for these aligning actions may well resist such efforts to define the nature of the conduct in question or the identity of its perpetrator. A professor, for example, may refuse to accept the excuse of one who is repeatedly late to class because of problems with transportation, arguing that the excuse is too frequently used and is therefore worn out. The professor may fear that too ready acceptance of the excuse deprives him or her of any leverage over the student's conduct. If there is no penalty for coming late—not even an altered identity—then the conduct is likely to recur. Likewise, the recipient of extraordinary help may find it in his or her interest to minimize its importance or downplay the key role of the helper. To accept the latter's claims about the crucial character of his or her help is to incur a debt that might later have to be repaid.

EMOTIONS AND SOCIAL LIFE

Thus far our discussion has emphasized the *cognitive aspects* of defining the situation, role making, and role taking. Social interaction entails more than cognitive activity, however, for in addition to using knowledge to make matter-of-fact calculations about what they will do, people also experience emotions. As they interact, people respond with *feelings* of diverse kinds — with fear, hate, love, empathy, embarrassment — and these emotions play an important part in shaping their conduct.[19]

What is emotion? In everyday speech people use the term to refer to a number of feelings — such as love, hate, or anger — that they think of as being naturally or spontaneously aroused under particular conditions. Thus, they say that they "love" or "hate" certain individuals, or that in certain situations they are "afraid." The commonsense view of emotions often treats them as antithetical to rationality. When people are being emotional, people say they are being irrational, not in full command of themselves and their actions. Although emotions are seen as a normal part of life, they are often defined as feelings that should be brought under control. Thus, an individual who is frightened may be urged to conquer his or her fear; a bereaved person may be encouraged to stop grieving after a certain period of time. There are other occasions when people are encouraged to give vent to their feelings, when they are reassured by others that it is acceptable to cry or to shout in anger. In any case, the emotion is thought to be a natural, individual response to the situation in question.

The sociological conception of emotions differs from the commonsense view. Emotions are an important element of behavior, but not because they stand in opposition to rational conduct. Instead, emotions frequently accompany and support rational behavior. People do not just pursue their goals; they do so with accompanying feelings, such as passion or dedication, that may well enhance their capacity to get what they want. Similarly, when human beings engage in role taking and thus form attitudes toward themselves, their attitudes are affective as well as cognitive, and thus influence self-esteem as much as self-image or identity. Crucially, in the sociological view, emotions are not merely individual responses to particular individuals or situations. Instead, emotions are imbedded in the fabric of social life: They are meaningful experiences as much as any other form of behavior, and their origins and effects are likewise social and not merely individual.

Emotions have two major components:

- First, emotions are associated with physical sensations; they are physiological responses to situations.

Fear, for example, entails an increased rate of respiration and pulse, as do several other emotions, such as anger, anticipation, or generalized excitement. Similarly, sadness appears to be associated with a depressed psychological and physiological state: tiredness, lack of interest or animation, and the inability to concentrate or sleep. Whether characterized by elevated or depressed physiological activity, however, emotions are grounded in noticeable physical states.

- Second, emotions are named, and their names shape and sometimes determine how we experience them.

"Fear" and "sadness" are not only experienced as physical sensations but also named and talked about, both by those who experience them and by others who witness people experiencing them. One can have the physical sensation associated with a particular emotion without naming it, but in doing so one experiences only a fragment of the emotion. Emotional experience requires self-objectification as much as any other form of human experience. Thus, to experience fear one must not only have the sensations associated with fear, but also label those sensations as "fear." In doing so, the person experiences fear in a self-conscious way, seeing himself or herself as "afraid" by taking the perspectives of others. One is afraid when one is followed on a dark street in unfamiliar territory, for example, not only because fear is a natural reaction to the situation, but also because one takes the role of the person following one (and of the generalized other) and recognizes fear as an appropriate response and as an appropriate label for what one feels.

The fact that emotions are both physiological and meaningful responses to situations has led to some controversy about the relative importance of each component. Some argue that there is an identifiable physiological state that corresponds to each named emotion; others argue that the same physiological states underlie all emotions, and that the only thing that differentiates one emotion from another is the label and its implied expectations of behavior and feeling. The extreme physiological view ignores similarities in physical sensation between differing emotions, such as fear and guilt, and it ignores variations from one culture to another in the labels attached to emotions. The extreme social constructionist view tends to ignore differences in sensations between such emotions as fear and anger.

Theodore Kemper has advocated a compromise position.[20] According to Kemper, it is possible to identify four *primary* emotions, each of which has evolutionary significance, is grounded in a different and identifiable physiological state, appears relatively early in the development of the individual, and appears in every culture. *Fear, anger, depression,* and *satisfaction* are the four primary emotions. Fear, for example, can be seen as an evolutionary adaptation that energizes the animal in the face of danger; it is associated with the action of a specific neurochemical, epinephrine, on the sympathetic nervous system; it can be identified quite early in infancy; and it appears in every culture. In contrast to these primary emotions, Kemper says, there are more numerous and varied *secondary* emotions, such as pride, shame, guilt, love, and gratitude. These emotions are grounded in the primary emotions, but the specific experience of them depends upon a set of shared social expectations. These expectations, as well as their names, are a product of culture and are therefore quite variable from one society to another. Guilt, for example, is based on the physiological responses of fear, but the nature and experience of guilt depends on the fact that we have learned to respond to certain social situations by labeling our physiological responses as "guilt."

Whether there are four primary emotions, or two, or six, emotions have their origins in social life; we experience emotion because of our participation in social interaction. Although the physiological states associated with various emotions can be induced by chemical means (pulse and respiration can be increased, for example, by administering epinephrine), these same states are also—and more significantly—induced by our normal involvement in social situations. Just as emotions originate in social interaction, they are regulated as people interact and by the same general processes that regulate our conduct in general.

How do the social processes that originate and regulate emotions operate? The emotion of *grief* shows how a symbolic interactionist analysis of emotions can be developed.[21]

In North American culture, as in many others, grief is the normal emotion created when a loved one dies. The feelings associated with grief are well-known: People feel sad, they are depressed, they cry, they feel sorry for themselves, they feel alone or left behind. These feelings begin shortly after the experience of bereavement, intensify, and then gradually diminish (or at least they are supposed to) with the passage of time.

How do we explain the emotion of grief? Since we will not be satisfied with an appeal to human nature ("That's just the natural way people feel"), how do we account for the character of this experience in our culture? One approach, a culturally deterministic one, would say that people experience grief simply because they are supposed to. That is, grief is culturally defined as a set of sensations people are supposed to have when someone close to them dies. When people have been appropriately socialized, they spontaneously have these sensations when someone dies, and they call them "grief." This explanation is appealing, because it emphasizes the role of culture, but it has some shortcomings. It does not provide an explanation of the physical sensations themselves. How can cultural expectations create bodily sensations? And it does not explain why people experience different levels of grief. Some wives grieve when their husbands die, while others may be relieved or happy. Also, grieving for parents, while culturally expected, seems to vary according to their parents' ages and the relative social distance that has grown between them and their children. We do not have the same feelings about the death of an aged and distant parent as we do about the death of a parent whose death comes at an age younger than expected or on whom we still depend. Thus, a simply cultural explanation does not do all that we might want it to do.

Symbolic interactionism provides some of the missing details and linkages to improve a cultural explanation. Death represents the loss of a member of society. For those who have been close to the deceased, it means much more. The death of a spouse, for example, means not only the loss of a companion, lover, and friend, but also the loss of a part of the self. When people who have been close to us die, we lose the supports for our own self-conceptions that those people provided. We lose part of our identity, part of the support for our self-esteem, part of what had buttressed our self-image.[22]

Naturally, that loss is greater for some than for others. It will be greater for a surviving spouse who has been very close to the deceased than for one whose relationship has been more distant. It will be greater for a child whose parent still looms large as a figure in his or her life than for an adult faced with the death of an aged and failing parent. Indeed, perhaps the loss will be greater for a woman who loses her husband than for a husband who loses a wife, since it may be argued that in "traditional" marriage arrangements in this society, female identity is much more tied to having a husband than is male identity tied to having a wife.

Lyn Lofland suggests that the level of significance of the other is defined by seven "threads of connectedness" by which people are attached to one another:

> We are linked to others by the roles we play, by the help we receive, by the wider network of others made available to us, by the selves others create and sustain, by the comforting myths they allow us, by the reality they validate for us, and by the futures they make possible.[23]

Where these linkages are spread widely among a large number of people, the loss of any single other may have little impact on the individual's membership in the group or on everyday activities. Where a few others command the greatest share of our attention, providing role partners, definitions of reality, and validation of ourselves, each other person is likely to be of very great significance, and thus the loss of that other is likely to occasion more intense grief.

As Lofland points out, the extent to which people feel a sense of loss may depend on their typical definitions of the situation of death. In the past, death rates were higher in general, first experiences with death tended to occur early in life, and people more commonly experienced the death of children. Under such conditions, death itself was more routine, and so the sense of loss attendant on any individual's death may have been less. In the contemporary world, where many people experience their first significant death when their grandparents die, death may be a more shaking event simply because it is so unfamiliar. With the greater emphasis on the individual in modern life and the greater opportunity for solitude and privacy, which may encourage the elaboration of grief as well as restrict the opportunities for its expression, the emotional impact of death and the sense of loss that attends it may be greater than in the past.[24]

Whatever variations in the sense of loss there may be, loss it remains. Metaphorically, death tears a hole in the self-conceptions of those left behind. This is where the linkage between social experience and physical sensations occurs. As a general rule, physical sensations are created when human acts are blocked. That is, when some circumstance interferes with the normal course of our activities and prevents us from bringing an act to consummation, there are normal physiological results. When I experience the pangs of hunger, for example, and go to the refrigerator only to find it empty, the result is to heighten my tendency to think about food and to increase the sensation of being hungry. So it is also with grief. The loss of a significant other, by disorganizing our social worlds and conceptions of self, creates many obstacles to ordinary, routine conduct. At every turn, we are faced with habitual actions that cannot be completed as before because a significant other is not present. The sensations associated with grief — depression, frustration, anger — seem normal and spontaneous responses to the fact that the loss blocks our everyday actions.

What is made of these responses is quite another matter. All such individual experiences occur in the context of culturally preestablished meanings, and those meanings are subject to social interpretation. We must therefore ask what labels culture makes available for such sensations, and how social interaction makes use of these labels to influence further the sensations themselves and the meanings attributed to them.

It seems nonsensical to say that the individual feelings associated with the loss of a loved one have to be labeled as grief before they are experienced as grief. In our culture, we take for granted that people feel grief when their loved ones die. No one has to tell us that we are grieving, and we think of grief as the natural label for the experiences we are having. This is not universally the case, however. Robert Levy, for example, reports that Tahitians discuss the feelings associated with the loss of a loved one in terms of illness, rather than as grief.[25] Their cultural definitions lead them to downplay feelings of individual loss, so that while they probably have the same depressive reactions as we do, they view them in a different way.

Culture thus provides us with a vocabulary of emotions; that is, each culture accumulates a set of terms that apply to and describe the sensations that are the products of various situations. There is both variation and uniformity among cultures in this regard. The underlying physical sensations associated with emotion are real, they are important, and they are probably provoked by similar situations across many different cultures. Although cultures may differ widely in their definitions of which individuals fall into the category of important, close relationships, the death of someone in such a category will provoke feelings of sadness and depression. This is so because the underlying processes of self and the construction of acts are the same in all cultures. Yet, all cultures do not label the resulting feelings in the same way. One may treat the feelings in terms of a concept of grief, while another downplays the sense of personal loss and treats those feelings as illness.

The existence of cultural vocabularies of emotion is a clue that people have expectations about who will have what emotional experiences under what circumstances. In American society, a woman whose husband dies is supposed to grieve. Not only is there a term to cover her experiences, but her friends and family act toward her on the basis of this concept, and they indicate their expectations about how she should behave and feel. They treat her as someone who can be expected to grieve, and their actions are oriented toward seeing to it that this grief finds appropriate expression as well as providing social supports.

Cultural labels and social action in terms of them give rise to at least two forms of *emotion work*.[26] First, part of our emotional experience is constrained by the presentation of self and by the situation of mourning. Even in those circumstances where individuals do not spontaneously feel the grief they are supposed to feel, they may arrange their self-presentations so as to appear as if they are grieving. Such presentations of self may range from overacted grief — dramatic displays of grief behavior that may leave no one convinced of their genuineness but do meet ritual expectations — to more carefully and artfully acted performances. Moreover, individuals are also constrained in their behavior by the actions of others and by the situation in which they find themselves. A woman who is relieved to see her philandering, good-for-nothing husband gone will be surrounded by others for whom his death is a real loss, and whose conduct will define the situation as one in which mourning is appropriate. That mood is itself constraining, for it makes behavior that departs from the mood seem drastically out of place. So the rejoicing wife may well be somber and sad not just out of concern for her appearance in the eyes of others, but also so as to fit with the situation of grief and mourning.

The second form of work on emotions entails efforts to create, and not merely feign, the very emotions that are culturally prescribed when they are not spontaneously felt. In our presentations of self, it is not uncommon for us to be drawn into our performances to the extent that we begin to take them seriously. In striving to assume a mask that others will believe truly represents our feelings, we come to have the very feelings represented by the mask. We put on displays of anger to achieve a certain purpose and then find that we are indeed becoming angry. Similarly, at funerals, we may find ourselves drawn into the solemnity of the occasion and, at first assuming the demeanor of the sad, we then actually become sad.

Many social situations seem arranged as regulators of emotion. In weddings and funerals, for example, the spontaneous and genuine emotions of some are managed and kept within bounds as they interact with others. At the same time, those who bring to such occasions only the appearance of proper emotional involvement may find it necessary to "act" so as to create the appropriate actual emotions. In both cases, it appears, emotions are not individual responses to events, nor are they antithetical to organized, rational social life. Instead, emotions are integral parts of social life, and like all other forms of behavior, they are not matters of unconscious responses to stimuli, but of socially constructed meanings.

Weddings, funerals, and other dramatic events illustrate the importance of what Arlie Hochschild has called *feeling rules*—that is, shared conceptions of which feelings are appropriate to a situation, and to what degree. The importance of such rules is not confined to unusual events, however. Candace Clark has demonstrated that the display of the emotion of *sympathy* is likewise subject to social expectations.[27] People who have had an experience—a personal misfortune or disaster, for example—that qualifies them to receive expressions of sympathy from others generally recognize that there are limits on the claims they may make. One should not try to claim too much sympathy, or be too eager to accept sympathy, or make unwarranted claims. In other words, one should not exaggerate or misrepresent the significance of a misfortune in order to gain the sympathy of others, one should recognize that there are limits to the sympathy others will give for any particular event, and one should not appear excessively needful of the sympathy of others. Those who are asked for sympathy are likewise mindful of such rules and will sanction departures from them—claiming, for example, that some people are "always looking for sympathy" and, like "broken records," routinely exaggerate the problems that life has handed them.

The management of emotions is a task that confronts people in their occupations and not only in their associations with friends or family members. In some occupations, as Arlie Hochschild demonstrated in her study of flight attendants, a considerable amount of emotional labor is part of the day-to-day work. Airlines expect flight attendants to be cheerfully attentive to passengers, for example, as well as calm in the face of possible crises. They must maintain their emotional composure—they must work hard to avoid producing the "wrong emotions"—in the face of passengers who are frequently unpleasant or demanding. Like waiters and waitresses, sales personnel, and others who have regular contact with the public, they must learn to put on a face that often betrays their true underlying feelings. Their capacity to do so is a part of the labor they sell to their employers.[28]

Whatever the specific situation or social context, the experiencing, display, and regulation of emotions is a key aspect of social life. People are guided in their actions not merely by cognition that focuses on definitions of situations and on role making and role taking, but by affective responses to situations, others, and themselves.

CONSTRAINT AND SOCIAL INTERACTION

One major topic remains to be examined to complete our analysis of social interaction and the formation of conduct: the nature and consequences of *constraint* in social life. Symbolic interactionists have often been accused of painting too fluid a picture of the social world, of overemphasizing the freedom of individual actors or groups of actors to resist or overcome the influence of society and culture. By stressing the processes of role making and role taking, as well as the need to define situations, critics argue that symbolic interactionists overlook the fact that conduct is in many ways constrained.

- Symbolic interactionists take the view that there is both freedom and constraint in social life. Human beings are not merely social and cultural automatons, but thinking, acting creatures who use the intelligence they have gained as members of society to solve the problems that confront them. Nonetheless, there are real limits to what humans can do to solve problems and to act in ways of their own choosing.

Constraint is everywhere in social life. People must form definitions of situations and interpret others' conduct in order to construct their acts, but they are typically limited in the definitions they can consider and in the interpretations they can make. They are constrained by limits to their knowledge of others and their purposes, by the power that others hold over them, by obligations to roles or to individuals who are not a part of the present situation, and by others' responses to their acts. Thus, the capacity to define a situation as one sees fit and to make a role as one chooses is far from unlimited, for the individual continually bumps into others, their definitions, and their purposes. In the remainder of this chapter we will consider several ways in which our actions are thus constrained.

Altercasting

The aligning actions considered earlier focus our attention on what Erving Goffman called the *presentation of self*—that is, the things people do in order to enhance or protect their conceptions of themselves and their status in the eyes of others. Thus, to describe a disclaimer as an effort to avoid the possible negative typifications of a particular act is to focus mainly on the perspective of the disclaiming person as he or she seeks to pursue a line of conduct while also maintaining a desirable self in the situation.

But the presentation of self is only one side of the process of role taking and role making. The roles made by participants in any situation are reciprocal, which is to say that the role made by one person has to "fit" that made by another. In the interaction between patient and physician in the examining room, for example, the two attempt to fit their respective lines of conduct to one another. They do this by imaginatively taking one another's roles and making their own roles accordingly. In studying the presentation of self, we focus on one side of this interchange, namely the efforts made by a particular individual to make a role and at the same time to put forth a self that the others present will regard favorably. Now we must examine the other side: the effects of one individual's acts on the other's *capacity* to make a role and preserve a valued conception of self. This process, whereby one person's acts constrain and limit what the other can do and be has been termed *altercasting,* a term that calls attention to the "casting" of the other into a particular role preferred by the altercaster.[29]

A familiar example of altercasting is found in the experience of being (or putting someone) "on the defensive." In a formal debate, for example, or in political campaigning, an effective strategy for controlling the definition of the situation is to force others to defend positions they do not want to defend or to put them in the position of having to answer charges. A candidate for president may complain vigorously about the "tax and spend mentality" of an opponent, or call his or her character into question, and in doing so force the other candidate into a defensive position, and thus indirectly confirm that the charge is worth discussing. By creating an issue, a politician forces an opponent to respond to it and thus implicitly to be associated with some of the alleged negative characteristics.[30]

In altercasting, people are constrained to act in certain ways—to make roles of a particular kind—because they are treated *as if* they were making particular roles. A politician treats an opponent as someone who *does* "tax and spend" or who *is* of dubious character and by this treatment forces the other to deny the charge and defend or explain his or her conduct. But the moment the other candidate defends or explains his or her conduct, he or she seems to accept the issue—to agree implicitly that what is charged is worth talking about and thus might actually be true.

Altercasting thus relies on a key feature of all social interaction: The imputation of roles to individuals, and action toward them on the basis of such imputation, powerfully constrains their conduct. The nature and origins of these constraints can easily be seen in another example. A common form of altercasting in everyday life occurs when one individual treats another as a more intimate friend or ally than either is accustomed to thinking of the other. Treating someone as a special friend, confidant, or intimate is a common form of interpersonal Machiavellianism. Although sometimes the intended victim of such altercasting is aware of its insincerity—recognizing, for example, that an employer is bestowing special favors and treatment only in an effort to cultivate a spy and thus find out what the employees are thinking about—the victim may be unaware of what is taking place. An employer who treats a subordinate with a show of intimacy in order to elicit employee secrets may be successful in deceiving the employee, or at least successful up to a point. A child who attempts to enlist one parent as an ally in order to influence the other may well succeed in keeping one or both parents in the dark as to what is going on.

What makes altercasting work? Why should an employee be more inclined to squeal on coworkers if the boss begins to act in a friendly way? Why should a parent whom the child treats as an ally begin to take the child's part and act as an ally? One simple explanation of the employer/employee example is that the subordinate perceives an *advantage* in responding reciprocally to the boss's overtures — perhaps anticipating a raise or promotion as a possible reward and thus acting without thought to the interests of fellow workers. Another explanation might be that the employee is responding to a general *norm of reciprocity.* Alvin Gouldner defined such a norm as the belief that one ought to help those who have been helpful, or at least avoid doing them harm.[31] By reducing interpersonal distance, the employer confers something of value on the employee and the latter feels obligated to reciprocate. Similarly, by treating the parent as an ally, the child benefits from the latter's reciprocal feelings of obligation.

A more fundamental explanation of altercasting can be found at a cognitive level. The employer who acts in a more intimate, friendly fashion toward a subordinate is defining a situation in a particular way, treating it as an occasion on which formalities can be put aside and people can treat one another as equals, not as superior and subordinate. In so defining the situation, the employer influences the objects that are present and toward which conduct will occur — in particular, the boss indicates "friendly social intercourse" and "friendship" as main social objects of the occasion. Once the situation has been so defined, it requires considerable effort by the subordinate to define the situation differently and to indicate other objects — to call attention to the formal relationship between the two, for example. To change the encounter's object from "friendly social intercourse" to "boss talks to wary employee" requires self-conscious effort. The employee must actively resist the boss's preferred definition, acting in the role of wary employee rather than in the role of friend. Just as physical objects may block one's passage through a room, so, in much the same way, a social object toward which a powerful individual is acting must be taken into account by those with less power. The employee is not only induced to act in the role of friend by the very considerable press of implication in the situation, but the employee also knows that the boss controls resources and can reward or punish the desired role performance.

The effects of altercasting are not limited to the immediate situations in which people interact with one another any more than the presentation of self is so limited. Just as repeated self-presentations shape the character of self-conception, so, too, the repeated altercasting of one person by others in a particular way will affect self-conception. In many families, for instance, one individual — often, though not always, a child — is repeatedly treated as the scapegoat for everything that goes wrong. Systematically blamed and regarded as responsible for undesirable events and calamitous circumstances, the child very likely will develop a self-conception that reflects such treatment.

Altercasting and the presentation of self are two sides of the same coin. Both involve efforts to define situations by establishing identities and roles. The concept of presentation of self calls attention to the fact that people try to define situations in ways they think desirable by showing themselves in a favorable light to others. The concept of altercasting reminds us that what one individual does in a situation places limits on the roles and self-presentations of others. The effects of altercasting and the presentation of self are not limited to manipulation, Machiavellian schemes, or negative consequences for self-conceptions. Both may be employed for benign as well as malevolent purposes. Thus, for example, the teacher who believes that a child's performance will be improved by positive rewards and encouragement is altercasting every bit as much as the employer who seeks the confidence of an employee.

Power

Sociologists generally define power as the capacity of one person to achieve purposes without the consent of or against the resistance of others. Altercasting is thus a way of exercising power, since the successful altercaster is able to induce others to make a particular role without their realizing it or being able to resist doing so. Like all forms of power, altercasting involves the control of resources — in this case, control over the role of the other. Altercasting is not the sole means by which people pursue their goals, nor is the relevance of power for social interaction limited to the use of such techniques as ways of exercising control over the roles of others. Power depends on a variety of resources and is exercised in a number of ways that must be understood if our portrayal of interaction is to be complete.

In social interaction, the exercise of power depends in part on the control by one party of resources — goods, tools, knowledge, money — that are valuable to and desired by others. When people interact, they pursue individual as well as collective ends; they cooperate in the pursuit of common goals, but they also sometimes compete for scarce resources or engage in conflict over which actions to take. Thus, for example, members of a business organization cooperate with one another in furthering the organization's goals, but they also compete for advancement within the firm, and sometimes they fight over issues they consider important, such as whether to produce a new product or enter a new market.

In such contexts it is unlikely that all will be equal in their control of important resources. Managers, vice-presidents, and department heads have more power than those whom they employ. That is, they have the power to hire or fire, make unilateral decisions, withhold information from some and share it with others, and increase the budgets for some projects and cut them for others. Superordinates also possess *authority*—that is, they claim the *right* to exercise control over the actions of others, who concede that they have this right.[32] Leaving authority aside, however, there are other inequalities of power: Some members have been around longer than others and thus know more about how the organization works; some have developed close relationships with their superiors and can more readily gain a hearing for their proposals; some control key departments, such as data processing or personnel, and can thus make their influence strongly felt.

The exercise of power involves the same processes of defining the situation, role making, and role taking as more cooperative forms of social interaction. The more powerful person must role take, estimating what resources the other commands in order to predict how he or she will respond to an effort to use power. The more powerful person must also role make, forging a performance that will convince the other that here is someone to be reckoned with, who will not hesitate to use power ruthlessly if the need arises. Likewise, the weaker individual also must role take and role make, discerning whether the other's power is real or apparent, responding in ways that do not yield more than necessary.

Accurate role taking is, indeed, itself a resource of power. To the extent that one can accurately gauge the reaction of another to one's own contemplated act, one can calculate the act so as to secure the best advantage for oneself. If I know that an associate will abandon a course of action at the slightest hint of resistance, I can influence his or her conduct with a minimum use of my own power. If I can accurately anticipate spirited resistance, I can deploy my own resources to greatest advantage. The more accurately I can role take— imputing intentions and the definition of the situation to the other—the more leverage I have over that person.

Although role-taking ability enhances power, the possession of power, and especially authority, to some extent lessens the need to role take with accuracy. The person who exercises authority can generally get away with less accurate role taking than the person over whom it is exercised. Parents, for example, are in a position to command their children's compliance, at least within certain limits, and can thus afford to be less sensitive to their children's evaluations of them or even to their children's definitions of various situations.[33] The parent can be considerably less concerned with how the child will respond; the child, in contrast, has to learn accurate role-taking skills in order to predict the responses of powerful parents.

This link between role taking and authority should not obscure the basic fact, however, that some degree of role taking is always involved in social interaction. When a parent disciplines a child for doing what has been expressly forbidden and again forbids the child from doing it, role taking has occurred.

That is, the parent has made an imputation about the child's conduct in the past and probable behavior in the future. Indeed, the very recognition by a parent that a child has done something untoward requires role taking, for the parent's interpretation of the child's act requires that the situation in which it occurred be viewed from the latter's perspective. Has a child deliberately broken a rule, or did the forbidden conduct occur by accident? The answer to this question — even the act of raising it — rests on parental role taking, on the imputation of motives to the child, and the perception of the situation as the child saw it.

One of the less obvious ways people exercise power in everyday life is through their control of the physical setting in which interaction occurs. Role making and role taking do not occur in a vacuum, but in the midst of props, physical objects, machines, locations, buildings, and habitats that have human meaning and usually are human creations. People do not merely interact in social spaces provided by roles, but in banks, stores, homes, physician's offices, schools, parks, automobiles, beaches, factories, and myriad other places, each with its objects, colors, sounds, and other physical attributes.

People act in and toward such physical settings to some extent on the basis of habit. That is, they react both to specific places they have been before as well as to certain colors, sounds, or other aspects of their physical surroundings on the basis of conditioned responses rather than self-consciously. Some people are put at ease by soothing colors and canned music in a dentist's office, made to feel a sense of awe as they sit amidst the grandeur and ritual of a large cathedral, or impelled to feel somber by furnishings, casket, dress, and the serious demeanor of attendants at a funeral home. Even the route by which a person customarily drives to and from work generally is a setting in which many habitual responses occur — stopping at a particular traffic light, for example, or being especially alert at a dangerous intersection.

To the extent that people do respond habitually to certain settings and physical conditions, it follows that whoever has the power to control the physical elements of a situation also has considerable power to control how people in that situation will act. Indeed, this is the rationale that underlies the widespread use of canned music, controlled lighting in factories and offices, and similar practices. To influence conduct, in this view, one must control the stimuli to which people habitually respond.

Although it is doubtless true that some degree of control over conduct can be achieved through such manipulation of stimuli, of greater importance are efforts to control definitions of situations by physical means that rely on people's *interpretations* of physical settings. Donald Ball described the physical setting of an illegal abortion clinic along the California-Mexico border during the 1960s as an effort to create a "rhetoric of legitimation."[34] Faced with clients contracting for what was then an illegal service, who were therefore likely to be frightened or recalcitrant, the clinic arranged its setting and the appearance and manners of its staff in such as way as to assuage the fears of clients, keep them reasonably satisfied with the service, and provide a favorable image of self for both patrons and staff. The setting itself—waiting room, equipment, and facilities—was arranged to contradict the prevailing stereotype of an abortion clinic as a shabby, shady, back-alley operation. Moreover, staff were dressed to convey strongly the impression of competent medical treatment. Even though the observer noted serious departures from genuinely competent medical treatment, the overwhelming *impression* was of luxury, cost, and good medical practice. The impression depended in part on clients' interpretations of the physical setting itself as indicative of these qualities.

Awareness Contexts

Our discussion of social interaction has so far assumed that people present themselves genuinely and role take with reasonable accuracy. For numerous routine situations, it is quite valid to assume that there is no deception and that role taking is generally accurate. Parents and children, doctors and patients, teachers and students—most of these people, most of the time—interact in a context where roles are mutually and accurately understood and taken for granted. People trust others to be who they appear to be, and they act genuinely from the perspectives of their own roles.

Many situations in everyday life are, however, characterized by ignorance, suspicion, or pretense, and not by openness. People deceive one another about their true intentions. Spouses are unfaithful. Seemingly dedicated government employees turn out to be spies. How does social interaction work under such conditions? Do the same fundamental processes of defining the situation, role taking, and role making operate in such contexts?

Barney Glaser and Anselm Strauss approached this topic through the concept of the *awareness context,* which they developed in a study of the interaction between dying patients and their families, physicians, and hospital staff. They define an awareness context as "the total combination of what each interactant knows about the identity of the other and his own identity in the eyes of the other."[35] In an *open* awareness context, each participant knows the others' true identities—that is, the roles others intend to make in the situation—and his or her own identity in their eyes. In a *closed* awareness context, one interactant is ignorant of either the others' identities or his or her own situated social identity. In *pretense* contexts, interactants are aware of one another's identities but pretend not to be; in *suspicion* contexts, participants suspect that one another's identities are not what they appear to be.

Examples of these awareness contexts in the real world are numerous. When friends suspect one another's loyalty, for example, they are in a suspicion awareness context. A married couple, each of whom is carrying on an affair and knows the other is also doing so, but who pretend that everything is normal, are sustaining a pretense awareness context. The dying patient who does not know about his or her impending death and is not told by family or physician is a part of a closed awareness context.

Description and analysis of awareness context are essential to a full understanding of how people interact and of the outcomes of their interaction. The operations of a confidence scheme, for example, depend on a particular kind of awareness context. From the standpoint of the con artist, the task is to keep the mark unaware of the deception being perpetuated—but also to insure that the mark is not really a police officer in disguise. Awareness—knowing who knows what about whom—is an object of prime importance to the success of the scheme, whether it involves bilking a widow out of her life savings or persuading a business executive to buy worthless or stolen securities.

In general, when the awareness context is not open, considerable energies are devoted either to opening it up or keeping it closed. Thus, in the hospital context described by Glaser and Strauss, considerable effort goes into the engineering of a closed context by the staff. Physicians and nurses talk to dying patients *as if* they were going to live; they control their outward manner in order to keep from giving away the show; and often they minimize their contacts with the patient so as to reduce the risks of discovery. Moreover, patients who suspect the worst about their true condition may become devoted to the task of discovering their actual prognosis.

Suspicion and pretense awareness contexts represent occasions in which a great deal of interaction is focused on the definition of the situation. Although such situations are marked by doubt or pretense as to whether others are actually who they seem to be, it is more basically the definition of the situation itself that is at issue. If one's partner is a con artist and not a helpful new friend, then one is a victim of a con, not a beneficiary of friendship, and the situation is a con operation, not an exchange of benefits. If one is being conned, one acts toward the object of getting back one's money, or of going to the police while enduring the embarrassment of having been successfully deceived. If one is being helped by a friend, the object is to think of a way to reciprocate. It is the situation, as well as objects and identities, that is being defined.

Awareness contexts constrain interaction. That is, what people know, do not know, suspect, or pretend with respect to one another constrains how they will interact. Wives who suspect their husbands of philandering will concentrate their efforts on discovery and proof. Nurses seeking to deceive a dying patient will guard every word lest they disclose information that would reveal the patient's true condition. Con artists who think the mark may be an undercover police officer will be careful about what they promise. Ignorance, suspicion, and pretense shape definitions of situations and set the conditions within which role making and role taking occur.

Conventional and Interpersonal Roles

A final consideration in our analysis of constraint and social interaction requires a distinction between two fundamentally different kinds of roles. As Tamotsu

Shibutani pointed out, people interact with one another in two capacities.[36] On the one hand, they interact on the basis of standardized, known, and labeled positions in various situations. People are mothers, physicians, store clerks, assembly line operators, police officers, men, women, and so on. In the myriad situations in which people act, they have a grasp of the situations as wholes and of the positions of various participants expressed in terms of such *conventional roles.* Much of our sense of the structure of routine situations in everyday life stems from our capacity to identify one another as acting from the standpoint of such roles.[37]

On the other hand, people do not interact with one another merely as makers of conventional roles, but also as unique human beings. A child does not relate merely to a "mother," but to "my mother" — a specific and in some ways unique human being with whom the child has had sustained contact. When people engage in repeated interaction with one another, networks of interpersonal relationships develop in which people have a sense of mutual position that reflects individual peculiarities and their history of contact with one another. That is, they come to define and make *interpersonal roles.* When two friends meet, each is responsive to a set of expectations, claims, and obligations with respect to the other. Each has a sense of position — and of the structure of the encounter as a whole — that is informed by the interpersonal role of friendship rather than by a particular conventional role.

In some situations, people simultaneously make conventional and interpersonal roles. Parents and children respond to one another on the basis of fairly standardized expectations of how parents and children typically behave. This is especially true of the parents, whose wider experiences have exposed them to general typifications of parental conduct. At the same time, children and parents make and take roles on the basis of a unique set of relationships that build up over time and are a central part of their interaction. Similarly, coworkers in an office make conventional roles assigned to them in the hierarchy of office life; at the same time, they are friends, enemies, rivals, colleagues, lovers, shirkers, stooges, partners, and the like.

The overlay of conventional and interpersonal roles is responsible for some of the complexity of social life. People simultaneously typify one another's acts on the basis of the two sets of roles, and they must decide in any given situation which should be the controlling typification. Is my partner in interaction acting as my enemy? Or as my subordinate? Even though sociologists frequently describe such situations in terms of role conflict or role strain, which presumably people seek to avoid, it should not be supposed that they always attempt to do so. Quite the contrary, such situations provide the basis for office intrigue, warring factions, academic politics, love triangles, and a great many other forms of interaction that, although often painful and embarrassing for people, also add spice to their lives.

Each type of role is constraining, but in a different way. Conventional roles constrain us not only because they pose a set of obligations we must meet, but also because they shape our view of social reality. They are the source of our most basic images of social structure and of our location within it. In some instances — gender roles are a good illustration — conventional roles generally seem like natural and inevitable features of the social world. Moreover, they are also so deeply merged with the self that they seem to be the essence of the person as well.[38] Indeed, gender roles can be so constraining that they override other roles in a situation, as, for example, when a male cannot see past the gender role in order to interact appropriately with a female physician or boss.

Interpersonal roles also constrain. Like conventional roles, they present us with duties and obligations — but to individuals rather than to abstract conceptions of what we should or must do. They are likewise sources of our images of social structure. They point to the fact that our sense of structure is composed not just of the formally labeled roles of a group or society, but also of the unique way in which, over time, we have come to see ourselves in relation to others in that structure.

SUMMARY

- Human conduct is situated; it is formed in concrete situations and cannot be fully explained or understood outside the situations in which it occurs. A situation is a kind of container within which people act. It is an assembly of people, roles, objects, and joint activities at a particular point in social time and social space.

- People act on the basis of their definitions of situations. What one does at any given moment — indeed, whether one knows what to do at all — depends on one's capacity to establish and maintain a definition of the situation in which one is located. A definition of a situation is an organization of the person's perception, an overall grasp of the objects, meanings, people, roles, and activities that are present. The definition of the situation tells the individual what others are present, what kinds of acts are taking place, and what is expected of him or her. As the person acts on the basis of an initial definition of the situation, that definition is either confirmed or called into question by the responses of the others who are present. If it is confirmed, action can continue; if it is not, those present must act to reestablish the definition of the situation.

- Most conduct occurs within routine situations where social acts and objects can be readily anticipated, the roles to be made and taken are known in advance, and people can rely to a great extent on habit. Indeed, the characteristic attitude toward familiar situations consists of the assumption that what people think is happening is what is really happening, that participants share the definition of the situation, and that there is therefore no reason to verify the definition. Even in routine situations, however, there is always the possibility that something unexpected will happen. People do unexpected things, become involved in conflict with others, misunderstand one another, and in other ways introduce novelty into the midst of routine. Thus, conduct is powerfully shaped by the definition of the situation, but is not simply determined by it. Sometimes people have to work to establish or to reestablish their definitions.

• The capacity to engage in role making and role taking within the boundaries of defined situations rests on the possession of several kinds of knowledge or ways of knowing. These include knowledge of typifications, probability, causality, means and ends, normative standards, and substantive congruency. For every social role, situation, object, and social act, there is a more or less commonly shared typification that establishes the usual and familiar forms of that role, situation, and so forth. When people interact they rely on their stock of typifications to grasp the meaning of others' actions, their own appearance in the eyes of others, and so on. In addition to typifications, those who share a culture share a set of ideas about the things that are likely to occur in given situations; the causes and consequences of various events, including their own actions and the acts of others; useful means of attaining their ends; and the normative standards in terms of which acts may be evaluated. When the actions of others do not seem to fit the definition of the situation, people try to verify that the definition of the situation on the basis of which they are acting is the same as the definition held by others.

• Social life is filled with events that challenge definitions of situations, the identities of participants, or both. People behave in unexpected ways, violate norms, and do countless things that at least momentarily disrupt the uneventful flow of situations. Such occurrences give rise to aligning actions—efforts to maintain situational definitions, preserve situated identities, and link conduct to cultural standards. When people anticipate doing things that might disrupt a situational definition or injure their identities in the eyes of others, they are likely to *disclaim* their impending acts, seeking to have what they are about to do defined as nondisruptive and not a sufficient basis for retypifying them. When people are called to account for their transgressions, they must give *accounts* that explain why they have acted as they have. These and other aligning actions are means of preserving definitions of situations, the identities of participants, and the culture itself.

• Although social interaction is a cognitive activity in which people must determine what is going on in order to decide for themselves what to do, there is also an affective or emotional side of social life. People respond to situations, events, the actions of others, and to themselves with anger, joy, sadness, grief, elation, and other emotions. Indeed, emotion is not only a response to social situations, but is in many ways a part of the very definition of the situation and of the roles of its members. Grief, for example, is not merely a spontaneous reaction to the death of an intimate, but is an expected part of the role performances of the bereaved and a part of the definition of the situation of mourning. Thus, people engage in role making and role taking designed to maintain grief — and many other emotions — within socially prescribed boundaries. The very experience of emotion is shaped by cultural definitions and by a vocabulary that encourages the expression of some emotions and restricts the expression of others.

• Although the symbolic interactionist approach seems to grant people a great deal of freedom and to emphasize the fluidity of conduct, many things constrain how people can act. Whether intentionally or unintentionally, for example, when people make roles they shape the role performances of others. The concept of altercasting emphasizes that the way in which one person acts toward another constrains the other's conduct in many ways. Moreover, human beings frequently interact under conditions of unequal power — that is, where the resources of some people are greater than those of others and can be used to control the definitions of situations or merely to reduce their need to take the interests, goals, or feelings of the other into account. Although much social interaction takes place in contexts where each member is fully aware of the identity of others and of his or her own identity in their eyes, social life also includes situations where ignorance, pretense, or suspicion are more the rule. Finally, role definitions are themselves constraining. This is true not only of the conventional roles people perform, but also of interpersonal roles that emerge as people interact with one another repeatedly over time and come to develop unique and very personal expectations of one another.

ENDNOTES

1. The concept of definition of the situation developed here is influenced by the work of Peter McHugh, *Defining the Situation* (Indianapolis, Ind.: Bobbs-Merrill, 1968), which in turn depends on George H. Mead, *The Philosophy of the Present* (Chicago: Open Court, 1932) for its emphasis on emergence and relativity.

2. It is important to understand that although one habitual form of conduct may be disrupted when novel events occur, other habits will continue to guide us. If I encounter a friend who unexpectedly and sharply disagrees with me in a conversation, my habitual attitudes toward that person are disrupted and my interaction will become more self-conscious. Other habits will continue to guide me: I rely on my accustomed style of arguing, my habitual stance and tone of voice in disputes, even though I am dealing with an unexpected opponent.

3. George H. Mead, *The Philosophy of the Act* (Chicago: University of Chicago Press, 1938), pp. 6ff.

4. Sometimes this is an assumption, sometimes a deliberately chosen stance. See Joan P. Emerson, "Nothing Unusual is Happening" in *Human Nature and Collective Behavior: Papers in Honor of Herbert Blumer,* ed. Tamotsu Shibutani (Englewood Cliffs, N.J.: Prentice Hall, 1970).

5. McHugh, *Defining the Situation* (Note 1).

6. See McHugh, *Defining the Situation* (Note 1); Harold Garfinkel, *Studies in Ethnomethodology* (Englewood Cliffs, N.J.: Prentice-Hall, 1967); and Alfred Schutz, *On Phenomenology and Social Relations,* ed. Helmut Wagner (Chicago: University of Chicago Press, 1970).

7. See Schutz, *On Phenomenology and Social Relations,* pp. 111–122 (Note 6).

8. See Gregory P. Stone, "Appearance and the Self: A Slightly Revised Version," in *Social Psychology Through Symbolic Interaction,* 2nd ed., ed. Gregory P. Stone and Harvey A. Farberman (New York: Wiley, 1981), pp. 187–202.

9. See Peter Berger and Thomas Luckmann, *The Social Construction of Reality* (Garden City, N.Y.: Doubleday Anchor, 1967), pp. 42ff.

10. For critiques of this simplistic formulation, see Dennis Wrong, "The Oversocialized Conception of Man in Modern Sociology," *The American Sociological Review* 26 (April 1961): 183–193; Thomas P. Wilson, "Conceptions of Interaction and Forms of Sociological Explanation," *The American Sociological Review* 35 (August 1970): 697–709; and Randall Stokes and John P. Hewitt, "Aligning Actions," *The American Sociological Review* 41 (October 1976): 838–849.

11. Randall Stokes and John P. Hewitt, "Aligning Actions," *American Sociological Review* 41 (October 1976): 838–849.

12. C. Wright Mills, "Situated Actions and Vocabularies of Motive," in Stone and Farberman, *Social Psychology,* p. 326 (Note 8).

13. John P. Hewitt and Randall G. Stokes, "Disclaimers," *The American Sociological Review* 40 (February 1975): 1–11.

14. Marvin Scott and Stanford Lyman, "Accounts," *The American Sociological Review* 33 (December 1968): 46–62.

15. For an excellent effort to broaden and extend the concept of aligning actions and create a systematic classification, see Christopher H. Hunter, "Aligning Actions: Types and Social Distribution," *Symbolic Interaction* 7 (Fall 1984): 155–174.

16. See Nicholas Tavuchis, *Mea Culpa: A Sociology of Apology and Reconciliation* (Stanford, Calif.: Stanford University Press, 1991).

17. Hunter, "Aligning Actions: Types and Social Distribution," p. 157–158 (Note 15).

18. See Barry Schlenker, "Impression Management," *The Self-Concept, Social Identity, and Interpersonal Relations* (Monterey, Calif.: Brooks-Cole, 1980). I follow Hunter's usage in writing of "acclaimers" (to parallel "disclaimers") instead of Schlenker's "acclaiming."

19. The following account of emotions draws on several sources, chiefly Steven L. Gordon, "The Sociology of Sentiments and Emotion," in *Social Psychology: Sociological Perspectives,* ed. Morris Rosenberg and Ralph H. Turner (New York: Basic Books, 1981) pp. 562–592; Susan Shott, "Emotion and Social Life: A Symbolic Interactionist Analysis," *American Journal of Sociology* 84 (May 1979): 1317–1334; Arlie R. Hochschild, "Emotion Work, Feeling Rules, and Social Structure," *American Journal of Sociology* 85 (November 1979): 551–575; Theodore Kemper, "Social Constructivist and Positivist Approaches to the Sociology of Emotions," *American Journal of Sociology* 87 (September 1981): 336–362; and Kemper, "How Many Emotions Are There? Wedding the Social and Autonomic Components," *American Journal of Sociology* (September 1987): 263–289. In addition to these works and others cited below, useful studies include the following: Cheryl Albas and Daniel Albas, "Emotion Work and Emotion Rules: The Case of Exams," *Qualitative Sociology* 11 (Winter 1988): 259–274; Arlie Hochschild,

The Managed Heart: Commercialization of Human Feeling (Berkeley, Calif.: University of California Press, 1983); Theodore Kemper, *A Social Interactional Theory of Emotions* (New York: Wiley, 1978); Trudy Mills and Sherryl Kleinman, "Emotions, Reflexivity, and Action: An Interactionist Analysis," *Social Forces* 66 (June 1988): 1009–1027; and Thomas Scheff, "Toward Integration in the Social Psychology of Emotions," *Annual Review of Sociology* 9 (1983): 333–354.

20. Theodore Kemper, "How Many Emotions Are There?" (Note 19).

21. For an interesting symbolic interactionist analysis of grief and mourning as well as many other topics in the area of death and dying, see Cathy Charmaz, *The Social Reality of Death* (Reading, Mass.: Addison-Wesley, 1980).

22. In their study of the impact of bereavement, for example, Lund et al. found that the death of a spouse reduced the "social anchorage" of the self-concept in the elderly surviving spouse, and that the reduced social anchorage was evident even after two years of bereavement. See Dale A. Lund, Michael S. Caserta, Margaret F. Dimond, and Robert M. Gray, "Impact of Bereavement on the Self-Conceptions of Older Surviving Spouses," *Symbolic Interaction* 9 (Fall 1986): 235–244.

23. Lyn H. Lofland, "The Social Shaping of Emotion: The Case of Grief," *Symbolic Interaction* 8 (Fall 1985): 175.

24. Ibid.

25. See Robert I. Levy, *The Tahitians* (Chicago: University of Chicago Press, 1973).

26. The phrase and elements of this analysis are drawn from Hochschild, "Emotion Work" (Note 19).

27. See Candace Clark, "Sympathy Biography and Sympathy Margin," *American Journal of Sociology* 9 (September 1987): 290–321.

28. See Hochschild, *The Managed Heart* (Note 19). For an analysis of feeling rules and emotion management in relation to gender issues, see Hochschild, *The Second Shift: Working Parents and the Revolution at Home* (New York: Viking-Penguin, 1989); and Hochschild, "Ideology and Emotion Management: A Perspective and Path for Future Research," in *Research Agendas in the Sociology of Emotions,* ed. Theodore D. Kemper (Albany, N.Y.: State University of New York Press, 1990) pp. 117–142.

29. See Eugene Weinstein and Paul Deutschberger, "Some Dimensions of Altercasting," *Sociometry* 26 (December 1963): 454–466.

30. Peter M. Hall, "A Symbolic Interactionist Analysis of Politics," *Sociological Inquiry* 42 (1–2, 1972): 35–75.

31. See Alvin W. Gouldner, "The Norm of Reciprocity: A Preliminary Statement," *The American Sociological Review* 25 (February 1960): 161–178.

32. For an analysis of various processes of power, see Peter M. Hall, "Asymmetric Relationships and Processes of Power," in *Foundations of Interpretive Sociology: Original Essays in Symbolic Interaction. Studies in Symbolic Interaction, Supplement 1.* ed. Harvey A. Farberman and R. S. Perinbanayagam (New Haven, Conn.: Jai Press, 1985), pp. 309–344.

33. See Darwin L. Thomas, D. Franks, and J. Calonico, "Role-taking and Power in Social Psychology," *The American Sociological Review* 7 (October 1972): 605–614.

34. Donald W. Ball, "An Abortion Clinic Ethnography," *Social Problems* 14 (Winter 1967): 293–301. For a recent effort to show how settings are managed in legal clinics, see Mary K. Zimmerman, "The Abortion Clinic: Another Look at the Management of Stigma," in Stone and Farberman, *Social Psychology,* pp. 4–52 (Note 8).

35. Barney G. Glaser and Anselm L. Strauss, "Awareness Contexts and Social Interaction," in Stone and Farberman, *Social Psychology,* pp. 5–63 (Note 8).

36. See Tamotsu Shibutani, *Society and Personality* (Englewood Cliffs, N.J.: Prentice Hall, 1961), pp. 324–331.

37. For empirical studies of various kinds of roles, see Louis Zurcher, *Social Roles: Conformity and Creativity* (Beverly Hills, Calif.: Sage, 1983).

38. Ralph H. Turner, "The Role and the Person," *American Journal of Sociology* 84 (July 1978): 1–23.

▶ 6

Social Psychology and Social Order

A symbolic interactionist social psychology attempts to create a theory of action emphasizing the situated nature of social interaction and conduct formation. But the situations in which action occurs are embedded in a larger framework of people, groups, organizations, social classes, institutions, and society as a whole. Many of these larger units are far removed in time and distance from the immediate situation and yet have a significant impact on conduct. Our analysis is incomplete, therefore, until it shows how its theory of action is linked to broader questions of social structure and social change.

SOCIETY AND ITS STRUCTURE

A question of social order—"How is society possible?"—lies at the root of sociological inquiry. In our everyday lives we take the existence of society for granted, because the communities and groups of which we are members and the patterned activities in which we participate seem like fixed and natural features of the world. The social scientist, in contrast, takes society as something to be explained. How are such larger entities as groups, organizations, and society produced by the activities of individuals interacting with one another in everyday life? How do these larger realities, in turn, constrain the conduct of these interacting individuals?

The question of how society is possible has been approached by asking a number of different questions:

- How is it possible for individuals to subordinate their interests and goals to those of the groups to which they belong or those of society as a whole, so that they accept social guidance and constraint?
- How are various groups, organizations, communities, and other elements of society linked together in a coherent, organized way?
- How do the conflicts that arise between various groups, organizations, and other social units shape the social order?

The premise of the first question is that the interests and dispositions of individuals are not necessarily harmonious with those of the social groups, organizations, and communities to which they belong. Although individuals are creatures of society and derive their goals from society, they are also prone to self-interested behavior. The process of socialization produces human beings who can recognize that what others wish is not always what they themselves want to do, and who are able to say "No" to social demands. As a result, there is always the possibility that people will act contrary to the interests of others.

The second question is concerned primarily with coordination. Its premise is that in any society, but especially in complex societies, some mechanism for coordinating the activities of members is necessary, since all are involved in a complex division of labor in which no individual or family controls the means for producing a livelihood independent of others. In simpler societies, the activities of individuals are coordinated within relatively small groups of people who are intimately familiar with one another. In more complex societies, however, the activities of many groups and organizations somehow must be linked together.

The premise of the third question is that conflict is an inherent feature of social life. Even in simpler societies, the interests of one family are not necessarily consistent with those of another. There may very well be competition for scarce land or resources. In more complex societies, many groups and organizations arise, and the interests of each may conflict with the interests of others. The possibilities of conflict among individuals and social groups are multiplied by the social inequalities that seem invariably to arise in human life. Some individuals, families, groups, and organizations acquire more land, goods, weapons, knowledge, and other resources of power and seek to maintain their advantage and control the lives of others.

There are a variety of ways to explain how society gains and maintains the upper hand over the individual, how social life is coordinated, and how conflict shapes the forms and varieties of social life. Sociological "functionalists," for example, tend to regard society as a self-regulating system in which various "structures" — such as groups, organizations, social roles, social classes, and institutions — function together to provide guidance to the individual, maintain a productive division of labor, and limit destructive social conflict. Conflict sociologists argue that the important question is how those individuals and social groups with power exercise it so as to secure their own ends and organize and control the activities of others.

It is not the task of social psychology to answer all of these questions about social order, or to decide whether a conflict view of social life is to be preferred over a functional view. In the scholarly division of labor, the concerns of social psychologists are necessarily more microscopic than those of sociologists interested in the study of social organization on a large scale. Our task is to formulate a theory of action consistent with what sociologists have learned about the social order. An effective way of carrying out this task is by examining how the social order is produced and reproduced by the activities of everyday life.

A symbolic interactionist approach to the question of social order begins by noting the dangers of reifying society. We engage in the fallacy of *reification* when we treat an abstraction as if it were a thing, endowing it with a solidity or a capacity for action that it does not possess. In the case of such terms as *society* and *social order,* this fallacy is difficult to avoid. When we label something as *society,* we create and act toward an *object,* in the interactionist sense of this term. As we have already pointed out, human beings tend to act toward such abstract objects in the same way that they act toward more tangible objects, treating both as real and constraining. Even to speak or write of "society," therefore, is to imbue this theoretical abstraction with solidity and to treat it as if it had some autonomous capacity to act independently of the will of its members.

We can turn this practice of reification to theoretical advantage, however, by taking it as a starting point for understanding how society is possible. Social order exists, in part, because the *members* of a given society perceive that it exists. *They* reify it. Social order is as much a human *construction* of reality as it is an objective characteristic that can be described and analyzed by sociologists or other scientific observers. This is not to say that the social order is *only* a product of reality construction, for such a position ignores the fact that from the standpoint of its members, society is an external and constraining reality that seems quite objective and real. It is to say, however, that we can begin to understand the nature of this reality and how it constrains action by examining how its members collectively define it and uphold their definitions in their everyday activities.

SOCIAL ORDER AS A CONSTRUCTED REALITY

From the standpoint of its individual members, a society is a thing with an existence independent of themselves, even though its continued being depends very much on them and their behavior. The society has a name—the United States, Canada, India—that established its corporate existence; it is thought by its members to possess a more or less distinctive way of life expressed in its values, practices, beliefs, and political institutions. For the most part the society to which any of us belongs appears as a massive, durable, and given part of the world, a reality taken for granted as we go about everyday life. It is there when we are born, it affects our life chances for better or worse, and it will continue to exist after we are dead.

A society, in short, is an *object* toward which its members act, and to a great extent the fact of social order is simply the fact that people act toward and so constitute this object in a stable, orderly fashion. Thus, for example, Americans act toward the United States in a variety of ways that serve to constitute it as a stable, persisting object. Reciting the Pledge of Allegiance, reading about the role of the United States in the Middle East, talking about what's wrong with this country, or extolling "the American way of life" in political speeches are all ways in which people constitute and act toward a particular kind of object, a nation-state. In large part, their acting toward it defines it, constitutes it, and causes it to persist.

What is true of a society as a whole also is true of the smaller groups, organizations, communities, institutions, and other units that make it up. The orderly and stable existence and persistence of these units depends in part on the fact that people act toward them as objects. General Motors, the city of New York, the American Medical Association, the institution of the family as well as any particular family group, the friends of Joe Smith who lives in Peoria—all are more or less stable and orderly social units within the larger society. To be sure, their existence depends on people coordinating their conduct in particular situations. Five days a week Joe Smith goes to work in a factory that produces parts for automobiles manufactured by General Motors. That he does so is one key basis of GM's continued existence, but the corporate giant also continues to exist because Joe Smith and others like him act toward it as an object. They talk about what GM will do in the upcoming contract negotiations or how many workers it will lay off if sales don't improve. They conceive of it sometimes as very much a threat or sometimes as an omnipresent force controlling their lives, and they hate it or feel loyal to it. So, too, Joe Smith's family or circle of friends persist because he and they act toward one another in certain ways at particular times—but also because they are conscious of being a family or a group of friends, and so constitute themselves as social objects.

Talking

One of the key ways the members of a society constitute and uphold the social order is by talking about it. Everyday life is filled with occasions when people simply talk to one another, situations in which the chief social object is simply conversation. Chance encounters, coffee breaks, cocktail parties, formal conferences and seminars, speeches, religious gatherings, radio and television talk shows and interviews, informal get-togethers, and numerous other contexts are marked by talking as the central and most observable form of behavior.

These encounters may seem sociologically unimportant, because they sometimes appear to their participants merely as devices for passing time and thus as unrelated to the real work of society. We are prone to think that what really matters sociologically are actual transactions between buyers and sellers in the marketplace, and not what people say to one another about the high cost of housing or automobiles. Talk is so commonplace that we tend to regard it as nothing more than a reflection of more important processes and developments. After all, we might say, what counts is not what people say about a candidate or about the electoral process, but whether and how they actually vote on election day.

Talk may be cheap, but it is nonetheless sociologically important. Its very ubiquity makes it an important part of the cement that binds the social order. Whatever the situations in which it occurs, talk is a primary means by which people sustain the world of objects in which they live. This is especially true of abstract objects, such as institutions, groups, values, principles, organizations, and the society as a whole, because we do not experience these abstract objects in quite the same way we do more tangible things. One can touch a chair and act toward it by sitting in it or using it as a footrest, but people experience and act toward abstract objects such as institutions, groups, and values primarily by talking about them.

Talk thrives on problems. In the preceding chapter, for example, we saw that aligning actions — specific forms of talk that center on actual or impending violations of rules and other forms of untoward conduct — arise in response to the problematic. People account for their conduct when others define it as problematic or when they think they are likely to do so. They disclaim when they have reason to think others will typify them in undesired ways. In these instances, talk is stimulated by a sense that something is or might be problematic about social interaction.

Talk is stimulated by a great variety of problems. One of the most common forms of talk, for example, takes the form of complaints, griping, and expressions of disaffection. The state of the economy, the dizzying pace of inflation, the presumed decline of the family, the corruption of politics, the faults of ethnic groups other than one's own, the disloyalties of supposed friends, the difficulties people have with their cars and appliances, the high cost of medical care — such complaints about life constitute a major topic of conversation, debate, and disagreement. People may occasionally say that the world is a delightful and perfect place, but they spend much of their conversational time talking about problems, troubles, difficulties, and disasters.

Talk shapes our view of social order, but people obviously do not discuss problems for the sake of social order. People gripe, criticize one another, worry about conspiracies, argue, and in other ways confront the problems they face, not in order to construct social reality, but simply because they face real or imaginary problems. Other people do nasty things, ambition and effort go unrewarded, children misbehave, employers and teachers treat us unfairly. In dealing with and especially talking about these matters, we give shape and substance to our ideals, our values, and our conceptions of how things work in the society and how we think they should work.

The way people talk about problematic events and situations is to some extent culturally and historically variable. One culture, for example, may encourage people to keep a stoic silence about personal problems, while another may encourage discourse about them. In addition, a single culture may present different faces at different times. In the 1950s, for example, a number of books and articles appeared that expressed concern about a growing American tendency toward conformity. Scholars such as David Riesman wrote books about the decline of *inner-direction* and the rise of *other-direction.* By the 1970s and 1980s, the attention of social critics shifted to *narcissism,* and they worried that Americans were becoming too wrapped up in themselves, too selfish, too inattentive to the needs and interests of others. Although there is no evidence that the culture itself changed dramatically over the intervening years, the way in which some social critics perceived problems did change. The focus of their discourse, however, remained on the problematic relationship between the person and the social order.[1]

Although variable from one era to another and from one society to another, the propensity to talk about the problematic is itself inherently human. It is when a line of conduct is blocked that the distinctively human capacity for its conscious, deliberate control comes clearly to the fore. People tend to take their activities for granted until something interferes with their capacity to attain their goals. They are apt to talk about the high cost of medical care when they experience it or see others whose savings have been eaten away by a major illness. They are apt to talk about the state of the economy when their aspirations for a better standard of living seem thwarted. Under such circumstances, talk is a major way by which people attempt to restore their lines of conduct or redefine their goals.

People do not talk only about problems, of course, nor merely about the present. Often they talk about the past — about important events, fond memories, where they used to live or work, their travels, and other matters in the recent or distant past. Such talk is also significant in constructing the social order and linking the person to it.

One of the more interesting forms of talk about the past is what Fred Davis has termed "decade labeling," that is, naming calendar decades and assigning dominant or significant characteristics to them.[2] "The Roaring Twenties," the "Turbulent Sixties," and the "Me Decade" of the 1970s are examples of this social practice of decade labeling. Led by the mass media of communication, who with relish conduct such discourse as the end of each decade nears, people tend to impute distinctive qualities and characteristics to calendar decades. Thus, they see the 1950s as a decade of boring conformity, the 1960s as a time of social turbulence and upheaval, and the 1970s as an era of excessive narcissism or self-preoccupation. Once a decade has been so labeled and constructed, people remember events or experiences that fit the label more readily than those that do not; thus, we remember the Vietnam War or the assassinations of President John Kennedy and of Martin Luther King as events of the sixties more readily than other, less turbulent events.

Although it would be erroneous to depict each of these three decades as objectively the same—there were particularly dramatic events during the 1960s, after all—neither should one assume that the collective construction of the decade is merely a reflection of objective "facts." As Davis points out, decade labels and characteristics seem to follow a kind of plot or "moral narrative." Thus, the boring, conformist decade of the 1950s (which is also remembered as the decade of the Cold War) is seen as having been followed by the upheavals and protests of the 1960s, when people are thought to have resisted the materialism, social inequality, and appetite for war of the preceding decade. And the 1970s and 1980s were constructed as a decade during which people withdrew from concern for the welfare of others or the society as a whole into their own families and selves, where they pursued essentially private purposes. Decades seem to be depicted in terms of qualities that reflect important values, beliefs, and aspirations, and not just in terms of what actually occurred.

Talk about decades gives shape and meaning to the present social world and one's position and experiences in it by linking it to the past. As the sixties receded, for example, the conception of that era as turbulent and socially unsettled could serve as justification for a retreat into more selfish and private pursuits. As the 1980s ended, teachers, members of the clergy, and social critics would use its characterization as "selfish" in their efforts to flog the public into more community-minded activities. Such talk, and the remembering of important events to which it gives rise, also links the person and his or her biography to the social order. When people remember where they were when President Kennedy was assassinated or when the first people landed on the Moon, they connect themselves to the social order they are engaged in constructing.[3]

Explaining Disorder

In addition to talking about problems or about the past, people also talk about social order itself, largely by trying to *explain* disorder. In a common type of everyday conversation, people try to explain to their own satisfaction the causes of a problematic situation, whether it is one in which they are participants or one they observe from a distance. Such situations take many forms, but they have in common the fact that people see them as problematic. A married couple who quarrel repeatedly; a riot or some other disturbance; the delinquency of one's own or a neighbor's child; seemingly inexplicable, bizarre conduct by a public official—each of these situations may be viewed as problematic by somebody, and each may be the topic of a conversation in which people seek to explain the nature and causes of the problematic occurrence or situation.

What makes a situation as a whole problematic? One mark of a problematic situation is that people see it as *disorderly,* as somehow falling outside the usual bounds of social experience. In nonproblematic situations, social order is taken for granted—the situation is well-enough defined that people are able to interact more or less routinely, even when some untoward event occurs that merits an account or a disclaimer. Problematic situations, in contrast, are those in which social order no longer is taken for granted. The definition of the situation as a whole is called into question and viewed as requiring special effort to comprehend and define what is taking place.

Not all problematic situations elicit efforts to explain what has gone wrong. A crowd that gathers on a street corner, for example, represents a problematic situation to a police officer, who must define the situation in order to decide what action to take. A sudden disturbance and rush toward the exits of a large auditorium likewise is a problematic situation to those present, who must define it in order to know whether to call the police or fire department, leave the building, or merely return quietly to their seats. In situations such as these, people define the situation in order to act in it, and explanations are of secondary importance.

People construct explanations when their chief focus is on disorder itself, which they perceive exists when they cannot make sense of a situation in terms of their customary stock of knowledge. In making sense of one another's acts, people ordinarily rely on their conceptions of typicality, probability, causality, means-ends relationships, normative requirements, and substantive congruency. In role making, for example, the stock of knowledge enables people to know what is expected of them and how others will respond to their conduct; in the giving of accounts and disclaimers, the stock of knowledge guides the selection of a disclaimer or the framing of an account. Social disorder exists when the usual processes of motive talk, accounting, and disclaiming do not sufficiently restore routine—when people persist in behaving in an undesirable way, for example, despite the fact that they have repeatedly been called to account for their conduct, or when they persist in behaving in ways that seem unlikely to lead to the goals they say they have.

So defined, social disorder is a construction of reality, a belief that things are for some reason not working the way they usually are thought to work, or a perception that something is amiss in social relations. A married couple, for example, may find themselves quarreling so frequently that the arguments themselves become a matter of concern, to others as well as to them. The frequent quarrels may be viewed as strange in several different ways—as atypical of this couple, considering their past history of marital adjustment; as harmful to their children; or as improbable in the light of their recent accomplishments and successes. On whatever grounds the perception of disorder is based, the effect is to impel a search for an explanation—some convincing statement of how this problem has been produced and what is likely to remedy the situation.

Quasi theorizing is a name for one process in which people construct such explanations.[4] It is a peculiar kind of explanatory process, however, for it runs counter to our commonsense notions about how we should find explanations. Ordinarily, we suppose, we begin with something to be explained and then seek a plausible account of its causes. In quasi theorizing, however, people tend to identify the cause *before* the effect and to construct the reality of the latter in terms of the former. In other words, they perceive a set of conditions that match the cause they have settled on, rather than finding a cause that can account for an observed set of conditions.

Consider the case of our quarreling couple. At a certain point in their relationship they may have come to the realization that they argue too much, that they don't very much like this state of affairs, and that something ought to be done. Having arrived at the point where they view their arguments as problematic, they seek to construct an explanation, a process that occurs in a series of steps. First, they agree on a *solution* to their problem. "We have to learn to communicate better," one may say. This statement is a tentative basis on which to construct the reality of their problem. If the other agrees, perhaps saying, "You're right, because sometimes I don't think you understand what I'm talking about," we have the beginnings of a quasi theory of communication as an explanation of their discord. In the next phase of the process, the reality of their problem is perceived in terms that mirror the solution on which they have agreed. In developing a quasi theory of communication, people will say that most of their disagreements *really* are problems of communication and understanding, that the issues about which they have quarreled—money, sex, life style—really are superficial, and that when the problem of learning to understand one another's views is solved, the things on which they agree will outweigh the few matters on which they still disagree. At some point in their discussion, they will invoke generalizations about the importance of communications in human affairs: "Most disagreements are caused by failures of communication," they may say, thus effectively subsuming their particular case under a more general rule.

At this point it is likely that the participants will buttress their explanation in two additional ways. First, the couple may begin to rewrite their past history of quarrels, reinterpreting them in the light of the new insight about communication. They will look to the past and find examples of other quarrels in which they thought they understood one another's points of view, but in fact did not. Second, they will introduce other values and beliefs in support of the explanation. They may agree, for example, that since they have remained together in spite of their quarreling, it must mean that they are really alike and in agreement, that they really belong together, and that their communication problem is only temporary.

Quasi theorizing thus produces an explanation of social disorder. It is a hopeful explanation (from the perspective of its creators) since it holds out the possibility that the disorder will yield to order if the solution is applied. It is not merely a simple explanation, of course, for in the process of explaining social disorder the quasi theory also creates its reality. The situation of the married couple is transformed from an undesirable and disorderly condition of too many quarrels into one of unnecessary quarrels caused by failure to communicate.

Paradoxically, the focus on explaining social disorder found in such forms of talk as quasi theorizing plays a role in sustaining a sense of social order, for it is in such problematic situations that important parts of the social stock of knowledge are given new life and sustained in memory. Such talk affords an opportunity for the standards of social order to be exercised, for familiar aphorisms to be used and once again proven "correct," and for important beliefs and values to be affirmed. Distinctions between right and wrong, the typical and the atypical, the desirable and the undesirable are preserved by *use*, and so it might be argued that occasional failures in social order play a positive role in its maintenance by affording such opportunities.[5]

Quasi theories, along with disclaimers, accounts, and other aligning actions discussed in the previous chapter, are also an important means whereby the members of a society reaffirm and preserve their culture—that is, the world of objects in which they live and with which they must contend. When people explain disorder, give accounts, or use disclaimers, they attend to and thus also reaffirm important cultural objects. For example, the value placed on "honesty" is reaffirmed by an attempt to explain why a child is persistently dishonest; likewise, an excuse or apology for dishonesty calls attention to "honesty" and asserts its significance. When people verbalize their values through aligning actions, they act toward them as objects and thus bring them to life even in circumstances where conduct has violated them. As a result, these objects continue to form part of the landscape—part of what people notice, attend to, feel they must respect, and take into account in their conduct.

The social construction of social order depends on this continual reaffirmation of culture. A sense of social order depends not only on people's capacity to coordinate their conduct or on their ability to understand and remedy the occasional problematic situation, but ultimately on the conviction that there is a reasonably stable reality that they can take for granted. Humans seem to want not only the sense that they can predict one another's conduct but also the sense that the world is a more or less familiar and stable place. To construct social reality, therefore, they must continually reaffirm culture.

Social Problems

Talk about disorder and problems is not limited to day-to-day occurrences in which people construct explanations of problematic situations. There is a larger, more macroscopic way in which social reality is constructed through discourse about *social problems*. A social problem may be defined as a collective object of concern, a condition felt to pertain to society as a whole or to important parts of it and believed to be both undesirable and changeable. Such a collective construction of reality defines some condition — such as divorce, crime, homelessness, or child abuse — as a serious problem worthy of attention by officials, the media, and the public. Definitions of specific conditions as social problems are advanced from time to time by various social groups, and they tend to demand and get a great deal of attention for a period of time before the public focus shifts to some other problem.[6]

Collective definitions of social problems do not simply reflect an underlying set of objectively problematic conditions. Poverty and homelessness have long existed in the United States, just as alcoholism and child abuse have long existed. Conditions such as these are "discovered" as social problems from time to time, and as attention to one problem wanes, another is discovered to take its place. Thus, for example, poverty was rediscovered as a social problem during the 1960s, the environment during the 1970s, and child abuse and homelessness during the 1980s.

To point to the parade of social problems that seems to characterize American society is not to deny their reality, nor to be callous to the pain and suffering of the afflicted. Poverty, environmental decay, child abuse, and homelessness are not figments of the collective imagination, but the objective conditions that underlie such problems are generally shrouded in many layers of social definition. As a result, problem definitions tend to undergo change. If poverty is now thought to result from discrimination and other barriers inhibiting access to economic opportunity, it was earlier thought to result from cultural deprivation, and, before that, to be a moral failing of the poor themselves. The present environmental movement, which emphasizes environmental quality, superseded an earlier conservation movement that focused on the wise use of natural resources. Similarly, at least some parental use of physical punishment that would have been tolerated in earlier eras might well be viewed today as child abuse.

Given the diverse problems that may be discovered from time to time, it is difficult to generalize about the conditions under which certain problems will be emphasized or about their fate once attention is paid to them. It is, however, useful to examine in some detail the beliefs and perspectives that generally characterize the collective definition of a problem, for these have an important bearing on how people construct social reality.

Collective conceptions of social problems have at least three important dimensions. First, such conceptions generally treat some major object as the core of the problem. Poverty is one such object; environment is another. Negatively defined objects such as poverty or crime represent a set of facts, conditions, and circumstances that are to be attacked and eliminated. Positively defined objects such as environment are themselves regarded as under attack, threatened, or endangered, and so must be defended and restored.

Social problems objects are the focus of attention and action in several ways. Intellectuals and scientists theorize about them and conduct research. Government agencies are legislated into existence in order to deal with them. They become important political symbols, usually lending themselves to diverse uses in the arena of political debate. Sometimes, social problems objects take on a nearly universal symbolic value, appearing almost everywhere in society. Whether the object is the environment, child abuse, or homelessness, it is a ubiquitous social presence. The nightly news is filled with talk about the problem of drugs and proposals to wage war on it. Governmental units such as the Environmental Protection Agency become the focus for the discussion of environmental issues. Political debate focuses on the urgent need for action to deal with problems such as poverty or homelessness, and charges of inaction or overreaction fly back and forth. Advertisers promote "natural foods" and put pictures of missing children on milk cartons.

The second important dimension of problem definitions is that human activity is treated as causally related to the problem. Neither fate, the intervention of the gods, nor other supernatural forces are accepted as the causes of social problems. Rather, problems are felt to exist because of what people do or (in some instances) are unable to do. Thus, the environment is said to be endangered because people pollute it; poverty exists because people are denied opportunities to better themselves.

Sometimes collective efforts to define social problems focus on the basic institutions of a society—alleging, for example, that poverty exists because it is in the interest of an exploitative capitalist class to perpetuate poverty and thus keep wages low, or that resource depletion and environmental degradation are caused by a wasteful system of production that must continually expand if it is not to collapse. More typically, however, people reject social problems claims that attribute causality to basic social institutions, preferring to focus on relatively superficial aspects of underlying conditions and to ignore the possibility that inherent faults of the social order are responsible for the problem. Thus, poverty is seen as society's failure to include everybody in its opportunity structure rather than as a basic feature of the operation of the social system.

The third aspect of a problem definition is that it emphasizes the possibility of human solutions. Since people produce problems, human solutions are both necessary and possible. Even though conceptions of social problems focus on difficult, negative, and undesirable conditions, there is a basic optimism in the assumption that such problems can be remedied. "Solution" is implicit in the very conception of an undesirable set of conditions as a "problem." Given appropriate changes in human conduct and the right social policy, it is assumed, the problem can be eliminated. Provide people with equal access to opportunity and poverty can be made to disappear; encourage people to stop polluting the environment and its quality will improve.

How do these elements of a problem bear on the view of social order held by the members of a society? In spite of their emphasis on human and social failings, definitions of social problems provide a society with *unifying* objects, thus offering a basis for agreement (even if temporary or superficial) on the nature of the good society. To agree that child abuse is an evil that ought to be eliminated is, of course, to admit that society is not all that it could be, but it is also to specify what a good society should be. However it is defined in relation to a specific social problem, the good society is an idealization of social order, a collective vision of the kind of society to be sought. Social problems objects thus provide at least the potential for unifying diverse interests, ideas, and aspirations.

There is something of a paradox in the unifying effects of social problems objects, for they generate disagreement as well as unity. The environment, for example, is an object of considerable controversy. Where jobs are at stake, environmental quality may seem a secondary consideration; and environmentalists and their opposition go to great lengths to portray one another respectively as utter fools more interested in birds than people and greedy villains more concerned with profits than the quality of life. Yet the environment is also a potent contemporary symbol to which environmentalists, advertisers, oil companies, and lumbering interests all pay homage, in slick advertising if not always in concrete behavior.

Social problems thus provide a supply of unifying objects — implicit conceptions of what the social order ought to be. Such conceptions are *ends,* goals toward which individuals can think of themselves as striving as they go about their everyday affairs. In this sense, social problems afford a means by which people can identify with the society and so interpret their own activities in valued social terms. Social problems reflect more consensus on ends, however, than on means. It is easier to achieve agreement that the environment should be protected or that homelessness should be ended than on how to achieve such goals. This lack of consensus on means is partly what gives the problems object its unifying effect. If people disagree on what will solve the problem, then each person can identify his or her conduct as a potential solution. General Motors can point to its catalytic converter for automobiles, while the average citizen takes pride in his or her participation in efforts to recycle newspapers and glass bottles.

That social problems are seen as both caused by and to be remedied by human efforts also contributes to an orderly conception of social reality. The conditions around which definitions of social problems are built — drugs, crime, violence, urban decay, pollution, homelessness — are reminders that the world is an uncertain and sometimes hostile place, and that the human capacity to mold the physical and social environment is limited. Such conditions threaten to undermine the human sense of purpose, control, and meaning. The inherent optimism of social problems definitions — the belief that solutions can be found — is a means of reaffirming faith in human control. We treat crime and pollution as problems, organizing actions against them, not only because they are objectively harmful but also because our strategies of control and solution help to preserve a belief in human mastery over the world.

A social problems conception of environmental problems, for example, helps to preserve faith in the power of technology. It is because of human technological prowess that some environmental problems, such as air pollution and resource depletion, exist. At the same time, such environmental problems lend themselves to the belief that they are amenable to technological solutions. Resource depletion? Pollution? Invent processes that will use abundant resources (cheap energy from the sun, for example) and that will control and render harmless (or, better, recycle) wastes now dumped into rivers. Such technological fixes to environmental problems may or may not succeed. They clearly do, however, help to sustain a conception of human beings as masters of their world, so technologically competent as to be able to endanger the environment, but also powerful enough to repair the damage they have done.

In creating definitions of social problems, as in other aspects of their lives, individuals and the groups to which they belong do not have equal chances to influence prevailing conceptions of problems. The frequent emergence of the welfare system as a social problem, for example, reflects neither a careful process of discussion nor the objective weighing of evidence pertaining to the welfare system. Instead, the efforts of politicians to arouse public concern about welfare abuses may be a calculated means of deflecting attention from their own more serious abuses of power or of enlisting the support of voters. Michael Lewis argues that the strong American emphasis on material success, coupled with the fact that most people do not really achieve it, tends to make the poor and their alleged moral failings a key part of our vision of the society.[7] The fact that some people are visibly worse off and the belief that they are so because they lack energy or motivation provide evidence for others that they are worthy and relatively successful. Indignation about a host of characteristics attributed to the poor and unsuccessful — welfare dependency, promiscuity, family deterioration, laziness — is a way of dramatizing their failure, and therefore also one's own success. Put simply, the social construction of the reality of social problems reflects the interplay of power and social interests and rarely is a benign or disinterested process.

SOCIAL ORDER AS COORDINATED ACTIVITY

The social construction of reality is an important aspect of social order, but it is not the only one. If we could stand outside society and look at the activities of its members, we would see their actions as regular, patterned, and coordinated. In this sense, social order is an objective reality. That is, several dispassionate scientific observers, provided they could agree on the proper techniques and concepts of observation, probably also would agree on what they see in society. They could agree on such matters as the distribution of income, the attitudes and values of different groups in the society, or how people raise their children.

When we stand *inside* the society as members, we do not have anything like a dispassionate and objective perspective. We see things from the standpoint of our own gender, social class, religion, age, or region, viewing reality not in a scientific way but from a commonsense perspective. For this reason the social order we perceive *is* largely a matter of the social construction of reality by the means we have shown. Yet, of course, the fact that we create and sustain social order by acting toward and talking about it does not mean that we can construct any reality we please. If I am destitute, it takes some doing to see myself as wealthy or life as fair — I must denounce worldly possessions and substitute something else, such as spiritual purity or moral virtue, in their place. To put this another way, the individual can neither control nor define away many conditions that result from the actions of others. As a child confronting my parents or as a consumer confronting the highly organized and powerful automobile industry when I go out to purchase a new car, I must contend with an external reality that in important ways is beyond my control.

Social order is thus a double reality. First, it is something we construct as we confront the external realities that face us and as we attempt to make sense of them. Second, it can be portrayed as coordinated social activity, as the total network of persons, groups, and organized activities that make up a society and that can, at least in theory, be described from the perspective of someone standing outside society.

A note of caution is necessary here. When sociologists talk about social order as coordinated activity they are apt to use the term *social structure*.[8] Structure is a useful metaphor in this context, for it conveys a sense of firmness and solidity in the organization of social life. This often is an apt image of what the individual is up against in life — other people, their activities, their wishes, their decisions, and their commands that are firm and unyielding to any resistance. Structure can also be a misleading metaphor, for it encourages us to forget about people and their acts and to concentrate only on the patterns we observe in their conduct and on the ways they are constrained. It is essential to remember that social structures do not act, that only people act, and that people act not simply in relation to and under the constraint of an objective social order, but in relation to the social order they think exists because of how they construct its reality.

We can describe several ways in which people coordinate their social activities and thus produce social order or social structure. The countless situations in the everyday lives of people who do not know one another and who are separated by time and space are nevertheless sewn together into a complex social fabric. Although we cannot describe it fully here, we can suggest some of its outlines.

Consider first such varied activities as banking transactions, religious services, lectures, wars, and congressional debates. Each of these is what Herbert Blumer has called a *joint action*—an organization of several different acts of many participants into a single whole. A joint action,

> while made up of diverse component acts that enter into its formation, is different from any of them and from their mere aggregation. The joint action has a distinctive character in its own right, a character that lies in the articulation or linkage as apart from what may be articulated or linked. Thus the joint action may be identified as such and may be spoken of and handled without having to break it down into the separate acts that comprise it.[9]

A lecture to a university class, for example, consists of many articulated acts of a professor and several students—speaking, listening, taking notes, asking questions, answering questions, and the like. The identifying mark of the joint action we call a "lecture" is not any one of the specific acts in which individuals engage, but their articulation with one another in a particular defined situation.

Just as we (both as social scientists and as participants in social activities) can speak of various joint actions and thus constitute them as objects in our experience, we similarly can speak of and constitute the collectivities that engage in such joint actions. We speak of bankers and their customers, priests and congregants, professors and students, the United States Congress, workers at General Motors, or Joe Smith's family, each of which is a named collectivity, comprised of, but also more than, the individuals that make it up. Just as the interlinkage of individual acts is what constitutes a joint action, so the interlinkage of individuals, rather than the specific persons themselves, is what constitutes a collectivity.

From the perspective of symbolic interactionists, society consists of extended interlinkages of joint actions and collectivities in which diverse people and activities are interconnected over space and time. If we examine a society as a whole, we find that banking transactions, religious services, university lectures, wars, congressional debates, and other joint actions, along with the collectivities in which they take place, are linked with one another in complex and highly systematic ways, whether viewed at a particular point in the history of a society or over the course of its development from one time to another. Economic, religious, educational, military, and political institutions — each of which is itself a complex network of joint actions — are related to one another in a variety of ways. Religious beliefs justify economic activities, for example, and political affairs are influenced by military activity.

How is this complex of joint actions, collectivities, and institutions held together? How are the activities of one sector coordinated with those of another? What makes for the seeming persistence of patterned and stable joint actions, collectivities, and institutions over time? The coordination of a whole society and its component parts and activities rests on a number of important social processes, only a few of which can be considered here. From a social psychological point of view, the concepts of problem solving, negotiated order, horizontal linkages, and careers are particularly useful in accounting for the interlinkages among joint actions, collectivities, and institutions.

Problem Solving

Sociologists generally emphasize the patterned and repetitive nature of social life, stressing that the vast majority of problems that arise in everyday social life have predetermined solutions, which have been found by previous generations and codified in the social stock of knowledge. In this view, the typifications, causal propositions, and other forms of knowledge we discussed in Chapter 5 are more or less routinely applied, and nothing much is new or different in day-to-day life.

If any activity could be accurately so characterized, it would occur in the small and isolated societies of the past in which there was a stable relationship between people and their environment, few options for individuals to depart from routine patterns of behavior, and few events that might disrupt everyday routine. There is considerable doubt that any society has ever been quite so stable; certainly modern societies are not. Although students and critics of contemporary society probably vastly exaggerate the amount of social change that is underway, as well as its potentially disruptive consequences, it is clearly more accurate to portray modern society as one in which people confront a series of problematic situations in which they must be inventive than as one dominated by numbing routine. Much of modern life is not clearly and routinely prescribed, but is, instead, left open and negotiable. As Blumer argued, these areas of "unprescribed conduct are just as natural, indigenous, and recurrent in human group life as are those areas covered by preestablished and faithfully followed prescriptions of joint action."[10]

Symbolic interactionists see a problem-solving orientation as inherent in the symbolic organization of human conduct. Because people are not tied to a limited set of responses to an environment, but must instead interpret their world in order to respond creatively to it, the world is inherently open rather than closed, and susceptible to definition in terms of the problematic rather than fixed and immutable. A moment's reflection will suggest the extent to which attention to problems is a constant feature of everyday life. Those occasions on which activities are utterly routine are few and far between. More commonly, problems of diverse kinds arise and are solved in everyday activities. Cars won't start, people fail to show up for meetings, tasks seem difficult to understand, others' feelings are hurt, parties have to be organized, ball games are canceled and rescheduled, unexpected deaths occur, marriages get into difficulty, people disappoint us, employers are unfair, babies get sick, and so the list could be extended into a catalogue of the problems of everyday life.

To take this perspective is to argue that social order depends in part on the joint orientation of people to the solution of everyday, practical problems. A great deal of joint action, in this view, consists of the articulation of individuals' lines of conduct around problems that confront them. Some institutions and organizations, of course, are particularly concerned with organizing responses to problems; science, medicine, the other helping and teaching professions, and safety and security forces are noticeably problem-centered. Their everyday work routines regularly call upon them to respond to conditions that others define as problematic. But even in the most routine activities and occupations, difficulties must frequently be overcome and problems solved.

People's efforts to *solve* their problems in a practical way are just as important to social order as is their routine conduct in culturally established and predictable lines. What, after all, is a family, which is a social unit we might well consider fundamental to social order? To characterize it as a set of roles, rules, and social relationships focusing on the bearing and raising of children is sociologically appropriate. To treat it as an object constituted by people's talk about it is also accurate. Yet people in their everyday lives experience and conceive of their families to a great extent as a series of situations in which they confront and solve practical problems. In this sense, a family (depending on one's age, religion, ethnicity, social class, and the like) is changing diapers on a child who ought to be toilet trained, managing to feed a family on a limited budget, achieving some kind of mutually satisfactory sexual adjustment with another person, coping with the occasional rebelliousness of children (or of oneself or one's spouse), deciding whether to buy a new television set or how to pay for expensive medical care for a chronically ill child, and responding to a host of other problems. A family is a set of situations to be confronted and problems to be solved.

The propensity to organize in the face of the problematic is fundamental to social order, not any particular organized solutions. As Blumer reminded us, the standard solutions to commonly experienced human problems, as well as those solutions invented in response to situations in which there are few prescriptions for conduct, depend on the processes of indicating and interpreting objects in the environment. A food server taking the last of many orders during a busy day, cleaning tables, serving food, and making change is engaged in a process of social interaction that depends on meaning, objects, and interpretation, however routine it may seem, every bit as much as a family organizing to cope with the death of its breadwinner. It is a crucial fact that

> the meanings that underlie established and recurrent joint action are themselves subject to pressure as well as to reinforcement, to incipient dissatisfaction as well as to indifference; they may be challenged as well as affirmed, allowed to slip along without concern as well as subjected to infusions of new vigor. . . . It is the social process in group life that creates and upholds the rules, not the rules that create and uphold group life.[11]

Negotiated Order

In the standard sociological vision, social order seems to flow spontaneously from the fact that people obey rules, play their roles appropriately, and use standard procedures for dealing with the problems of everyday life. Coordination is seen as a consequence of adequate socialization, for if people have mastered their roles and the relevant stock of knowledge, their activities will mesh smoothly — men will know how and when to be fathers, breadwinners, or husbands, and their conduct will be coordinated with that of women as well as with other men. When, for one reason or another, conduct fails to be appropriate to a role, mechanisms of social control will come into play: People will be sanctioned for their departures from the norms, and efforts will be made to resocialize them.

However straightforward such a vision may seem, it scarcely does justice to what actually happens in everyday life. Coordination and social order are as much the results of people's self-conscious efforts to produce them as they are the spontaneous, unconscious products of their activities. Everywhere in social life we see bargaining, negotiation, deliberation, agreements, temporary arrangements, suspensions of the rules, and a variety of other procedures in which the accomplishment of social order and coordinated activity is a deliberate undertaking. The life of a middle-class family in American society, for example, seems well described as an effort to negotiate an orderly set of relationships among people who sometimes have conflicting interests, competing demands on their time, and divided loyalties. Keeping peace among the children, finding time to do things around the house as well as to earn a living, securing agreement on where the family will take a vacation or whether the husband's or wife's job will take precedence in determining where the family will live — organizational tasks such as these are the stuff of everyday life.

If much of human group life is oriented toward the solution of practical problems, the coordination of individual and group activities undoubtedly is among the major problems to be faced in any society or organization. Negotiation is one of the most characteristic human responses to such problems. The concept of the *negotiated order* was developed by Anselm Strauss and his associates to account for how the ongoing activities of a complex organization, such as a hospital, are coordinated so as to pursue its paramount goal, helping sick people to get better.[12] Although the concept pertains explicitly to organizational life — hospitals, schools, corporations, government agencies, universities, and the like — it can, as Peter Hall suggests, be extended to the societal level, where it provides one useful model of what social order is like and how it is attained.[13]

Theoretically, organizations such as hospitals coordinate the activities of their members by inventing rules and formal procedures. These specify the activities of various personnel so that they can coordinate their efforts on behalf of their patients. They describe duties, obligations, rights, limitations, and other requirements pertaining to the various roles that are played in the organization. They specify who has what kind of authority over whom, and presumably give members a fairly comprehensive picture of the work that is to be done.

In actuality the situation is considerably more complicated. Even though all members may agree in theory on the abstract value of making sick people well, they conduct their everyday organizational lives amidst a myriad of details that often seem remote from this lofty objective. The goal is a sort of organizational cement, symbolically useful but of little concrete guidance in the day-to-day activity of nurses, physicians, dietitians, orderlies, and others who must coordinate their efforts on the patients' behalf. In addition, individuals and subunits may hold a number of additional values or goals that from time to time take precedence over the chief goal of the organization. Nurses and physicians are interested in their pay and social status as well as in curing the sick; department heads are apt to think of their domain as more beneficial or important than others, and so compete with one another for a larger budget; physicians are private practitioners and researchers as well as hospital affiliates, and so must divide their time; some support personnel, such as orderlies and aides, often are overworked, asked to do jobs that go beyond their training, and are badly underpaid; and so the list of complicating conditions could be extended.

The important point is that in the ongoing operation of an organization, no simple, easily achieved coordination of activities can be found. There are too many competing aims, individual interpretations of organizational goals, divided loyalties, internal disagreements over resources, and other complexities. Although organizations formulate rules and procedures to cope with such matters, no set of rules will be absolutely clear about lines of authority, responsibilities, or rights. Constitutions, bylaws, procedural rules, "the book" — these apparently unambiguous devices for the coordination and regulation of activity usually are far from definitive. No set of rules can cover all possible contingencies, and so, by common consent, rules are broken from time to time, even by people pledged to uphold them. Because organizations experience turnover in personnel, no one is likely to know all the rules that are theoretically in force – sometimes rules are made to deal with situations and then forgotten as new personnel and new problems arrive on the scene.

How, therefore, is social order accomplished? Strauss's answer is that an ongoing process of negotiation takes place, one in which agreements, contracts, and understandings among various members of the organization, made from time to time and occasionally renewed or allowed to lapse, serve as the basis for coordinating activities. Since rules may be ambiguous or even lacking, members agree on certain interpretations, exceptions, or new rules. If jurisdictions seem to overlap, as between physicians and nurses, participants will seek to develop understandings about who is entitled to do what and when they are supposed to do it. If the responsibilities of several categories of personnel directly responsible for patient care – registered nurses, licensed practical nurses, nurses' aides, and orderlies, for example – are ambiguous, working agreements will be created to specify approximate lines of responsibility.

Negotiation does not, of course, occur in the same ways in all contexts, nor is its importance equal in different kinds of organizations. On the basis of research in public schools and a review of other studies of negotiation, Hall and Hall suggested a number of circumstances that influence how much negotiation occurs and how important it will be.[14] First, they argued, where teamwork and coordination are required and where activities are public and involve some novelty, there will be more negotiation than under circumstances where people do their work alone and where it is very routinized. Special education teachers, for example, who move from classroom to classroom or who must coordinate their work with that of regular classroom teachers find they must engage in more negotiation than regular teachers, whose work is isolated in one classroom and tends to be quite routine. The propensity for negotiation is also fostered by organizational size and complexity (the larger and more complex the organization, the more likely there will be competing subunits that must negotiate); by the broader dispersion of power and feelings of equality or efficacy (teachers are more likely to negotiate with one another than with superiors); by the delegation of authority by the organization's leadership; by actual or planned changes in the organization that require existing arrangements to be renegotiated; and by the presence of professionals (such as physicians or psychologists) who think of themselves as autonomous and therefore as entitled to negotiate the terms and conditions of their work.

Negotiation is ubiquitous, not only *within* the many organizations that make up the society as a whole, but at the societal level as well. Given the fact that a complex society such as the United States or Canada is made up of regions, ethnic and religious groups, social classes, organizations, groups, social movements, and many other units with like, common, and competing interests, social order depends on the ongoing negotiation of orderly relationships among them. Two elements of this societal level of negotiation are especially noteworthy.

- *Self-interest.* Given the multitude of units and individuals that make up a society, the interests of particular units or individuals are rarely felt (by them) to coincide with one another, and often not with those of the society as a whole.
- *Power.* Individuals and collectivities are not equal in their capacity to influence one another or to pursue their interests successfully.

The pursuit of self-interest, along with the need to negotiate between competing interests, is inherent in the problem of maintaining social order. Self-interest manifests itself in a variety of ways and contexts. In the hospital organization, for example, physicians may feel greater loyalty to their profession than to the particular hospital in which they have privileges. In the larger society, Roman Catholics may find it in their interest to support state aid to private schools, while Protestants oppose such assistance, perhaps on constitutional grounds, or perhaps only because it will aid Catholics. City politicians may oppose changes in the distribution of state or federal assistance to cities if such changes will reduce their control over how the money is spent or eliminate its value as political patronage. In each of these cases, various processes of negotiation are employed to reach agreement among contending parties.

In the course of their negotiations, individuals and groups attempt to exercise power over one another—that is, to bring to the negotiations whatever resources they can in order to achieve their goals at least cost or without the consent of others. The resources of power are varied, ranging from naked force to the control of information and knowledge, the dispensation of rewards by controlling jobs and financial resources, and the manipulation of symbols. However power is exercised, and no matter by whom, it is an important determinant of social order. It influences who will be able to bargain successfully, whose definitions of the rules will prevail, and how individuals and collectivities will define and pursue their self-interest.

To provide a full analysis of the negotiation of social order in the political process, or of the nature of the groups that form any given society as well as their interests and the distribution of power, is far beyond the scope of a book in social psychology. What must be stressed here is that power, negotiations, and self-interest are central to interactionist conceptions of social order, and that such phenomena are important concerns of social psychology. When we examine the situations people define, the roles they make and take, the objects toward which they act, and the routine and problematic circumstances they confront, we discover that these elements of social life are inextricably bound up with inequalities of power, the pursuit of individual and collective interests, and the ongoing negotiation of social order, whether in any of the numerous units that make up a society or at the societal level itself.

One cannot, for example, understand either the dynamics of American society as a whole or the lives and selves of individual members without grasping the patterns of competition, conflict, and cooperation that have developed among various ethnic and religious groups. In ethnically and religiously diverse societies such as the United States and Canada, a negotiated order among such groups is a crucial aspect of the structure of the society that shapes individual lives.

Americans, for example, have historically taken three differing approaches to the negotiation of relationships among ethnic groups and to their status in the society as a whole. One, which was perhaps the dominant view during the nineteenth century, assumed that the United States was fundamentally an Anglo-Saxon culture, and that newly arriving immigrants should adopt this culture as quickly as possible. A second, which came into favor later, argued that the United States was a "melting pot" that would, through a mixture of citizens of diverse origins, produce a new, hybrid culture. And the third, which also emerged as the tides of immigration swelled in the late nineteenth and early twentieth century, was based on a belief in a pluralistic society in which no group would be forced to abandon its culture and in which all would be free to live as they saw fit.

Each of these views of ethnicity constitutes a different negotiating position on the basis of which groups relate to one another and to the society as a whole. If, for example, those who are white, Anglo-Saxon, and Protestant believe that their culture is the "true" American culture and that other groups ought to assimilate it, they are likely to act to persuade or coerce others into doing so. They will seek to "Americanize" immigrants, by which they mean that immigrants should learn and subscribe to their definitions of what constitutes American culture. Such efforts occur, for example, when groups try to have English declared as the nation's "official" language. Often efforts of this kind are stimulated by large-scale immigration into a particular area, which arouses in existing groups a sense that their position is being threatened. This occurred dramatically in South Florida, which experienced significant immigration of Spanish-speaking people from Cuba beginning in the 1960s.

In recent decades, the vigorous and self-conscious pursuit of civil, economic, and political rights by African Americans has helped to reinforce consciousness of ethnic affiliation and identity in the United States. During the same period, pluralism has also gained a wider measure of support. In place of an emphasis on assimilation or on the melting pot has come a greater emphasis on the positive aspects of ethnic heritage, the contributions of each ethnic group to the society as a whole, and the right to maintain ethnic differences. Furthermore, it is likely that the growth of ethnic pluralism improved the negotiating position of other groups, such as gays and lesbians, in their quest for social redefinition by making the existence of diversity seem more normal.

The position of the individual in the society or any of its constituent units cannot be grasped apart from the negotiated order of ethnic, religious, and other groups that exists at any given time. For African Americans, for example, the growth of ethnic pride probably has been of considerable aid in combating a historic problem of self-hatred and its consequent sapping of individual and social energies. For Jews, a greater acceptance of pluralism in the society has meant an increasing willingness to be openly Jewish and therefore different from the putative American cultural "mainstream." To take a different example, white males currently construct their conceptions of self under circumstances very different from what they once were. White Protestant men once could assume that they were and had the right to be the central and dominant figures in the society. Now they have lost the sure sense of ownership and entitlement they once possessed, and they often feel themselves under attack from African Americans, women, and minority groups of all kinds.

Horizontal and Vertical Linkages

Negotiation does not occur only *within* particular organizations as people with formally specified responsibilities and particular interests negotiate the actual day-to-day operation of factory, university, or hospital. In a complex society, there are many linkages or interconnections *between* organizations, groups, social classes, and institutions. Professionals and their associations are linked to clients on one side and to the organizations in which they work on the other side. Organizations that manufacture basic products like steel are connected to other organizations that utilize these materials to manufacture washing machines, automobiles, and other consumer goods. Companies producing goods are linked to those that wholesale or retail them. Small groups such as families, as well as large entities such as political parties, are linked to a variety of other units: work places, communities, governments, churches, schools, and the like.

These linkages are both horizontal and vertical. Social units are linked *horizontally* because individuals are simultaneously members of different units. I am at the same time a professor in a university and a husband and father within my family. It is likely that what I do in one context will have a bearing on what I do in the other. The amount of time I devote to my family, for example, sets some limits on the amount of time I can devote to my job. Moreover, people are linked one to another in personal networks of friendship or acquaintance that often fall outside organizational or group boundaries. These ties provide channels of communication and thus part of the coordination of activity in everyday life.[15]

Sociologists have treated this kind of linkage in terms of such concepts as role conflict and role strain, and the chief question of social psychological interest is how individuals manage their personal economies of time and energy to cope with the competing demands of different social units in which they participate. Groups and organizations make demands on individuals, who must decide how to respond — how much time to allocate to particular organizations or activities, for example, or which activity to give priority. Frequently the individual's response is worked out in various negotiations. The employee who wants to put family first will have to negotiate or renegotiate a place in the work organization, finding some way to retain a job while putting in less vigorous effort (and probably also settling for fewer rewards from the job). The spouse who wants to devote more time to work will have to secure the cooperation of his or her family.

Horizontal linkages between social units also exist because such units participate in various exchange relationships. Thus, companies sell products and raw materials to one another. Charitable organizations, such as the United Way, contract with employers to run charity campaigns and to have deductions made from their employees' paychecks. In these and countless other linkages between organizations, negotiations take place *between* one organization and another. More precisely, the representatives of such organizations negotiate and reach agreements about how their organizations will interact.

The study of the patterned interconnections among larger social units in a society is not the main concern of social psychologists. Even so, such matters are not beyond the scope of interests of social psychologists. This is because when we think of large organizations interacting with one another, the actual negotiation that takes place is between individuals and groups of people, not between organizations as such. A company, a state legislature, and a political party are not acting entities. Organizations do not act; people do. Although one need not study the actual points of contact between organizations to see how they are linked to one another in general terms, frequently the study of how real people in differing organizations actually deal with one another is very revealing about how negotiation between organizations takes place.

Social units are also linked *vertically* — or hierarchically — because the activities of some control or strongly influence the activities of others. Harvey Farberman provides a fascinating illustration of such vertical linkages, as well as of the way organizations interact with one another, in his study of the automobile industry.[16] This study examines linkages among automobile manufacturers, new car dealers, and used car dealers. It is a study of a context of organizational negotiation where relationships among social units are very unequal, with the manufacturers dictating a set of conditions within which others in the industry must operate.

Farberman examines how certain illegal operations in the retail and wholesale automobile business are linked to the operating policies of automobile manufacturers. According to Farberman, the auto manufacturers force their dealers to earn profits on new car sales in a high-volume, low-margin operation. The manufacturers want to sell a large number of cars in order to realize their own economies of scale, and they force their dealers to maintain large inventories of cars and pressure them to sell them at a slim margin of profit.

This is costly to dealers, not only because the per car profit is low, but also because they incur large interest costs in maintaining large inventories of expensive cars. Thus the dealer has to keep the cars and the cash moving in order to stay afloat.

These conditions, Farberman shows, foster a number of illegal practices. Faced with limited profits on new car sales, dealers cheat on repairs – charging for repairs not done, submitting false warranty claims, overcharging the customer – as a way of increasing profits. Moreover, they must also quickly turn over their inventory of used cars taken in trade on new cars in order to generate the flow of cash they need to maintain their new car inventories. To manage this turnover, dealers hire used car managers whose job is to retail the good used cars taken in trade and to sell the remainder at wholesale. The latter cars are sold to used car operations, which themselves will sell some cars at retail and wholesale the rest.

The process of disposing of used cars sets the stage for additional illegal activities. First, used car dealers find that they must pay kickbacks to the new car dealers' used car managers in order to be sure of an adequate flow of used cars to their operations. This practice is overlooked by new car dealership owners, even though it costs them profits, because they desperately need the cash. Second, the used car dealer needs a ready source of cash with which to pay the kickbacks – since one can't pay an illegal kickback by check. This cash is generated in part through the practice of the "short sale." The customer is charged a certain amount for a car, but only part of that amount is written on the bill of sale. The customer pays the difference in cash "under the table." This practice gives the used car dealer the cash needed to pay kickbacks (it is tax-free as well). It also saves the customer some money, since the sales tax on the car is based on the price of the car listed on the bill of sale.

The system is complex, involving linkages between several different organizational units – manufacturers, new car dealers, used car dealers, and customers. These organizational linkages are not abstract, of course, but are established by real people, each with self-interests as well as the interests of their organization in mind. Each negotiates on behalf of self or organization, and in the process forges linkages – in this case involving criminal acts – between them. Note that the definitions of the situation on the basis of which people act at one level may have little connection with the definitions that exist at other levels. The customer who sees an opportunity to save a few dollars on the sales tax through a short sale probably has no idea of the place this act has in the larger, vertical linkages of various levels of the automobile industry.

Careers

A fourth way in which joint actions are coordinated and organized at various levels involves the temporal dimension of human activity. Herbert Blumer has pointed out that "any instance of joint action, whether newly formed or long established, has necessarily arisen out of a background of previous actions of the participants."[17] Just as an orientation toward the solution of everyday problems and the ongoing negotiation of social order link people horizontally and vertically, joint actions are linked temporally. The concept of *career* captures the nature of this linkage.

In the simplest sense, the background of earlier experience out of which any joint action arises consists of previous instances of such joint action. Today's transaction with a banker is much like yesterday's; managing a religious service is pretty much the same from one week to the next; the routines of dealing with one patient are similar to those for dealing with another for a physician and office staff. This temporal character of social activity is important to social order, for the recognition of various activities as typical of similar activities carried on at other times is essential to preserving a sense of orderly joint action.

The concept of career points to the fact that the temporal organization of activity runs deeper than merely the recognition of similarity between past and present joint actions. We usually think of a career in relation to an occupation or profession, where it denotes the course of an individual's expected and actual occupational activities from one stage to another, often involving increasing responsibility and pay. Careers have timetables—that is, members are expected to spend a certain amount of time in each stage and then to advance to the next stage within a limited period of time. A new member of a university faculty, for example, typically spends six years as an assistant professor, at which point he or she is either given tenure and promoted or let go.

Sociologists have come to use the concept of career somewhat more broadly to denote the temporal sequencing of joint actions in any sphere of life and not merely in reference to occupations. Thus, while we can talk about the careers of teachers, automobile workers, or musicians, we can also discuss the shorter-term careers of people in such institutions as mental hospitals, universities, and military service, in deviant activities like theft or prostitution, in political affairs or public life, in love affairs and friendships, and in a great variety of other activities. In essence, this broadened concept of career points to the fact that people organize their own participation in joint actions, as well as organizing their interpretations of others' actions, with an eye on various points in the past and future.

The joint action of a patient and physician in the latter's office provides a good illustration of the concept and its import for social order. For the patient, a particular encounter with a physician is not simply an isolated, single situation in which the task is to make an appropriate patient role. This particular encounter is embedded in a temporal sequence of joint actions in at least two ways. First, this office visit occurs between past and future visits, for each medical problem itself has a career around which treatment is organized. The patient interprets what is done today within the framework of what has already happened and what is thought will take place next. Second, this visit, as the others, constitutes a joint action that is temporally connected with joint actions involving people other than the physician. Before seeking medical help, one is likely to discuss the matter with family or friends, considering the potential impact of the news one might receive from the physician. Will the prognosis be favorable or unfavorable? Will an illness interfere with plans already made? Will the patient be alive a year from now? After the visit, the patient considers the implications of the news for his or her future.[18]

The physician also views the illness in terms of its career, or "course," and sees a particular visit in that context — as part of an effort to diagnose what is wrong, or as an occasion to deliver effective treatment or assess the efficacy of treatment. The physician also views this patient in relation to patients seen earlier and later in the day, for each day has its temporal flow. And an encounter or a series of encounters with a particular patient also is an event in the professional career of the physician. Perhaps this patient has a rare disease that will offer the physician an opportunity not only to treat the patient but also to do research that will further a promising career. Or, perhaps this patient is one more routine case in a career filled with uninteresting and unchallenging cases, and thus a source of confirmation for the physician's growing feeling that medicine hasn't turned out to be as exciting as hoped or anticipated.

One reason for the importance of careers to social order is that people regularly develop expectations about what they will be doing at various points in their lives. Patients expect that they will recover over a course of treatment. Physicians expect that their incomes will grow as their reputations increase. Professors expect that they will be promoted to higher ranks, and they have a fairly precise idea of when that should occur. Psychiatrists expect that mental patients will exhibit a predictable sequence of reactions to the course of therapy. People involved in love affairs expect increasing degrees of intimacy with the passage of time.

The social order, thus, is supported by a framework of expectations geared to the passing of time. Individuals are tied to the social order because they organize their efforts in relation to such expectations. Social order thus rests, in part, on individuals' biographies — on their ordering of joint actions in a variety of contexts in relation to their own careers. To see a society as a set of interlocked joint actions is thus to portray a set of conditions across time as well as among people at any given time.

Socialization Redux

Career expectations are not necessarily fulfilled. A sociologist in his or her twenties who looks forward to promotion to professor by age thirty-five may not be able to achieve this goal. The aspiring actress may never get the break that propels her into a series of increasingly successful roles. The young baseball catcher who starred in the minor leagues may never perform as well when he reaches the majors, and even if he does, no spot may be open for him.

Career expectations run up against a variety of objective realities: inadequate performance, aging, limited opportunities, injury, economic changes, wars, and the like. When this happens and the individual encounters circumstances that make it impossible to realize career expectations, he or she must make adjustments. The individual who has embarked on an occupational career with certain mobility aspirations and who has built a self-conception around them, must now remake the self in accord with new realities. The position actually attained must be reinterpreted, viewed no longer as a stepping stone on the way to the top but as a satisfactory accomplishment in its own right.

In a study of professional hockey players and orchestra musicians, Robert Faulkner detected a number of themes that people invoke as they come to terms with immobility.[19] Seemingly locked into a particular position, the individual can emphasize its benefits against the costs that would have to be paid for moving on and up. "I like it here, and going somewhere else for a better job would involve too much politics and too much scrambling," one might say. One may redefine one's expectations for esteem on the job, expressing satisfaction at doing a good job and giving up the quest for the peak of one's profession. One may redefine the job so that it looms less large in one's life, giving more importance to family. "I could do better," one might say, "but my spouse and children would suffer if I tried."

The individual is not the only one who must adjust to the realities of limited opportunity within the organization, for it is a problem for the organization itself. Just as individuals become oriented toward progression through a career, organizations rely on those expectations to motivate individuals' efforts. As individuals find their horizons closing in and learn to make their adjustments, their reduced aspirations and commitments become organizational problems. The university, for example, must find a way to maintain the loyalty and effort of faculty members whose high aspirations have been thwarted, just as baseball teams must win the efforts of all their players, not just the stars. Thus, the resocialization of individuals to confront new circumstances is not only an individual problem but also one that affects organizational success.

Just as important, these examples suggest that socialization is associated with orderly *participation* in social life just as much as with *preparation* for it. The adult confronts many circumstances that demand new learning. From the individual perspective, resocialization—by adjusting to limited success or by learning new skills—is a matter of adjustment to life circumstances. From an organizational perspective, successful resocialization is just as crucial to the organization's efforts to maintain itself. Indeed, from the perspective of social order, socialization in adulthood is as crucial to the coordination of social activities as is the learning of basic knowledge and social skills in childhood.

INSTITUTIONAL AND COLLECTIVE BEHAVIOR

As we have sought to make clear, symbolic interactionists place considerable emphasis on the ways people respond to problematic situations. In addition to the topics we have already discussed, there is one more important form of conduct in problematic situations that demands attention and without which our portrayal of social order is incomplete — *collective behavior.*

Sociologists customarily distinguish between *institutional behavior* and *collective behavior.* Institutional behavior is a term applied to conduct that is well organized by the expectations associated with various roles and by the organizations and situations in which those roles are made. The conduct of parents and children in the family or of workers and managers in the factory are examples of institutional behavior. The joint actions that occur in such contexts are familiar, the problematic situations that arise are more or less predictable, and there is agreement on how people ought to act in various circumstances. Collective behavior, in contrast, is a term applied to conduct in situations that are not well defined, that represent novel and often challenging circumstances for which routine joint actions are not available. The behavior of various kinds of crowds, responses to disaster, public opinion, and social movements are examples of collective behavior.

The distinction between institutional and collective behavior actually is less absolute than these definitions and examples make it seem. An orientation to the problematic is an intrinsic part of social order itself. Even when we consider the most ordered and routine aspects of social life, problems continually arise, including the very basic problem of negotiating orderly social relationships. Even routine forms of conduct depend on people's ability to maintain meaning — to preserve orderly definitions of situations and the objects and people they contain. Thus there is an element of collective behavior in many of the routine situations of everyday life.

Just as attention to the problematic is an important part of the creation and maintenance of social order, so, too, the phenomena usually associated with collective behavior cannot be grasped except in relation to the organization of a society. Many of the specific instances of crowd behavior, for example, in which unexpected and unusual events take place, start off as relatively routine instances of joint action. A panic that develops in an audience confined in an auditorium when a fire breaks out, for example, or a hostile reaction to police by those present when one of their number is arrested constitute forms of collective behavior occurring in situations that are themselves embedded in organized contexts of social interaction. A social movement, which may be defined as a conscious effort to bring about (or prevent) change in the social order, can be viewed by its members and opposition alike only in relation to the social order it seeks to revise (or maintain). Indeed, the activities of members of movements rely on the same techniques of negotiation and stock of knowledge as those used by others in the society.

John Lofland has suggested several criteria that help distinguish between what is and is not collective behavior:[20]

- Collective behavior entails the redefinition of a situation from routine to problematic, so that people begin to feel that things are not as they usually are.
- Participants agree that the situation *must* be defined.
- The redefinition involves a relatively large number of people, not just one or a few.
- Collective behavior is accompanied by increased emotional arousal.

As Lofland suggests, our typical attitude in everyday life is that things are going pretty much as they usually go and that "nothing unusual is happening."[21] In collective behavior this attitude changes, and people come to believe they are faced with unusual circumstances that *demand* unusual actions. Such redefinitions occur many times in everyday life, of course, but do not constitute collective behavior: People experience personal crises, they are mugged on the streets, their marriages fall apart, they lose their jobs. Collective behavior requires a fairly large number of people as, for example, when a crowd is roused to a state of anger and then goes on an angry rampage. Although emotion is an important aspect of much collective behavior, there is more to the matter than fear, anger, or ecstasy. In situations of collective behavior, people do not abandon rationality and simply embrace crowd emotions; rather, emotional arousal gives force and direction to their collective actions.

Collective behavior is a matter of degree rather than all or nothing. The emergence of a belief that something very unusual is taking place is the minimum requirement for collective behavior to get under way. However, various forms of collective behavior involve differing numbers of people, who are emotionally aroused in different ways and to varying degrees, and whose agreement with one another is variable in extent and duration. This last point is especially important. As Ralph Turner and Lewis Killian point out, there is often an "illusion of unanimity" in crowds and other forms of collective behavior. That is, the collectivity *appears* to be united in its definition of the situation and those members of the collectivity who are not emotionally aroused or who do not share the emerging definition of the situation think they are exceptions.[22]

Collective and institutional behavior are characterized by the same essential processes. Roles are taken and made, objects indicated, and situations defined. Self is central, both as a process of behavior and an object of conduct. The accounts and disclaimers that can be observed in routine interaction in families and stores also can be seen in such forms of collective behavior as riots or social movements. Indeed, the typifications and other parts of the stock of knowledge that are the basis of routine social interaction also are central to collective behavior.

What is crucially different about the two forms of conduct is the extent to which objects, roles, meanings, and definitions of the situation are taken for granted by participants. Behavior is institutional when people know in advance the identities of the others with whom they are going to interact, when they bring to the situation a definition they assume others share, and when the other aspects of a situation are taken for granted as routine and normal. To the extent that objects, roles, meanings, and definitions of the situation are *emergent* — when their existence is not taken for granted but depends on the self-conscious efforts of people to create them — we have collective behavior.

Crowds and Panic

The crowd is perhaps the form of human association most commonly associated with collective behavior. A crowd is a particular kind of collectivity, one that does not possess the degree of organization and self-consciousness of a group or organization, but whose members nonetheless have a collective sense of themselves as belonging to a unit. According to Turner and Killian, crowds are marked by a number of features.[23] First, they exist in ambiguous or undefined situations in which there are no clear-cut guidelines for conduct or in which there is not even a grasp of the objects toward which conduct will occur. Second, this ambiguity is accompanied by a sense of urgency — a general feeling that something must be done to resolve the situation. Third, the mood and imagery of the situation are rapidly communicated among those present, who indicate to one another the urgency of the situation and what they feel ought to be done. Fourth, there is an emerging sense of constraint, a feeling that all present ought to conform to the common definition of the situation that is becoming manifest. Fifth, there develops what Turner and Killian call *selective individual suggestibility,* which amounts to a "tendency to respond uncritically to suggestions consistent with the mood, imagery, and conception of appropriate action that have developed and assumed a normative character."[24] Finally, the crowd is selectively permissive, for some actions and attitudes that would ordinarily be prohibited are possible within the context of crowd behavior.

Crowds can be classified on a number of dimensions.[25] Some (such as riots) are compact, existing within a fairly well-defined space; others (such as followers of a fad or fashion) are more diffuse, spreading out over a larger territory and often interacting indirectly rather than face to face. Some crowds (such as lynch mobs) have a specific object of action; others (such as crowds that celebrate the home team's victory in the World Series) are expressive, serving more to give voice to a collective mood or sentiment than to attain a specific goal. Some crowds (again, a lynch mob is a good example) are solidaristic, with a collective goal that could not be attained by individuals acting alone; others (such as an audience that panics) are individualistic, with goals pursued by individuals in parallel with one another. Some crowds are spontaneous, coming into existence in a novel situation that members have never experienced before; other crowds are conventionalized, occurring predictably on certain occasions, such as sports events or rock music concerts.

One form of crowd behavior that has attracted considerable attention involves the phenomenon of *panic,* such as that attendant on fires or similar incidents in crowded public places. Panic refers to "individualistic and competitive behavior . . . [that] . . . arises when the members of a collectivity are each trying to gain an objective whose attainment is problematic for each of them."[26] In a panic resulting from efforts to escape a burning building, for example, several circumstances combine to produce behavior that is individualistic, competitive, and self-defeating. If people are both threatened and entrapped (because the number of exits is limited), panic arises when there is both a partial obstruction of escape routes and a breakdown of communication from front to rear. Such a breakdown prevents the fact that the exits are not open from being communicated to those in the rear who, striving to make their way to the exits as quickly as possible, exert strong pressure on those in front. This is what produces the trampling effect characteristic of such disasters.

Behavior in panic situations—as with many occurrences associated with crowds, such as hysteria, riots, looting, and lynching—seems on the surface to be the epitome of social disorder. Yet conduct in such situations is formed on many of the same grounds that characterize institutional conduct. People must define their situation, taking into account the available stock of knowledge; they must, for example, decide what is likely to happen in a fire, or, indeed, whether their own perception of the situation as serious is shared by others. People carve out roles for themselves in crowd situations—becoming leaders and followers, for example—just as they make roles in everyday life. The crucial difference from routine conduct, then, lies in the fact that in crowds and other forms of collective behavior, the definitions, normative constraints, and plans of action emerge (and often very quickly) in the course of conduct rather than being taken for granted in their basic outlines in advance of the situation.

Social Movements as Social Order

Another form of collective behavior—larger in the scope of its activities and longer in duration—is the *social movement.*[27] We can define a social movement as a collective effort to bring about some change in society or a part of society (or to resist such a change sought by others). The change may involve a return to earlier ways of doing things or to values that, in the eyes of movement participants, have been abandoned or neglected. The ideologies of conservative political movements or religious revival movements often have this quality. The movement may seek to prohibit some form of activity that has gained widespread acceptance. The temperance movement in the nineteenth century and the anti-abortion movement of today are examples of this kind of movement. Social movements may have very particular goals, such as racial equality or environmental protection, or more general ones, such as moral revitalization.

Whatever their goals, ideologies, forms of organization, and methods, social movements are oriented toward social change. They seek to restructure the society, to alter its values, beliefs, practices, and modes of organization. Thus, it would seem, there is a simple relationship of opposition between the social order the movement would like to create and the social order that exists and against which it struggles. In the United States of the 1950s and 1960s, there existed a social system in which blacks were legally excluded from jobs, educational opportunities, and public accommodations. At the same time, there was a civil rights movement opposed to that social system and dedicated to reforming it so that people would enjoy equal opportunity and equal social treatment.

Although adequate in general terms, this view of social movements as forms of collective behavior standing in opposition to social structure is also potentially misleading. For, indeed, social movements are in some ways very intimately tied to the social order they seek to change, and under some circumstances social movements can even be said to form a part of social order.

The values of social movements, for example, are often closer to the dominant values of the society than they seem. The women's movement, for example, seeks (among other goals) to overcome discrimination against women in employment, opening for them the same kinds of careers that are open for men. The goal runs counter to prevailing discriminatory practices, but it also accepts the widespread belief that occupational success, which often plays a dominant and oppressive role of its own in the lives of men, is what really counts. In opposing one aspect of the social order, the movement implicitly lends its support to another.

Moreover, social movements, although they seek to change dominant modes of social organization, themselves use organizational means to attain their ends. A movement is not just a set of ideas or a program of objectives, but also a set of organizations, each with members, leaders, resources to be secured and allocated, and methods of internal and external negotiation. In short, social movement life is organizational life. Movements find they must organize their activities, and in so doing they provide structure for the lives of their members. They are the source of opportunities, careers, rewards, and disappointments. Even movement organizations committed to maintaining their flexibility and to resisting ordinary hierarchical forms of organization find they confront the same problems as any organization. Things have to get done, procedures have to be adopted for getting them done, and people have to be motivated to do them.

Movements are also linked to existing social arrangements, because they negotiate with existing social groups and organizations. The image of a movement as the opposition can obscure the fact that movement leaders are in frequent contact with those whose politics they oppose, developing close professional and sometimes also personal relationships. In the town in which I live, leaders of various movements at the local level are seemingly as integral to local government as elected officials and appointed boards and committees. Such leaders attend meetings, make presentations, are addressed on a first-name basis by officials, and often seem to feel entitled to and are accorded the right of special attention when they testify at hearings or otherwise participate. This is not to say that such groups get what they want, or that such victories as they win are well received by the establishment. It is only to suggest that they are an important part of the local landscape: They are as visible and sometimes as permanent as more formal political institutions.

The same is true at the national level. Congressional hearings on environmental legislation, for example, will frequently include invited testimony from various social movement organizations, such as the Sierra Club, the National Wildlife Federation, or the National Parks and Conservation Association. Such groups are invited because they have gained status as legitimate political actors and are thus accorded the right to speak on behalf of the environmental movement.

In this sense, it sometimes seems that social movements are an integral part of social structure. Particularly in recent decades in the United States, social movements have become so plentiful that their very existence on the social landscape is taken for granted. Moreover, they are an important part of the process whereby decisions are made. They are yet movements, for they define themselves as such and see their objectives as being substantially at variance with contemporary social practices. Their presence not only influences decisions, but also seems to be a necessary part of the process whereby decisions are made. Thus, for example, it is hard to envision policy decisions about environmental matters being made without the participation of environmental movement organizations. Not only do social movements thus participate in the coordination of social activities, but by their visible presence they also shape the social construction of reality.

SUMMARY

- Although it is not the job of social psychology to theorize about or study social structure from a macroscopic perspective, it is nevertheless important for a theory of action to take into account the fact that human beings act in situations that are shaped by larger structures. Moreover, the everyday actions of people produce and reproduce society and culture, and it is the job of social psychology to show how this is accomplished. This chapter deals with such questions of social order in three ways: by showing how people socially construct the social order in their everyday activities; by examining how social life is coordinated beyond the immediate situations of social interaction; and by examining the nature of collective behavior.

• The social order exists in part because people act toward it, much as they act toward any object, by talking about it. They name their groups, organizations, and other social units and, in naming them, confer on them part of their solidity and stability. Thus, conversations in which people talk about their activities and about themselves have the effect of continually refreshing the collective consciousness of the groups, organizations, and other social units to which they belong as well as of their identities as members.

• Talk about social order is especially likely to occur in response to problematic events and situations. When people encounter problems, they talk about them. When problems persist, they seek to construct explanations that will make the problems understandable and that will provide some basis for acting to remedy them. A considerable amount of effort in American society is devoted to the definition of undesired conditions as social problems. Talk and action focusing on problems has the effect of reminding people about their conceptions of the ideal society and of providing objects that unite the members of the society or one of its constituent groups in opposition to the problem.

• Social order is thus maintained in part because people talk about it, focus on those situations where it seems threatened, and thus are able to maintain images of what it should be. Social order is not only a result of the social construction of reality, but also of the variety of ways in which members of society coordinate their activities with one another. This coordination takes a number of forms.

• Much of the coordination of joint actions occurs as people seek to solve everyday, practical problems. Culture does not provide us with ready-made solutions to all of the problems of life, nor do our habits fully suffice to enable us to get along from day to day. Much of our conduct is self-consciously focused on the practical solution of this or that problem. Indeed, to a certain extent the groups and organizations in which we coordinate our conduct with others are experienced as a set of problems to be solved and obstacles to be overcome. Problems provide the common focus of joint efforts, and encountering and solving problems marks the passage of time in collective life.

• Social order is also accomplished in everyday life through various processes and in numerous contexts of negotiation. The established rules of social life that people talk about and that become enshrined in laws and organizational regulations are not in themselves sufficient to organize everyday life. Circumstances are too varied, there are too many unanticipated problems, and people are faced with conflicting demands on their time and energy. As a result, the life of groups and organizations often centers around the negotiation of specific agreements on what will be done, when it will be done, and who will do it. Viewed from this angle, the social order is a mass of negotiated agreements that are constantly being enacted, renewed, or negotiated. Such negotiations occur not only in the families to which people belong or the organizations in which they work, but also in the larger context of the society itself, as ethnic groups, religions, social classes, and other social units vie with one another for relative position, dominance, or simply acceptance.

• Social coordination also depends on complex horizontal and vertical linkages between and among various social units. Groups and organizations are linked horizontally because they share members and enter into economic and other relationships of exchange with one another. They are linked vertically because some of these organizations exert powerful controls over others. Such linkages between social units constrain the actions of the individuals who are their members.

• Social coordination also rests on the fact that individuals organize their lives around temporal expectations. The activities in which one engages in a given situation are not only linked to the activities of others in the same or different situations, but are also related to what one did in the past and to what one expects to be doing in the future. Within the situation, each joint action has a career in the sense that it is organized temporally as well as spatially. Individuals have careers of various kinds in the sense that acts in the present are meaningfully linked to their own past and future acts and to the past and future acts of others. Social order is accomplished at the level of everyday action, in part, simply because people share approximate conceptions of what they will be doing and when they will be doing it.

• Finally, to grasp social order, and perhaps especially the ways in which it may be transformed, we examine collective behavior, which occurs when some collectivity defines a situation as problematic and calls for unusual forms of action. Collective behavior is of both long and short duration and involves varying degrees of emotional arousal. The concept thus embraces phenomena as diverse as the panic crowd and the social movement. All forms of collective behavior, however, even though they may involve great departures from the usual routines of a society, are ways of accomplishing social order—that is, of coordinating the conduct of the members of a group, organization, or society as they strive to secure their individual and collective goals.

ENDNOTES

1. For an analysis of this form of talk about the self, see John P. Hewitt, *Dilemmas of the American Self* (Philadelphia: Temple University Press, 1989).

2. Fred Davis, "Decade Labeling: The Play of Collective Memory and the Narrative Plot," *Symbolic Interaction* 7 (1984): 15–24.

3. Remembering the past is aided by a great variety of monuments, memorials,

and markers that call attention to past events and persons and give them present significance. For an interesting analysis of the process of memorializing, see Stanford W. Gregory, Jr., and Jerry M. Lewis, "Symbols of Collective Memory: The Social Process of Memorializing May 4, 1970, at Kent State University," *Symbolic Interaction* 11 (1988): 213-233. For an analysis of the creation of a major political character, see Barry Schwartz, *George Washington: The Making of an American Symbol* (New York: Free Press, 1987).

4. See John P. Hewitt and Peter M. Hall, "Social Problems, Problematic Situations, and Quasi-Theories," *The American Sociological Review* 38 (June 1973): 67-74; and Hall and Hewitt, "The Quasi-theory of Communication and the Management of Dissent," *Social Problems* 18 (Summer 1970): 17-27.

5. This discussion of the positive contributions of social problems and disorder to the maintenance of order bears a family resemblance to the classic position of Emile Durkheim that crime is normal "because a society exempt from it is impossible." This view is founded on the premise that collective sentiments are maintained in part by the fact that crime arouses them — just as ours is premised on the view that social disorder highlights the nature of social order. See Emile Durkheim, *The Rules of Sociological Method,* 8th ed., ed. and trans. G. Catlin, S. Solovay, and J. Mueller (New York: Free Press, 1964).

6. For an excellent formulation of social problems theory, see Malcolm Spector and John I. Kitsuse, *Constructing Social Problems,* Rev. ed. (New York: Aldine de Gruyter, 1987). For studies of the construction of social problems, see *Images of Issues: Typifying Contemporary Social Problems,* ed. Joel Best (New York: Aldine de Gruyter, 1989); Joel Best, *Threatened Children: Rhetoric and Concern about Child-Victims* (Chicago: University of Chicago Press, 1990); and Joseph Gusfield, *The Culture of Public Problems* (Chicago: University of Chicago Press, 1981).

7. Michael Lewis, *The Culture of Inequality* (Amherst, Mass.: University of Massachusetts Press, 1978).

8. For analysis, critiques, concepts, and discussions of the symbolic interactionist approach to social structure, see the following: Robert Day and JoAnne Day, "A Review of the Current State of Negotiated Order Theory," *Sociological Quarterly* 18: 126–142; Norman Denzin, "A Case Study of the American Liquor Industry: Notes on the Criminogenic Hypothesis," *American Sociological Review* 42 (December 1977): 905–920; Harvey Farberman, "A Criminogenic Market Structure: The Automobile Industry," *Sociological Quarterly* 16 (Autumn 1975): 438–457; Gary Alan Fine, "Negotiated Orders and Organizational Cultures: Qualitative Approaches to Organizations," *Annual Review of Sociology* 10 (1984); Gary Alan Fine and Sheryl Kleinman, "Network and Meaning: An Interactionist Approach to Structure," *Symbolic Interaction* 6 (Spring 1983): 97–110; Peter M. Hall, "A Symbolic Interactionist Analysis of Politics," *Sociological Inquiry* 42 (1–2, 1972): 35–75; David R. Maines, "Social Structure and Social Organization in Symbolic Interactionist Thought," *Annual Review of Sociology* 3 (1977): 235–259; Richard O'Toole and Anita Werner O'Toole, "Negotiating Interorganizational Orders," *Sociological Quarterly* 22 (Winter 1981): 29–41; Anselm L. Strauss, *Negotiations* (San Francisco: Jossey-Bass, 1978); Strauss, "The Articulation of Project Work: An Organizational Process," *Sociological Quarterly* 29 (2, 1988): 163–178; and Jim Thomas, "Some Aspects of Negotiated Order, Loose Coupling, and Mesostructure in Maximum Security Prisons," *Symbolic Interaction* 7 (2, 1984): 213–231.

9. Herbert Blumer, *Symbolic Interactionism: Perspective and Method* (Englewood Cliffs, N.J.: Prentice Hall, 1969), p. 17.

10. Ibid., p. 18.

11. Ibid., pp. 18–19.

12. Anselm L. Strauss, D. Erlich, R. Bucher, and M. Sabshin, "The Hospital as a Negotiated Order," in *The Hospital in Modern Society,* ed. Eliot Friedson (New York: Free Press, 1963), pp. 147–169; Strauss, *Negotiations,* 1978 (Note 8) is a major extension of the concept of negotiation and is a rich source of theoretical and empirical insight and analysis. See also *Urban Life* 11 (October 1982), which is devoted to the topic of negotiation.

13. See Hall, "Symbolic Interactionist Analysis" (Note 8), for another extension of negotiated order to the societal level and for an excellent general discussion of the utility of symbolic interactionism in the analysis of political phenomena.

14. Peter M. Hall and Dee Spencer-Hall, "The Social Conditions of the Negotiated Order," *Urban Life* 11 (October 1982): 328–349.

15. See Fine and Kleinman, "Network and Meaning" (Note 8).

16. Farberman, "Criminogenic Market Structure" (Note 8).

17. Blumer, *Symbolic Interactionism,* p. 20 (Note 9).

18. For an empirical account of the experience of chronic illness in relation to the self, see Kathy Charmaz, *Good Days, Bad Days: The Self in Chronic Illness and Time* (New Brunswick: Rutgers University Press, 1991).

19. Robert R. Faulkner, "Coming of Age in Organizations: A Comparative Study of Career Contingencies and Adult Socialization," *Sociology of Work and Occupations* 1 (May 1974): 131–173; other useful work on careers and adult socialization includes Howard S. Becker, "Personal Change in Adult Life," *Sociometry* 27 (March 1964): 40–53; Orville Brim, Jr., "Adult Socialization," in *Socialization and Society,* ed. John A. Clausen (Boston: Little Brown, 1968), pp. 183–266; and Diane Mitsch Bush and Roberta G. Simmons, "Socialization Processes over the Life Course" and Viktor Gecas, "Contexts of Socialization," both in *Social Psychology: Sociological Perspectives,* ed. Morris Rosenberg and Ralph H. Turner (New York: Basic, 1981).

20. See John Lofland, "Collective Behavior: The Elementary Forms," in *Social Psychology,* ed. Rosenberg and Turner, pp. 411–466.

21. See also Joan P. Emerson, "Nothing Unusual Is Happening," in *Human Nature and Collective Behavior,* ed. Tamotsu Shibutani (Englewood Cliffs, N.J.: Prentice-Hall, 1972).

22. Ralph H. Turner and Lewis M. Killian, *Collective Behavior,* 3rd ed. (Englewood Cliffs, N.J.: Prentice-Hall, 1987).

23. Turner and Killian, op. cit., pp. 77–78.

24. Ibid., p. 78.

25. Ibid., especially Chapters 6–8.

26. Ibid., p. 81.

27. For an analysis of social movements, see Ibid., Part 4.

▶ 7

Deviance and the Social Order

Deviance is a complex and difficult sociological concept, yet one that is crucial to our efforts to understand the relationship between the person and the social order. The concept is troublesome because it embraces forms of conduct so diverse that they do not seem to belong in the same category. From a commonsense perspective, for example, such crimes as rape or assault seem to merit the label *deviance,* for they depart from widely shared ideas about desirable and undesirable conduct and they appear obviously harmful to their victims. Other forms of conduct that are sometimes called deviant, such as homosexuality, present a more complex picture. In some cultures, homosexual acts seem to be of little concern; while in other cultures, they provoke considerable fear and are thought to constitute a serious threat to society. Other forms of conduct that the sociologist is apt to study under the rubric of deviance — prostitution, labor racketeering, the use of such drugs as alcohol or cocaine, antitrust law violations, and mental illness — seem to have origins and social consequences so diverse that they should not be grouped together.

Yet these forms of conduct do have *something* in common, for all raise questions in the minds of the members of society about the stability or security of the social order they take for granted. The murderer provokes not only the anger of the victim's family, but a more widespread public outrage. The circumstances under which prostitution or drug use are condemned are more complex and variable, but from the perspectives of those who condemn these forms of conduct, the underlying issues are much the same. Drug use is constructed as a threat to normality, as a form of conduct that will, if permitted to go unchecked, undermine social life by promoting violent and property crime, destroying individual careers, and even addicting newborn babies. Similarly, prostitution, income tax evasion, and even mental illness seem, at least to some members of society at some times, to constitute threats to an established sense of how social life ought to be arranged.

The essence of deviance as a sociological category does not lie in any particular form of behavior itself, but in the way that behavior is viewed by the members of society and the way those who engage in it are treated socially. The study of deviance thus provides clues about the nature of social order and the way it is maintained and reproduced by the members of society. To grasp the social psychology of social order we must look at the underside of social life represented by deviance. In this sense, this chapter is a continuation of the previous one. Its focus is not so much on what causes people to commit deviant acts, but rather on how deviance is socially constructed and perceived, and on how it is linked to the construction of social order and the coordination of conduct.

DEFINING DEVIANCE

What do the various forms of behavior ordinarily classified as deviant have in common? Theft, armed robbery, shoplifting, aggravated assault, rape, grand larceny, fraud, homicide, suicide, homosexuality, drug use, price fixing and other violations of the antitrust laws, child abuse, treason, disturbing the peace, juvenile delinquency—the list could be extended considerably. It would differ from one society to another and also historically within any particular society, but in any society at any given time, one can find a category of activities classified as fundamentally different and threatening.

What, if anything, makes these phenomena alike? If homosexuality is tolerated in some cultures and rigidly condemned in others, whereas violence against *most* categories of people is fairly universally considered wrong, what is the warrant for putting them in the same category? Sociologists once thought there was a relatively straightforward answer to this question, that deviant behavior could be defined simply as behavior that violates social norms, whether the informal norms of everyday life or those formally codified in law and sanctioned by the state. This seems like a simple enough matter, since most instances of conduct that fall into the category of deviance are typically considered to violate some part of the legal code, which is itself often (although not always) supported by widespread normative sentiments. Thus, for example, theft and homicide are against the law and also run counter to most people's conception of right and wrong.

When it is defined this way, deviance seems to be an *objective* phenomenon. That is, an act either *is* or *is not* deviant, regardless of who commits it, whether it is detected, why it is committed, or the circumstances under which it takes place. Even though definitions of what is deviant vary from one society to another, within a particular society the status of an act as deviant, from this sociologically "objective" perspective, is a matter on which the members of that society agree. The act is deviant, and it is so without much regard to who does it or the circumstances under which they do so. Thus, for example, a theft committed as a part of a career in crime is deviant in the same way as a one-time act committed by a desperately poor individual seeking money to buy food for his or her family. Both violate the law and therefore fall into the deviance category.

This view of deviance as a quality inherent in the deviant act itself — as an objective phenomenon that can be described, analyzed, and explained — is typically accompanied by two other ideas. The first is the idea that the person who commits the deviant act is objectively different from "normal" persons, just as his or her act is objectively different. The second is the idea that *social control* — that is the detection, apprehension, legal processing, and punishment of deviance — is merely a response *to* deviance. Both ideas are deeply imbedded in commonsense notions about deviance, and both were once explicitly or implicitly shared by many sociologists.

The idea that the deviant is qualitatively different takes many forms, but in essence it asserts that those who commit deviant acts have characteristics that clearly differentiate them from those who do not. If homosexual acts are basically different from heterosexual acts because they depart from community standards of appropriate sexual conduct, then homosexuals themselves must in some ways be different from heterosexuals. Perhaps they have failed to develop "appropriate" sexual identities and have fixed on the "wrong" sex as the object of erotic impulses, whether because of "pathologies" in the families in which they grew up or because of genetic or psychological differences from heterosexuals. Since armed robbery is against the law, the armed robber must somehow be different from the rest of us, with different values, motives, goals, normative allegiances, or behavioral propensities.

The idea that violations of laws *lead to* social control is also a major part of our commonsense views of deviance and to some extent assumed by a sociological view of deviance as an objective reality. The network of police, courts, and the sanctions of the legal system, as well as the less formal control mechanisms of everyday life, are viewed as organized social responses to the phenomenon of deviance, designed to reduce the amount and seriousness of deviant conduct wherever it occurs. In this view, deviant acts prompt formal or informal responses; people are arrested, criticized, tried, convicted, jailed, ostracized, put to death, all in an effort to prevent such acts from occurring again.

A Critique of the Objective Approach

There are a number of difficulties with such an objective definition of deviance; indeed, the symbolic interactionist approach to deviance arose in part from a critique of the objective approach. An understanding of this critique is thus essential in order to grasp how interactionists view deviance and why they think it is significant.

Perhaps the most serious weakness of the objective approach is its insistence that deviance consists objectively of violations of laws and norms. Even though this idea seems to make common sense, it in fact distorts the way in which norms and laws enter both everyday experience and the formal procedures of social control agencies. It assigns to norms rather more importance than symbolic interactionists believe they deserve.

Norms (as we point out in Chapter 5) are but one element in the stock of knowledge people bring to the situations in which they act and interact. Although sociologists often describe both role making and role taking as heavily dependent on social norms for guidance, norms are less central than they are made out to be. In most situations, norms rarely are problematic. People go about their everyday tasks with their attention fixed on a great many different objects, and not only or even primarily, on the norms. People tend to *state* what they think the norms are when a violation occurs or seems to occur, but even then there is considerable flexibility in the application of norms to conduct. People sometimes acquire a license to break the rules, particularly if they acknowledge in advance that they are going to do so and disclaim any connection between the violation and their fundamental identities. When violations do take place, accounts usually are demanded or offered, and perhaps the most frequent outcome is not the disruption of an occasion by a charge of deviance, but the restoration of orderly social interaction. Norms *may* be objects of individual, private consciousness more often than they are objects of talk, for people do indicate norms to themselves as they role take, but even so they probably are not the most central elements in the process. We indicate to ourselves the expected responses of others to our own conduct using a variety of standards, such as typifications and probability knowledge, and these probably are collectively more important than norms.

Moreover, there is no one-to-one correspondence between acts and norms. Whether a particular act is a violation of a norm usually is a matter of dispute or negotiation and not simply of objective certification. If a person makes a statement known by others to be false, they do not automatically classify the act as a lie, which is a violation of everyday normative sentiments and in some cases also a violation of the law. Instead, people usually negotiate the matter. People claim that they bent the truth in order to avoid hurting someone, or that they did not really lie but merely failed to reveal everything they knew. A government official charged with lying to a congressional investigating committee may claim successfully that he or she did so in the interest of national security; or the person may take an altogether different tack and claim that the lie was unintended, that important facts were temporarily forgotten, or perhaps never known, or that the committee did not ask the right question.

If social norms are less central to conduct than both sociological and common sense suppose, and if the status of a particular act as a violation of a norm or law often is in doubt, then the objective definition of deviance is basically flawed. Deviance cannot be easily defined as "violations of the norms and laws" if those whose norms and laws are violated do not easily and automatically agree on the objective status of an act as a violation. Deviance cannot be seen as an objective quality of an act if the act is sometimes deviant and sometimes not, sometimes treated seriously and at other times lightly dismissed. The meaning of an act as deviant or not is a matter of negotiation, it would seem, and thus we cannot assert that acts are objectively either deviant or not deviant. They are deviant or not *if* people agree that they are or are not.

The negotiable character of deviance can be observed in the formal procedures of the law as well as in everyday social interaction. In many instances of crime, for example, the facts available to police, public prosecutors, or judges lend themselves to multiple interpretations. That is, an act can be interpreted as a violation of several different (or related) laws. As David Sudnow shows, this is an important part of the context within which plea bargaining takes place.[1] If a man is charged with *statutory rape* (having sexual intercourse with a minor female, with or without her consent), he may agree to plead guilty to a lesser offense, *contributing to the delinquency of a minor,* in order to avoid prosecution and possible conviction on the greater charge. The lesser offense is "necessarily included" in the greater — that is, it is impossible legally to commit statutory rape without also contributing to the delinquency of a minor — but the individual cannot be simultaneously charged with or convicted of both on the basis of the same set of facts. If the defendant can be convinced of the certainty of his conviction under the greater charge, and if the prosecutor wishes to avoid a lengthy trial and thus dispose more quickly of the case, a plea bargain may be struck — the defendant pleads guilty in return for a lesser charge.

In a case of this sort, there is clearly an act — sexual intercourse between an adult male and a minor female — considered wrong by the law and by most ordinary people. (The defendant and his victim may or may not agree that the act was wrong.) The meaning of the act is not fixed in the act itself, however, but in its definition by others — police officers, young women, their parents, district attorneys, judges, and the public. Contributing to the delinquency of a minor is a lesser charge than statutory rape, not merely because it entails a shorter maximum prison sentence, but more fundamentally because it involves a different set of assumptions about the seriousness of the act and perhaps even about the partial culpability of the victim. The police may well treat a minor female whom they have typified as delinquent differently than one they regard as a "good girl," and in the former case a charge of statutory rape may be less likely than in the latter. Plea bargaining is simply one procedure by means of which the formal, recorded meaning of the act is decided.

Moreover, just as everyday life is replete with situations in which accounts are used to negotiate the character of an untoward act, so, too, the law is filled with principles that focus on the question of when a specific act is or is not a crime. The law recognizes that circumstances may extenuate the commission of an act and render it not a crime. The act of taking the life of another human being is a good illustration. "Thou shalt not kill" is a firm moral precept in the Judeo-Christian world, and Western societies have complex laws describing various degrees and forms of homicide and manslaughter. Yet many acts of killing do not constitute punishable criminal offenses, for the law takes intent and circumstances into account in defining the nature of an act of life-taking. A police officer's use of a weapon in the performance of duties, for example, may result in death, but it is rarely treated as a crime. Soldiers in war are not charged with homicide when they kill the enemy, except in very carefully defined circumstances, such as those involving noncombatants. Likewise, surgeons whose operations lead to the death of their patients are not charged with manslaughter. Circumstances clearly affect the meaning of various acts in the eyes of those concerned—the offenders themselves as well as the agents of social control and the public.

Another problem with the objective view of deviance stems from the excess of actual violations of the law and other norms over the number of prosecutions and convictions. Not only do people violate everyday norms of conduct and get away with it, feeling no particular remorse at having done so, but they frequently violate more serious norms and laws in the same spirit. Most people probably have violated many laws in the course of their lives—ranging from actions that could be constructed as theft (taking office supplies home for personal use), to fraud (cheating on their income taxes), to assault and other offenses against persons, as well as more common but undetected and unpunished violations of the motor vehicle code such as speeding or making illegal turns. Most such activities are not detected, and for the most part the people who commit them do not think of themselves as thieves, conspirators, rapists, criminals, speeders, or deviants, but rather as upstanding citizens who have managed to get away with something that "isn't really anything." Hockey players regularly fight during games, often rather violently assaulting one another, yet the decision of a local prosecutor in Minnesota to press charges against the perpetrator of one such incident in 1975 produced an outcry. Fans and players alike were mystified by this redefinition of a form of conduct they previously took for granted as a normal part of the game.

The fact that violations occur with greater frequency than prosecutions raises the question of how the criminal justice system operates to detect, prosecute, and punish various offenses. Is the detection of criminal acts governed solely by chance, so that in theory any violator is equally likely to be detected, prosecuted, and punished? Or is there some more systematic process of selection, so that some people are more likely than others to be detected or prosecuted? If detection and prosecution were essentially random, then we might be more likely to consider deviance as an objective phenomenon, since in theory anyone caught would find his or her act treated as deviant. If principles of selection are at work (whether explicit or implicit), then the objectivity of deviance is in doubt. If, for example, an act is more likely to be considered seriously deviant if the perpetrator is a member of a minority group (for example, if we punish homicides by black people more severely than those by whites), then clearly the act is considered deviant (or a particularly serious instance of deviance) because of *who* the perpetrator is rather than because of what the *act* itself is.

There are also good reasons to doubt the commonsense assumption that those who commit deviant acts are qualitatively different from those who do not. Sociologists recognized quite early that normal motivations and social experiences could induce people to engage in deviant acts. Robert Merton's classic theory, for example, sees at least some deviant behavior as the result of barriers to full participation in the society.[2] Americans are strongly urged to value material and status success, the theory argues, but many are prevented from attaining it. Inequalities of income, education, access to knowledge, and other barriers make it more likely for some to succeed than others. Adaptations to real or anticipated failure—to the discrepancy between limited access to opportunity and the universal emphasis on success—may take several forms. People may ritualistically adhere to everyday routines and affirm the value of success even when they really have given up the effort. They may withdraw from social participation, seeking comfort in various forms of retreat, perhaps including the use of drugs or alcohol, even suicide, or they may engage in criminal activity as a way of securing material success. The point, of course, is that quite ordinary motives may prompt conduct that under some conditions will be defined and treated as deviant; the point is *also* that conduct that seems quite normal or "non-deviant" may in fact stem from motives that are not so ordinary. Thus, the mobster may seek the same financial rewards as the corporate executive; and the person who goes through the motions of striving for success without much appetite is at least outwardly indistinguishable from the individual who craves success.

Finally, the objective interpretation of deviance as activity that *stimulates* organized social efforts to control it—and the corollary assumption that societies try to eliminate deviant conduct wherever and whenever it occurs—can be challenged. In many instances the exact nature of the threat to society entailed in a particular form of deviance is difficult to ascertain. Laws against the sale or use of marijuana, for example, may be socially justified on the grounds that the drug is medically harmful and saps the energy it takes to pursue a career or makes the person less competent to perform such mundane activities as driving an automobile. Such arguments are difficult to prove or disprove, but even when they are correct, they do not show that the social control of marijuana is simply a response to its recognized dangers. Laws against marijuana, which existed in only a few states until the early 1930s, became harsh and punitive starting with the Marijuana Tax Act in 1937. After receiving vigorous enforcement and considerable public attention during the late 1960s and early 1970s, concern and enforcement efforts began to wane. In the late 1980s there was another drug scare, this time focused on the spread of crack cocaine, and public officials declared a "war on drugs." The rising and falling tides of concern with drugs are not always closely correlated with actual rates of use. Thus, a view of social control merely as a response to deviant conduct is a vast oversimplification of social reality.

This possibility gains strength if we consider that in some instances the very agencies charged with the social control of criminal and other deviant activity seem to be a part of its perpetuation. Prisons are not notoriously successful as agencies of correction, but they do seem to aid the preservation of criminal subcultures. That is, the prison provides a context for criminal socialization — for the knowledge, ideas, theories, and techniques of crime to be transmitted from one person to another. Efforts to control deviance seem often to have the unanticipated consequence of fostering it or at least of further shaping its forms and varieties.

We can thus argue that the image of social control as a response to deviance is only partly correct—that, equally important, we must see deviance as in part a response to or product of social control. This position suggests— although not without qualification—that deviance exists to the extent that laws exist, and that the mechanisms and agencies of social control crucially affect the shape and character of deviance in a given society. Where laws are harsh and restrictive, and especially where they attempt to prohibit widely practiced conduct, there will be a great deal of deviant behavior. Laws governing the use of drugs, including alcohol, marijuana, and more recently cocaine, are a prime example. The laws not only create a category of illegal behavior, drug use, but in some instances also generate a criminal underworld whose economic function is to supply drugs.[3]

An Interactionist Conception of Deviance

How can we analyze the phenomenon of deviance to avoid the inherent limitations of the commonsense and orthodox sociological views and take its great complexity into account? Any definition of deviance that is to serve as the basis for analysis must accomplish several tasks:

- It must show the conceptual logic of treating very diverse forms of conduct under the heading of deviance.
- It must somehow account for the variable and negotiable character of deviance, as well as the process used to define acts as deviant.
- It must take into account the fact that participation in various forms of deviance has variable effects on the selves of those involved.

A number of sociologists identified with what has come to be known as the *labeling perspective* — which is closely allied to symbolic interactionism but not equivalent to it — attempted to define deviance in a way that took these problems into account. Howard S. Becker, whose writing and research on deviance was influential in the development of labeling theory, was among the earliest to recognize some pitfalls of the conventional sociological view and to propose a new approach. "Social groups," Becker wrote,

> create deviance by making the rules whose infraction constitutes deviance, and by applying those rules to particular people and labeling them as outsiders. From this point of view, deviance is not a quality of the act a person commits, but rather a consequence of the application by others of rules and sanctions to an "offender." The deviant is one to whom that label has successfully been applied; deviant behavior is behavior that people so label.[4]

Becker's approach to deviance clearly attacked some of the major issues we have identified. Instead of treating deviance as a quality of the person or of his or her acts, it regarded it as a quality or qualities *imputed* to the person and his or her acts by social classification. It also recognized that the categorization of acts and people as deviant is not an automatic process, but one of conflict, negotiation, bargaining, and often power. It is the *successful* application of labels that creates deviance, not merely the attempt to do so or the act that provokes the attempt.

Becker's definition of deviance is not wholly satisfactory. Although it successfully captured the variable nature of deviance and the impact of deviant labeling on individuals, it did not well characterize the essence of deviance itself. As Edwin Schur pointed out, the definition of deviant behavior as "behavior that people so label" does not specify the grounds on which they do so.[5] What kinds of conduct do they "so label"? Any kind? Or are there limits on what may be called deviant? Even though it is clear that conduct is not so automatically called deviant as the objective view suggests, neither is its definition as deviant at random. Becker's formulation is open to the criticism that it permits *any* conduct to be labeled as deviant, even though it appears that there are *some* restrictions on what usually goes into the category.

Kai Erikson approached the thorny issue of what may or may not be called deviant by regarding deviance "as conduct which is generally thought to require the attention of social control agencies — that is, conduct about which 'something should be done.'"[6] Although this definition does not fully solve the problem of what *kinds* of conduct are likely to fall within the category of deviance, it does offer at least the beginnings of a standard: a sense that somebody ought to do something about the conduct in question. Conduct that in some or all cultures or under some or all circumstances is susceptible to classification as deviant is conduct that somehow arouses a sense of concern, a belief that something is amiss with the conduct or the person engaging in it.

Exactly what this "something" may be is more difficult to specify. As we have already argued, it is not *merely* the violation of a norm that constitutes an act as deviant — for norms and laws can be violated without encouraging a sense that something ought to be done. Moreover, whatever the something is, we can be fairly certain that it is variable from one culture to another and from one historical era to the next. Particular acts do not always arouse this sense of concern, they do not do so in every culture, and not all members of a particular society exhibit the same degree of concern that something ought to be done in response to particular behavior. Family violence — both child and spouse abuse — is currently a matter of great public concern, but acts (such as the corporal punishment of children or wife beating) that nowadays elicit widespread condemnation were once rather widely tolerated and even supported. Clearly there is a "something" of variable and changeable character.

We can focus the definition of deviance by suggesting that the belief that "something must be done" is aroused when a breach of *social order* is sensed by those with the power to apply deviant labels or to enlist those who can. A "breach of social order" is not itself very definitive of the object of concern, but it does help to narrow our focus somewhat to a concern that the normal, usual, typical, and routine round of activities in the society or some part of it is threatened. Moreover, breaches of social order may be perceived in a variety of ways, not merely in response to violations of normative sentiments, but also in relation to threats to self-interest or power.

Defining deviance as a set of labels applied to conduct that appears to someone to constitute a breach of social order permits a variety of behavior to be seen as *possibly* subject to such labels, yet gives conceptual unity to the category. Any conduct targeted as a breach of order, and any individual held responsible for it, may be labeled deviant. Long hair on men, for example, can be seen as possibly subject to definition as deviant (as it was for a time in the United States in the 1960s), because it can be treated by some people as evidence of rebellion against the established social order they support. Ordinary conceptions of crime also seem to fit well into the category. Killing constitutes deviance when it is directed against an orderly, upstanding member of the society, but less so when it is directed against an outsider, as in the case of war, or against an actual or possible criminal, as in the case of someone shot by a police officer in the line of duty. Moreover, the approach permits the inclusion of what can be termed *political deviance,* which includes allegations of subversive activity against the state as well as various occasions on which charges are more or less trumped up against political enemies. The Chicago Conspiracy Trial of those who participated in the 1968 demonstrations against the war in Vietnam at the Democratic National Convention is a good illustration of the latter.[7]

Defining deviance in terms of the perception of breaches of social order calls attention to the fact that the social construction of reality – and often the politics of reality – is at the very heart of any attempt to apply a deviant label. A crucial element of deviance in almost any society is that people do not always find themselves in harmonious agreement with any particular label or its application under given circumstances. Many Americans readily agree that social protest against war or against racial injustice is an attack on the very foundations of social order; others feel as vehemently that even violent protest is moral in the context of immoral activities. Those who use and supply cocaine and other illegal drugs say that they see nothing wrong with their activities and that those who use legal drugs such as alcohol or tobacco are being hypocritical in making other drugs illegal; those who oppose the use of illegal drugs see the very future of the society at risk unless they can be eradicated. If the police and public prosecutor think a man is guilty of the first-degree murder of his wife, he and his counsel may argue for a verdict of not guilty on grounds of temporary insanity.

Whether a particular form of conduct or a particular act is viewed as deviant, therefore, is the outcome of various processes of negotiation and social definition. The boundaries between legal and illegal protest are not fixed, but rather shift from time to time depending on court decisions, the activities of local police and district attorneys, and the willingness of judges and juries to entertain defenses such as the "necessity defense," which argues that protesters have the right to violate laws if they believe their actions are necessary to prevent a larger wrong from occurring. It is not the inherent character of substances, but rather social processes that determine at any given time which drugs are legal and which are illegal, as well as how the use of these drugs is socially defined. Further whether a killer is guilty of murder or not guilty of an act by virtue of insanity – and therefore what the act *is* and how much a threat it is perceived to be – reflects negotiations between attorneys, the court, and other parties.

The perception of social disorder is only one element of deviance, for just as various acts come to be regarded as threats and classified as deviant, so those who commit them are seen as threatening and called deviants. As Jack Katz suggested, the attribution of a particular kind of status to the deviant is fundamental to the phenomenon of deviance. Katz argued that

> the sociological existence of deviant phenomena is constituted by the imputation of deviant ontological status to human beings. The ontological status imputed to deviants is a negative essence, which is analytically the mirror-image of imputing to human beings a positive essence, or charisma. The one is an imputation of subhuman nature, the other of superhuman nature.[8]

This idea carries us to the heart of the phenomenon of deviance: not merely a category of behavior defined as a breach of social order (though that is an essential part of it), deviance also is a category of persons, viewed as somehow not fully normal, not in possession of normal human capabilities or dispositions, and perhaps not even fully human.

Deviance, Katz emphasized, is in many respects the opposite of charisma.[9] Some members of any society come to be defined as better than average, possessing superior capabilities, dispositions, or motives, whereas others become defined as worse than average, filled with undesirable motives or socially destructive capabilities, or perhaps simply lacking the capacity to act in appropriate ways. That people become so viewed is, of course, a function of socially imputed qualities and characteristics. Even though the concrete accomplishments of the charismatic figure may be the grounds on which he or she gains charisma, its maintenance rests equally on the *belief* in its existence. Similarly, deviants acquire negative essence because of their acts, but their badness, ill will, corruption, uncontrollability, and danger are sustained as much by public imputation as by anything they subsequently do. Even the reformed criminal or recovered mentally ill person is feared in many quarters, just as the retired charismatic military hero or social movement leader retains the luster of charisma even after the glory days are past. Both negative and positive essences, once attached, tend to stick.

Deviance is thus sociologically identified by the perception of threat to social order *and* by the attribution of negative being to individuals. If an automobile suddenly veers onto a crowded sidewalk and kills several people, for example, we do not consider it deviance if we later discover that the car's brakes failed through no fault of the owner or the manufacturer. We see the event as tragic, but not as deviant. If, however, we learn that the driver was drunk, then the act becomes deviant: We attribute a negative essence to an individual who, in disregard of the safety of others, operates an automobile that he or she is unable to control because of a decision to drink too much alcohol. We perceive this event as threatening in a broader sense, for we are apt to see the public safety as threatened by a more widespread problem of drunk driving, of which this is but one instance. Likewise, if the cause of an airplane crash in which hundreds die is found to be faulty maintenance by the airline or poor design by the manufacturer, the definition of the event as involving deviance comes into play.

A crucial element of this approach to deviance is the insight that neither the perception of threat nor the attribution of negative essence simply reflects the *discovery* of reality, although it often seems that we are uncovering the truth rather than socially constructing it. Clearly there are many instances where it seems like there is little leeway for the "discovery" of any but the obvious "truth." If we observe someone who has previously threatened another take out a gun and shoot and kill that person, it seems fairly obvious to all concerned that this is a premeditated killing, that it represents a threat to the social order, and that a person who commits such an act is different from the rest of us. Even here, however, the act is judged deviant because there is widespread social agreement that such acts are criminal and that something needs to be done about those who commit them. One can imagine other circumstances — such as the late nineteenth century American Western frontier community or perhaps even the contemporary urban scene — where some people are far more tolerant of such individual acts of violence and more inclined to see the perpetrator as acting from legitimate motives. The issue of what is threatening and what is not cannot be settled by appeal to the objective meaning of the act itself; here, as in social life generally, the meaning of an act lies in the response it elicits from others who have the capacity to do something about it.

One benefit of this approach to deviance, then, is that it makes it somewhat easier to understand why a variety of forms of conduct can fall under the sociological rubric of deviance. The way we deal with the mentally ill (that is, those whose behavior earns them the modern label of mental illness) so closely resembles the way we treat other forms of deviance precisely because mental illness seems to elicit both a perception of threat to social order and the attribution of negative essence. Those classified as insane or deranged are quite often perceived (in the majority of cases, wrongly so) as a threat to community order. Their behavior arouses fear, distaste, or simply a desire to keep one's distance. The mentally ill are often viewed as strange, dangerous, behaving in unpredictable ways for unfathomable reasons, and therefore as different from the rest of us. Despite the redefinition of insanity as illness, a movement founded on a concern to treat persons afflicted with mental illness more humanely, the mentally ill are still perceived as a danger and an inconvenience. Perhaps this is because their definition as ill does not substantially alter the negative quality of the essences imputed to them. As earlier experience with such diseases as tuberculosis and cancer, and more recently AIDS, has shown, medical conditions can easily arouse fear of contamination and loathing of the potential contaminator, even when people rationally understand that the problem is medical and not moral.[10]

The *perception* of behavior as deviant relies on the perception of threat and the attribution of responsibility to the deviant. *Discourse* about deviance often — but by no means always — incorporates an additional element: normative conceptions. That is, the vocabularies with which we discuss deviance rely heavily on conceptions of right and wrong, even though the underlying reality is formed by perceptions of disorder and the attribution of individual cause. People do not merely talk about the threat that violent crime poses to upstanding citizens and decry the evil motives of criminals, for they also organize their conceptions of and their talk about crime in terms of right and wrong. "It is wrong to steal," we say; "it is sinful to have sexual relations with another of the same sex," some assert; "drugs are dangerous and lead us to do things we should not do," many people feel.

From the interactionist perspective, normative talk about deviance is an expectable but by no means inevitable practice, and it does not define the essence of the phenomenon. As we pointed out, norms frequently are violated without any allegations of deviance. The mark of deviance is that a breach of social order is perceived and attributed to the act of a specific individual. The act may be real or imaginary, and even the deviance may be, for a time, hypothetical, as when a murder has obviously been committed, but there is not yet a suspect. Even though most acts are subsequently classified by people in reference to the norms, *not all acts are so treated.* Mental illness, for example, is marked by the perception of individually attributed acts that breach social order, yet is not usually seen in normative terms. Indeed, the very classification of certain kinds of behavior as the result of *illness* suggests an effort to avoid defining them in normative terms. Defining conduct as a violation of norms usually implies that the violator's act will be seen as willful and knowledgeable unless shown to be otherwise. When we say that someone has broken a rule, we usually imply that he or she did so with knowledge of the rule and also with full intent to break it. To describe conduct as the result of mental illness, however, is to imply the lack of voluntary, knowledgeable violation. Yet, it should be noted, the person said to be mentally ill is judged no less a threat to social order, nor is that person's ontological status thereby made less negative.

One final note is in order. Deviance is in many cases a matter of degree and not of all-or-none classification. As Edwin Schur pointed out in his definition of deviance, behavior is deviant

> to the *extent* that it comes to be viewed as involving a *personally discreditable* departure from a group's normative expectations, *and* it *elicits* interpersonal or collective reactions that serve to "isolate," "treat," "correct," or "punish" *individuals* engaged in such behavior.[11]

Schur's definition recognizes that deviance is a variable phenomenon, not an absolute one—that any given act is more or less deviant, depending on whether noticed; and if noticed, taken seriously as a departure from group standards and attributed to the individual; and, if so taken, it elicits a social reaction, whether an informal sanction in everyday life or the formal sanctions of police and courts.

With this interactionist conception of deviance in place, the task now is to explore some of its dimensions in more detail. Why are some acts perceived at some times as threats to social order and at other times as quite normal— that is, what makes actions threatening? What causes people to engage in acts that become perceived as threats to social order and treated as the basis for altering our view of the person? And what is the impact on the person of the attribution of negative essence—what difference does it make for future conduct if one is labeled deviant?

VARIABLE RESPONSES TO SIMILAR ACTS

The interactionist perspective on deviance rests on the premise that the meaning of an act as deviant or not is contained in the social response it meets rather than merely in the act itself. This should come as no surprise, for it represents an extension of a basic symbolic interactionist position that has recurred several times in this book. Objects take on meaning according to how people act toward them, and deviant acts are objects of concerted definition and action by audiences, whether formal agents of social control or people in various everyday situations.

Thus, what is true of all acts is true of deviant acts: Any act lends itself to a great variety of interpretations, depending on the context of the act and the imputations others make about it. A wink may signify a multitude of intentions, as may prolonged eye contact between members of the same or opposite sexes. Moreover, more complex acts may be subject to a variety of interpretations. Is a woman taking a typewriter home from work in order to do work or to steal it? Is a youngster driving a car on his or her way home in the family automobile or taking a ride in a stolen vehicle? The meaning of such acts depends in part on the intentions of the actor, but it is also a function of how observers act toward them and how acting persons in turn respond.

Given this basic perspective, it becomes a matter of some significance to determine the general processes at work in defining the acts of particular individuals in particular cultures as deviant. Two basic questions face us:

- Why are some acts and not others perceived as possible breaches of social order and treated as reasons to single out individuals and impute negative characteristics to them?
- Why are the acts of some individuals apparently more likely to be regarded as deviant than those of others?

In order to understand why some acts are regarded as deviant in a given culture and others are not, it may be helpful to return to an earlier discussion. Definitions of deviance are often (though not always) couched in terms of social norms, statements of universally or situationally proscribed conduct. Why should this be so? What determines which social norms will be invoked and in relation to which forms of behavior?

One possible answer is that some forms of conduct are so universally perceived as willful breaches of social order that traditional normative conceptions invariably grow up around them. The taking of human life, for example, may be perceived as a fundamental threat to social order in any society. We could say that a sense of outrage at homicide is a natural, existential response, species-wide in its distribution, and that the development of norms or rules against it is thus a natural phenomenon. This approach has something to recommend it, for in spite of the fact that every society has systematic rules for excluding certain categories of people (enemies, strangers, those not considered fully human) from the general rule that murder is wrong, the act itself seems inherently a threat to social order.

It is somewhat more difficult to see the definition of an act as deviant as a simply "natural" occurrence, however, when we move much beyond murder and other violent acts against persons. In order for theft to constitute deviance, for example, conceptions of property rights must be fairly specific — that is, there must be normative conceptions of who owns things and who has the right to use, destroy, move, or otherwise dispose of them. If the social order is founded partly on beliefs that individuals are entitled to call certain forms of property their own to dispose of as they wish, then a perception of theft as a breach of order is natural for that society. Where property is shared freely among the members of a community, theft cannot by definition exist as a form of deviance.

Mental Illness

Mental illness provides another illustration of conduct where we can readily grasp why a sense of concern about social order is aroused. Indeed, as Morris Rosenberg persuasively argued, symbolic interactionism enables us to pinpoint precisely what it is that people find unusual about at least one particular form of mental illness, psychosis.[12] We call certain behavior "insane," Rosenberg said, because we are unable to grasp the perspective from which the person exhibiting this behavior has acted — our efforts at role taking are unsuccessful — and we attribute this failure to the other's conduct and not to our own inability or unwillingness to try to understand it.

Rosenberg argued that the criteria that psychiatrists use to identify psychosis, although sound and useful from a medical point of view, don't really tell us much about why we find psychotic behavior disturbing. Psychiatrists rely on such criteria as "subjective distress" and "impairment of functioning" to diagnose this and other forms of mental illness. People in many circumstances, however, experience subjective distress or their normal functioning is impaired and yet we do not consider them mentally ill. The loss of a job or the death of a child are occasions on which people are upset and don't function as they normally would, for example, but we don't therefore consider them psychotic. Indeed, we find these reactions quite typical and would be surprised if they did not occur.

Yet mentally ill people clearly do exhibit distress and impaired functioning. The psychiatric view tends to treat their behavior, thought, and affect as objective indicators — or symptoms — of illness. The problem, however, is that behavior that under some circumstances is treated as evidence of psychosis is viewed entirely differently under other conditions. Rosenberg used the example of a wealthy movie star who was arrested for shoplifting and whose behavior was later psychiatrically diagnosed as kleptomania. The same behavior from a poor youth living in a slum would probably be regarded as sane and not as evidence of illness. If conduct under the former circumstance is considered symptomatic of insanity, but not under the latter condition, then what makes the act sane or insane is not the act itself but rather the way others interpret it. Similarly, whether a belief in ghosts indicates insanity or not depends on one's cultural surroundings; to believe seriously in ghosts or leprechauns in a culture where these beings are assumed to exist is to be sane; to believe seriously in such beings in contemporary North America might well raise questions about one's sanity. To be depressed when a spouse has died is considered normal in our culture, whereas to be depressed for no apparent reason is taken as a sign of illness.

Whether behavior, thought, or affect is regarded as "sane" or "insane" depends on whether and how an observer makes sense of it. We cannot understand why a wealthy person would shoplift from a store, whereas we can grasp a poor individual's reasons for stealing. In the former case, we cannot successfully role take — that is, we cannot impute any perspective or motives to the other that would enable us to see the conduct as an expression of the person's role. In the latter case, we can do so — we can grasp the perspective of a poor person as one from which theft is a possible act and perhaps even a necessary one. Likewise, we can successfully put ourselves in the shoes of the grieving survivor and understand why he or she is depressed. Depression seems to us to be a likely and reasonable reaction to a loss, but sometimes we observe that people are depressed even though there seems to us to be no good reason for them to be. When role taking fails in this way, we are inclined to take their depression as an indication of mental illness.

Role-taking failure does not invariably lead us to view the other's conduct as indicative of insanity, but only when we believe that the failure is not our own fault. As Rosenberg pointed out, we don't consider babies insane, even though their behavior is often difficult to fathom. Rather we assume that *we* just haven't been able to figure out why the child behaves in a particular way. By the same token, we don't consider physicians insane, even though they do things — shining lights at us, using terms we find unintelligible, poking and prodding in strange ways — we cannot fathom. We assume, instead, that they know what they are doing even if we, due to our ignorance of medical procedure, do not.

Under some conditions we attribute our failure of role taking to the behavior of the other rather than to ourselves. If we think we should observe conduct that is typical of an individual or a role incumbent and if the behavior we observe seems atypical, improbable, and inexplicable, then we are likely to say that the fault lies with the acting person. If a friend begins to act depressed and we cannot interpret his or her mood as typical of this person, as a likely response to experiences he or she has had, or as a rational response to the situation in which we find the person, then we are apt to think something is wrong with the individual. We may not immediately jump to the conclusion that the individual is mentally ill—people seem to avoid applying this label as long as they can—but we are at the very least suspicious that something may be amiss, and that the problem lies with them and not with us.

Rosenberg's approach to mental illness fits well with the general approach to deviance developed here. That is, social suspicions or judgments of insanity or mental illness seem to focus on the *individual* whose behavior is in question and they seem to attribute to that person a special and not very positive status. Although it is the puzzling behavior of others that strikes us as noteworthy, once we have begun to think of the behavior as insane we also consider the *person* to be insane. Mental illness, much like other forms of deviance, is a label that, once applied because of our inability otherwise to understand a person's behavior, comes to apply to the whole person and not just to the behavior. Once this happens, all of the negative stereotypes—such as unpredictability or violence—attached to mental illness become attached to the person.

Moreover, not only do we attribute a deviant ontological status to the person as a way of accounting for his or her conduct, but a sense of threat to social order is also mobilized. It is difficult and uncomfortable to deal with people when we cannot successfully role take. Our normal expectations about how people will behave are not met, and so there is a sense of discomfort, at the very least, and often of more serious threat. People who address us in a babble of incoherent words or who seem depressed when there is no reason to be depressed disrupt our usual assumption that we are living in a world where people understand one another and interact in an orderly fashion. Because stereotypes have grown up about the conduct of the mentally ill—that they are dangerous and prone to violence, for example—there is also a deeper sense that we might be harmed if they are not isolated and controlled.

Moral Enterprise

Beyond such fundamental and very widespread definitions of deviance as murder, theft and other offenses against property and persons, and mental illness, however, there lies a far more ambiguous realm of rules, categories of deviance, and perceived breaches of social order that we cannot as readily account for. If a response to the taking of human life seems to flow quite naturally from the basic conditions of human existence, a category such as delinquency does not. Conceptions of murder and thievery have been on the human scene for a long time; juvenile delinquency is a comparatively recent social invention. Although Rosenberg's approach introduces a good deal of conceptual order into the nature of insanity as a folk judgment, mental illness is likewise a relatively recently created social category.[13]

The question is, why are such categories invented? To speak of them as inventions, of course, is *not* to argue that the conduct to which they point does not in some form exist. Juveniles do occasionally engage in thoroughly bad conduct. Some people do have such major difficulties coping with life that the category of mental illness seems well suited to them. These kinds of behavior surely exist — but they exist in part because a category exists into which we have learned to classify certain acts, and in terms of which we have learned to think about these acts and to encourage those who commit them to think about them. The question is, why?

A fundamental insight of symbolic interactionists has been that the creation of deviance categories as well as the making and enforcing of rules against various forms of conduct results from both individual and collective enterprise. Categories and rules do not emanate automatically from the culture; they do not spontaneously appear on the scene. Rather, rules are the result of collective efforts of definition and redefinition. Howard Becker stated the point forcefully:

> Wherever rules are created and applied, we should be alive to the possible presence of an enterprising individual or group. Their activities can properly be called moral enterprise, for what they are enterprising about is the creation of a new fragment of the moral constitution of society, its code of right and wrong.[14]

Becker illustrates this view by showing the use of such moral enterprise by the Federal Bureau of Narcotics in seeking passage of the Marijuana Tax Act of 1937, which rigidly controlled marijuana by heavy taxation. Officials of the bureau sought to bring marijuana within their official jurisdiction and waged a sustained public relations campaign in order to gain congressional support. Their campaign was ultimately effective not only in securing legislation but also in widely publicizing the alleged dangers of the drug.

Before the bureau's campaign, law enforcement officials had expressed little concern about marijuana, and few states had laws prohibiting it. There was, in other words, no widely perceived breach of social order in the use of this drug until a group of moral entrepreneurs — perhaps motivated as much as anything by a desire to see the powers and budget of their bureau expanded — succeeded in creating such a public perception. The evils of the drug were dramatized, rules against its sale and possession formulated, and the perversities of its users highlighted, not by the spontaneous responses of people to an obvious breach of order, but because of moral enterprise.

Analyzing the American Temperance Movement, Joseph Gusfield showed that such moral campaigns are closely related to how the constituent groups of a society view one another.[15] Rural Protestants, who had traditionally dominated American culture and had upheld temperance norms, began to feel more and more threatened by urban, Catholic, and working-class immigrants as the nineteenth century wore on. Increasingly, temperance-oriented Protestants turned their attention away from a humanitarian concern for the victims of alcoholism and toward a more combative, coercive effort on behalf of the prohibition of alcohol. The use of alcohol became seen not merely as a violation of the Protestant conception of moral conduct and a practice with unfortunate consequences, but as a potent symbol of the decline in status and influence of the older Protestant groups relative to those of newcomers. The successful passage of the prohibition amendment provided a way for Protestants to assert what they felt was their legitimate "moral ownership" of American society in the face of their declining actual status and power.

Moral enterprise is by no means a phenomenon confined to the past, for the creation of various forms of deviance continues. In recent years moral entrepreneurs have focused their attention on a plethora of social problems, such as child abuse, elder abuse, drug use, family violence, and even smoking. Often the motives that underlie efforts to arouse public concern about a form of deviance seem to have little to do with the conduct itself. The news media, for example, discovered a "crack epidemic" in the late 1980s. At the same time, politicians joined in the battle against this apparently renascent menace to the social order. Although there can be little doubt about the deleterious effects of crack, the reporters and television anchors who publicized crack probably did so before the use of crack drastically increased rather than after. Was it, therefore, concern for the welfare of crack users that motivated these moral entrepreneurs? Or, did they seek to sell newspapers and increase their ratings? Was crack defined as a serious form of deviance because of its objective threat to social order, or because it came to symbolize the perceived threat to order posed by urban black sellers and users? Did politicians seize on the drug issue as a way of mobilizing political support? [16]

These examples suggest that definitions of deviance, like social problems more generally, may often be the product of the actions of specific individuals and groups with goals that go well beyond the particular form of deviance in question. In such cases, threats to the social order are either manufactured to serve the interests of particular groups and organizations as with the Federal Bureau of Narcotics and their stance on marijuana, or seized on as a way of providing symbolic support for the values and social standing of groups that feel threatened, as in the case of rural Protestants and their campaign for temperance.

THE CAUSES OF DEVIANCE

An approach that finds the reality of deviance in a combination of perceived threats to social order and attributions of personal essence clearly complicates the problem of identifying the "causes" of deviance. Rather than being an objective reality, a fixed and given part of the social world, deviance is to a great extent a product of human definitions of what the world is like. This is not to say that there are no causes of deviance apart from social definitions. People kill and steal from one another for a variety of reasons and in many different circumstances; they use drugs sometimes because they are taught to do so and sometimes because the drugs allow an escape from painful realities; they develop homosexual or bisexual rather than exclusively heterosexual orientations for reasons that are scarcely understood; and so a list of "deviant" forms of behavior might be elaborated and the potentially diverse causes of each specified.

The symbolic interactionist approach eschews any effort to find any simple set of causes of deviance or to view deviance as a form of conduct sharply differentiated from the ordinary. The same processes of situation definition, role taking, and role making that are found in everyday life also underlie deviant conduct. Those who engage in deviance have goals and purposes just as do those who avoid deviance. The self is as crucial an object in the experience of one who engages in deviant forms of conduct as it is in the life of one who does not. Moreover, if deviance arises from the same processes and circumstances as ordinary conduct, there are no simple keys to its explanation and control. It is an unavoidably diverse phenomenon that resists simple explanations.

The applicability of standard symbolic interactionist concepts to the study of deviance is illustrated in Lonnie Athens's intensive study of violent criminal acts and actors, which relies primarily on in-depth interviews with violent offenders convicted of such crimes as homicide, rape, and robbery.[17] Athens found that, contrary to conventional assumptions that depict violence as the result of unconscious motivations or emotional outbursts, people "commit violent criminal acts *only after* they form violent interpretations of the situations which confront them." The violent criminal actors in Athens's study assessed the situations in which they found themselves and self-consciously came to the conclusion that violence was an appropriate or required course of action. Athens also found that the person's self-image affected the assessment of the situation. Those with nonviolent self-images committed violent acts only in those situations in which their interpretation called for physical self-defense; those with violent self-images interpreted a wider range of situations as calling for violent actions.

Athens's study points to the necessity of taking actors' definitions of situations into account in explaining their deviant conduct. It also underscores the *decisional* nature of much deviance. The origins of many forms of deviance seem to lie in the assessments and interpretations of people as they act in their social worlds rather than in some more uniform and hidden causes that, if discovered, might make the control of deviance easier. If even such clear-cut acts as rape or assault are the result of conscious (and in some sense even "rational") decisions to act in a given way, then it is difficult indeed to grasp the causality of deviance. People may define situations in novel, unexpected, and mistaken ways; as a result, any given situation may provoke a variety of definitions and acts.

In a similar vein, Jack Katz has also argued that in order to understand crime we must see it as the criminal sees it. Katz feels that many forms of criminal activities seduce the criminal through their own rewards and excitements. Various crimes—from the thrill-seeking crimes of adolescents who vandalize, joyride in stolen cars, or shoplift to cold-blooded and seemingly senseless killings— hold positive attractions for those who perpetrate them. Although they may recognize what they do as wrong and even be ashamed of it, the actual doing of the particular crime may be interesting, exciting, gripping, and ultimately compelling. In addition to its particular emotional rewards, each crime entails a particular set of joint actions that must be completed, and it fosters a distinctive understanding of oneself in relation to others. Thus, Katz writes that often for adolescents

> shoplifting and vandalism offer the attractions of a thrilling melodrama about the self as seen from within and without. Quite apart from what is taken, they may regard "getting away with it" as a thrilling demonstration of personal competence, especially if it is accomplished under the eyes of adults.[18]

For these and other crimes, the perpetrator sees himself or herself faced with a particular challenge, and the crime is a way of meeting it.

The hypothesis that deviant conduct has multiple causes—and that it may for some people become an inherently attractive way of life—seems at least as plausible as any of the current theories of particular forms of deviance that see them in singular terms.[19] Indeed, it is this hypothesis that accounts, in part, for the appeal of the symbolic interactionist perspective, which permits the apparent diversity of causes of given forms of deviance to be accommodated with the fact that each form often seems to us in commonsense terms to be uniform, to have certain identifiable and inescapable characteristics. The social construction of deviance as a category of act and person is what accounts for the apparent uniformity of deviance, not its underlying causes.

Indeed, this point must be made more generally about all human conduct. An exceedingly complex set of situations, biographical experiences, individual motivations, and combinations of persons interacting with one another can be assumed to lie behind each observable act or sequence of acts. As I sit at the typewriter composing this paragraph, for example, a multitude of factors impinge on and help to shape my act. While I am acting within my definition of the situation—writing a book—I also am subject to other kinds of influences.

The telephone may ring, a student may knock on my door to ask a question or just to chat with me, or my mind may wander away from my situated role and into other aspects of my life. Thus, how I actually write this paragraph, what I end up typing into the computer, results from a great number of influences, many of which really have little or nothing to do with the act of writing.

An observer would have little difficulty seeing my conduct as typical of someone in my position. No one else can fully penetrate my mind and predict what I am going to do, where I will get my examples for a point I am trying to make, or what I will end up saying. I cannot even fully predict these things myself. Yet somehow the end product of my conduct appears meaningful and expectable. It can be seen as sensibly related to the definition of the situation I am in, as living up to the expectations associated with my role, and as typical of me as an individual. Put simply, no matter how complex the actual causes of my conduct, it often seems very simple and straightforward when viewed from the perspective of someone who shares my definition of the situation.

We should emphasize that putting people and their acts into categories is not just a phenomenon of deviance but of all human conduct. In our efforts to make sense of the world we inhabit, including our own conduct in it, we sort people into categories, such as insane, criminal, homosexual, exceptional, or abnormal. That the causes of conduct that lead people to become categorized in such terms are diverse should give us a clue that perhaps the causes of any conduct are multiple. Even though the extraordinary character of the kinds of conduct we call deviant and of the persons we call deviant tends to make us pay attention to them and look for underlying causes, we should not forget that all conduct has exceedingly complex antecedents and situational influences. We label good guys, the average person, and heroes just as much as nuts and crooks. In either case, the categories we use and the assumptions that lie behind them exert a powerful influence on what we see and how we explain it, not only as ordinary people but as sociologists looking for the causes of given forms of behavior.

Deviance and Identity

The social categories of deviance also affect the lives and future conduct of those to whom they are applied. Because they prompt the attribution of negative essence, deviant acts reflect negatively on the situated, social, and personal identities of those who engage in them. It is individuals who are held responsible for their acts and who are targeted for correction, rehabilitation, punishment, isolation from society, and other such responses intended to root out the causes of the behavior from the individual and to protect the society from him or her. This social treatment establishes and sometimes controls the identities of those who are labeled as deviant.

Most people make a variety of roles in their day-to-day affairs, and so have a variety of situated identities. They are office workers and fathers and husbands and volunteer firefighters and many other things. Their social and personal identities are constructed out of these situated identities. Although some roles are much more important than others as bases for viewing and defining individuals — and for their defining themselves — few roles prevent them from making other roles. Being a woman, for example, makes it more difficult to make some roles; to the extent that people think that women cannot be competent engineers or truck drivers, they will find it difficult to enter such roles and build them into their identities. Gender is thus a very powerful identity — that is, an identity that strongly affects the way others view the person and the way the person views himself or herself. Still, both men and women make a variety of roles and thus have a variety of situated identities.

Deviance often confers not just a powerful identity, but a controlling identity. If an individual is identified as deviant in some respect — as a homosexual, a bank robber, a juvenile delinquent, or a psychotic — that identification tends to become the main or even the sole basis on which others define and relate to the person. The establishment of a deviant identity in the eyes of others tends to negate all or most other possible identities in the eyes of those others who regard the deviance category in question as particularly grave. That other identities are negated means that the individual is seen as incapable of assuming them. Regardless of whatever identities the person *announces,* others *place* him or her in the deviant identity. Thus, for example, someone who is accused and convicted of murder becomes — at least in the eyes of the public — a "murderer," someone whose very essence is defined by this label and whose other possible roles and identities thereby become inoperative. Likewise, if an individual is publicly labeled as homosexual, the result will be that some people will be unwilling to regard the person in any other capacity except as a homosexual. That is, their attitudes toward the person would be profoundly shaped by the knowledge of his or her homosexuality, they might tend to see homosexual motives underlying most of the person's conduct, and they might try to prevent the person from assuming other identities (being a neighbor in an apartment building, for example, or a coworker on the job).

In many forms of deviance, formally constituted agencies of social control — police, courts, probation officers, attorneys, and the like — attach deviant identities to individuals. Thieves and murderers are apprehended, indicted, tried, convicted, and incarcerated; and each step in this process is not only a part of the application (or misapplication) of justice, but also the attachment of an identity to a person. The "due process" to which the Fifth Amendment to the Constitution entitles people in the United States is not only a matter of law, but also of attachment and certification of identity.

Deviant identities are not only attached by official agencies, but also in less formal ways. The thief or murderer comes to have a criminal identity as much through the efforts of the mass media as through the operation of the criminal justice system. This is perhaps especially true of "leading" criminal figures, those who acquire a substantial local or national reputation, such as Al Capone and other gangsters of the 1930s or Mafia leaders in more recent years, as well as mass murderers and other well-known killers whose activities are sensationalized by the media. Moreover, even when particular forms of deviance go unattended by the police, their discovery in informal social circles is sufficient to attach and sustain a deviant label. Except for those involved in "tearoom sex" (the making of impersonal homosexual contacts by men in public places), most homosexuals are not formally charged or processed by the police or courts for sex offenses, even though laws against "sodomy" remain on the books in many states. Yet the discovery of an individual's homosexuality by friends or associates is sufficient to give that person a new identity in their eyes, particularly if they disapprove of homosexuality. Where attitudes are rigidly homophobic, redefinition of the individual concerned is likely to be substantial and to entail considerable imputing of negative essence. Even where attitudes are relatively "tolerant," some redefinition is likely, if only to the extent that the individual now becomes someone "whose homosexuality we understand and accept because *otherwise* he is normal."

When a deviant label is applied, whether through formal or informal means, there is frequently a process of *retrospective interpretation* of the person's conduct on past occasions. This may be especially true of homosexuality, where the pressure of homophobic attitudes and behavior has led many gays and lesbians to conceal their sexual orientations from their straight friends and acquaintances. When the person's identity is discovered (whether accidentally or because the person decides to "come out of the closet") and a label of homosexuality is applied, others are apt to reinterpret past conduct in the light of the new identity. Based on his interviews with a sample of college undergraduates about their experiences with homosexuals, John Kitsuse concluded that a reinterpretation of the past behavior of homosexuals is especially likely to occur if the previous relationship was more than casual. Subjects reported that they searched for and generally were able to find past conduct that now made sense to them in the light of the new discovery that the person was homosexual.[20]

If the individual acquires membership in a deviant category—and is assigned a situated identity as deviant—as a result of legal processing, public labeling by others, or retrospective reinterpretation, how does this fact shape the person's social and personal identity? Are deviant labels applied only by others, or are they also self-applied? Does the person build a deviant label into his or her social or personal identity? If so, how does this affect subsequent conduct? Does labeling itself become one of the causes of deviance? Can the person under some circumstances resist a deviant label?

Labeling an individual as deviant implies several *possible,* but not inevitable, developments. To grasp them, we must first grasp the distinction between *primary* and *secondary* deviance. Primary deviance, Edwin Lemert argued, arises out of a variety of factors—"social, cultural, psychological, and physiological"—and it has little to do with the person's sense of self.[21] For various reasons, individuals perform acts that are considered deviant: Adolescents get in fights, for example, or people drink too much or use other powerful drugs. Secondary deviance, in contrast, consists of "deviant behavior or social roles based upon it which becomes a means of social defense, attack or adaptation to the overt and covert problems created by the societal reaction to primary deviance."[22] Primary deviance arises out of diverse causes; secondary deviance arises because of the way others react to this primary deviance. What processes might be at work?

First, because the person to whom a deviant label is attached is thereby placed in a category of people who are similarly labeled, there is at least implicitly some pressure to identify with others who are so labeled. To impute a negative essence—whether "criminal," "homosexual," or "insane"—is to situate the person relative to those who are not so labeled. Others may tend to avoid this person, to exclude him or her from their social circles, and to refuse to give the person a job or sell or rent housing. Labeling also encourages a sense of "membership" in the deviance category and thus some degree of identification—a sense of likeness and common purpose—with others who are deviant. The labeled deviant is pushed out of conventional situations and associations and pulled toward deviant ones.

Those who are labeled may indeed perceive some advantage in such identification. Lumped in with other adolescents who are called "delinquents" the young person may feel that he or she can be fully accepted only among such others. Despised or rejected by those who hold strongly homophobic attitudes, the gay or lesbian individual may conclude that only by socially identifying with a gay or lesbian community will he or she truly feel at ease, be accepted by others, and thus have any sort of normal opportunity for maintaining self-esteem and constructing a personal identity.

Second, because categorization as deviant frequently offers the person only one role to perform and one situated identity to claim, there are also some pressures to learn to think, feel, and act in fairly standardized ways implied by the label itself. To be labeled deviant is to experience the pressures of altercasting—that is, to be handed a role and to be subtly (and sometimes not so subtly) pressured to accept it. In part these pressures are effective because they encourage the individual to think of himself or herself solely in terms of the proffered role and identity. The labeled delinquent, in this view, comes to think of himself or herself as delinquent, and this conception of self prompts the individual to enact a delinquent role.

By the same token, the person who is able to maintain a self-definition as "normal" is likely to be the one who can resist this altercasting. It is important to grasp that individuals do not necessarily or automatically accept the identities that are handed them through deviant labeling. Delinquents assert that they are not really bad; homosexuals maintain that the only thing that differentiates them from others is sexual preference. Relying on a combination of inner resources, in the form of previously established personal and social identities, and support from others, labeled deviants are able to resist accepting some or all of the implications of the new identity that others try to attach to them. Their success in doing so also depends on their capacity to engage in successful aligning actions — to excuse, justify, and otherwise account for their actions in ways that leave their identities relatively unharmed.

Yet *any* labeling of an individual will have at least the effect of generating doubt where previously there was an unproblematic conception of self.[23] A young boy who gets into trouble with the police may be treated as an ordinary delinquent — as typical of the hundreds of juveniles they have dealt with. Even though the police may act toward the youth *as if* he has the usual delinquent propensities — lying, being disrespectful, being ready to go out and get into trouble again — this one episode of labeling probably will not lead to a substantial change in self-conception, but it will probably raise some doubts and anxieties. Subsequent episodes are sure to do so. The boy who has never before encountered any official sanctions and then, through bad luck or circumstances, has one or two run-ins with the police, may experience a subtle change in self-conception. Where previously no question had ever been raised, he may now ask, "Is there something wrong with me?" Told by police that "all you kids are alike," he may begin to wonder if, in fact, this is so.

Some evidence exists that whether labeling affects the self depends on where the individual is located in the social structure. Gary F. Jensen's studies of delinquency, for example, seem to indicate that being labeled as a delinquent has more effect on whites than on blacks.[24] Given the systematic exclusion of many African Americans from educational and occupational opportunities and their frequent devaluation and denigration by whites, they may be less inclined to doubt themselves on the basis of labels that are commonly applied by whites. The more a person is integrated in a given social order, the more its labels have significance for the self; the less a part of that world the individual feels, the less he or she feels compelled to regard its judgments as significant.

It is also important to recognize that self-labeling may be as significant or more significant than labeling by others. The delinquent whose primary offense goes undetected by police may nevertheless be aware that he or she has broken the law and even consider himself or herself a delinquent because of this. To be sure, the act would have a different meaning had it been detected by others — an act is, in the terms of Schur's definition quoted earlier, "more deviant" if others see and label it than if the person alone thinks he or she is a delinquent. In some cases, the application of labels to the self is *the* crucial basis for establishing a deviant identity. This is true of homosexuality, where people very early learn to avoid displaying what at first seems to them a very unusual sexual orientation, and then later come to think of themselves as gay or lesbian, often seeking to conceal this fact from audiences who might publicly label them as homosexual.

Others' formal and informal responses to deviance may thus contribute to the elaboration of deviant conduct and thereby become one of its causes. Although we should not ignore this aspect of the deviance process, neither should we overemphasize it. Labeling contributes to deviance, but it is not its only cause. As we have argued, there is no more sense in asserting that deviance has a single cause than in asserting that any other form of conduct has a single cause. The human social world is complex, and the forces that influence what we do are likewise complex.

SUMMARY

• Symbolic interactionists are interested in deviance not only because we can use the concepts and ideas of this perspective to help explain this phenomenon, but also because an understanding of deviance adds to our grasp of how social order is constructed and maintained. The commonsense (and often the conventional sociological) approach to deviance regards deviant behavior as qualitatively different from conforming or nondeviant behavior, and it tends to view those who commit deviant acts as different from those who do not. In this approach, deviance is viewed as an *objective* quality of certain acts. This view of deviance involves many problems, including its overemphasis on normative definitions of deviance, its inability to deal with existence of far more instances of violations of social norms than of certified instances of deviance, and its exaggeration of the extent to which many forms of deviance constitute real threats to the social order.

• The symbolic interactionist conception of deviance emphasizes not the inherent quality of the act but the way that act is socially defined and treated. An interactionist conception emphasizes that deviance is in some degree the result of people making rules, the violation of which constitutes deviance. That is, to some extent, deviance is a product of the specific configuration of laws and other prohibitions and the way they are applied and enforced. Deviance is not simply a product of rules, however, for certain forms of conduct are singled out as requiring the attention of social control agencies while many other forms of conduct are not. What leads to a collective sense that something ought to be done about a particular form of conduct is a sense of threat to an established social order. This order may be (and often is) defined in normative terms, as, for example, in relation to acts of physical violence. Further, the definition of the social order and of what constitutes a threat against it may also be constructed in political terms. In this latter sense, definitions of deviance are as much or more the result of the distribution of power and the capacity to have certain acts defined as deviant than the result of any genuine sense of collective outrage over an act.

• Deviance labeling attaches meaning to the person who commits an act as well as to the act itself. Those who are accused of some form of deviant conduct find themselves imbued by others with a negative essence. They are viewed as dangerous, corrupt, bad persons who are to be feared and about whom something ought to be done. The deviant person is thus thoroughly discredited by the ascription of a deviant status, and deviance is apt to become a controlling identity in relation to which the person's whole life and being are apt to be reinterpreted. Thus, to be labeled deviant may in some circumstances promote deviance, for a deviant label may become the basis for a defiant identity on the basis of which the person subsequently acts. Primary acts of deviance may arise from diverse causes, but under some conditions a career of secondary deviance may result from labeling.

• The definition of some acts or categories of acts — such as homicide or assault — as deviant reflects a natural, existential response by the members of a society to these forms of conduct. That is, it seems legitimate to view such acts as quite naturally and universally precipitating a sense of concern for social order as well as for individual well-being. Other definitions stem from particular social and cultural arrangements — property crimes are possible and important where property itself is privately held and of great significance. In the case of mental illness, it seems to be the inability of others to role take and thus to make sense of a person's act that leads to the attachment of a label of "mental illness" or "insanity." Finally, many of the rules whose violation constitutes deviance are the result of individual and collective enterprise. They exist not as the result of a spontaneous sense of moral outrage by the members of a community or because of an inability to comprehend conduct, but because some people have persuaded others that they ought to feel outraged by the behavior in question.

• The causes of deviance, as of all forms of social behavior, are quite diverse; no single principle or theory can assimilate all of the phenomena of deviance. This is so for two reasons: First, deviance is itself a category produced by social definitions and not by any objectively sociological qualities of certain forms of behavior. Deviant behavior is called deviant by the members of a society at a given time, and so variable a category can hardly have a single or even a simple cause. Second, even when we focus on a single type of behavior, such as violent crime, it seems likely that people engage in such acts for diverse reasons and that the basic processes of defining the situation, role making, and role taking underlie their deviant acts as much as they do the acts of ordinary people. If this is so, deviance is quite an ordinary form of behavior and, like most other ordinary kinds of behavior, arises from diverse motives and situational definitions and gets its reality as much from the way we perceive and define it as from anything intrinsic to the conduct itself.

ENDNOTES

1. David Sudnow, "Normal Crimes: Sociological Features of the Penal Code," *Social Problems* 12 (Winter 1965): 255–270.

2. See Robert K. Merton, "Social Structure and Anomie," in his *Social Theory and Social Structure,* rev. ed. (New York: Free Press, 1957), pp. 131–160.

3. This is not to say, however, that it automatically follows that the solution to the drug problem is simply decriminalization. To argue that deviance is not simply an objective phenomenon and that laws help to create it does not necessarily support the conclusion that there is no objective harm in drugs or that the problem will disappear if laws are removed from the books.

4. Howard S. Becker, *Outsiders* (New York: Free Press, 1963), p. 9.

5. See Edwin Schur, *Labeling Deviant Behavior: Its Sociological Implications* (New York: Harper and Row, 1971), p. 23ff.

6. Kai Erikson, "Notes on the Sociology of Deviance," in *The Other Side,* ed. Howard S. Becker (New York: The Free Press, 1964), pp. 9–21.

7. For an analysis of the political construction of deviance, see Paul G. Schervish, "Political Trials and the Social Construction of Deviance," *Qualitative Sociology* 7 (Fall 1984): 195–216.

8. Jack Katz, "Deviance, Charisma, and Rule-Defined Behavior," *Social Problems* 20 (1972): 192.

9. Charisma, in Max Weber's words, is "a certain quality of an individual personality by virtue of which he is set apart from ordinary men and treated as endowed with supernatural, superhuman, or at least specifically exceptional qualities." See Max Weber, *The Theory of Social and Economic Organization,* trans. R. A. Henderson and Talcott Parsons, ed. Talcott Parsons (New York: Oxford University Press, 1947), p. 358.

10. Raymond L. Schmidt and Tiffani M. Schmidt have examined the intense emotions that are aroused by AIDS in a study of the responses of local school officials to a young student who had acquired the disease through a blood transfusion. "Community Fear of Aids as Enacted Emotion." Unpublished paper.

11. Schur, *Labeling Deviant Behavior,* p. 24 (Note 5).

12. This discussion of mental illness relies on Morris Rosenberg's "A Symbolic Interactionist View of Psychosis," *Journal of Health and Social Behavior* 25 (September 1984): 289–302. Readers of earlier editions of this book will note a change in its approach to mental illness. I have been convinced that Rosenberg's analysis is the more fundamental one so far as symbolic interactionism is concerned, and that there are some flaws in the labeling approach espoused by Thomas Scheff. See Scheff, *Being Mentally Ill: A Sociological Theory,* 2nd ed. (New York: Aldine, 1984).

13. See the historical study of mental illness by David J. Rothman, *The Discovery of the Asylum* (Boston: Little-Brown, 1971), which deals with the development of institutions for the care of the dependent in the Jacksonian era. On the discovery of

juvenile delinquency, see Anthony Platt, *The Child Savers: The Invention of Delinquency* (Chicago: The University of Chicago Press, 1969).

14. Becker, *Outsiders,* p. 145 (Note 4).

15. Joseph Gusfield, *Symbolic Crusade* (Urbana, Ill.: University of Illinois Press, 1963).

16. For a discussion of the "war on drugs," see Craig Reinarman and Harry G. Levine, "The Crack Attack: Politics and Media in America's Latest Drug Scare," pp. 115–138 in *Images of Issues: Typifying Contemporary Social Problems,* ed. Joel Best (New York: Aldine de Gruyter, 1989).

17. Lonnie H. Athens, *Violent Criminal Acts and Actors: A Symbolic Interactionist Study* (London: Routledge and Kegan Paul, 1980).

18. Jack Katz, *Seductions of Crime: Moral and Sensual Attractions in Doing Evil* (New York: Basic Books, 1988), p. 9.

19. For a survey of several different theories of deviance and evidence pro and con, see Allen E. Liska, *Perspectives on Deviance,* 2nd ed. (Englewood Cliffs, N.J.: Prentice Hall, 1987). Chapter 5 deals with the labeling perspective.

20. John Kitsuse, "Societal Reactions to Deviant Behavior: Problems of Theory and Method," *Social Problems* 9 (Winter 1962): 247–256.

21. Edwin M. Lemert, *Human Deviance, Social Problems, and Social Control* (Englewood Cliffs, N.J.: Prentice Hall, 1967), p. 40.

22. Ibid., p. 17.

23. For an analysis of this point, as well as a generally excellent discussion of theories of deviance, see David Matza, *Becoming Deviant* (Englewood Cliffs, N.J.: Prentice Hall, 1969).

24. Gary F. Jensen, "Delinquency and Adolescent Self-conceptions: A Study of the Personal Relevance of Infraction," *Social Problems* 20 (1972): 84–102.

▶ 8

The Value of
Social Psychology

What good is social psychology? What is the value of symbolic interactionism as an approach to the study of social life? Does it offer anything that the ordinary person can put into practice in order to make the human condition better — or even make his or her own life better? What is the point of all this theorizing and empirical research?

These questions have no easy answers. Social science does not enjoy a particularly good reputation in the contemporary world, among either students or the public at large. It often seems to express murky ideas in turgid, jargon-laden prose, or to tell us only what everybody already knows. Sometimes it seems bent on reducing the complexity of human experience to crude formulas, or on stripping away any sense of mystery about life and portraying human beings as naked economic creatures. Moreover, the very idea of scientific knowledge itself is under attack from various quarters. Some argue that science — particularly social science — does nothing more than legitimize existing social inequalities and power arrangements. Others think that any quest for empirical generalizations or for explanations of human behavior is foolish, and that any scientific effort to describe social reality distorts it.

I work from a symbolic interactionist perspective because I think it offers the best hope of a humane science — one that avoids distorting our diverse human natures into particular and narrow caricatures, but also one that respects and emphasizes the value of theoretically guided empirical inquiry as one of the best hopes of humankind for creating a better world. In these last pages I will try to explain why I hold this conviction. I will begin by reviewing some of the most central ideas of symbolic interactionism. Taken together these basic symbolic interactionist images of human beings and their world shape the way we view the nature and uses of social science.

THE SIGNIFICANCE OF SYMBOLS

Symbolic interactionists seldom tire of pointing out that it is the capacity for symbolic communication that endows human beings with their distinctively human capabilities. Symbols enable us to name the objects and situations that we confront and then take useful, adaptive action in or toward them. Our symbols name a complex social and physical world, one that is as much abstract and therefore "unseen" as it is material. Moreover, they expand the framework of space and time within which humans live, making it possible for us to remember the past and anticipate the future and to respond to real or imagined events at a considerable distance from us as well as those close at hand. Symbols also increase both the capacity and the necessity for social cooperation. In the course of human evolution, they fostered more precise communication and at the same time sped us on a course in which the social world became the necessary source of both individual learning and the satisfaction of individual needs. Most dramatically of all, symbols give rise to the consciousness of self by making it possible for human beings to become objects of their own experience and action. These consequences of symbol using shape our human natures, both as participants in everyday life and in that particular contemporary way of being we call "social science."

Human beings share with all other living creatures the propensity to survive in the world in which they find themselves. Their "prime directive" (to borrow a phrase from the contemporary version of "Star Trek") seems to be to engage their environment actively, to struggle with it, and to achieve such mastery over it as they can in order to stay alive. The world with which they struggle is a complex one, a world that is in some ways far more challenging than that faced by other creatures. It is one that encompasses not only immediately present situations and stimuli to which people must respond, but also distant and imaginary ones. We are stimulated to act not only by problems or opportunities we can see, but also by those we cannot see and can only imagine. Thus, a real threat or insult from another human being prompts us to respond, but so does an imagined slight. The smell of a freshly baked loaf of bread on a winter day stimulates our hunger, but so also may the imagined applause of our peers for an accomplishment that still lies in the future. We throw ourselves not only into concrete tasks such as baking bread or writing books, but also into more abstract and elusive ones such as "loving" or "doing our duty."

To be a symbol-using creature who is free to range in fact and imagination across wide expanses of space and time, and to respond to the imagined as if it were real, is to gain considerable freedom from determination by the surrounding world. Faced with immediate problems or challenges, human beings do not need to respond only in terms of the objects that are at hand (nor need they always respond immediately) but can instead think of alternative courses of action and the tools with which to accomplish them. We can choose to bide our time and respond to a real or imagined insult at some later time; we can even choose to disregard an insult by thinking of it as unintended. We can have fantasies of future success or anxieties about whether we will ever achieve it, but we can also channel fantasy and anxiety into constructive actions that will help us get what we imagine we want. We can transform the merely biological act of eating bread into an act of cooperation or emotional solidarity with others.

Symbol-using creatures can do these things because they act toward *objects* rather than merely in response to stimuli. Before we human beings can act toward the world we must name it; that is, we must attach significance to the stimuli that confront us at any given time, and we must formulate objects toward which we subsequently act. "I don't get mad, I get even," we may tell someone who has injured us. We transform images of success and applause into plans of action, and then we undertake these plans as a way of finding "success" or "fulfillment" or whatever object we have named as our goal. We say to others, "Let's share this meal and celebrate being together." The very fact that we can name the world toward which we act opens myriad possibilities of action toward it.

Furthermore, naming the world in order to act toward it is not merely something we human beings *can* do, it is something we *must* do. Much of the time we have little or no choice in the matter. Human beings are not mere biological creatures with a fixed set of behavioral capabilities, a limited number of instincts, and the comfort of learning a relatively fixed repertoire of conduct that will enable us to cope with a relatively stable environment. We live in a cultural world that is itself a human creation. We live in a world of names we have created and used. We live amidst complexities of meaning and of social organization that both rest on our capacity to use symbols and that are the result of hundreds of centuries of our actual use of them. Although we surely rely on habit for a great many of our everyday responses — how could we ever act at all if we had to deliberate about everything? — we nonetheless must frequently interpret and name events that confront us if we are to act successfully toward them. We must recognize an insult as such if we are to decide how best to answer it; we pursue an ambition by naming our goal and continually reminding ourselves of it. Human beings are, in short, *required* to interpret the world in order to act in it. Life confronts human beings with problems and opportunities, and in order to solve the former and take advantage of the latter, they must give them meaning. Moreover, a creature who must find meaning in events in order to act is in a sense *driven* to find meaning. We construct meaning in order to solve problems, but we also sometimes look for meaning, even where it does not exist, because it is in our symbolic nature to look for it. The quest for meaning enables us to adapt, therefore, but sometimes it also makes us crazy.

What we know — as individuals and as participants in social life — arises out of our individual and collective efforts to find meaning as we try to solve the problems and to utilize the opportunities that the environment presents to us. Our individual and collective capacity to discover useful meaning—that is, to interpret or name problems and opportunities and the objects we will use to confront them—depends upon what we *know*. The members of any given society share a considerable body of socially created knowledge that has proven useful in solving the problems and meeting the opportunities they have repeatedly faced. Each individual masters a portion of this knowledge and applies it in the particular circumstances with which he or she is confronted. In either case, knowledge of all kinds—theoretical as well as applied, general as well as particular—has a highly practical character. Human beings are problem-solving creatures driven to create practical knowledge.

Human beings are also intensely social creatures. Having created a complex symbolic world, we inhabit it together. We depend upon one another in order to learn what we must know in order to adapt to the world and solve the problems it throws at us. We can survive infancy and the extended period during which we have little or no capacity to take care of ourselves only because we live in the company of and are cared for by others of our kind. Although many other animals are social and their offspring must learn a great deal from them in order to survive in their world, we humans have magnified and intensified our social natures through our dependence on symbols. We not only must learn how to respond to and act successfully or adaptively in the world in which we live but also we must learn a very great deal about that complex, abstract, and often distant or invisible world. We must learn a host of names for material and abstract objects; we must learn a cognitive map of the social relations in which we ourselves are implicated and on which we depend; we must learn both the names of the things we can see and the invisible "things" associated with names we hear, but for which there are no concrete referents.

Our intensive sociality has two consequences that bear particularly on our understanding of the nature of knowledge. First, the stock of knowledge accumulated by a society constrains the way its individual members "know" their world. The individual's knowledge depends upon the social stock of knowledge and its distribution in any given society. And second, our human sociality and our socially created knowledge open up the possibility—though not the inevitablity—that we can discover the ways in which our participation in human life constrains what we know and can be.

The knowledge that we human beings acquire as members of a society constrains the ways we can imagine the world and respond to its problems and opportunities. This is so, first, because our ways of knowing the world inevitably incline us to notice some things and fail to see others. If we collectively "know" that people either succeed or fail in life according to their abilities and their willingness to work hard, then we will view those who succeed as industrious and those who fail as lazy, and we will probably not even recognize the existence of obstacles that make it difficult for some people to succeed. If we "know" that people commit crimes because they have been denied legitimate opportunities for success, then we may not see that perhaps some individuals find the opportunities and excitements of crime to be greater than more legitimate forms of activity could ever be. Our everyday, socially shared knowledge of the social world is a basis for blindness as well as insight into its operation.

This is essentially what George H. Mead meant when he argued that we grasp what is problematic in social life over and against the background of that which is not problematic. Our grasp of problems — of others' actions that may be insulting or threatening, or of others' apparent failure to work as hard as we think they should — is always formulated relative to ideas, beliefs, and other forms of knowledge that we think are secure. When we attempt to create new knowledge in an effort to deal with some problem, we do it by relying on what we already know and understand. There is really no escape from this fact, for we cannot question everything at once or make everything problematic at once. Human beings need some secure place to stand when they try to solve the problems that confront them, and that place is provided by the knowledge they feel they can take securely for granted.

Moreover, much of what we know and understand is effectively hidden from us, because it is embedded in the language we speak and therefore in the names we are prepared to attach to objects in our world. Contemporary Americans, for example, respond to some problematic forms of behavior by calling them "alcoholism," by which they mean a kind of disease in which the victim finds it impossible to control his or her consumption of alcoholic beverages, with frequently destructive consequences for the individual and those around him or her. Embedded in the word "alcoholism" is a more complex set of attitudes toward the "alcoholic," attitudes of which we are scarcely aware when we use the term, even though they dispose us to act toward that person in specific ways. That is, the term inclines us to look for "treatment" and to apply to this "disease" the same assumptions we might apply to any disease, namely that steps can be taken to control it, if not to cure it. Once we learn and routinely use a set of terms to describe the world, the actions we can take are in many ways constrained by the words, the objects they denote, and the forms of action these objects invite.

Moreover, the words we use to designate the objects in our environment did not necessarily arise out of a collective and democratic process in which everybody participated equally. We speak of "alcoholism" not because the term more or less spontaneously arose out of various human efforts to cope with a perceived problem by giving it a name and an interpretation. Rather, we think of the excessive consumption of alcoholic beverages as a "disease" essentially because a variety of people, including physicians, have convinced us that it is a disease. Medicine, with its conceptions of disease and cure, is a general way of "knowing" the world, and in the course of the last century or so its practitioners and their allies have employed it to think about a wider variety of phenomena than merely the illnesses and infirmities of the body. A variety of individual and social problems have been medicalized, including alcoholism, drug use, and many other behavioral difficulties and problems of adjustment. "Mental illness" is one of the more obvious illustrations of how the medical model of human conduct and problems has been extended.

As these illustrations suggest, what people "know" is subject to influence by those who have an interest in having people "know" the world in a particular way. The medical establishment has power over us because we have come to share their ways of knowing the body and its various problems. Likewise, psychologists and psychiatrists exercise power over us because we have been persuaded to think of our behavior in the language they provide. Contemporary people worry about their self-esteem or pursue self-actualization because they have "learned" from psychologists that these are real and important phenomena. In a similar vein—but with far deeper penetration of our consciousness and more serious consequences for our behavior—our "knowledge" of what is natural or possible for men as compared with women, or black as opposed to white or yellow or brown people, or those who are poor versus those who are middle-class, reflects a variety of ways in which we have been taught to regard, understand, and speak about the social world and our own place in it.

No one should underestimate the extent to which our "knowledge" of the social world is also "ignorance" of it, or the degree to which particular social classes, professions, or organizations exert unseen power by shaping the very language with which we grasp ourselves and the social world in which we live. Such forms of "power" are far more subtle than the exercise of naked force. One ordinarily has no difficulty knowing when one is being forcefully conscripted into military service, or when one lacks the wherewithal to purchase a decent place to live or food for one's family, or when one is denied opportunities solely because of one's color or gender. When we "know" that women are "emotional" and that the care of children is their sole "natural" vocation, we are powerfully constrained in our actions in a way that is more diffuse and far less obvious.

There is another side to this coin—a basis for at least some optimism about the capacity of human beings to avoid being duped. Human beings are capable of "knowing" their world as one in which they may be deceived; they can make their secure knowledge itself problematic and ask whether what they take for granted ought not to be. To put this another way, we human beings seem to be capable of thinking about ourselves as the potential victims of our own assumptions as well as of the "knowledge" that various others would have us possess in order to foster their interests. If we are susceptible to influence by professionals bent on extending their influence and prestige by shaping the way we solve problems and the kind of help we seek in doing so, we are also capable of seeing and talking about that very susceptibility.

Human beings have the capacity to make our own "knowledge" of the world problematic partly because the flow of problems that confronts us is never ending. Although it may be true that in the distant past culture and society changed at a glacial pace, in the contemporary world things seem to happen more quickly. We seem no sooner to recognize and formulate a social problem than another comes along; actions we take to solve one problem have unanticipated consequences, and today's solution thus becomes tomorrow's problem. No human society on the face of the earth has ever been in such stable equilibrium with its human and material environment that it achieved a stable and finite body of "knowledge" that could definitively solve all of its problems. The contemporary human condition especially seems to be one of ceaseless change and an unending parade of problems. Thus, perhaps more now than at any time in history, everything we "know" can be in question, subject to revision, open to doubt.

There is another, more fundamental reason why human beings have the capacity not only to develop new knowledge about the world but also to become conscious of the limits of knowledge. Human beings are creatures with *selves*. Thoroughly social creatures, permeated by socially created and controlled knowledge, we are nonetheless creatures with individual self-consciousness. This fact has enormous implications for both knowing and acting.

The conception of the individual human being developed by George Herbert Mead and to a large extent shared by his friend and mentor John Dewey is distinctive in its ability to portray both the tension and the fine balance between the individual and the social world. On the one hand, this view of the person makes the self a product of the social order. Mead explains the emergence of individual self-consciousness as a product of membership and participation in the social world. We have consciousness of self because we are born into the stream of social life and come to share its names and knowledge and apply them to ourselves. We learn to see ourselves as others see us, and we do so by adopting the language and the organized social perspectives made available in the social world around us. We seem to be thoroughly social creatures.

On the other hand, symbolic interactionism also views the self as a social force in its own right. Socialization endows the individual with the capacity to cooperate in social acts with others, but it does not create an automaton who unfailingly reproduces the meanings and actions he or she has been taught. Joint actions—handshakes, cocktail parties, social movements, wars—exist because individual actors who share a conception of what they are doing come together and assemble their individual contributions into a social whole. It is the *individual* who acts, who does the interpreting, naming, and coordinating that permits joint actions to proceed or that disrupts and derails them. To have a self, therefore, is not merely to be a thoroughly programmed agent of society, but just as important, to be one who chooses, decides, and exerts control over his or her own conduct and that of others.

One important consequence of the existence of a self, then, is that it endows the individual actor with the capacity to recognize and act in the pursuit of his or her self-interest and to conceive of himself or herself in opposition to the social world and not just as dependent on it. When symbolic interactionists say that the self is a social object, they imply not just that we constitute this object by seeing it and acting toward it from the imagined perspectives of others but also that we come to value this object and to feel that we own it and must protect it. The self is something we create and sustain jointly with others, and in that sense its "locus" is not strictly speaking within the body or brain but in the social world that surrounds us, nourishes us, and often challenges us. Still, it is the particular living and breathing organism who lies at the center of this social world, who experiences impulses, and who exerts control over his or her conduct. Indeed, the influence of the surrounding social world upon us depends on our *imagination* of it; when we engage in role taking in an effort to form our conduct, we respond to our imaginations of others and our interpretations of their words and deeds. There is, in short, a sentient being who is as much responsible for the creation of the self as is the surrounding social world.

Moreover it is the individual who experiences the problematic situation and who initiates the knowing and problem solving. The sense that a situation is problematic, that there is something that needs to be done, that there is some gap in knowledge or understanding that needs to be filled arises first in the *individual* mind. Human conduct, including efforts to confront and overcome problematic situations, is thoroughly a social affair because it is based on shared assumptions and perspectives, shared knowledge, and some form of social coordination (whether cooperative, competitive, or conflictful). Yet this so intensely social and problem-solving conduct ultimately rests on what transpires within the single individual as much as upon what transpires between individuals. Through their capacity to rebel, innovate, resist social influences, and apply social knowledge creatively in an effort to solve problems, individuals make felt their influence on the social world.

Although this reading of Mead is often slighted in favor of one that merely emphasizes the social nature of human beings, I believe his social theory encourages us to see the individual and the society as always in a potential state of tension, and the individual as the potential innovator, inventor, and creator of new forms of conduct. In the last analysis, every human act begins with an impulse over which the person has no control and that often takes the person by surprise. To be capable of self-consciousness is to have the ability to subjugate this impulse to social demands, and that is perhaps what we most typically do. A creature with a self can also see the possible value of this impulse, both to self and to others, and allow it to be completed in behavior.

THE USES OF KNOWLEDGE

The interactionist conception of human beings and of the way they know themselves and their social world implies a way of viewing the knowledge of social science. Although a full account of how symbolic interactionists study the social world, what they feel they may learn about it, and what they think they and others ought to do with this knowledge would fill more than this chapter, I can outline a few principles that offer useful guidelines.

First, human beings seek knowledge in order to solve problems, and the test of knowledge — of its truth — lies in its practical consequences for our lives. The quest for knowledge of any kind is no mere idle pastime that we undertake because we have nothing else to occupy our time. The effort to know arises in those situations where for one reason or another something interferes with our effort to do something. This statement is as true of scientific knowledge as it is of everyday affairs, and it is as true of our quest for religious or philosophical knowledge as of the search for practical understanding. We seek to know in order to act successfully in our world, and we believe we have achieved truth when we are able to do so.

This pragmatic conception of truth seems obvious when we apply it to the knowledge we seek and use in our everyday lives, but perhaps not so obvious when we apply it to such spheres as religion or literature. One wants to learn about how an automobile works, for example, so that one can drive it well enough to get a driver's license and then put the car to use. If the car fails to start, one wants to learn what is wrong with it so as to get it started as quickly as possible. But in what sense does religious doctrine constitute practical knowledge? Those who are committed to a particular version of religious truth probably prefer to think of religion as a matter of faith or of revelation from a supernatural being, not as something that exists to solve practical problems. Many who write novels would perhaps say that their stories express truths about the human condition, but would deny that they write them to solve particular problems.

Yet religion and literature — and, for that matter, music and art — are ways of "knowing" the world, and people act on the basis of the knowledge these disciplines produce. Religious faith usually dictates that people act in certain ways. It may do so through an explicit set of commandments, whether the Ten Commandments of the Jewish and Christian Bibles, or the larger set of specific directives contained in the Book of Leviticus and still followed scrupulously by observant Orthodox Jews. Those who believe such "truths" attempt to act on the basis of them. Religious beliefs may also indirectly influence conduct. Early followers of the Swiss theologian John Calvin (whose contemporary religious descendants include Baptists) believed that God had preordained that some people would find salvation in the hereafter, whereas others were doomed to external damnation and could do nothing to be saved. Such beliefs make people anxious about their eventual fate — each person wonders whether he or she is among the elect who are predestined for salvation or those unfortunates who will burn in Hell. The Calvinists also believed that even though there was nothing one could do in order to earn salvation, one's success in earthly pursuits nevertheless could be interpreted as a sign that one was among the elect. The result was indirectly to encourage efforts to succeed in worldly pursuits, for in doing so one could find reassurance that God had decided that one would spend eternity in heaven. Religious forms of "knowledge" thus form grounds for action just as much as more practical forms; their "truth" likewise depends upon their capacity to promote action.

What about science itself? Does it also represent a quest for practical knowledge? It seems clear that the birth of contemporary scientific inquiry during the seventeenth century in England and Europe was stimulated in part by considerations associated with the rise of industry, warfare, and other practical concerns. In the contemporary world, the practical consequences of scientific knowledge are visible everywhere. Modern technologies are grounded in scientific discoveries. Although much science is conducted without any particular interest in or concern for the immediate practical uses of the knowledge that might be gained, even theoretical inquiries are "practical" in the sense that they attempt to organize and make sense of accumulated scientific discoveries. Even such theoretical endeavors as the effort by physicists to create a general theory of the universe are motivated by an effort to solve a problem. The problem is a highly abstract one — how to make sense of complex and often contradictory data about the universe — but it is a problem, nonetheless, and the practical value of a theory is precisely that it makes sense of those data. It is true to the extent that and so long as it continues to make sense of the data.

Social science likewise arose as a response to problems. As industrialization transformed human societies in the eighteenth and especially the nineteenth century, old patterns of human life were disrupted and new ones were created. Sociology in particular arose in the late nineteenth and early twentieth centuries in the United States in an effort to understand and cope with the social problems associated with industrialization, the growth of cities, and large-scale immigration from other countries. Throughout this century sociologists have pursued their discipline not only in an effort to answer questions raised by their own research and theories, but also in an effort to contribute in a practical way to the solution of social problems.

The question, then, is how a symbolic interactionist social psychology seeks to make a practical contribution to human affairs. What does this approach offer to those who study it and grasp its view of the social world?

Although in principle I think symbolic interactionism can contribute to the solution of problems in a variety of ways, here I want to advance the idea that an important component of its contribution involves the teaching and learning that goes on (or should) in colleges and universities. Symbolic interactionism proposes a method for the empirical study of social life, and it provides a perspective on the social world. Its method and perspective are valuable not merely because of any specific solutions to social problems they may produce, but more importantly because they offer a different platform from which each of us can understand our own lives and those of others.

The special method that symbolic interactionism recommends is participant observation, so-called because the social scientist is both an observer of some sphere of social life and (in some way) a participant in it. Symbolic interactionists believe that we cannot study the social world from a distance, and that if we want to examine and understand it we must do so at close hand. The reason, of course, lies in the interactionist view of conduct as dependent on meanings. If people form their conduct on the basis of meaning as they interact with one another, then one must grasp their meanings in order to explain why they act as they act. We must discover what lies in the minds of those whose conduct we would scrutinize, and doing so requires us to interact with them, to live cheek by jowl in their worlds, at least for a time, in order to see how and why they define situations, make and take roles, and interpret their worlds as they do. Symbolic interactionism encourages its practitioners and their readers alike to enter into the worlds of those whose lives they would understand.

The special perspective of symbolic interactionism I have in mind here has to do with its capacity to help people to understand not only the lives and perspectives of others, but also the ways in which each individual life is linked to the surrounding social world. Symbolic interactionism tries to reveal the social origins of the self, the nature of social constraints, and, crucially, the ways in which the social order depends on the actions of individuals with selves. It seeks to show how society forms us, how it limits us, how it makes us what we are. At the same time it portrays a human actor who is capable of changing the very social order that has formed him or her.

Both the method and the perspective of symbolic interactionism, in my view, foster the capacity to appreciate the diversity of the world we live in and the common humanity that unites all of us. To study the worlds of others by entering them and constructing, as best we can, an account of their members' lives and problems that can be communicated to others who live outside those worlds is to help convey a sense of what it means to be human in the many ways it is possible to be human. We study the lives of others—various minorities and majorities, women and men, children and adults, the oppressed and their oppressors—so that we may grasp the diversity of human life and, in grasping it, perhaps learn to take a somewhat more humble and less chauvinistic stance toward our own lives. To study the worlds of others is to learn something of our own humanity as well as theirs. It is to learn that the world has formed and shaped us, that problems that seem unique and private may also be the concerns of others, that we have much in common as well as much that divides us.

No one can fully penetrate the social worlds that others have constructed and communicate a completely accurate or totally undistorted view of them to those who live outside. No one can fully grasp his or her own life experience in relation to the surrounding social world, nor communicate that experience fully to others. Neither are the worlds of others intellectually or emotionally accessible, however, only to those who live there. To argue that no outsider can depict, or has any right to depict, the lives of any particular group of human beings, it seems to me, is to abandon any hope that human beings can live in both diversity and harmony. To argue, for example, that no man can possibly understand the world as a woman understands and lives it, or that whites should never try to speak or write about the experiences of blacks, is in effect to say that the barriers that divide one group from another are too great for understanding to pass between them.

Symbolic interactionism asserts that human beings share a social psychology—our dependence upon symbols and our distinctive capacity for selfhood—and that we can transcend those social and cultural barriers. One way of transcending them is to understand that they exist, to attempt to depict life behind those barriers, and to show how each of us, no matter where or how we live, participates in a common humanity. The practical value of social psychology, then, lies partly in its capacity to reveal this common humanity through research and analysis. To act on the basis of this knowledge is to increase one's capacity to appreciate diversity and to grasp one's own dependence upon and responsibility for the social world in which one lives.

The second principle is that any form of knowledge—everyday knowledge, religious knowledge, scientific knowledge—is partial and tentative. In our everyday lives, we act on the basis of what we know about driving cars or raising children and tend to believe that we can generally regard such knowledge as sure and certain. To one degree or another, however, we are prepared to question that knowledge and learn new ways of behaving. In matters of religious belief, we are perhaps more likely to cling to a faith once we have arrived at it, and certainly those whose whole lives are invested in a particular religious faith will cling to their faith with particular conviction. Even religious faith wears thin for some people—the precepts of their religion seem to lead them astray, they find their faith unsatisfying, or another faith seems more appealing—and so they seek a new faith or perhaps discard the idea of religion entirely. We approach scientific knowledge particularly with the idea that it is always tentative and subject to revision. Scientific knowledge is based on the belief that the ultimate test of truth is a process of empirical inquiry in which hypotheses and theories are tested against the real world. Indeed, the ideal of scientific procedure is to look for instances in the world that will contradict a hypothesis. In that sense it differs from other forms of human knowledge, since it intentionally questions its own validity and always looks for evidence that it might be in error.

Clearly the rigor and care with which human beings scrutinize their knowledge and the standards they apply in evaluating it vary among different forms of knowledge. In everyday life we are concerned with the immediate practical results of what we do. We are not interested in assembling the various bits and pieces of our practical understanding of the world into a coherent, meaningful system. We are content to use a more fragmented approach, relying on bits and pieces of knowledge about how to drive cars, discipline children, bake cakes, conduct weddings, and perform the countless important tasks of everyday life. We are very empirical in our approach—we want knowledge that works—but not very theoretical. In matters of religious faith or philosophical belief, we may be considerably more theoretically oriented; we want our various beliefs to fit together in some coherent way, to make sense as a general way of looking at the world. In matters of religion we are not very empirical—we do not make systematic observations of the world to test our religious beliefs, but more or less rely on faith rather than what we believe will ultimately turn out to be true. In matters of science, we tend to be both theoretical and empirical; we want to generalize about reality, to create theories that will explain the world, to form hypotheses about the world, and to test these hypotheses against our empirical observations.

Symbolic interactionists believe that the tentative and problem-centered character of human knowledge means that there can never be a final or complete body of knowledge. We do not believe that it is possible to assemble a picture of the natural or the social world that is in every way complete, final, and total, so that there is no additional knowledge to be sought or gained. Rather, because new problems continue to confront us, we must continue to grapple with the world and seek new knowledge of it. As a result, the body of knowledge we possess is always changing; old "truths" are continually being shed as they cease to "work" and new "truths" are discovered as we confront new problems. No symbolic interactionist would argue that scientific knowledge progressively assembles a more and more complete picture of the world, and that doing science of any kind is therefore like putting together the pieces of a jigsaw puzzle. Rather, the shape of the puzzle keeps changing as we approach it from first one angle and then another; it is never complete.

Still, interactionists believe that some knowledge is better than none, especially if that knowledge is a result of the empirical study of the social world based on verifiable, public methods of inquiry that can be understood by and checked by others. Symbolic interactionism yields knowledge of social worlds and social processes that is open to empirical verification and revision. This knowledge—of how others conspire to hide their identities from us or to manipulate us, of the social sources of self-esteem, or of the way individual transactions in the automobile business are shaped by industry-wide practices—holds no panaceas for the solution of social problems. The knowledge is short-term and may have to be revised. Still, it is knowledge and provides us with some basis for acting in the world in which we find ourselves and solving the problems that arise within it.

Symbolic interactionists believe that empirical knowledge is a good thing. They believe that it is a valuable thing to have in spite of the fact that such knowledge is never complete or perfect and never can be. They hold no illusion that the mere possession of knowledge can compel others to yield to its truths. Knowing that the course of the transaction in which one buys a used car has been influenced by a chain of connections at one end of which lies a powerful industry and at the other end a weak consumer will not get one a better price for the car. Nor will that knowledge by itself bring about a change in the way the industry acts. But it seems worth betting that knowing is better than not knowing in this situation, and that with knowledge one is more likely to be able to take effective actions to change the situation. A little knowledge is potentially a very useful thing and not necessarily or even typically a dangerous thing.

A third principle is that our knowledge of reality shapes that reality. We human beings seek knowledge in order to solve problems, and then act on the basis of what we learn. Our actions, in turn, shape or influence the conditions under which we live. Symbolic interactionists believe that the relationship between human beings and their world is one of mutual determination—the environment, social or material, influences and constrains us, but our actions toward it also influence or shape it. If this is so, then in a general sense what we "know" about the world influences the "reality" of that world.

Perhaps an example will clarify this general idea and show why it is significant. Contemporary Americans are struggling with the apparent fact that the primary and secondary schools don't seem to do a very good job of educating many children. Standardized test scores have been declining, many students do not read at grade level, and competence in science and math also seems lower than educators and parents alike feel that it should be. A variety of explanations for poor school performance have been advanced by educators, critics, politicians, parents, and others. Among them is an explanation that has gained considerable attention in recent years, namely that a principal cause of the problem lies in the low self-esteem of some children. Those who have low self-esteem, it is argued, do not learn very well. They usually believe they are going to fail; they are always too anxious about their performance to do what they must to learn; they quickly abandon hope and become poorly motivated. Those who advance this explanation argue that the school achievement of such children can best be improved by teaching them to have higher self-esteem—to think better of themselves—so that they will then have the motivation and energy to learn.

Although such an explanation of school failure vastly oversimplifies the nature of the problem and its possible solution, the truth or falsity of the explanation is not what is at issue here. Rather, the question is how this kind of "knowledge" influences conduct and thereby shapes the social world within which students and teachers live. It is clear that it does influence conduct: Many teachers believe the self-esteem approach to education, and therefore design at least some of their classroom activities in an effort to "teach self-esteem." Their activities range from efforts to structure learning so that each child has at least some opportunities to succeed and thereby gain in self-esteem to more simplistic and perhaps more questionable efforts to bolster each child's self-esteem regardless of how well the child is doing in school. Moreover, once "low self-esteem" is available to teachers as an explanation of school failure, it is also available to the children themselves and to their parents. That is, it becomes a part of their vocabularies of motive, a way for children to account for their own failure or for parents to blame themselves or teachers for their children's failure.

Knowledge, then, has consequences, not only for the actions we take on the basis of it, but also for the nature of the world in which we live. Even as we create explanations of problems, we provide people with a basis for acting to solve them as well as a way of perceiving their social world. Even as we seek to understand the motives on the basis of which people act, we provide them with motives for acting and with ways of understanding their own actions. When we seek to "know" the social world, therefore, we are not learning about a reality that is simply "out there" fixed and final. Rather, we are engaged in creating that reality even as we seek to know and understand it.

If scientific knowledge is tentative and at the same time consequential, should we ever act on the basis of it? If we can never know anything with certainty, since what we know today is likely to be untrue or irrelevant tomorrow, then perhaps we ought to abandon any pretense at objective empirical inquiry. If the actions we take on the basis of what we think we know are likely to have consequences, many of which we cannot anticipate and may be quite different from what we intended, then perhaps we ought to do nothing out of fear of doing something wrong.

I can imagine no conclusions more inimical to what symbolic interactionism stands for. We do influence the social world when we study it and produce knowledge on the basis of which we and others act. Sometimes we are wrong or think we know more than we do. Yet what alternative is there but to act as intelligently as we can on the basis of what we think we know? The symbolic interactionist approach to knowledge is a humble one. It recognizes that there may be many ways to truth and that each is prone to error. It grants that behind particular versions of truth there always lurk particular interests and unequal power to pursue them. Still, it believes empirical truth is worth pursuing, that we are worse off without it, and that the pursuit of such truth in the long run may offer the best hope of reconstructing a human world in which all can live in dignity and peace.

Much has occurred in the world since 1976, when I wrote the concluding words to the last chapter of the first edition of this book. Notwithstanding those changes, the rise and fall of various versions of utopia, and what seems to be an unrelenting attack on the values of Western enlightenment and the worth of social science from within the academic world itself, I think those ideas still hold true, and so I close this chapter in much the same words as I have in each of the five previous editions of this book.

Sociology promises, in the words of C. Wright Mills, "an understanding of the intimate realities of ourselves in connection with larger social realities."[1] But what the sociological imagination promises it does not easily deliver. If sociology and social psychology represent potential contributions to the advancement of human intelligence—and to the betterment of the human condition—they do so only if exercised. They are not storehouses of facts and formulas to be applied mechanically to human problems, but ways of looking at the reality of the human condition. As such they are everyone's property and responsibility, a set of tools not only for those with power, but also for those over whom it is exercised.

It is thus in the things individuals might do on the basis of its insights that I think the greatest value of social psychology lies. The only final advice an author can give is to urge readers to struggle with these ideas and to use them to good ends. That is not revolutionary advice; indeed, both revolutionaries and reformers will find it wanting, since it appears to hope that a better society can come about through the struggles of informed and educated people. In a world brimming with ideological movements whose leaders seek to impose their own utopias on the rest of us, and with professional reformers who underestimate the magnitude of their task and think the world will easily yield to goodness, it is not popular advice. Still, the democratic ideal of informed people struggling with their world and its problems seems to me a good one, and this book has sought in a small way to contribute to it.

ENDNOTE

1. C. Wright Mills, *The Sociological Imagination* (New York: Oxford University Press, 1959), p. 15.

Index